P9-CKY-032

DATE DUE

DEMCO 38-296

TECHNOLOGY AND INDUSTRIAL DEVELOPMENT IN JAPAN

HOKKAIDO
• Sapporo

Hakodate

SEA OF JAPAN

Sendai

Niigata

Kanazawa

HONSHU

Tokyo

Yokohama *Tokyo Bay*

Kyoto

Nagoya

Kobe

Hiroshima

Nara

Shimoda

Shimonoseki

Osaka

Fukuoka

Nagasaki

SHIKOKU

KYUSHU

PACIFIC OCEAN

Kagoshima

| 0 | 100 | 200 miles |
| 0 | 100 | 200 | 300 km |

Technology and Industrial Development in Japan

Building Capabilities by Learning, Innovation, and Public Policy

HIROYUKI ODAGIRI
and
AKIRA GOTO

with a Foreword by
Richard R. Nelson

CLARENDON PRESS · OXFORD
1996

Riverside Community College
·97   Library
AUG   4800 Magnolia Avenue
Riverside, California 92506.

HC 465 .T4 O3 1996

Odagiri, Hiroyuki, 1946-

Technology and industrial
development in Japan

Street, Oxford OX2 6DP

York

gkok Bombay

es Salaam Delhi
Florence Hong Kong Istanbul Karachi
Kuala Lumpur Madras Madrid Melbourne
Mexico City Nairobi Paris Singapore
Taipei Tokyo Toronto
and associated companies in
Berlin Ibadan

Oxford is a trade mark of Oxford University Press

Published in the United States
by Oxford University Press Inc., New York

Copyright © Hiroyuki Odagiri and Akira Goto, 1996

All rights reserved. No part of this publication may be reproduced,
stored in a retrieval system, or transmitted, in any form or by any means,
without the prior permission in writing of Oxford University Press.
Within the UK, exceptions are allowed in respect of any fair dealing for the
purpose of research or private study, or criticism or review, as permitted
under the Copyright, Designs and Patents Act, 1988, or in the case of
reprographic reproduction in accordance with the terms of the licences
issued by the Copyright Licensing Agency. Enquiries concerning
reproduction outside these terms and in other countries should be
sent to the Rights Department, Oxford University Press,
at the address above

This book is sold subject to the condition that it shall not, by way
of trade or otherwise, be lent, re-sold, hired out or otherwise circulated
without the publisher's prior consent in any form of binding or cover
other than that in which it is published and without a similar condition
including this condition being imposed on the subsequent purchaser

British Library Cataloguing in Publication Data
Data available

Library of Congress Cataloging in Publication Data
Data available

ISBN 0-19-828802-6

Typeset by Graphicraft Typesetters Ltd., Hong Kong
Printed in Great Britain
on acid-free paper by
Bookcraft, Bath Ltd., Midsomer Norton, Avon

Contents

List of Figures

List of Tables

Foreword by Richard R. Nelson

Understanding Japan's rise as an economic and technological power is important for several reasons. First, Japan was the first major nation, outside the Western mainstream, to take aboard the technological and organizational advances that occurred in the West in the century after the first industrial revolution. More, Japan was the first non-Western nation to establish itself as fully able to tap into and contribute to the sustained and broad technological advances that began to occur in the twentieth century as science became harnessed to technology. Second, while Japan's success was followed nearly a century later by the rapid technological and economic development of a few countries like Korea and Taiwan, much of the world remains technologically backward and poor. And Japan's economic development remains a model for many countries who have not yet been able to master modern technology and organizational forms. It therefore is extremely important to understand just how Japan achieved what it has.

It is hard to exaggerate the contribution of this book to that understanding. So much of the current writing about Japan starts the story at the close of World War II. Yet Japan had achieved rough technological parity with Western countries, across a broad industrial front, by World War II. This book provides by far the most detailed account and analysis written thus far on Japanese technological development in the century after the Meiji restoration.

The technological and economic development of Japan not only is a topic of major interest in its own right. Knowing what happened in Japan can contribute importantly to our broader understanding of economic growth in the modern era. This book, therefore, can be seen as making a major contribution to economic growth theory. The theoretical exposition is verbal, not mathematical. But the key variables and relationships that lie behind Japan's remarkable economic assent, as these are seen by the authors, are laid out carefully and clearly. The key elements are as follows.

Japan had a well educated and technologically sophisticated population as far back as the mid-nineteenth century. Japan's investments since that time in improving human capital have matched or exceeded those in Western Europe, and the United States. The authors make an analytically persuasive case that large investments in human capital are an absolute requirement for catching up and staying up with the advance of technology in the modern world.

While the presence of significantly superior Western technologies and organizational forms provided Japan with the opportunity for rapid economic growth in the early days after the Meiji restoration, there was nothing easy or automatic about taking aboard these more productive techniques. The Japanese were extraordinarily open and creative in searching out and learning to use modern technologies.

The managers of many Japanese business firms were highly entrepreneurial. They aggressively sought out and took aboard foreign techniques, and did the hard work of tailoring these to the Japanese scene. The investments and risks were substantial. And Japanese firms, after taking aboard new technology, made the further continuing investments needed to stay up with its development worldwide, and increasingly contributed their own invention and innovation to those developments. The development of Japanese industry has been, from the beginnings, marked by intra-industry competition, and in many cases by aggressive entry of new firms when there were niches left by established ones. And, from the beginning, except for an interlude overlapping World War II, Japanese firms have had to fend off foreign competition and have sought their markets abroad as well as at home.

From the beginnings of the Japanese catch-up, the Japanese government has played a strong supporting role. That role has included active and effective development of economic and technological infrastructure and, from time to time, providing the market, and protection from foreign competition, to enable Japanese firms to get their footing in a field. However, the role of public policy in Japan needs to be understood as providing support for aggressive competitive business enterprise, and facilitating business entrepreneurship, rather than as providing a substitute.

A number of macroeconomic analyses of Japanese economic growth have recognized that very high rates of investment in human and physical capital have been involved, and have tried to calculate how much of Japan's growth has been simply the result of these investments, as contrasted with technological advance measured by growth of total factor productivity. The Odagiri–Goto analysis sharply illuminates why this attempt to divide up the credit for Japanese growth between investments and technological improvements is misconceived. As the authors reveal, high investments in human and physical capital were an essential part of the process by which Japan took on board more advanced technology. At the same time, it was the continuing innovation and learning that was going on that kept returns to these investments high and induced their supply. But while the authors view these sources of growth as strong complements, there is no question as to what they see as the key driving force. It is entrepreneurship and learning combined.

Thus the broad perspective on economic growth here is Schumpeterian, not in its emphasis on large firms—the authors highlight that in the early days of Japanese development the entrepreneuring firms were young and small—but in its emphasis on continuing innovation involving firms venturing into terrain unfamiliar to them. The authors see their analysis as very much in the spirit of evolutionary growth theories, and I certainly would agree.

The role of a foreword is to tell why a book is important, and to lead the reader into it, and not to steal the authors' thunder. It is time now for the reader to get into the real thing.

Acknowledgements

This book is concerned with Japan's historical development: we thus begin by describing the historical development of the book itself. This, we believe, is the only way to properly acknowledge our debt.

The study started when Richard R. Nelson held the first of a series of conferences on the 'National Innovation Systems'. Goto had been invited to present his view on Japan but, owing to illness just a week before the conference, he asked Odagiri, then at the London Business School, to attend the conference in his place. This experience led the two of us to present a paper together on the 'Japanese System of Innovation' at the second conference in Maastricht, The Netherlands. Fortunately, we received a number of insightful comments at this conference. Especially instrumental in deciding the future course of our study was Christopher Freeman, who observed with amusement that 90 per cent of the American paper written by David Mowery and Nathan Rosenberg was about the past, and 10 per cent about today, whereas 90 per cent of the Japanese paper was about today and 10 per cent about the future. He rightly suggested that the Japanese paper should pay more attention to the historical aspects.

Accordingly, we decided to add a historical discussion of technological development in Japan. In our view, some of the major players, if not *the* major players in shaping the Japanese innovation system (if there is in fact a *Japanese* system), have been the entrepreneurs and industrialists. Believing that their role can be fully understood only through case studies, we studied three industries (iron and steel, electrical equipment, and automobiles) besides Japan's industrial and technological development in general. The result was our chapter 'The Japanese System of Innovation: Past, Present, and Future' in *National Innovation Systems* (ed. R. R. Nelson, Oxford University Press, 1993).

Through this investigation of the process of Japan's technological accumulation and industrial development, we learned much and decided to pursue the study further by adding several new case studies, expanding the previous case studies, and aiming to give a detailed and comprehensive view—not necessarily an orthodox one—of the process of Japan's development. The result is this book.

This lengthy story shows how much we are indebted to Dick Nelson and other participants of the National Innovation Systems project, especially Chris Freeman. Dick not only had us participate in the most stimulating conferences but also gave constructive criticisms to our draft conference papers and to this book. It has been, therefore, an immense pleasure and honour that he agreed to write a foreword for this book. Among other participants of the conferences, we are particularly indebted to Hugh Patrick, Keith Pavitt, and Nathan Rosenberg.

To the present volume, Ronald Dore, Martin Fransman, Leslie Hannah, and Jon Sigurdson, as well as Dick Nelson, gave comments and encouragement. We have also benefited from discussions with Takahiro Fujimoto, Seiichiro Yonekura, and other participants of the 'Innovation in Japan' conference, which produced a book entitled *Innovation In Japan: Empirical Studies on the National and Corporate Activities* (ed. A. Goto and H. Odagiri, Oxford University Press, 1996). This book is complementary to the present volume, as the main focus there is the analysis of the *current* situation whereas our focus here is historical.

Writing this book took more time than we had expected, mainly because of administrative and other duties in our universities, and we thank Oxford University Press for their patience. Certainly it took more time than when Odagiri wrote his previous books in the USA and England, reminding him of the unfavourable research environment of Japanese universities. We will return to this topic in the concluding chapter.

Quite possibly we might have given up this research project were it not for the constant encouragement and support of our families, Mari, Kosuke, and Shinsuke (Odagiri) and Mitsuko, Koichi, and Minami (Goto). To all of them, we give our heartfelt thanks.

H.O. & A.G.

Tsukuba and Kunitachi, Japan
Summer 1995

1

Introduction

1.1   THE ISSUE

Three strands of thought have emerged during the past decade to explain how the economy, industry, and business develop. Among these, probably the most sympathetic to the neoclassical economic theory is the so-called new growth theory or the endogenous growth theory. This theory recognizes technical progress as a major force in economic growth and tries to formulate an equilibrium growth model in which technical progress is generated as an endogenous outcome of an economic system (see Romer, 1990, 1994; Grossman and Helpman, 1991, 1994). For an earlier effort in this direction by one of us, see Odagiri (1981).

The second, which is more in line with the Schumpeterian view, is the evolutionary theory proposed by Nelson and Winter (1982). They do not assume that firms maximize profits over well-defined and exogenously given choice sets. Instead, these firms are assumed to have certain *capabilities* and *decision rules* at any given time. 'Over time these capabilities and rules are modified as a result of both deliberate problem-solving efforts and random events. And over time, the economic analogue of natural selection operates as the market determines which firms are profitable and which are unprofitable, and tends to winnow out the latter' (Nelson and Winter, 1982: 4).

The concept of capabilities has been also emphasized by Chandler in his discussion of the development of industry and business in the USA, the UK, and Germany since the mid-eighteenth century. To him, 'at the core of this dynamic [in the development of modern capitalism] were the organizational capabilities of the enterprise as a unified whole. These organized capabilities were the collective physical facilities and human skills as they were organized within the enterprises. . . . But only if these facilities and skills were carefully coordinated and integrated could the enterprise achieve the economies of scale and scope that were needed to compete in national and international markets and to grow' (Chandler, 1990: 594). That is, to create, maintain, accumulate, and utilize capabilities is the challenge to the management but 'such organizational capabilities, in turn, have provided the source—the dynamic—for the continuing growth of the enterprise' (ibid.). In his view, this dynamic has been the main engine behind the expansion of industrial capitalism.

Notwithstanding the different emphasis and methodology among these authors, they agree in their dissatisfaction with the existing theories that ignore technology, skills, and capabilities or, at best, regard them as exogenous. Such capabilities have to be consciously and carefully accumulated, even though, particularly in the views of Nelson, Winter, and Chandler, the process of accumulation may be the result more of trial and error than of rational calculation. Without an investigation of such a process of accumulation, they all say that the dynamics of industrial development cannot be fully understood.

We take a similar view in this book. We believe that the development of Japanese industries since the mid-nineteenth century can only be fully described with a discussion of how they acquired technology and how they accumulated capabilities. Particularly because, when Japan started its modernization effort in the mid-nineteenth century, it was technologically (as well as organizationally) behind the Western nations, its first priority was to accumulate sufficient technological and organizational capabilities to catch up with them and, hopefully, surpass them eventually. Much emphasis will be placed, therefore, on the analysis of how the firms acquired and accumulated technological capabilities over the course of development.

The question of how they acquired technologies cannot be separated from the question of who was willing to take risks to enter into unfamiliar business fields and to pursue the often enormously difficult task of acquiring unfamiliar technologies. In other words, we have to ask who the *entrepreneurs* were. Similarly, we have to ask how the managers and workers accumulated their capabilities, because an entrepreneur alone cannot develop a business without capable managers and workers. It is important to answer these questions just as it is important to answer what role the government policies played.

In other words, a study of the process of industrial development has to be a study also of how the businesses and industrial organization evolved in the course of development. There have been a few studies on the development of the business system in Japan, for instance Hirschmeier and Yui (1975), and a few industrial case studies, some of which will be cited in later chapters. In our view, however, none has made a comprehensive study of the process of the acquisition of technology, the building of capabilities, and, as a consequence, the industrial re-structuring and economic development. Such a comprehensive study of Japan's industrial development, admittedly a huge task, is the aim of this book.

We will challenge this task by means of both a general historical study (Chapters 2–3) and industrial cases (Chapters 6–11). We will also discuss the evolution of the management system (Chapters 4–5) in a belief that the technological and industrial development of Japan cannot be fully understood without knowledge of its microeconomic and managerial foundations.

1.2 THE BASIC VIEW

When Japan ended its Seclusionism in 1859 (see Section 1.7 below for the precise meaning of 'Seclusionism') and started a new non-feudal government with the Meiji Restoration of 1867, the leaders realized how far behind Western countries Japan was in many aspects of technology. The government, therefore, made efforts to import superior technology, hire engineers from abroad, educate its people, and encourage the entrepreneurs to assimilate foreign technologies and apply them into Japanese factories. In addition, the government was determined to catch up with the West in its military capacity, thereby having a strong incentive to support technological catch-up and make domestic procurement feasible.

It is easy to attribute Japan's rapid development to latecomer advantages and active government policies. One can, for instance, easily make a list of intellectual and scientific import. Although the language itself is more or less original, in writing the people use characters, *kanji*, imported from China. They also created their own phonetic characters, *kana*, by deforming Chinese characters. In religion, Buddhism has the largest following, which was imported from India via China. Furthermore, Confucianism, imported again from China, at one time prevailed although now less so. These religions and thoughts have been also transformed, sometimes intentionally by those in power (Morishima, 1982) and sometimes to satisfy the wishes of common people.

Scientific knowledge was also imported; mostly from China in the early periods, sporadically from The Netherlands during the Tokugawa era, and then from America and Europe since the Meiji Restoration. Thus, for instance, in the case of pharmaceuticals discussed in Chapter

11, the medical doctors at first practised the Chinese method except for a few who practised the Dutch method during the Tokugawa era, and then following the Meiji Restoration, virtually all the doctors started to practise the Western medical method, most importantly the German one.

One should not conclude, however, that Japan has been totally dependent on imported knowledge and technology, or that Japan imported them without cost. Any country has to possess capabilities, often at a surprisingly high level, to be able to absorb and fully utilize technology; that is, there must be an absorptive capacity there. Such capabilities were present in Japan, partly inherited from its own indigenous technology and partly fostered through education and other conscious efforts. One aim of this book, therefore, is to demonstrate how indispensable such capabilities were and how Japan had accumulated them.

The government of course contributed to this accumulation, by creating industrial infrastructure and encouraging investment, besides establishing the education system. In the early Meiji, namely the latter half of the nineteenth century, the government raised the slogan of *Fukoku Kyohei* (enriching the nation and strengthening the military) in order not to become subordinate to Western power. They have taken a number of policy initiatives towards this end (see Chapter 2). Similarly, after the defeat in World War II, the maintenance of necessities for the large population and the recovery of the pre-war production level were the main concern of the government. Certain policies have been taken (see Chapter 3).

However, the government alone could never bring the industrial development that Japan has achieved. It also needed the initiative of the private sector to endeavour to accumulate sufficient technological capabilities, to take risks in making investment, particularly to enter into unfamiliar and uncertain industries, and to make the right managerial decisions. Only with such private initiatives and capabilities could government policies achieve the desired effects. Only with them could the economy overcome any undesirable effects the policies might have had on the market mechanism. Active entrepreneurial activities were needed, which were actually there in surprisingly many instances during the course of Japan's development. As a consequence, a high degree of contestability and competition was maintained, no doubt fostering the efficiency and growth.

Hence, both the private sector (the firms) and the public sector (the government) played indispensable roles in Japan's development,

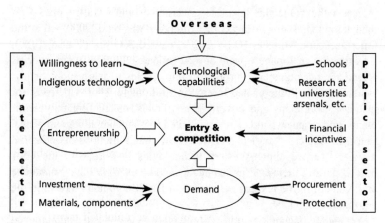

FIG. 1.1. Technology and industrial development in Japan: the basic view

together with the inflow of information, capital, and other resources from overseas. A very simplified picture of this mechanism is shown in Figure 1.1. We emphasize that the market mechanism of entry and competition played the vital role of fostering efficiency and stimulating dynamism. What supported such entry and competition are the three elements of growth—technological capabilities, entrepreneurship, and demand—which we will discuss in some detail below. One may wish to view these as representing, respectively, technology, supply, and demand sides of economic growth.

1.3 TECHNOLOGICAL CAPABILITIES

Scientific and technological knowledge was transferred into Japan in many ways. Most apparently, the transfer took place when information itself was imported through licensing agreements of patents and knowhow, including that on production, accounting, and other management systems. The transfer was also made by bringing in people from abroad and sending Japanese abroad.

In the early Meiji period, Americans and Europeans hired by the Japanese government and by industry were many and provided not only scientific, technological, and engineering knowledge but also expertise in designing social infrastructure, such as education, law, and administration. The exorbitant salaries paid to these hired Westerners clearly indicates the value the Japanese government and industry placed on their knowledge. For instance, one foreigner was paid 2,000 yen at the time the Prime Minister (*Dajo Daijin*) earned 800 yen (Yuasa, 1980).

A number of Japanese went abroad to learn. Some of them, such as scientists and engineers, enrolled in universities to learn more or less systematically. Some visited foreign institutions for shorter periods; for instance, politicians and government officials visited foreign governments, and managers and engineers visited foreign companies and plants. Later, in our case studies, we will show that a number of industrial pioneers learned about Western technologies in Europe or the USA before starting their enterprises in Japan. The examples are Yamanobe and Kikuchi in the textiles industry, and Hashimoto and Aikawa in the automobile industry.

Yet another technology transfer took place as goods and capital moved into Japan. The imported products were often disassembled and copied, that is, 'reverse-engineered'. Technological knowledge was also embodied in the imported machines and equipment, raising the productivity level.

Direct investment into Japan also caused the transfer of technology. The transfer was most prominent in many cases of capital participation by foreign companies because, from the Japanese viewpoint, the acquisition of technology through licensing and guidance was the main purpose of seeking the participation. The most typical is the case of the electrical and communications equipment industry (see Chapter 8). Even in the cases of fully-owned subsidiaries, such as the pre-war Japanese subsidiaries of Ford and General Motors, many technologies spilled over to the suppliers and the workers in a number of ways.

In these examples, we will show that technology transfer can be effectively made only when the receiving country makes sufficient investment, is motivated to learn, and is intelligent enough to understand the acquired knowledge. The expenditure by the Meiji government to hire foreign experts and to send many Japanese abroad was no doubt a huge investment for the still poor country. The country also allocated a large proportion of its limited budget to create a national education system from elementary education, which became compulsory around the turn of the century, to higher education (see Chapter 2).

The education level can never be raised, however, by government investment alone. It also requires the willingness of pupils and students to learn, and the willingness of parents to bear the cost of education, including the cost of lost earnings during schooling, a major expense in a still underdeveloped country. Such willingness was abundant in

Japan; otherwise the enrolment ratio of nearly 100 per cent would not have been attained, however compulsory the elementary education was supposed to be.

In addition, the technological skills accumulated through the Tokugawa era cannot be ignored. Some of these came from Dutch books and doctors because the relationship with The Netherlands was maintained even under Seclusionism. Others came from indigenous technology. Although one may argue that the indigenous technology was not based on scientific knowledge and, hence, was hardly related to the imported Western technology, it still helped the Japanese to grasp the mechanism or the basic idea behind it. For instance, master craftsmen who had been trained during the Tokugawa era could utilize their skills in copying imported machines and equipment, for instance telephone receivers (see Chapter 8).

Furthermore, the choice of technology had to be made with the geographic, climatic, and socio-economic conditions taken into account, and knowledge of indigenous technology helped to understand these conditions. On many occasions, imported technology had to be adapted to achieve the desired effect, which again required a certain level of knowledge and skills. In iron-making, the first Japanese to build a blast furnace based on Dutch technology did not simply copy the technology from the book; he adapted it to the indigenous iron-making technology so that the new technology would fit the local conditions (see Chapter 7). Without such knowledge and without such willingness and capability to adapt the technology, his attempt would have failed.

Thus, technological capabilities cannot be developed simply by investing in technology importation and in education and training. There has to be a certain background facilitating the absorption of imported technology, and there has to be a willingness on the part of the industry to make necessary investment and innovate. To this latter topic we now turn.

1.4 ENTREPRENEURSHIP

Schumpeter (1942: 82) once argued that 'capitalism . . . is by nature a form or method of economic change and not only never is but never can be stationary.' There is hardly any other time or any other nation in which this statement fits better than the turbulent years in Japan following the Meiji Restoration and following World War II. The process of 'creative destruction', as Schumpeter called it, was there, which destroyed much of the old and traditional, from businesses and markets to social customs and institutions, and created the new. At the core of this process was the presence of entrepreneurship.

Entrepreneurship, in essence, is the willingness to undertake something new and unfamiliar. Anyone undertaking such an enterprise is constrained by the lack of knowledge and resources. One has to strive, therefore, to gain the necessary technologies as well as the financial and human resources in order to come up with products, production processes, channels of marketing them, sources of supply, and methods of organizing the business. That is, one has to *innovate* however time-consuming, costly, and formidable it is expected to be. The willingness to challenge such a task is the essence of entrepreneurship.

Other related obstacles are the uncertainty and the risk associated with any new enterprise. The uncertainty may be scientific or technological; for instance one may not know whether and how one can solve technical problems. It may be economic; for instance the demand for a new product may not be known in advance. It may be social; for instance the society may be sceptical, or even hostile, to the new enterprise. It may be even political; for instance the government may try to prevent a new venture which, in their eyes, would cause a disorder. Therefore, the majority of the population, which may be safely assumed to be risk averse, would opt to not undertake such an uncertain enterprise. Still, there must be some people who are willing to challenge it—who are less risk averse or who have a more favourable subjective probabilistic expectation.

The function of entrepreneurs as undertakers of innovation was emphasized especially by Schumpeter (1942) and that of risk-takers by Knight (1921), although these two functions are rarely separable in reality. Both Schumpeter and Knight were aware that the number of entrepreneurs is limited and that their availability is one of the key factors, if not *the* factor, of economic development. Knight, for instance, argued that 'the supply of entrepreneur qualities in society is one of the chief factors in determining the number and size of its productive units' (ibid.: 283).

Similarly, Marshall (1923: 645) wrote: 'progress has been effected on the scientific side by students and by business men: on the practical side by those business men, who have been alert to invent or adopt new ideas; to put them into practice, bearing the risks of loss; to improve on them, and again to improve on them'. Although he did not use the word 'entrepreneurs', he clearly implied that their presence is indispensable in economic progress.[1]

In Japan, a number of entrepreneurs appeared in nearly every industry despite (or because of) a large technological gap behind the West and enormous uncertainty surrounding new opportunities. After the Meiji Restoration, a number of former *samurai*, who had been relatively educated but became unemployed following the Restoration, turned entrepreneurs, struggling to innovate (see Chapter 4). In the early post-World War II period, the business risk was still high but the opportunities to introduce new technologies were there. A number of entrepreneurs eagerly took the risk and worked hard to expand their businesses by means of innovation. Ibuka and Morita of Sony, and Honda and Fujisawa of Honda are well known. Among the lesser known are Kondo and Tsuzuki in the textiles industry. Some post-war managers of existing firms undertook entrepreneurial innovation and investment, for instance, Nishiyama of Kawasaki Steel. As will be repeatedly argued throughout this book, the rapid catch-up of Japanese industries would have been impossible were it not for such abundant entrepreneurship.

Entrepreneurs have to be distinguished from mere managers. The distinction was made by Knight as well as by Penrose. According to the latter, 'entrepreneurial services are contrasted with managerial services which relate to the execution of entrepreneurial ideas and proposals and to the supervision of existing operations' (Penrose, 1959: 31).

Such managerial capability is indispensable in industrial development, because one has to run businesses after innovation is introduced and investment made. Financial resources must be secured and human resources must be recruited, educated, organized, and motivated. Relational skills may be needed to deal with the government and the military, or with foreign firms and governments. The company system and the internal labour system need to be created and adapted to changing environments. An economy, therefore, cannot grow continually unless adequate corporate and labour systems are there. These aspects of Japan's development are the main themes of Chapters 4 and 5.

1.5 THE ROLE OF GOVERNMENT IN SUPPORTING DEMAND AND PROMOTING INDUSTRIES

Technological capabilities and entrepreneurship that characterize the technological and supply conditions of an economy have to be supported by market demand. Demand is partly created by entrepreneurs themselves through investment in production facilities and the purchase of materials and components. The government can also play an important role through public investment and consumption; for instance, investment to create a system for the telegraph service led to an expanding demand in telegraph equipment and wire, and that for the railway in rolling stock and rails. Military procurement was a big source of demand for several industries, including shipbuilding, aircraft, automobiles, and communications equipment. The procurement by semi-government organizations, such as Nihon Denshin Denwa (Nippon Telegraph and Telephone, NTT), Nihon Hoso Kyokai (NHK, Japan Broadcasting Corp.), Nihon Kokuyu Tetsudo (Japan National Railways, JNR; now privatized as Japan Railways, JR), and Nihon Kouku (Japan Air Lines, JAL), was also often made with certain policy aims.

In addition, the government influenced market conditions by controlling foreign trade and investment. Import restriction was a particularly important means of protecting markets for domestic producers. In fact, some of the industrial policies of the Japanese government may be best understood with this emphasis on the demand effects. Also, the stoppage of imports from America and Europe during World War I and in the years immediately preceding World War II caused a huge demand increase to some of the domestic producers.

By no means, however, were the Japanese markets always closed. In the early Meiji era, protection was minimal because under the Unequal Treaties that the Tokugawa Shogunate government signed under duress in 1858 with several Western countries, the government had no discretion to set tariffs. Some of the American and European economies were surely more closed at the time.

More recently, the trade and capital liberalization during the 1960s forced the government to abandon most of the means of market protection that it used to have. Thus, beyond a few still regulated industries such as agriculture, the main means with which the government tried to exert its influencé had become a less coercive measure of administrative guidance (*gyosei shido*) to the industries.

The government has occasionally provided financial incentives, such as subsidies, tax credits, and low-interest loans, to encourage technological accumulation and market entry. For instance, the pre-war automobile industry received a subsidy for developing government-approved 'standard' cars (see Chapter 9). After the war, a number of industries received tax credits and other benefits. Also, many of the research associations, to be discussed in Chapter 3, were subsidized.

The effect of these financial incentives is difficult to evaluate because we never know how the industries would have evolved without them. There are a number of cases which failed despite receiving them and a number of cases which grew despite not receiving them. It is also noted that, despite a seemingly large technological lead and a dominant market power of government enterprises in the early period, for instance, Yawata Steel Works (see Chapter 7), there were a number of market entries of a purely private nature. The presence of such active entries is a clear indication that ample entrepreneurship was there in Japan.

1.6 THE ORGANIZATION OF THE BOOK

A study of technological and industrial development necessarily entails a study of industrial organization as well. We have discussed the basic demand and supply conditions, including technological capabilities, entrepreneurship, and government policies, as the determinants of the speed and course of industrial development. They are also the determinants of industrial organization and, since they are neither exogenous nor stationary, the industrial organization is also bound to change according to internal forces. The purpose of this book is to approach this complex issue through a study of Japan's experience since the mid-nineteenth century. Such a study, we believe, is essential in order to know if there is any peculiarity with Japan's experience and to consider if there is anything from which the present developing countries can learn.

The book consists of three parts. In Chapters 2 and 3, we discuss Japan's economic and technological development in general, with details of government policies. We then discuss the evolution of management system in Chapters 4 and 5 because, in our view, industrial development would be hindered without a parallel development in the management systems, such as the legal status of a company, the internal labour system, and the financial system. Then, starting with Chapter 6, we study the development process of six major industries. These case studies are intended to give a more accurate understanding of how the technological capabilities were developed and the industrial organization evolved. Finally, as a conclusion, we summarize and discuss the observations and lessons from our study of Japan's past experience. For the readers' convenience, a brief chronology of Japan's history is included in an appendix. A map of Japan appears at the front of the book.

Throughout the book, Japanese names are given with surnames first, following the Japanese convention (except our names on the cover of this book): as usual, surnames follow first names for Western names. Japanese company names, when they appear for the first time, are usually given by the Japanese original names with the English translation in parentheses. Thereafter, either the Japanese name or English name is used.

1.7 INITIAL CONDITIONS: ACCUMULATION OF TECHNOLOGICAL CAPABILITIES UP TO THE MID-NINETEENTH CENTURY

The discussion in the subsequent chapters focus on the development since the mid-nineteenth century when, in 1854, Japan started to have diplomatic relationship with Western countries (besides The Netherlands with which the Tokugawa government kept a relationship even under its seclusionist policy) and when, with the Meiji Restoration of 1867, a non-feudal central government under Emperor Meiji was established. We discuss here, albeit briefly, the development of Japan's industrial and technological bases up to the mid-nineteenth century.

By focusing on the post-Meiji development, by no means do we imply that the technological base was insignificant until then or that the development since the Meiji era was a discontinuous jump from the earlier one. Actually we believe otherwise; that is, we believe there was a substantial base accumulated even during the two and a half centuries of feudalism and seclusionism. There were quite a number of cases, even then, of Japan either importing technology for adaptation or inventing and improving its own indigenous technology, showing a rather astonishing similarity to the way it accumulated technology after the Restoration. Without the technological and industrial bases thus accumulated, the post-Restoration development would have been much more difficult. We will later observe that, in a number of industries, the technological knowledge accumulated during the Tokugawa era was utilized to understand imported modern technologies and adapt them to fit to Japan's natural and social conditions.

Major importation of cultural, scientific, and technological knowledge before the Tokugawa era (1600–1867) took place twice, first in the fifth to ninth century, when the emperor's government still had the real power, and then in the sixteenth century, when feudal lords (*daimyo*) fought against each other. Chinese characters and Confucianism are believed to have reached Japan around the fifth century and Buddhism, the sixth century. Knowledge of the calender, medicine, pottery, and weaving also came around the same time. Around 600 AD, the emperor, following Prince Shotoku's advice, sent envoys to China under the Sui Dynasty, both to trade and to import culture and technology. Envoys were sent eighteen times in all until the mid-ninth century. The knowledge thus imported gave an important impact on the art, architecture, religion (Buddhism in particular), literature, and technology in construction, textiles, pottery, and many other fields. For instance, the first clock was made with imported technology.

Although the emperor's envoys were not sent after the mid-ninth century, occasional contacts with China (under the Tang, Sung, and Ming Dynasties) and Korea took place, in particular for the purpose of trade, which brought valuable knowledge to Japan. For instance, tea-drinking is believed to have come to Japan in the twelfth century.

The first contact with the West took place in 1543 when a Portuguese ship was hit by a typhoon and drifted ashore on Tanegashima, a small island in the south-west. They brought guns at the time when a series of fierce wars was taking place among several feudal lords. Not surprisingly, these lords soon started using guns to defeat rival lords, which created a strong demand for guns. A number of blacksmiths, with the order or encouragement of these lords, started producing guns either by copying foreign guns or with the help of Portuguese gunsmiths who started to arrive in Japan. The technological level in guns, ships, and other arms production seems to have soon caught up with the West, indicating the presence of absorptive capacity even in this early period. Besides gunsmiths, a number of Europeans arrived in Japan around this time. The majority of them were Portuguese but some came from Spain, England, and The Netherlands. Some of them came for the purpose of trade while some were missionaries. It is important and perhaps ironic to note that the first main European export to Japan was weaponry and Christianity.

The internal war ended when Toyotomi Hideyoshi conquered every part of Japan and then, after Hideyoshi's death, his son was defeated by Tokugawa Ieyasu. Ieyasu was nominated to be a *shogun* by the emperor and, with the real power now residing in shogun (a hereditary position), started the government in 1603. The Tokugawa government, sensing that Christians might disobey their rule, prohibited Christianity, deported Portuguese and Spanish, and restricted foreign trade to the

Chinese, the Korean, and the Dutch only. Under this policy of Seclusionism, the only Western contact that the Japanese maintained was through a number of Dutchmen allowed to live in Nagasaki in Kyushu, the westmost of Japan's four major islands (see the map at the front of the book). The Tokugawa government monopolized the trade, though evidence suggests that some of the powerful feudal lords (*daimyo*) did trade with Chinese and other foreigners.

By request of the government, the Dutch regularly provided information on foreign affairs and science, some of which was spread to other lords. The Dutch in Nagasaki were also a source of information on many aspects of science and technology, such as medical science, biology, and geography. Several Dutch books were translated into Japanese, and a number of Japanese studied with Dutch doctors or other scientists living in the Dutch quarters of Nagasaki. Thus, Seclusionism by no means implied a complete seclusion from foreign scientific and technological knowledge. In fact, the knowledge learned from the Dutch contributed to a rapid absorption of the Western economic system and technologies when the Tokugawa government opened the country to other Western nations in 1854. For instance, the first Western-style iron furnace was made by a samurai who had studied a Dutch book (see Chapter 7).

In terms also of indigenous technology, the Tokugawa era was hardly a static period. Because of the importance of agriculture and mining for the feudal lords' finances, productivity increase in these areas was encouraged and many improvements were made and diffused. Particularly, because of the steep flow of rivers and the climatic conditions (rainy season in June–July and typhoons in September–October) and because of the importance of water in rice cropping, a large investment was made to improve rivers and make irrigation systems. Consequently, the technological level in civil engineering is believed to have been high.

Machine engineering was another area for indigenous technology at the time. The innovators were called *karakuri* masters because karakuri, a moving mechanism, was the most essential part of any machine. These mechanisms were applied to many sorts of machines and tools, ranging from dolls and clocks to textile looms and rice-polishing machines.[2] Again, we will show later that there was a continuous development from such indigenous technology to imported Western technology after the Meiji Restoration. Tanaka Hisashige, probably the most important karakuri master toward the end of the Tokugawa era, was one of the first to make a steam engine using Western technology and became a pioneer in the electrical equipment industry. Toyoda Sakichi invented internationally copied looms.

Therefore, although the Japanese failed to invent steam engines among other things, their technological level was not far behind the West. This fact should be emphasized because it is in marked difference from the cases of many developing countries today. In addition, the educational level during the latter Tokugawa era was high—probably higher in elementary education than the USA, Britain, France, and Germany, though lower in higher education because in these countries science education in universities had started by the early nineteenth century.

Basically, there were two school systems. The first was the schools owned by feudal local governments, which were usually compulsory for the children of *samurai* (i.e., the employees, as warriors and officials, of respective local governments). Many of them also admitted the children of wealthy farmers and merchants. The second was private schools, called *terakoya*, since many of them were run by Buddhist temples (*tera*). The length of education varied but, most typically, it went from the age of 6 to 12, similar to the present elementary school system. They mainly taught reading, writing, and the use of *soroban* (abacus) to calculate.

In addition to these schools for children, there were a number of private or public higher education systems. Some of these taught purely Japanese or Chinese studies, for instance, Confucianism. However, there were private schools teaching medical science using Dutch books. The best-known was Tekijuku, a private school in Osaka taught by Ogata Koan who had learned Dutch medical science in Nagasaki. Among his students were Fukuzawa Yukichi, who later introduced Western democratic thoughts and commercial practices to Japan (see Chapter 4) and established one of the first private universities, Keio; Nagayo Sensai, who later played a major role in establishing the regulatory framework for medical services and in founding the first Western-style pharmaceutical company in Japan (see Chapter 11); and Ohmura Masujiro, who later designed the Meiji military system but was assassinated before the system was completed. We will discuss Ogata's activity again in our study of the pharmaceutical industry.

There were not many terakoyas and other schools in the early Tokugawa era but they became more and more popular and, according to a very rough estimate, there were almost 10,000 such schools in Japan towards the end of the era. Many of them were small with ten or fewer children, but there were schools with more than 500 in big cities such as Edo (later renamed to Tokyo) and Kyoto. The ratio of school enrolment (or attendance) varied among estimates and among regions, ranging from about 25 to almost 100 per cent for boys while the percentage was lower for girls (Umihara, 1988). These estimates can be misleading because they may include those children enrolled as pupils but who seldom went. Nevertheless, the ratio of, let us say, 50 per cent under the non-compulsory system was surprisingly high and showed the eagerness of the parents to invest in education. This fact suggests that the literacy rate in Japan in the seventeenth and eighteenth century was probably higher than in Europe and America. The introduction of the public education system in the Meiji era would have been more difficult were it not for this broad educational background.

2

Economic and Technological Change from the Meiji Restoration to World War II

2.1 OVERVIEW

We begin with an overview of the general Japanese history from the mid-nineteenth century to World War II. This overview merely purports to provide background knowledge. A more detailed discussion of its economic development will be given in the next two sections, so those familiar with modern Japanese history could skip this section.[1]

In 1868, young samurai and court nobles overthrew the Tokugawa Shogunate which had ruled Japan for two and a half centuries. Their central cause was to restore the imperial rule, but the real power was in the hands of these young lower-ranking samurai and court nobles. They were the leaders of the new Meiji government. Several years prior to the Restoration, European countries and the United States had threatened Japan with their overwhelming military power in order to open its ports and start trade. Japan had to accept Unequal Treaties, as they are called there, which allowed the USA, the UK, The Netherlands, France, and Russia extraterritorial privileges and deprived Japan of the right to set its tariffs. These treaties were similar to the one they forced upon China, a country that had been practically reduced to semi-colonial status by the West. The leaders of the Meiji government were keenly aware of this appalling situation in China and, hence, fervently started a modernization effort.

The government started building up military forces; investing in social and economic infrastructures such as roads, railroads, ports, a postal system, and a banking system; building and running factories, and developing mines; and investing heavily in developing the national school system. All of these efforts necessitated the learning of Western systems and technology.

After two decades of trial and error, Japan's modernization drive bore fruits. The economy started to grow continuously, and the country had somehow acquired the military power to fend off the threat from the West. The Constitution was promulgated in 1889 and the first election in 1890 established a bicameral parliament system.

Even though, at least partly, Japan had started its zealous modernization effort for fear of imperialistic expansion by the Western nations, it started to play the same game itself. It invaded Taiwan briefly as early as 1874, and forced Korea to accept an unequal treaty (as Japan itself had been forced to accept before the Restoration). In 1894, Japan fought the Sino-Japanese War against China over the control of the Korean peninsula and, ten years later, fought another war, the Russo-Japanese War, this time against Russia over the control of Korea and Southern Manchuria. Surprisingly, the small island nation, which had started the modernization effort less than forty years before, triumphed in both wars and became one of the major powers in the world, even though the wars exhausted the nation. In 1914, World War I broke out in Europe, which gave Japan a further opportunity for expansion. Japan, with the Anglo-Japanese Alliance of 1902, declared war on Germany and seized the German interest in China and the Pacific islands with little effort.

Through these years to the end of the 1920s, the Japanese economy grew on average at around 3 per cent per annum, with post-war booms followed by recessions. The industrial structure changed throughout this growth process. Although the textiles industry remained the largest industry in terms of production and exports, the so-called heavy industries, such as steel, shipbuilding, machinery, and chemicals, expanded rapidly, especially during World War I. The growth of these industries was partly induced by the military build-up: it also reflected the natural process of economic maturation and sophistication.

In the 1920s, the Japanese economy experienced a prolonged recession. The growth rate of the first half of the 1920s fell to a level below 2 per cent, and a number of banks went bankrupt. In 1930, the Great Depression hit Japan. Under these economic conditions, the unemployment rate increased and a number of bitter labour disputes erupted. The rural areas were hit particularly hard because of a sharp drop in the price of rice and silk. Despite these general conditions, the heavy industries kept growing. In some of these industries, larger firms acquired smaller firms, and research and development as well as scientific management techniques were emphasized, as will be discussed later in more detail.

On the political front, parties became active and a parliamentary government took hold. The foreign policy was characterized by a series of Disarmament Treaties, negotiated under the American leadership. The society had also undergone drastic changes during this decade. The emerging middle class in urban areas enjoyed literature, music, and movies made at home and abroad. Baseball became a national pastime.

In the 1930s, the tide changed. The Japanese Army overran Manchuria in 1931 and established a puppet state, Manchukuo, the following year. Despite the government's intention not to further the aggression and despite the criticism from abroad, the military invaded Mongolia and Northern China in 1933/4. At home, several *coup d'etat* attempts were made by the right-wing extremists and military officers. They captured the empathy of the people, especially those in rural areas who were perplexed by the rapid social changes and suffered badly from the prolonged recession of the 1920s. They also exploited the populist sentiment against the 'greed' of big businesses, which increased with the growth of heavy industries. The increasing dependence of the Japanese economy on foreign countries for natural resources and as the outlet for its products gave another reason for its outward military expansion.

The military gradually took control of the nation away from party politicians and elder statesmen who had survived the Meiji Restoration, and continued the aggression. The full-scale war Japan started against China in 1937 led to the Pacific War four years later, two years after World War II started in Europe. The economy was accordingly transformed to a wartime control system. In 1938, the National Total Mobilization Law (*Kokka So Doin Ho*) was enacted, allowing the government to mobilize manpower, materials, capital, and other vital items that were needed to continue the war. Price control was imposed in 1939, and the rationing of necessities such as sugar and matches was introduced in 1940.

Japan surrendered in 1945 after the airdrop of two atomic bombs. About two million people died during the war, and the major cities were destroyed. It was seventy-seven years since Japan started its modernization drive following the Meiji Restoration.

2.2   CATCHING-UP AND FORGING AHEAD

Following the brief exposition of the general history in the previous section, let us now discuss Japan's industrial and economic development from the Restoration to World War I (this section) and from World War I to World War II (next section) in more detail. Simply speaking, this development was the process of 'catching-up and forging ahead', using Abramovitz's (1986) expression.

The end of Seclusionism in 1854 and the inauguration of a non-feudal central government fourteen years later prompted Japan to catch up with the West economically and militarily. The government thus started an organized effort to modernize the country, including the provision of infrastructure for transportation, communication, utilities, education, and finance.

In the late 1860s and early 1870s, telegraph, railroad, and a modern postal system were introduced for the first time into Japan.[2] With their expansion, regional markets were gradually integrated into the national market in many industries. In 1887, the first electric power company was established. As the network of electric power spread, the use of electric motors increased in factories. According to Minami (1976), the amount of horse power generated by electric motors surpassed that of steam engines by 1917.

The modern tax system based on land tax was introduced during 1873–81, which gave the new government a means to finance the investment for infrastructure. However, because of a vast increase in government expenditure to finance such investment, to promote industries, and to finance the 1877 Civil War (*Seinan War*) to defeat the rebels in former Satsuma Clan, the money supply increased sharply, causing the prices to rise rapidly in the late 1870s. Drastic measures were taken to control this inflation during the early 1880s under the leadership of the finance minister, Matsukata Masayoshi, including tax increases and severe spending cuts. In addition, the Bank of Japan was established as the central bank in 1882 to secure an institutional foundation for a healthy monetary policy. Owing to these policies, the inflation was successfully contained by the mid-1880s, but the economy had to go through a severe recession.

The new government also made an effort to establish a country-wide education system. As discussed in the previous chapter, Japan already had a fairly well-developed elementary education system before the Restoration. Even so, it was a strenuous task to spread elementary education nation-wide in a short period of time. There were only about 20,000 schools in 1874, which was less than half of what the government had planned. As will be discussed in more detail in Section 4, it took two to three decades before the system became firmly established.

In the 1870s and early 1880s, as a means to promote industrial development, the government built and owned plants and factories in such industries as mining, railroad, shipbuilding, machinery, textiles, cement, and glass. Such a policy was taken because it was still difficult for the private sector to finance the required investment and take risks. In addition, personnel with advanced Western technological knowledge were scarce in the private sector. Nevertheless, the government's investment programme in these industries was neither quantitatively spectacular compared, say, to that of today's developing countries, nor always successful. In fact, as will be seen in later chapters, major government-owned factories, such as the Tomioka silk-spinning factory and the Kamaishi steel works, suffered losses. Such loss was partly inevitable because these factories and works were partly aimed to function as demonstration plants. Their purpose was not necessarily to make profits but to establish modern plants with which people could learn and acquire the necessary technological and managerial capabilities, and encourage the private sector to follow.

No government can sustain loss-making enterprises for long, however. With the tight government budget owing to the Seinan War and the mounting criticism against government enterprises, the government changed its policy and started to privatize them, except those related to the military and the public infrastructure. They were sold to the emerging private entrepreneurs through the 1980s and 1990s. Some of them became the foundations of *zaibatsu*, large conglomerates discussed in Chapter 4.

The role of these government-owned factories in Japan's early development should not be over-emphasized, because their scale was limited and so was the period of their existence. These factories contributed to easing the financial and technological difficulties inevitable at the early stage of industrialization, thereby making it attractive for entrepreneurs to buy them upon privatization. The government also shouldered the high initial risk associated with the start of advanced industries. Yet our case studies will suggest that such a contribution can be (and has been) easily over-emphasized. The experience of government investment in cotton spinning was apparently not as useful as, for instance, the knowledge Yamanobe Takeo gained in England before he and Shibusawa started the first large-scale cotton-spinning plant in Osaka on a purely private basis. When Tanaka Chobei started iron-making in Kamaishi, he did not use the unsuitable furnace the government had earlier built but opted to build more appropriate and smaller furnaces himself. Only after he and his staff had acquired sufficient capabilities did they restart the government-built furnaces, but they had to modify them first.

The economy was put on a course for sustained growth in the mid 1880s, after about two decades of the Restoration during which the foundations had been laid for modern economic growth. Gross National Expenditures (GNE) more than doubled and per-capita GNE grew 1.6 times during the thirty-year period of 1885 to 1914, the year World War I started: see Table 2.1. Even taking account of the low initial level, these high growth rates are impressive; they were one of the highest among the countries that started economic growth during the nineteenth century.

In terms of industrial composition, food processing and textiles were the largest manufacturing industries before the turn of the century. Food processing was mostly a traditional industry made of small firms, and was based on agriculture. Textiles started similarly but evolved into an industry of large-scale firms with international orientation in terms of the export of the product and the import of materials (see Chapter 6). The combined share of iron and steel, and machinery in the total manufacturing production was just 15 per cent in the mid 1880s.

The metal, machinery, and chemical industries (the so-called heavy industries) started to grow fast after the turn of the century. As will be discussed in later chapters, many companies in iron and steel, electrical machinery, and pharmaceuticals had been established by the mid-1910s and had started to grow. Military-related production occupied a significant portion of Japan's economy at the time, because the Meiji government was keen to build up its military capacity to defend the nation from the threat of Russia and other countries that were colonizing China.

In 1907, the largest operation in machinery industry (including shipbuilding, vehicles, general machinery, tools, and parts) in terms of the number of blue-collar workers, was the Naval Shipyard in Kure with about 21,500 employed, followed by another naval shipyard and two arsenals (Sawai, 1990). The largest private plant, Mitsubishi's Nagasaki Shipyard, ranked fifth with less than 10,000 employees, whose most important customer was again the Navy.

The military-owned plants were also a centre of technological development. They hired a large proportion of scarce engineers and imported advanced machinery from abroad. Their technology was subsequently transferred to the private sector as the engineers and skilled workers moved from the military plants to the private sector, especially during the disarmament period following the Russo-Japanese War of 1904/5.

TABLE 2.1 Gross national expenditures and production: 1875–1940

	Levels (at 1934–6 prices)					Annual growth rates (%)				Composition (%)				
	1875	1885	1900	1915	1940	1875–85	1885–1900	1900–15	1915–40	1875	1885	1900	1915	1940
Population	35,036	38,176	44,056	53,110	71,933	0.9	1.0	1.3	1.2					
GNE (million yen)		3,852	6,238	8,522	22,848		3.3	2.1	4.0		100.0	100.0	100.0	100.0
Personal consumption expenditure		3,284	5,270	6,806	13,389		3.2	1.7	2.7		85.3	84.5	79.9	58.6
Government consumption expenditure		283	538	769	3,377		4.4	2.4	6.1		7.3	8.6	9.0	14.8
Gross domestic fixed capital formation		346	703	1,176	7,070		4.8	3.5	7.4		9.0	11.3	13.8	30.9
Surplus on current account		–61	–279	–224	–988		10.7	–1.5	6.1		–1.6	–4.5	–2.6	–4.3
Exports and factor income from abroad		68	275	1,020	3,973		9.8	9.1	5.6		1.8	4.4	12.0	17.4
Imports and factor income paid abroad		129	554	1,244	4,961		10.2	5.5	5.7		3.3	8.9	14.6	21.7
GNE per Capita (yen)		101	142	160	318		2.3	0.8	2.8					
Production (million yen)														
Mining	7.1	21.3	90.3	290.6	763.7	11.6	10.1	8.1	3.9					
Coal	4	9.2	53.2	145.5	399.8	8.7	12.4	6.9	4.1					
Manufacturing	742.6	877.9	2,101	4,029.4	20,210.2	1.7	6.0	4.4	6.7	100.0	100.0	100.0	100.0	100.0
Food	457.5	454	1,018.5	1,356.3	2,634.7	–0.1	5.5	1.9	2.7	61.6	51.7	48.5	33.7	13.0
Textiles	64.1	129.7	508.7	1,133.6	3,454.3	7.3	9.5	5.5	4.6	8.6	14.8	24.2	28.1	17.1
Chemicals	75.6	99.1	186.4	427.6	3,342.3	2.7	4.3	5.7	8.6	10.2	11.3	8.9	10.6	16.5
Machines	4.9	12.2	68.9	362.2	5,580.5	9.6	12.2	11.7	11.6	0.7	1.4	3.3	9.0	27.6
Iron and steel	2.3	3.2	5.8	89.1	2,494.8	3.4	4.0	20.0	14.3	0.3	0.4	0.3	2.2	12.3
Nonferrous metals	6.1	13.8	22.7	145.4	556.2	8.5	3.4	13.2	5.5	0.8	1.6	1.1	3.6	2.8
Other	132.1	165.9	290	515.2	2,147.4	2.3	3.8	3.9	5.9	17.8	18.9	13.8	12.8	10.6

Source: K. Ohkawa, M. Shinohara, and M. Umemura (eds.), (1988), *Estimates of Long-Term Economic Statistics of Japan since 1868*. Tokyo: Toyo Keizai

The military at first produced within its own shipyards and arsenals, but gradually started procuring arms, munition, vehicles, and other products from the private sector. Since the military preferred to procure them domestically for obvious defence reasons, the procurement gave a chance for domestic producers in shipbuilding, steel, machinery, electrical equipment, and others, which were under a competitive threat from larger and technically advanced foreign firms, to increase their production and accumulate knowledge through experience. It should be noted that, as discussed earlier, Unequal Treaties with the West deprived the government of the right to set tariffs to the imports. In fact, in the 1870s, the ratio of duties collected to the value of dutiable imports was less than 3 per cent in Japan (Kinoshita, 1968) but about 45 per cent in the USA (Myers, 1970). Thus, until 1911 when the treaties were revised, the government had little means to protect domestic producers from foreign competitors except preferential procurement; that is, the budding Japanese manufacturing firms had to compete with the competitors of the developed countries without tariff protection.

2.3   THE ADVANCE OF HEAVY INDUSTRIES DURING THE INTER-WAR PERIOD

During the three decades from the start of World War I to the end of World War II, the Japanese economy transformed itself significantly. Some of the consequences of this transformation persisted in the postwar period and may have formed the foundation for the current Japanese economic and management systems.

In the latter half of the 1910s, the economy enjoyed an unprecedented boom. The export more than tripled during 1914–18 owing to the war-related demand from Europe and the USA, and to the increasing export to Asia—the supply from Europe and the USA being severely curtailed because of the war. European and American export was also reduced to the Japanese market, which was expanding owing to the increased military spending. These conditions boosted the demand for Japanese firms tremendously, particularly in the heavy industries, which were still at an early stage of their development and had been struggling to compete against more advanced European and American firms. Zaibatsu expanded and new firms entered. Many of these new firms failed to survive the prolonged recession in the 1920s but Matsushita

Denki (Matsushita Electric Industries), Komatsu, Nihon Kogaku (now Nikon), and a number of other firms survived and expanded.

The war caused the stoppage of critical imports, such as advanced equipment and materials, and this stoppage convinced the policy-makers and the industries of the importance of domestic production. Various measures were taken to support the production and strengthen the technology base as will be discussed in Section 2.5.

The heated boom ended in 1920 as the stock market collapsed, and the Japanese economy entered the prolonged recession that persisted during the 1920s. The stock-market collapse caused a sharp drop in the prices of commodities, such as silk and rice, leading to the financial difficulty of the firms and banks involved in the trade of these commodities. In 1927, Suzuki Shoten, a conglomerate which had expanded rapidly during and after World War I went bankrupt (see Chapter 6) and the Taiwan Bank, which had been supporting Suzuki Shoten's expansion through its generous loans, was on the verge of collapse. People started to withdraw their deposits and the entire financial system was endangered. The Bank of Japan had to provide special loans to solve the crisis. In 1929, the collapse of the stock market in Wall Street, New York, triggered a further depression. The wholesale price and export price dropped 30 per cent and 47 per cent, respectively, during 1929–31.

During the 1920s, the machinery, chemical, metal, and other industries struggled to compete against imports. In addition, the demand was low owing to the prolonged recession and the arms reduction following the Washington Naval Disarmament Conference of 1921–2. Many small firms went bankrupt or were acquired by larger firms, thereby increasing concentration. Major firms in a number of industries formed cartels to eliminate the excess supply situation. Mishima (1980) reports that seven cartels were formed by 1914; twelve during 1915–26 and twelve during 1927–9.

The effectiveness of these cartels has been questioned, however. In the cotton-spinning industry, where the first cartel in the country was formed, the cartel may have actually accelerated investment because it restricted only the operation of existing machines (see Chapter 6). In the sugar industry, the cartel restricted the production within mainland Japan (excluding Korea and Taiwan, then Japan's colonies), which propelled the firms to re-import the sugar they had exported to Korea (Arisawa, 1967). That is, the inherent force of market competition seems to have often prevailed over the restrictive force of cartels.

Nevertheless, in a belief that cartels should help to 'rationalize' the industry through stable business performance, the government implemented the Vital Industries Control Law (*Juyo Sangyo Tousei Ho*) in 1931. This law required cartels in designated industries to be notified to the government. Moreover, if the majority of the firms belonged to the cartel and two thirds of them agreed, the cartel was allowed to force the outsiders to obey the cartel agreement. Although such enforcement of the outsiders was rarely exercised, the law fostered a pro-cartel atmosphere; consequently, many cartels were formed and industrial associations usually played a central role in monitoring cartel agreements. The voluntary character of cartels and associations became very thin and, in 1937 when the war against China started, there were 1,173 diverse industrial associations and 109 cartels (Hirschmeier and Yui, 1975). The road to wartime control was thus paved and some authors argue that the effect remained to the post-war period (see Chapter 4).

Several measures of industrial policy were also adopted to rationalize and modernize the industries. Perhaps most importantly, the procurement by the Army, the Navy, the Ministry of Railways, the Ministry of Telecommunications, and other government agencies was an important source of demand in the machinery, automobile, shipbuilding, aircraft, and communications equipment industries (as will be discussed in the case studies), and domestic firms were favoured in such procurement despite the poorer quality and higher cost. The 'Buy Japan' campaign was also organized by the government to encourage the consumers to buy domestic products.

Technological support was provided to the industries by government laboratories, the arsenals, and the naval shipyards. Often, engineers moved from these institutions to private companies, thereby fostering technology transfer. In several industries, such as automobile, steel, and dye, specific laws were introduced to promote the industries.

In the early 1930s, the economy finally started to escape from the long recession of the 1920s. Takahashi Korekiyo was appointed to be the new finance minister in 1931 and adopted an expansionary fiscal policy. Increasing military build-up owing to the Manchuria Incident in 1931 and other hostilities caused an expanding demand in war-related industries. And the depreciation of the yen after the end of the short-lived gold standard raised import prices and fostered import substitution. Domestic industries benefited from this environment. Particularly, the heavy industries expanded rapidly as shown in Table 2.1 above. During the decade of 1934 to 1944, the production of steel more than doubled and that of machinery almost quadrupled. The share in total manufacturing production of heavy industries increased from 33.9 per cent in 1931 to 55.8 per cent in 1937, and then to 70.2 per cent in 1942 (Miyazaki and Ito, 1989).

These industries had been gradually accumulating technological capabilities through the long recession period of the 1920s and were now ready to take off. Many of the firms were led by engineers who were eager to import advanced technologies from abroad to achieve domestic production, or to accumulate their own technology through reverse engineering, learning from trial and error, and development efforts. They often had a strong nationalistic enthusiasm as well as scientific curiosity, and pursued technological catch-up with fervour. Many examples will be given in later chapters, such as Noguchi Shitagau of Nitchitsu chemical group (see Chapter 4), Odaira Namihei of Hitachi (see Chapter 8), Aikawa Yoshisuke of Nissan and Toyoda Kiichiro of Toyota (see Chapter 9), and Nakajima Chikuhei of Nakajima Aircraft (see Chapter 10). Noguchi and Aikawa, in particular, were the founders of the so-called 'New Zaibatsu' to be discussed in Chapter 4, together with Mori Nobuteru of Showa Denko, a chemical group, and Nakano Tomonori of Nippon Soda, another chemical group.

The government control on the economy was gradually intensified as the hostilities intensified and, finally in 1938, with the enactment of the National Total Mobilization Law (*Kokka So Doin Ho*), the economy was totally under wartime control. Since it has been argued that this control system was the origin of Japanese industrial and managerial systems such as the main bank system, the supplier system, and the close government-industry relationship, we will come back to this topic in Chapters 4 and 5.

2.4 ESTABLISHING THE EDUCATION SYSTEM

Recent theories of economic growth, most notably the endogenous growth theory, emphasize the role of education in economic growth. Therefore, let us go back to the early Meiji era and discuss how Japan built the education system in the early stage of its economic modernization.

As discussed in Section 1.7, the education level in Japan is estimated to have been fairly high even before the Meiji Restoration. This fact should be kept in mind in evaluating the government's role in the establishment and spread of a nation-wide public education system after the Restoration.

In 1874, seven years after the Restoration and two years after the government set off a series of efforts to establish a modern, nation-wide elementary education system, there were about 20,000 schools, less than half of what the government had planned. Some of these schools were converted from *terakoya* (the private elementary education institutions during the Tokugawa era: see Section 1.7) and taught by former terakoya teachers. The enrolment ratio was 46 per cent for boys and 17 per cent for girls.

By 1907 when a compulsory six-year education system was finally established following three decades of trial and error, the ratio had reached 99 per cent for boys and 96 per cent for girls. Thus, illiteracy among the youth was nearly absent by the beginning of the twentieth century. Secondary education became also commonly available and, by 1920, more than half of the children out of elementary schools proceeded to two-year or five-year secondary schools (Kaigo, 1971).

Needless to say, this rapid spread of elementary education would not have been achieved with the government effort alone. In fact, in the beginning, the attendance ratio remained at about 70 per cent among the 32 per cent who had enrolled, despite the government effort to encourage the parents to enrol their children and have them attend. The cause obviously was the high cost of education, including the loss of earnings, which was unbearable to many parents in the still poor economy. However, as the economic and social merit of education became known, the enthusiasm for education rose and the enrolment and attendance ratio started to increase.

Clearly, building schools is necessary but not sufficient in order to raise the level of education. The demand must be there as well. Even though the government can encourage school attendance by advertising the merit of education, it takes time for parents to be convinced of the merit. The presence of many schools (terakoya) during the Tokugawa era helped in this regard, because many parents were familiar with the concept of learning at schools. In addition, income has to reach a certain level for many parents to be able to afford the education cost.

For the higher education system, particularly in the field of technology and engineering education, a British influence was introduced. Kobusho (the Ministry of Industries), which was started with the advice of a British railway engineer, hired a Scotsman, Henry Dyer, to make a plan for an engineering college. In 1873, Kogakuryo (the College of

Engineering) was established and eight more British professors were hired besides Dyer himself who became the head. In the first year, it admitted fifty-two students between ages 15 to 18 for a six-year course. During 1879–85, 211 students graduated who had majored in the following seven fields (the number of graduates from each field is given in parentheses): civil engineering (45), mechanical engineering (39), telegraphy (21), architecture (20), practical chemistry (25), mining (48), metallurgy (5), and shipbuilding (8).

The eagerness and high quality of both the professors and the students made the college successful. It hired more foreign (mostly British) professors and then started to replace them with its own Japanese graduates. In 1877, Kogakuryo was renamed Kobu Daigakko and in 1886 merged with another college, established by the Tokugawa government, to teach science and technology, with the help of the Dutch, the French, and the Germans. This merger created the Engineering Department of Imperial University (later renamed the University of Tokyo). The College and the University produced graduates who later founded many of the major Japanese manufacturing companies (see Chapter 4).

That the college was supported by the Ministry of Industry also helped Dyer's objectives, partly because the facilities at the Ministry could be used and partly because the students received scholarships on condition that they would work at the Ministry for several years after graduation. Hence, they were eager to gain practical knowledge. The merger to become a part of the Imperial University implied a loss of this connection with the Ministry because it now became under the authority of Mombusho (Ministry of Education). The result, it seems, was some shift from practice to academism.[3]

It is noteworthy that Dyer later exported his Japanese experience of engineering education to his home town, Glasgow. He had been recommended to the Japanese government by a professor of the University of Glasgow, and went to Japan at the age of 25, after receiving a master's degree. The programme of study at Kogakuryo emphasized the interaction between classroom studies and on-site training at the laboratory within Kogakuryo as well as at the Ministry's works. This balance between the two aspects of education was uncommon in European schools at the time.

Dyer returned to Glasgow in 1882 and made efforts to introduce a similar engineering educational programme to a technical college. Apparently, the Japanese government placed an emphasis on practical engineering education at the time when pure science was regarded as being superior to engineering in developed countries (except, perhaps, the USA: see Rosenberg and Nelson, 1994). This background gave Dyer an opportunity to experiment with his ideas in engineering education and, only with this Japanese experience, could he persuade his own people of the importance of engineering education.[4]

Tokyo Imperial University was the only national university until 1897 when Kyoto Imperial University (now Kyoto University) was established. In addition, Tokyo Shokuko Gakko was established as a practical technical school in 1881, which later became Tokyo Kogyo Gakko and then the present Tokyo Institute of Technology. It offered a three-year course (plus a one-year preparatory course) for chemical engineering and mechanical engineering.

For business education, Tokyo Koto Shogyo Gakko, the predecessor to Hitotsubashi University, was established in 1885. Several private colleges were also established before the turn of century. In addition to Fukuzawa's Keio (see Section 1.7), the predecessors of Hosei, Senshu, Meiji, Waseda, and Chuo Universities were established during 1879–85, all of which taught law.

Later, during the 1920s and 1930s, more universities, both public and private, were established, including the Imperial Universities of Hokkaido, Tohoku, Nagoya, Osaka, and Kyushu. Professional higher education institutions, with shorter programmes, were also established in engineering, commerce, pedagogy, and other fields. As the high salary earned by university graduates became known, the attraction of university education increased and the race for admission became intense. What is known as *gakureki*-ism (educational careerism), or what Dore (1976) called 'diploma disease' resulted, although it is questionable if such enthusiasm for diploma really is *over*-education from an economic viewpoint (Odagiri, 1993). Dore argues that such 'disease' has not been unique to Japan but is observed in many developing countries.

2.5 TECHNOLOGICAL PROGRESS AND R&D ACTIVITIES

Technological progress was an important source of Japan's economic growth. Minami (1992) estimates that 65 per cent of the growth of per-capita production in mining and manufacturing in 1908–38 is accounted for by the residual factors, which include technological progress. The main sources of this technological progress were indigenous (traditional and domestic) technology and the technology imported from advanced countries. Indigenous technology was important not only for its own sake, particularly in traditional industries, but also in providing a capacity to select the most suitable among foreign technologies and to adapt them to domestic conditions. Later, we will show that in many industries, the knowledge of indigenous technology helped Japanese industries to make full use of imported technology.

This fact notwithstanding, the role of indigenous technology was limited and, in most modern industries, imported technology played a far greater role. As discussed already in Chapter 1, technology transfer from abroad was made through many channels. Many foreign engineers and specialists were hired, although they were gradually replaced by Japanese staff educated domestically or abroad. Other channels of technology transfer were importation of advanced machinery (and reverse engineering), licensing agreements, and foreign direct investment into Japan. The latter two have increased since the turn of the century because the government liberalized foreign direct investment (in return for the revision of Unequal Treaties) and also joined the Paris Convention, though the patent system itself was introduced as early as 1885.

The number of patents granted in Japan during July 1885 and February 1902 was 4,817 (Patent Office, 1955). In comparison, the number was 27,136 in 1902 alone in the USA, 13,714 in the UK, 12,026 in France, and 10,610 in Germany. Hence, the number of patents in Japan was hardly comparable with those of the Western countries. Among these 4,817 patents, 2,175 (45 per cent) were related to machinery, 728 (15 per cent) to chemicals, 52 (1 per cent) to electric equipment, and 1,862 (39 per cent) to miscellaneous. Therefore, in so far as we can infer from the number of patents, R&D in the machinery industry seems to have been relatively active around the turn of the century.

The country's scientific and engineering base started to be formed as the heavy industries started to grow. The education system, which had been expanded by this time to include several universities and other higher education institutions, started to supply many trained engineers. More and more skilled workers capable of handling advanced equipment became available. Some of them started their own enterprises. Academic associations were formed and professional journals started. Access to foreign technological information became easier through access to foreign books and journals, and through trading companies.

To enhance the scientific and technological base further, various proposals were made by industrialists, policy-makers, the military, and scientists to create basic research institutions, to increase national industrial laboratories, and to foster science and technology education. The industrialists felt a strong need to upgrade the scientific and technological capabilities to accommodate the growth of technology-based industries. The experience during World War I taught the government of the importance of technology, as it realized that advanced weaponry was used by European and American nations, and that the import of advanced capital equipment and material might stop during wars.

More universities and vocational schools were established by the public as well as the private sector. Several national research institutions were founded. Hiroshige (1973) counts thirty-eight national research laboratories founded during 1914–30 including those annexed to national universities and to the military.[5] Some of them were founded by reorganizing existing laboratories or testing institutions. For instance, Denki Shikensho (Electric Laboratory) was substantially expanded in 1918 by upgrading the laboratory within the Ministry of Telecommunications, which dates back to 1875 when Kobusho started a small laboratory to test insulators (see Chapter 8). In 1890 it had about thirty staff with seven engineers, the rest being assistants and shop workers. It studied technologies related both to electric power and communications, although its main duty continued to be the testing of various equipment procured by the Ministry.

Another example is Kogyo Shinkensho (Industrial Research Institution, the predecessor to the Agency for Industrial Science and Technology, AIST) established in 1900 with twenty staff. By 1920, it had expanded to 220 staff including forty-eight researchers and engineers. It had five departments: inspection; chemistry, such as japan (a type of lacquer) and matches; ceramics; dye; and, since 1909, electrochemistry. Other research institutions present or established during this period included those studying measurement, silk, geography, mining, fuel and airplane (within the Navy), besides several institutions related to agriculture (Kamatani, 1988).

One of the largest and most productive research institutions established during this period was Rikagaku Kenkyusho (Institute of Physical and Chemical Research, abbreviated to Riken). The proposal for Riken was first made by a chemist, Takamine Jokichi, with the aim of fostering scientific progress and thereby contributing to industries.[6] Thus the aim was not purely academic but also practical. After a long discussion involving businesses, the government, and academics, it was established in 1917 and funded by the government and the private sector (approximately half each), with twenty-two staff of which five were full-time (including both researchers and supportive staff). In four years, it increased to sixty-three staff with thirty full-time members. By 1945, its researchers had published 2,004 academic papers in Japanese and 1,164 in English and other foreign languages, and had produced about 800 patents in Japan and 200 overseas (Hiroshige, 1973). Some of these new technologies were developed into products, which Riken's subsidiary companies sold. These included chemical products, such as vitamins and sensitive paper, and machinery, such as piston rings and measuring equipment. In terms of the contribution to the national economy, these products were hardly as significant as, say, automobiles and electrical products.

To promote basic research, Gakujutsu Shinkokai (Science Council, abbreviated as Gakushin) was established in 1933 with funding from both public and private sectors. Its purpose was twofold: first, to increase research funds at universities and other research institutions and, second, to promote inter-organizational research collaboration. The research funds were granted both on an individual basis and on a project basis. In the beginning, most grants were given on an individual basis but, by 1942, more than 80 per cent were given on a project basis, with each project pursued by members from a number of universities and other institutions. Among the grants given on a project basis in 1942, approximately two-thirds were given to the projects in the field of engineering, and the rest to medical science, natural science, social science, and humanities. The top three projects in terms of research grants were jet-fuel, wireless communication, and atomic nucleus. The emphasis on military-related technology was thus apparent (Hiroshige, 1973).

Companies also started their own R&D laboratories. In 1923, there were 162 private R&D laboratories affiliated to companies, cooperatives, and other private foundations. Seventy-one were in chemistry (including pharmaceuticals, dye, paint, rubber, cement, ceramics, and paper), twenty-seven in metals and machinery, and twenty-four in food. Among the big companies having their own laboratories were Shibaura Seisakusho and Tokyo Denki (later merged to become Toshiba, see Chapter 8); Mitsubishi Shipbuilding (later Mitsubishi Heavy Industries, see Chapter 10); Nihon Kokan (now NKK, see Chapter 7); Oji Paper; and Takeda, Tanabe and Sankyo (all in pharmaceuticals, see Chapter 11). How many of them deserved to be called laboratories in the current sense is unknown. Most of them were small.[7]

The R&D activity intensified in the 1930s and 1940s with the afore-mentioned growth of technology-intensive heavy industries. Although the data reliability may be questioned, one survey in 1930 shows the number of research organizations (including departments and institutions within universities, government laboratories, Riken, and laboratories affiliated with private companies) to be 349, which spent 30 million yen or 0.22 per cent of GNP.[8] In 1942, the number of private research organizations was 711, employing 33,400 staff and spending 590 million yen or approximately 1 per cent of GNP. In addition, there were 443 public research organizations (including university departments, etc.) employing 16,160 staff and spending 296 million yen.[9]

These increased production and R&D activities enabled some of the Japanese manufacturing industries to start building world-class production facilities and developing advanced products; for instance, large-scale furnace and open hearth used in steel production, Zero fighter and other military aircraft, ships, alloys, and communications equipment. However, even these industries depended on American and European technologies in various ways, and Japan imported technologies actively until the late 1930s. The stoppage of technological flow from abroad during World War II had a serious impact, therefore, and the increase in R&D efforts at the time reflects Japan's desperate effort to fill the void created by this stoppage. Consequently, despite the increased R&D effort, the technological gap from the West widened in such key munitions industries as aircraft and shipbuilding, which had almost caught up with the world technological frontier before the war. This gap partly explains Japan's defeat in the war.

3

The Post-War Technological Progress and Government Policies

3.1 OVERVIEW

In discussing the economic change and technological progress since the end of World War II, we start with a historical overview: those familiar with Japan's post-war economic and political history could skip this section.

The impact of World War II on the Japanese economy was, needless to say, devastating. The production index in manufacturing fell to 26 per cent of the pre-war peak level (1934–6) in 1946 and the supply of food fell to 51 per cent. Even though about two-thirds of the plant and equipment built before and during the war remained intact, shortage of fuel, materials, and intermediate goods made continued production extremely difficult. Inflation caused by the decreased production and increased money supply was getting out of control: the consumer price index rose 195.2 per cent a year in 1947.

Some of the policies and changing external conditions helped the Japanese economy to recover from the post-war difficulties and to transform itself to an economy with sustained fast growth from the mid-1950s to early 1970s. Some policies were aimed at the supply side, for instance, to increase production by providing subsidies and other preferential treatment, especially to the coal and steel industries, called the Priority Production Policy (see Chapter 7). Other policies, such as price control, were intended to curve inflation. The price control, not surprisingly, caused black markets to spread and was often inconsistent with the supply-side policies. Nevertheless, the production level gradually recovered, and the production index in mining and manufacturing regained the pre-war level by 1951 while the annual rate of increase in consumer price index slowed down to 50.2 per cent in 1948.

In 1949, a series of drastic policy measures were implemented to contain inflation. These measures were called the Dodge Line after

Joseph M. Dodge, a banker from Detroit, who was invited by the General Headquarters (GHQ) of the Allied Power, the occupation forces, to advise on the economic policies needed for the recovery of the Japanese economy. Under the Dodge Line, subsidies to the industry were drastically reduced, the government budget was forced to balance, and the exchange rate was set at 360 yen per US dollar. These measures helped containing inflation, although the rate of inflation had already started to fall before the Dodge Line. By 1952, the rate of inflation fell to a mere 2 per cent.

These deflationary measures, however, put the economy in deep recession. Then, in 1950, the Korean War broke out, bringing a huge procurement demand to Japan. In the early 1950s, this procurement demand amounted to 600–800 million dollars per year when the total export was about 1.2–1.3 billion (Kosai, 1989). Not only did the procurement place huge additional demands on the struggling Japanese industries but it also allowed the industries to earn much-needed foreign currency with which they imported critical inputs such as fuel, materials, and intermediate goods. Unused production capacity gradually started to be put into operation as these inputs became available.

Under GHQ's initiative, a series of policies, summarily called the Economic Democratization Policy, were implemented. These included land reform, labour reform, the dissolution of zaibatsu (pre-war large conglomerates), and the divestiture of dominant firms. Absentee landlords were forced to sell their farmland to peasants at low prices. Workers' right to organize was legitimized, and regulations on workplace safety and minimum wages were introduced. Zaibatsu were dissolved and some of the dominant firms, such as Japan Iron & Steel, Mitsubishi Heavy Industries, Oji Paper, and Toyo Can, were split into a few firms each. In addition, Japan's first competition law, the Antimonopoly Law, was introduced. We will discuss more about zaibatsu dissolution and the divestiture in Chapter 5.

Supposedly, these reforms laid a foundation for the subsequent economic growth that was characterized by mass consumption by the middle class and competitive supply by industries. Yet, care should be taken in the evaluation of their contributions. For instance, land reform caused the division of farmland into numerous small plots under different owners, which was detrimental to the introduction of an advanced large-scale agricultural system (Kawagoe, 1993). The competitive market structure may have been the product of rapid market expansion that attracted entries rather than that of a one-time reform. Thus, the implication of the reforms is more complicated than it might appear at first sight (Kosai and Teranishi, 1993).

The economy grew at the rate of 8.6 per cent annually during the first half of the 1950s. On the demand side, the major driving force was consumption. Consumers were still short of basic necessities such as food, clothing, and other daily goods. The production of these items was mostly met by re-utilizing existing production facilities, and the rate of investment was rather low.

Between the mid-1950s and the early 1970s, the Japanese economy grew at around 10 per cent annually. The stable political environment at home and abroad helped, as well as the expanding world trade under the GATT–IMF regime, and the low and stable material prices. In the late 1960s, Japan's GNP surpassed that of West Germany, making Japan the second largest economy among capitalist nations, even though per-capita GNP was still lower than several European nations. This so-called High-Growth Era that spanned almost two decades was characterized by a high rate of investment supported by a high saving ratio. During the 1960s, investment accounted for more than 30 per cent of GNP. As we will discuss later, this active investment was accompanied by the introduction of advanced production technologies.

The investment was spurred by rapid expansion of demand for consumer durables, fostered by a large increase in the number of households, which was caused by the disintegration of large families and migration from rural farm areas to urban areas. Japan in 1955 was still a developing country with 40 per cent of the workforce engaged in the primary sector, such as agriculture. By 1975, the proportion became less than 15 per cent. In 1960, only 16 per cent of households owned a refrigerator, 1.2 per cent owned a car, and 46 per cent owned a washing machine. By 1975, the proportion reached 98 per cent, 41 per cent, and 99 per cent, respectively (Yasuba, 1989).

The first oil crisis of 1973 ended the high-growth era abruptly. In the same year, Japan moved to a flexible exchange-rate system, resulting in a major appreciation of the yen. The annual growth rate fell from roughly 10 per cent of the high-growth era to less than 5 per cent in the 1970s and 1980s. The immediate consequence was a rising general price level, recession, and current account deficit. Energy-intensive industries recorded huge losses. The second oil crisis of 1980 caused similar problems to a lesser extent, except that the current account deficit was larger than that in the first oil crisis.

The exchange rate, fixed at 360 yen per US dollar in 1949, remained at this level for more than two decades. Since the float of the yen in 1973, the trend had been towards appreciation of the yen, even though there were ups and downs. By 1994, yen per US dollar had fallen to the level below 100. Not surprisingly, the export industries suffered and many of them started off-shore production. On the other hand, lower import prices suppressed the rise of consumer prices, encouraging consumption.

Japan's current account surplus grew rapidly in the first half of the 1980s from the deficit of 13.9 billion dollars in 1979 (by fiscal year, which runs from April to March) to the surplus of 94.1 billion dollars in 1986. With the steep appreciation of the yen, it decreased during the latter half of the 1980s, but increased again after 1990 to exceed 100 billion dollars. This large current account surplus was the product of a combination of continued high level of savings (which increased further in the 1970s) and the reduced level of investment in the 1970s and 1980s. As is well known, this large current account surplus intensified trade conflict, which was aggravated by an increasing global interdependence of economic activity and Japan's increasing importance in the world market.

3.2   TECHNOLOGY IMPORTATION[1]

When World War II ended, Japan again found itself technologically lagging behind the West in many industries. The process of catch-up resumed. Yet, since the allocation of resources on R&D had been increased before and during the war to compensate for the severed technology importation, Japan's own technological capabilities had been maintained and, in some fields, even increased. These capabilities provided a basis for locating, assimilating, and, if necessary, adapting the advanced technologies imported from the USA and Europe. Furthermore, many workers, who had worked in the munitions plants and other war-related heavy industries during the war and, thus, had gained production experience, returned to civilian production. As Japan's military spending after the war was severely restricted by the new constitution, most of the human and other resources in these industries had to be transferred to civilian production. For instance, some of the former aircraft engineers were hired by automobile companies to design passenger cars (see Chapter 9) and some of the former navy engineers played important roles in the post-war development of the electrical equipment and electronics industries (see Chapter 8).

Technology importation was made through diverse channels and became a significant factor for Japan's post-war technological progress.

First, imported machinery and equipment helped many industries in a critical way to improve the product quality and productivity. For instance, the automobile industry imported machine tools and robots, the steel industry imported converters and rolling machines, and the electric utility industry imported generators. Domestic machinery manufacturers then tried to reverse-engineer, by copying the imported machines and equipment, and learning from them. Gradually, domestically manufactured machines started to replace imported ones.

Secondly, Japanese firms eagerly sought technological agreements with the USA and European firms. Most of the automobile manufacturers had some sort of technological agreements, except Toyota (see Chapter 9). Toshiba, Mitsubishi, and Fuji, three of the four largest electric equipment manufacturers, had extensive technological agreements with GE, Westinghouse, and Siemens, respectively (see Chapter 8). The steel industry introduced a new steel-making technology called basic oxygen furnace (BOF) from an Austrian firm (see Chapter 7). The textiles manufacturers eagerly sought to have technological agreements with American and European firms concerning the production of new synthetic fibres (see Chapter 6). Similar agreements were made in many other industries as well, through which Japanese firms obtained patent licenses and know-how. Often, foreign engineers were invited for their advice and instruction.

Thirdly, consultants, mostly Americans, were hired to help to modernize the production processes. For example, Nissan hired American consultants to plan a new plant at Oppama, which was completed in 1961.[2]

Fourthly, the purchase of blueprints was also common. Japanese firms even bought inventions that were still at an experimental stage, that is, those proved only in laboratories. The well-known case is the purchase of a mid- to low-density polyethylene production process by Mitsui Sekiyu Kagaku (Mitsui Petrochemical) from a German scientist. Mitsui is said to have paid 1.2 million dollars for two notebooks of experiment data, and eventually built a plant based on it.

Fifthly, Japanese firms routinely sent their top engineers abroad to seek promising technologies. Trade associations and institutions like Nihon Seisansei Honbu (Japan Productivity Centre) organized 'missions' to study the technological trends abroad and learn the business practices, often helped by the generosity of the US government and industries.

Sixthly, while many developing countries accepted (and even encouraged) direct investment as a major means of importing advanced foreign technologies, Japan restricted direct investment until the gradual liberalization in the late 1960s and early 1970s. There were several exceptions. Foreign-owned firms that had been established before the war were allowed to operate and some of them expanded rapidly. In addition, during 1956–63, the so-called yen-based investment system was adopted, under which foreign firms were allowed to invest in Japan on condition that they would not remit the profits or the revenue from property sales back to their home country (Komiya, 1972). Several foreign firms entered under this scheme, including IBM, Esso (Exxon), Mobil, Nestlé, Olivetti, and National Cash Registers (NCR). These firms brought new technologies and new ways of doing business into Japan. They were exceptional, however, and foreign investment in Japan remained at a low level until liberalization. In fact, despite liberalization, it still remains at a relatively low level.

These means of technology importation appear to have been used more actively and more effectively by Japan than by any other country. Four factors explain why. They are (1) the market conditions characterized by high growth and intense competition, which brought high rates of return to innovating firms, and misery to failing companies; (2) the presence of technological capabilities within the firms; (3) government policies; and (4) a favourable international environment. The first two will be discussed in detail in Section 3.3 and the government policies in Section 3.4. The last factor will be briefly discussed here.

Following the end of World War II, the international political situation remained stable because of, rather than despite of, the Cold War. The so-called Pax Americana, or Pax Russo-Americana, prevailed. International trade increased rapidly as the world economy grew, which in turn accelerated further growth in trade. The International Monetary Fund (IMF) and the General Agreement on Tariffs and Trade (GATT) provided an institutional framework for this process. The Paris Convention and the World Intellectual Property Rights Organization (WIPO) encouraged the international trade in technology to grow rapidly. From 1960 to 1965, the payments for technology importation by Japan, France, and West Germany combined grew 1.8 times. In 1960, Japan paid 94.9; France, 90.8; and West Germany, 127.5, all in million dollars, whereas in 1965, the amounts were, respectively, 167.0, 213.0, and 195.2, although payments for technology importation capture only a part of the entire technology transfer activity. Apparently, France and Germany imported technology as actively as Japan, and there was a large flow of technology from the USA to both Europe and Japan. The post-war political and economic environment was favourable to a growing world trade, including that of technology, at least within the capitalist block. The active importation of technology by Japan needs be considered in this context.

3.3   COMPETITIVE AND GROWING MARKETS, AND INDUSTRIAL R&D EFFORTS

In the mid-1950s, investment in plant and equipment started to grow, pulled by rapidly growing demand. The plant and equipment inherited from the war, such as old steel mills, became obsolete and insufficient. The changing demand structure created new industries, requiring new investment. This, in turn, created a strong demand for advanced technology. Existing firms expanded and new firms entered into existing industries, such as textiles and steel: these firms sought plant and equipment embodying the state-of-the-art technology. Furthermore, new industries emerged, such as petrochemicals and electric appliances. The automobile industry, which had existed before the war but was mostly limited to the production of trucks and taxi cars, started production of passenger cars for consumers. These new industries also required new investment and new technologies.

The growing demand for consumer durables and other commodities induced strong demand for investment in plant and equipment, and in advanced technology. This investment, in turn, enabled cost reduction and the introduction of new products, stimulating the demand further. Under these conditions, the profits of Japanese firms grew: the profit rate of the non-financial private sector, calculated from the national income account, more than doubled between 1955 and 1970 (Odaka, 1989). In many cases, the investment accompanied importation of advanced technology.

A few cases illustrate the high return on investment in imported technology and plant and equipment. Nissan, the second largest automobile manufacturer in Japan, made a technology agreement with Britain's Austin in 1952. At first, it was a knock-down operation where

Nissan merely assembled the parts provided by Austin, with the technological help also provided by Austin. Nissan built a plant for this operation and started production. According to a Nissan executive at the time, they could easily sell all the Nissan-made Austin cars at the price of one million yen, which brought them a profit of 200,000 yen per car (Ekonomisuto, 1984). The Nissan–Austin and other tie-ups in the post-war automobile industry will be discussed further in Chapter 9.

Another example is Toray. Toray (then Toyo Rayon) obtained a licensing agreement on the nylon manufacturing technology from Du Pont in 1951. The license fee was three million dollars (1.08 billion yen) in initial payments plus 3 per cent of sales up to 5 million pounds of production per year. The initial payment alone exceeded Toray's paid-in capital at the time, 750 million yen. But, the profits were enormous. Following two years of large loss, nylon brought Toray 500 million yen of profits during the first half of fiscal 1953 alone, and it grew continuously afterwards as the demand grew rapidly. Until the entry of a second firm in 1955, Toray was the only nylon producer in Japan, which allowed Toray to appropriate the return to its huge investment in technology importation. The third firm entered as late as 1963. The demand for nylon grew rapidly from the late 1950s to early 1960s, during which period the number of firms remained at two and the profit-sales ratio of Toray's nylon division remained above 10 per cent.

Clearly, rapidly growing markets for manufactured goods created a strong incentive and large rewards to firms investing in plant and equipment and upgrading the technology. Intense competition, on the contrary, heavily punished the firms failing to do so. As discussed in Section 1 and further in Chapter 5, the Economic Democratization Policy administered by the Occupation Forces broke up pre-war zaibatsu and a number of dominant firms in several industries. In addition, the Antimonopoly Law was enacted. These policies helped to create and maintain competitive markets, even though some of the firms that were split by the policy re-merged later, and the Antimonopoly Law was weakened several times until 1977 when it was strengthened again.

Perhaps more importantly, the rapidly growing markets induced entries, thereby intensifying competition. Cases such as Sony in electric appliances and consumer electronics, and Honda in automobiles, are well known, and there are many more cases of market entry discussed later. The number of firms in steel, aluminum, and petrochemicals increased and, in many industries, the numbers surpassed those of the USA despite the latter's much larger markets.

Even though the actual amount of imported manufactured goods and inward foreign direct investment would increase only slowly after the liberalization of trade and investment, the knowledge that trade and investment would soon be liberalized led the firms to upgrade their technology further so that they would be able to compete against the much larger and technologically advanced firms of the USA and Europe. That is, the potential threat from foreign rivals made the domestic markets contestable, forcing the firms to be efficient. Actually, the competition against foreign rivals was not only potential but also real, because many firms started intensifying their export efforts, thereby competing against foreign firms in international markets. Such export efforts were partly encouraged by the government which, at the time, was deeply concerned about the balance of payments.

Consequently, Japanese firms were exposed to intense potential or real competition against domestic rivals as well as foreign, supposedly technologically superior rivals in both domestic and international markets. However, even if these markets provided the firms with a strong incentive (or a desperate need) to import technologies and utilize them fully, they would not have been able to do so unless they had sufficient capabilities to select, assimilate, and, if necessary, adapt or improve the imported technologies. The need for such capabilities, often called an absorptive capacity, implied that, for a country to be able to exploit the advantage of being a latecomer by utilizing the existing technologies developed by advanced countries, the country must not be too backward. Post-war Japan, as discussed earlier, had inherited a rather strong technology base, accumulated through education and R&D efforts before and during the war. Further investment in R&D and education during the post-war period not only promoted Japan's own innovation efforts but also helped the effective use of imported technologies.[3]

Comprehensive statistics are not available on R&D expenditure during the early post-war years. Estimates by the Science and Technology Agency date back to 1953, indicating that the R&D expenditure started to grow rapidly in the latter half of the 1950s: during 1955–61 it grew at a rate of more than 20 per cent per year. As a percentage to the national income, it grew from 0.84 in 1955 to 1.73 in 1961 (Science and Technology Agency, various years).

This increase in R&D expenditure in the latter half of the 1950s coincides with the increase in technology importation. As mentioned earlier, technology importation started to grow in 1958. Domestic R&D and technology importation are positively correlated not only at the time-series level but also at the cross-firm or cross-industry level, indicating that the firm or the industry that actively imported technology also made an active R&D investment (Odagiri, 1983).

3.4 GOVERNMENT POLICIES CONCERNING TECHNOLOGY IMPORTATION

In addition to the profit incentive and capabilities of the private sector, government policies also influenced the process of technology importation. Most directly related to technology importation was the government control based on the Foreign Exchange and Foreign Trade Control Law of 1949 and the Foreign Investment Law of 1950. In principle, each application to import technology was reviewed by the Foreign Investment Council, except for imports with small payments that could be imported with the approval of the Bank of Japan. Actually, the screening was mostly done during prior consultation with government ministries, notably the Ministry of International Trade and Industry (MITI).

The restriction on technology importation was gradually liberalized, and the number of cases of technology importation subject to review decreased rapidly (Sekiguchi, 1986). The major steps for liberalization were taken in 1961, 1968, and 1972. The 1968 liberalization was particularly significant, because the importation of technology of less than 50,000 dollars became automatically approved, except for contracts that included cross-licensing agreements, contracts that involved foreign parent firms and their subsidiaries in Japan, and contracts in seven designated areas of technology: arms, ammunition, aircraft, space, computers, nuclear energy, and petrochemical. Finally, in 1980, the two laws mentioned above were consolidated into the Foreign Exchange and Foreign Trade Law, and all technology importation became liberalized except for that in twelve designated areas of technology. Even the importation in these designated technology areas could be freely made if the amount involved was less than 100 million yen.

When the importation of technology was still subject to individual government approval, especially before the 1968 liberalization, the government could influence the choice of technology to be imported and the choice of the firm to import it. The government also tried to help Japanese firms to obtain technology from foreign firms at favourable terms. For instance, Toray, as mentioned earlier, was allowed to import nylon technology from Du Pont. At the time, the industry was considered to be one of the key industries because clothing was a necessity, the product had export potential, and the need to import materials was modest. Toray was chosen from the applicants because it had been experimenting on nylon for many years, even before buying Du Pont's technology (see Chapter 6).

There were several rather vague criteria for selection, which changed over time. In the 1950s, the effect on the balance of payments was emphasized, along with the contribution to 'important' industries or public utilities. It was not clear which industries MITI regarded as important, but they seem to have included capital goods industries, industries with high export potential, and industries related to the production of basic necessities, such as the fertilizer industry (considered essential for food production) and the textiles industry. It was argued that imported technology should contribute to the improvement of balance of payments by reducing imports or increasing exports, and to the reconstruction of the nation, because the importation of technology required the expenditure of scarce foreign currency reserves. Thus, the applicants had to demonstrate how the technology to be imported would contribute to these objectives. They also had to show their capability in understanding and implementing the technology, and in successfully manufacturing and marketing the products.

These requirements were gradually dropped in the 1960s, as the economy grew and the balance of payments improved. The applicants were no longer required to show how the technology would contribute to the balance of payments, and such supposedly unimportant technology as the design of golf wear began to be imported. The new criteria for reviewing the application of technology importation established in 1961 included the following: (1) the imported technology should not disrupt the development of indigenous technology, (2) the imported technology should not disrupt the existing order of industry, (3) the imported technology should not cause difficulties for small firms, and (4) the importing firm should be able to use the technology technologically and financially. Again, these criteria could be interpreted in many ways.

To some of the readers, the balance of payments may appear to have been excessively emphasized as a justification for governmental review and, if necessary, intervention. In fact, the balance of payments was the overriding concern of the policy-makers until the late 1960s, because it was the limiting factor for economic growth. Economic booms tended to increase imports and worsen the balance of payments. Since the devaluation of yen was never considered as an option, the Bank of Japan had to raise the discount rate to slow down the economy and reduce imports. Booms would have lasted longer were the balance-of-payments ceiling relaxed. Thus, all efforts were made to improve the balance of payments. Probably, the control of technology importation itself reduced foreign-exchange payments only little; yet, it was an important reduction for Japan at the time. Furthermore, the importation of advanced technology was expected to contribute to a reduction of imported manufactured goods and materials and, in the long run, an increase in exports.

An important but difficult question is whether the government had the ability to choose the best technology and the best company to import. Although some argued that the government had a superior ability to gather and process information especially in the early years, there were cases where the government apparently made wrong decisions because of incompetence or because of political and bureaucratic reasons. A widely-known case is the long delay in Sony's obtaining approval to import the transistor technology, because a MITI official concluded that Sony, then a small start-up firm, lacked the capability to develop the untried technology (see Chapter 8). Thus, there seems no a priori reason to believe that the government made fewer mistakes than the market mechanism.

A related issue is whether the government intervention really changed the overall pattern of technology importation. Sony's case suggests that, though the approval was delayed and the manager had to spend long hours negotiating with MITI officials, even small start-up firms could eventually get the approval. In the case of nylon, Toray got the approval first and was practically guaranteed the monopoly position until the second firm was granted a similar approval. With delay, however, other firms also obtained approval. In many cases, therefore, those who wanted to import technology appear to have been granted the approval, however long the delay was. Still, we do not know how many firms, probably smaller firms, not as persistent as Sony, simply gave up their plans to import technology after MITI's refusal (or sabotage).

The same argument applies to the criterion of important industry. In the 1950s, the demand for capital goods and necessities such as food and clothing was strong, while the demand for luxurious goods, say, golf wear, was weak. Accordingly, the demand for technology related to the first category of products, namely, those of the so-called important industries, was stronger. More technology of this sort would, therefore, have been imported with or without government regulation.

Other criteria, namely, the protection of domestic technology and the avoidance of abrupt disruption of existing industrial order, often contradicted the overriding concern of the government, namely, the promotion of key industries. The first criterion reflected the view that the development of domestic, indigenous technology should be promoted so that the nation would not become technologically too dependent on foreign countries. In reality, however, the importation of foreign technology proved to be critically important in promoting domestic industries.

The significance of the criterion of protecting the existing industrial order is also unclear. It meant to prevent the situation where the technology-importing firm would dominate the market, or where the imported technology would change the product or production process so drastically that small parts manufacturers would lose their work. Actually, there were cases where the government helped to make arrangements under which all the major manufacturers had access to the advanced foreign technology; for instance, the importation of BOF (basic oxygen furnace) technology by the steel industry (see Chapter 7). There were also cases where the government tried to create a balance among competing firms; for instance, when one of the firms was granted permission to import synthetic-fibre technology, its competitor was allowed to import another synthetic-fibre technology. Obviously, in these cases, the government tried to avoid any abrupt change in the distribution of market share taking place as a result of its policy. As for the protection of small firms, it is unclear whether there really were instances where technology importation was denied on the grounds that it might lead to the collapse of a group of small firms.

Thus, the evidence is not sufficient to judge the significance and the effectiveness of the industrial-order criterion; actually, however, changes in market shares and the turnover of firms were drastic throughout the high-growth period of the 1950s and 1960s during which the demand structure and technologies changed significantly. That is, despite the government's intention to protect the *status quo*, changes were inevitable. Since the overriding concern of the government was to promote the domestic industry and, in many cases, the importation of advanced technology was essential for this promotion, the government rarely stopped the importation whether the existing order would be disrupted or not. The government instead compensated those affected, through subsidies or other measures.

These facts suggest that individual reviews of technology importation may not have had a significant impact on the overall pattern of technology importation: technologies to be imported were imported and firms that wanted to import did so, eventually.

To individual firms, however, the government intervention had a significant impact. In the case of Toray's importation of nylon technology, Toray, with its prior experience in nylon production, might have been a successful early importer even without government intervention. Still, the government's refusal for other firms to import nylon technology for several years after Toray's importation allowed Toray to appropriate the return to its development effort and also brought huge monopoly profits. In the case of the steel industry's introduction of BOF (basic oxygen furnace) technology, the industry-wide arrangement to share the imported technology was orchestrated by MITI, as mentioned earlier. Under this arrangement, the firms that had learned of the existence of the technology earlier and had been experimenting with it were deprived of the opportunity to gain technological advantages over the competitors, even though all the firms in the industry might have adopted the technology sooner or later with or without the government policy.

As Peck and Tamura (1976: 553) write, 'in a fast growing economy it can be of importance whether government policy delays or speeds up the use of a particular technology by only three or four years.' As a result, the government bureaucracy, especially MITI, possessed much power over the industry. Whether a firm could obtain a permission to import vital technology ahead of its rivals was one of the most significant determinants of the firm's profits.

The government control may have also affected the price Japanese firms paid to foreign firms, because the government may have prevented the royalty rate from escalating by reducing the competition among Japanese firms. As discussed already, MITI tried to reduce competition among the Japanese steel makers in the importation of BOF technology. In other cases, MITI selected the firms to import technology from many applicants, using the allocation of foreign currency as a tool. Consequently, the sellers of technology could not let Japanese firms compete against each other and bid up their prices. Peck and Tamura (1976) show that the percentage of agreements with high running royalty rates increased after the major liberalization of 1968. Similarly, Lynn (1982) estimates that the royalty rates that US producers paid to import the same BOF technology were higher than the rates paid by the Japanese producers, even after taking into account the inventor's failure to foresee the high rate of production increase that the Japanese firms actually achieved.

It should be also noted, however, that MITI intervened exactly because the competition among Japanese firms was so intense that the royalty rate, MITI worried, might sky-rocket. In the BOF case (see Chapter 7), Nihon Kokan (now NKK), the first firm to have learned of the technology, became serious only after its competitor, Yawata (now Nippon Steel), also started to pursue the technology. When an Italian firm invented a new type of synthetic fibre called polypropylene, almost thirty Japanese firms rushed to Italy to import the technology. MITI became concerned and tried to group the importers into three. Apparently, the intensity of competition, or what MITI regarded as *excessive* competition among Japanese firms, was behind MITI's intervention, and it is futile to separate the effect of government intervention from that of market competition.

The negotiation of technology importation involved not only prices but also other non-price factors. Sellers might attach various conditions, such as territorial restrictions concerning the sales of the products, and restriction on the improvement of imported technology. In addition, cross-licensing was increasingly required by the sellers of technology. The number of agreements that required cross-licensing increased from three in 1965 to thirty-seven in 1968. Although the proportion of this type of agreements was still only 2 per cent in 1968, the government became worried that technology importation would become increasingly difficult unless Japanese firms developed their own technologies that could be offered in return for importation. The agreements with sales territory restriction also increased during the late 1960s and 1970s. The proportion of agreements that prohibited the Japanese firms from exporting the products manufactured with the imported technology increased from 10 per cent in 1968 to 31 per cent in 1974. The trend was alarming to Japanese firms as well as the government because it could have reduced export potential.[4]

In addition, several other government policies affected the process of technology importation.

The first were the preferential tax measures used to encourage technology importation (Goto and Wakasugi, 1988). Two types of tax measures were included. One was to reduce the withholding tax on payments made to foreign corporations against import of technology. The other was to allow tariff exemptions on designated or highly efficient machines that could not be produced domestically. These tax exemptions were designed to encourage firms to import advanced technology and to import machines embodying advanced technology. Both measures were introduced in the early 1950s and the tax revenue lost due to these measures peaked in 1961 at 9.9 billion yen. They were abolished in the mid-1960s as the emphasis of technology policy shifted from importation to domestic R&D.

The second was the review of international technological agreements by the Fair Trade Commission (FTC). Section 6 of the Antimonopoly Law stipulates that 'no entrepreneur shall enter into an international agreement or an international contract which contains such matters as constitute unreasonable restraint of trade or unfair trade practices.' An entrepreneur entering into such an agreement or contract is required to notify the FTC which, if necessary, may request changes in the conditions or prohibit the agreements. The conditions that might be considered as violating the law included, among others, the restriction by the licensor on the export price, quantity, geographical area, or buyer of the product which was manufactured using the technology in question; grant-back clause mandating the licensee to provide the technology adapted or improved from the original licensed technology to the licensor; and the restriction on the technology or product competing against the licensor's. The FTC also monitored royalties to prevent 'excessive' royalties from being demanded by licensors. There was no such review system for licensing agreements between Japanese firms. Although the FTC's intervention on these grounds was intended to prevent unfair trade practices, it may have helped to enhance the bargaining position of Japanese firms *vis-à-vis* foreign firms. The size of this effect is unknown, however.

Thirdly, the policies on trade and inward foreign investment had a profound impact on technology importation. Trade liberalization started in the early 1960s and foreign investment liberalization in the late 1960s. Even after liberalization, however, the penetration of foreign firms to the Japanese manufacturing markets remained slow. In this circumstance, foreign firms with advanced technology opted to sell the technology to Japanese firms rather than export manufactured goods into Japan or establish their own plants in Japan. Japanese firms could buy only the technology, and sell the products made with it in rapidly growing domestic markets. These policies may have had a welfare cost as they limited competition against foreign rivals, although the intense competition among domestic firms may have compensated considerably for these costs. It is worth emphasizing again that the smooth and active technology transfer without direct investment was possible only because Japan had sufficient technological capabilities and made active R&D investment of its own.

In addition to these policies, which were more or less directly related to technology importation, various other policies had an indirect effect. For instance, various financial incentives, such as tax breaks and low-interest loans from semi-governmental institutions for investment in plant and equipment, encouraged the technology importation of the subsidized industries. Furthermore, the macroeconomic growth policy, such as the maintenance of low interest rates and tax incentives for household saving, affected technology importation by creating demand for advanced technology. Indeed, one may argue that the creation of a general environment conducive to the early introduction of new technology was the most important factor for successful technology importation. In this sense, all the policies that helped to create such an environment were important.

3.5 RESEARCH ASSOCIATIONS AND OTHER R&D-SUPPORTING POLICIES

Technology importation alone was hardly sufficient to raise the technology level to make Japanese firms competitive in the international markets following the trade and capital liberalization. In addition, foreign firms were expected to become less willing to sell their technologies to Japanese firms. The government, being fully aware of this difficulty, started several policies to encourage R&D activities by Japanese firms.

One such policy was a tax credit to incremental R&D expenditure, started in 1966, which allowed the firms to deduct a fixed proportion of their experimental research expenditure in the current year over and above the highest expenditure incurred in previous years (at present, 20 per cent of the excess amount is deductible, up to 10 per cent of the firm's total corporate tax payments). The amount of tax foregone by this credit (and other less important R&D-related credits) was 19 billion yen in 1970 and 38 billion yen (about 0.2 billion dollars) in 1980. The USA started a similar policy in 1981 and the revenue loss due to this credit was estimated to be 0.6–1 billion dollars in 1981, far higher than that of Japan (Mansfield, 1985).

The government also started several subsidy programmes to encourage R&D, the total amount of which was 11 billion yen in 1970 and 61 billion yen in 1980 (Goto and Wakasugi, 1988). A large portion of these subsidies was given through research associations, mainly because of the belief in scale economies by the government and industry. The government citing, for instance, the fact that the R&D expenditure of the six largest Japanese computer makers combined was a mere fifth of that of IBM in 1970, encouraged collaborative research among them and provided major R&D subsidies through this channel.

Since this scheme of research association in Japan has attracted considerable interest inside and outside of Japan (Fransman, 1990; Okimoto, 1989; Patrick, 1986), it deserves some discussion here. A fuller discussion can be found in Goto (1996).

Formally, these research associations are joint or cooperative research efforts based on the Law on Technological Research Associations in Mining and Manufacturing of 1961. The organization for joint research under this law is called *Ko-kogyo Gijutsu Kenkyu Kumiai* (Technological Research Association in Mining and Manufacturing), but it is commonly called *Kenkyu Kumiai* (Research Association). Hereafter, this research association will be abbreviated to JRA to distinguish it from the British research association to be discussed presently.

The number of JRAs by the year of establishment and by research theme is shown in Table 3.1. The distribution of these numbers reflects the various needs of the private sector and the policy targets. For instance, many large-scale JRAs were established in the computer and semiconductor industry, particularly in the 1970s, indicating that the need to catch up with IBM was the overwhelming concern of the industry and policy-makers at the time. After the oil crises (the impact of which on R&D will be discussed more in the next section), JRAs were also used to promote research in energy-intensive industries, such as aluminum and petrochemicals, and to develop energy-saving production technologies. Research on pollution control, traffic control, and medical equipment was also conducted under the JRA scheme.

Although this scheme used the British research association system as its prototype, there are two salient and noteworthy differences between the original UK model (Johnson, 1971/72) and the Japanese version.

The first difference was that, while the original research associations in the UK were established on an industry-wide basis, the Japanese research associations were organized to solve certain specific technological problems. The UK system, actually, was designed to establish

TABLE 3.1 The number of research associations by the year of establishment and by research theme

Research theme	Year of establishment						Total
	1961–5	1966–70	1971–5	1976–80	1981–5	1986–9	
Chemicals and petroleum refinery	2	0	2	4	13	2	23
Textiles	2	0	0	0	2	1	5
Iron and steel	2	0	2	0	0	0	4
Nonferrous metals and new materials	2	0	1	0	4	1	8
Computers and information	1	0	10	3	1	1	16
General machinery and precision equipment	1	0	0	3	9	2	15
Transportation equipment	0	1	3	1	0	1	6
Paper and pulp	0	0	0	0	1	0	1
Other	2	0	2	3	2	7	16
Total	12	1	20	14	32	15	94

Note: The numbers are for research associations under the auspices of the Ministry of International Trade and Industry. In addition, two associations have been established under the auspices of the Ministry of Transport, and eighteen under the Ministry of Agriculture, Forestry, and Fisheries.

Source: Kokogyo Gijutsu Kenkyu Kumiai Kondankai (1991), *Kokogyo Gijutsu Kenkyu Kumiai 30 Nen no Ayumi* [30 Years of Technological Research Association in Mining and Manufacturing]. Tokyo: Nihon Kogyo Gijutsu Shinko Kyokai

joint research institutions mostly in the traditional industries comprising small firms incapable of doing independent research. In sharp contrast, JRA's member firms were, especially after the 1970s, mostly large firms trying to enhance their technology bases, or to explore the possibility of tackling long-range, risky research subjects. Often, member firms came from different industries, usually from user and supplier industries.

The second distinct feature was that JRAs were designed to be dissolved after the completion of specific research targets. In most cases, they were dissolved when it became clear that their missions were impossible to achieve within a reasonable time frame. Whether successful or not, these R&D activities usually lasted for several years only. This time limit was important because participants were thereby assured that they need not commit their resources to the project infinitely. Of 114 JRAs established up to fiscal 1990, forty-five have been dissolved, or are in the process of being dissolved.

Actual research at JRAs was carried out in either of two ways. In the first case, the JRA established a joint research laboratory of its own. In the second case, the research subject of the collaborative project was divided into several sub-themes and these were assigned to member firms. Each member firm carried out its sub-theme in its own research laboratory and the members met occasionally during the course of collaborative R&D to exchange research outcomes.

Not many JRAs had their own joint research laboratories. Indeed, only twelve out of the 114 JRAs established by the end of fiscal 1990 had their own joint research laboratories or some sort of joint research facilities. The case of VLSI (Very Large-Scale Integrated Circuits) Research Association, whose joint research laboratory attracted wide attention, was truly exceptional, while the vast majority of JRAs were managed by dividing their respective research theme into several sub-themes and assigning them to member firms. Even in the rare cases where JRAs actually established joint research laboratories, most of the research was allocated to member firms and carried out separately at their respective laboratories. In fact, it was quite exceptional that researchers from various, often competing firms got together and conducted joint research as a team under the JRA system (Hayashi et al., 1989).

The resources of JRAs, that is, researchers and research funds, were procured in the following way. The arrangement for researchers varied depending on whether the JRA in question had its own laboratory or not. When it did not, the researchers of each member firm were simply assigned to the research subject allocated to this firm. When a JRA had its own laboratory, the staff of this laboratory comprised researchers on loan from member firms: no researcher was hired directly by the JRA. In addition, some researchers were dispatched from national laboratories, such as the Electro-Technical Laboratory to be discussed in Chapter 8. In the two well-known JRAs with their own laboratories, namely, VLSI Research Association and Opto-Electronics Research Association, the head was from a national research laboratory.

Research funds were shared by member firms. However, there was no standardized rule as to how the R&D costs should be divided among the members. In some cases they were divided evenly, whereas in others they were allocated in proportion to the sales of the member firms. Research carried out at each member's laboratory was financed independently, except for cases in which the equipment was bought on JRA's account.

Government subsidies were often, but not always, granted, depending on how important the subject of collaborative research was from the national policy viewpoint. When government subsidies, contingent loans, and/or national research contracts were nevertheless granted, they proved to be an important source of funds for JRAs. Yet, there has been no specific government subsidy programme linked to the JRA system and, instead, various existing R&D subsidy programmes were tapped, including the Basic Technologies for Future Industries Programme, the Large Scale Project Programme, and the Programme to Promote Computer and Information Processing. In 1963, there were nine JRAs, which spent 21 per cent of total government R&D subsidies. In 1983, forty-four JRAs were active in research and spent 64.4 billion yen, which was about 1.5 per cent of the total R&D spending in Japan that year. Among this expenditure, government subsidies amounted to 32.8 billion yen, or 51 per cent of the total JRA R&D spending. These subsidies to JRAs accounted for 46.9 per cent of the total government R&D subsidies of the year.

To apply for these major subsidy programmes, firms were often required to form a new JRA or join an existing one. If a firm was denied membership to a JRA financed by government subsidies, it in effect implied that the firm would be unable to get financial assistance from the government. Thus, JRAs were often dubbed the 'receptacles' of government subsidies. Special tax breaks, including a scheme of accelerated depreciation, were also provided to JRA member firms and to JRAs themselves.

Recently, the focus of research at JRAs has shifted gradually towards more long-range, risky research projects, more akin to basic research. However, as the focus shifted in this direction, firms started to rely less on JRAs as a vehicle to carry out their research. Research closer to the basic end, say, super conductivity and the fifth generation computer, has been made more often by jointly setting up research institute rather than through a JRA which would be dissolved after a few years. On the other hand, research closer to the commercialization end of the spectrum has been carried out more and more by independent firms.[5]

3.6   R&D IN THE 1970S AND 1980S: THE IMPACT OF OIL CRISES AND YEN APPRECIATION

The high-growth era was nearing its end in the early 1970s, but it was the first oil crisis of 1973 that really killed it. The price of imported oil jumped from 2.51 dollars per barrel in 1972 to 10.79 dollars in 1974. The second oil crisis of 1979–80 further pushed the price to 37.29 dollars in 1981.

The consequence on technology was twofold. First, developing energy-saving production processes became one of the major targets in R&D for many businesses. Such R&D, together with the accumulation of incremental innovation at production sites, made it possible for Japanese manufacturing industries to raise energy efficiency. For instance, the steel industry developed the so-called oil-less steel-making technology and reduced energy consumption drastically. This shift in emphasis towards energy-related R&D was also apparent in government R&D: the proportion of energy R&D among total government R&D funding increased from 7.5 per cent in 1975 to 16.3 per cent in 1985 (National Science Foundation, 1988). The Sunshine Project aimed to develop alternative energy-generating technology and the Moonlight Project to develop energy-conserving technology started in 1974 and 1978, respectively.

Second, the entire industrial structure shifted towards an energy-saving, technology-intensive, and high value-added one. Energy-intensive industries scaled down and high-technology industries expanded rapidly. The striking example of the former was the aluminum smelting industry. Japan was the second largest aluminum-producing country in the world in the early 1970s. By the end of the 1980s, the industry had been virtually wiped out. Out of fourteen plants that existed previously, only one is still in operation while the import soared

(Goto, 1988). By contrast, high-technology industries—semiconductors, computers, fine chemicals, and such—grew rapidly.

As a consequence of these responses to the increased oil price, the consumption of oil decreased in the absolute amount as well as relatively to the size of GNP. The amount of oil necessary to produce one yen of GNP dropped by 40 per cent between 1973 and 1982.

In addition to the sharp increase in oil prices, the exchange rate changed radically in the 1970s and 1980s. The yen appreciated 65 per cent against the US dollars in 1977–8, and 92 per cent in 1986–8. This rapid increase in the value of the yen raised the dollar prices of Japanese exports. Yet, in order to compete against the foreign rivals, Japanese exporters could not pass the impact of the yen's appreciation on to the export prices. They, therefore, had to increase their effort to cut costs again. This effort bore fruit as the percentage increase of export price in 1986–8 was about a half of that of the yen. The firms also introduced products with superior quality so that they could remain competitive in terms of quality, not just in terms of price. These products included video cassette recorders (VCRs), copying machines, facsimile machines, and small cars.

Thus, after the two oil crises and the sharp appreciation of the yen, Japan's less energy-intensive manufacturing industries found their shares to have considerably increased in the world export markets. This increase was most prominent in high-technology products where the Japanese share rose from 7.2 per cent in 1965 to 19.8 per cent worldwide in 1986. We may attribute this adaptability of Japanese firms to changing conditions to three factors.

The first is the high rate of investment in R&D and in plant and equipment. The R&D expenditure grew 4.4 times between 1973 and 1987 and, as a proportion to GNP, from 2.0 per cent to 2.8 per cent. The ratio of investment in plant and equipment to GNP fell gradually after the first oil crisis from the level of 19 per cent in 1970, but remained at 14–15 per cent, and then grew in the 1980s to reach 19 per cent again in 1990. The amount of investment in plant and equipment in Japan even surpassed that of the USA, whose economy was 1.8 times larger than Japan's. Such active investment in R&D and in plant and equipment reinforced each other, increasing productivity and improving product quality.

Second, the management system of Japanese firms contributed to their adapting to the rapidly changing environment. It emphasized the importance of accumulation of small improvements at the production site and the management system was designed to be conducive to this. These attributes enabled Japanese industries to achieve energy efficiency and high quality.

Third, the organizational aspect of Japan's manufacturing system probably contributed to the adaptability of Japanese firms. Unlike their US counterparts which have a high degree of vertical integration, Japanese manufacturers depend heavily on outside suppliers. Competition among suppliers allowed buyers (most commonly, assemblers) to reduce overall costs. Yet, the willingness for long-term cooperation was also there between buyers and suppliers, which led to quality improvement and quick product development. We will come back to this topic in Chapter 5.

3.7   R&D ACTIVITY IN TODAY'S JAPAN

We conclude the discussion of post-war technological development by summarizing Japan's current R&D efforts in comparison to those in other industrialized nations. Table 3.2 summarizes the essential indicators of R&D activity in Japan and other major R&D-performing countries. Japan is now the second largest in terms of R&D expenditure, which is about two thirds of that of the USA and more than twice as large as that of Germany, the third largest country. As a proportion to GNP, Japan devotes about 3 per cent to R&D, the highest among the nations. In terms of non-defence R&D expenditure, Japan's spending is 93 per cent of that of the USA. The ratio to GNP remains almost unchanged at 2.98 per cent in Japan, far above that of the USA at 1.92 per cent.

Japan's R&D spending relative to GNP has been high for quite some time. In 1958, Japan spent 0.97 per cent of its GNP on R&D. This was much lower than that of the US (2.4 per cent) or the UK (2.1 per cent) but nearly comparable to that of France (1.0 per cent), Canada (1.0 per cent), or West Germany (1.3 per cent). Given the size and the development stage of the economy at the time, Japan's figure is impressive.

Table 3.2 also shows that Japan's private sector is active in R&D while the role of the government is limited. One reason for this smaller government funding is the small defence-related R&D expenditure in Japan. Yet, as the table shows, even with defence-related R&D expenditure excluded, the proportion of government funds in total R&D expenditure is smaller than that in the USA, France, or Germany.

TABLE 3.2 Indicators of R&D in selected countries, 1991

	Japan	USA	Germany	France	UK
R&D expenditure (billion yen)	13,771.5	20,312.8	6,048.3	3,894.6	2,828.9
R&D expenditure (percentage of GNP)	3.00	2.63	2.65	2.43	2.10
Non-defence R&D expenditure (billion yen)	13,656.5	14,700.0	5,785.7	3,114.2	2,570.2*
Non-defence R&D expenditure (percentage of GNP)	2.98	1.92	2.54	1.94	1.83*
Government funds (percentage of total R&D expenditure)	18.2	43.2	36.6	49.5	34.2
Government funds (percentage of total non-defence R&D expenditure)	17.5	24.2	33.8	36.7	18.8
Government funds (percentage of total R&D expenditure by industry)	1.4	28.5	10.8	17.3*	16.7*
Number of researchers in thousand persons	5,82.8	949.3**	176.4**	129.2	113.1
Number of researchers per 10.000 population	47.0	38.4	28.4	23.0	20.0

Note: Figures with * and ** are those for, respectively, 1990 and 1989.

Sources: Science and Technology Agency (1994), *Indicators of Science and Technology*; (1993), *White Paper on Science and Technology*

The limited role of the government is also shown in the share of government funds in industrial R&D expenditure. It is a mere 1.4 per cent in Japan; that is, Japanese companies are financing almost all of their R&D out of their own funds. This makes a contrast with other countries where 10–30 per cent of industrial R&D expenditure is supported by government funds. Again, the gap narrows considerably if defence-related industries are excluded. When aircraft and missile industries are excluded, the comparable percentage for the USA reduces to 7.7 per cent (Eads and Nelson, 1986). Still, it is much higher than that of Japan.

Japan's R&D activity in terms of funding, as well as spending, had been dominated by the private sector. This tendency intensified during the 1980s. As mentioned previously, Japanese firms increased their R&D efforts in the 1980s to cope with the high energy cost and the slow-down of economic growth. They struggled to reduce costs by introducing more sophisticated production technologies and to produce quality goods. By contrast, government spending in general was under tight control in order to reduce the mounting government deficit, which reached 6.0 per cent of GNP by 1979. This contrast explains why the private sector's R&D funding tripled between 1980 and 1990, while that of the government increased only 1.6 times; consequently, the share of the government in total R&D decreased from 25.8 per cent to 16.5 per cent. The implication was mixed. The active R&D helped industries to gain competitiveness, while higher education and basic research suffered from lack of resources. We will return to this last topic in the concluding chapter.

Table 3.2 also shows the number of R&D personnel. The number of research personnel was more than one million in 1991, having trebled in the preceding two decades. Sixty-two per cent of them were working in industries. Although the number of research personnel is 61 per cent of that of the USA, Japan has more researchers per population than the USA or European countries. It is likely, however, that the number of Japan's R&D personnel is over-estimated because it is not adjusted to the full-time equivalent (FTE) basis, unlike that of the USA and Europe. In order to quantify the human resources devoted to R&D, the time that researchers spend on administration and teaching, for instance, has to be excluded. According to a rough estimate by the Science and Technology Agency, the number of FTE Japanese researchers in 1990 was approximately 360,000, or 65 per cent of the unadjusted figure, and the number of researchers per 10,000 population was 30, which was smaller than that in the USA (38).

One notable feature of Japanese research personnel is a relatively large proportion of engineers (247,000 out of total 504,000 unadjusted research personnel, or 49 per cent in 1990) than scientists (21 per cent). The same tendency exists for university degrees: the number of Ph.D.s granted in 1989 by Japanese universities was 876 in science and 1,774 in engineering. By contrast, these were, respectively, 8,927 and 5,691 in the USA and 4,886 and 1,400 in Germany. Although consideration must be given to the international differences in the degree systems, Japan's bias in favour of engineering appears consistent with the emphasis on engineering education in the Meiji era discussed in the previous chapter.[6]

Active R&D results in patents. The number of patent applications and the number of patents granted in Japan increased from, respectively, 130,831 and 30,878 in 1970 to 367,590 and 59,401 in 1990. This large number of patents was partly caused by the Japanese patent system: the scope of patent claim was narrower than that of the US system (Ordover, 1991). Until 1988, the number of independent claims in a single patent was limited to one in Japan, whereas, in the USA, several independent claims of a single invention can be grouped together for one application. For instance, a bicycle inventor would have to patent separate bicycle parts in addition to the bicycle itself under the Japanese system (Klemperer, 1990; Ordover, 1991). Furthermore, the scope of a patent was narrower in Japan. As a result, a number of related but slightly different inventions tended to be patented separately, causing a large number of patents in Japan.

As a way to compare the number of patents internationally, with the differences in patent system controlled, one may examine the number of patents granted in the USA to various nationals. As Table 3.3 shows, the share of patents granted to the Japanese in the USA has almost doubled during the last decade and reaching closer to one-third of all the patents granted in the USA. Clearly, Japan's increased R&D efforts have been bearing fruit.

3.8 CONCLUSION

In this and the previous chapter, we gave a general discussion of the economic and technological change since the mid-nineteenth century, including a rather detailed examination of the role of government policies, such as the creation of the infrastructure and the education system in the early Meiji era, and the policies related to technology importation

TABLE 3.3 The proportion of US patents granted by nationality of patent-holders (%)

Nationality of patent-holders	1980	1992
USA	60.2	53.6
Japan	11.5	22.5
Germany	9.3	7.5
France	3.9	3.1
UK	3.4	2.5
Other	11.7	10.8

Source: Science and Technology Agency (1993), White Paper on Science and Technology

and to research associations in the post-war era. The discussion is by no means exhaustive. We have not discussed, for instance, the industrial policy in general after the war. Excellent books already exist for this topic (e.g., Komiya et al., 1988).

The main theme in these chapters was Japan's accumulation of technological capabilities. No doubt, the major source of technology was overseas, both before and after World War II. It has been emphasized, however, that technology importation alone does not guarantee technological progress and the successful catch-up to advanced nations. The presence of entrepreneurship, as discussed in Chapter 1, is an essential condition, as well as the presence of competitive markets that reward those who have successfully introduced new technologies and punish those who have failed to do so.

Yet, entrepreneurship alone is not sufficient. Capabilities must be there to locate the appropriate technologies to import, to evaluate the merit of alternative technologies, to apply them at production sites, and, if necessary, to adapt them to surrounding conditions. These capabilities came from indigenous technologies, some of which had been accumulated through the Tokugawa era, from education, from the experience of learning through trial and error, and from research and development efforts.

The government can and did play an important role in this connection, for example, by establishing an appropriate education system, by allocating precious foreign currency to the import of technology, by providing subsidies and other financial incentives to industries, and by maintaining a general environment conducive to innovation and growth. The government, however, has to be flexible in the changing environment and failure to be so may hinder the development initiated by the private sector. As shown in Figure 1.1, government policies represent only one side of the mechanism behind industrial development, and the activities and organizations of the private sector have to be equally investigated. We now turn to this latter investigation in the next two chapters.

4

The Evolution of a Management System from the Tokugawa Era to World War II

4.1 THE RISE OF MERCHANTS IN THE TOKUGAWA ERA

The most famous entrepreneur in the early Tokugawa Era (the early seventeenth century) was Yodoya Tsuneyasu. Yodoya came to Osaka, then the capital of the government ruled by Toyotomi Hideyoshi. Yodoya made money as a building contractor for the Toyotomi government and then for Tokugawa Ieyasu, who overturned the rule of Hideyori, Hideyoshi's son. Yodoya and his descendants then made a prosperous business as traders of rice, vegetables, fish, and so forth. They prospered and lived so extravagantly that the irritated Tokugawa government ordered Yodoya's business to be closed in 1705 and confiscated all the wealth.

Yodoya made a fortune during the civil war by working for the lords who were fighting with each other. It was more or less a transitional period and Yodoya could accumulate wealth by making full use of his contacts with the lords and making a clever judgement as to who would win the civil war.

By contrast, most enterprises in later periods prospered from commercial demand. The biggest three were Konoike who started with brewing *sake* (Japanese rice wine), Sumitomo who started with copper refining and selling medicine, and Mitsui who started as a draper. They were all innovators in their businesses. Konoike succeeded in transporting sake from the sake-brewing centre near Osaka to a growing market in Edo (Tokyo), thereby enlarging the market tremendously. Sumitomo and their collaborator, Soga Riemon, started copper-refining with the technology they learned from a European merchant. They also pioneered the exporting of copper. Mitsui's innovation in retailing included marking prices, no discount, no credit sale, and selling cloth in any dimensions desired by customers, when none of these was a normal commercial practice. Clearly, all of them were innovators and entrepreneurs in the sense defined in Chapter 1.

As the businesses prospered, they diversified. Some of the businesses they started, for instance, Sumitomo's copper-mining and Konoike's development of rice fields, were risky. To support these enterprises, they wished to enter into a more secure business, which they found in finance. Through this business they became connected to the Tokugawa central government or local governments of feudal lords. In fact, these governments often had huge deficits and depended on the merchants for finance.

There were numerous enterprises, besides these three, both in indigenous manufacturing (craft) and commerce, in both urban and rural areas. Many merchants came from Ohmi (now Shiga Prefecture) and Ise (now Mie Prefecture) areas. They brought clothes, medicine, and other commodities to big cities, some of them, like Sumitomo and Mitsui, settling there. Commercial activities took place not only in the three big cities of the time, Edo (the site of the Tokugawa Government), Kyoto (the site of the Imperial Palace), and Osaka (the commercial centre) (see the map at the front of the book), but in nearly all the cities where local feudal governments located. Hence, many merchants of significant size were found all over the country.

Agriculture was overwhelmingly the largest industry. Even towards the end of the era, that is, the early nineteenth century, more than three-quarters of the labour force was in agriculture. Yet, many manufacturing activities took place in big cities as well as in rural areas. They were more or less traditional crafts, for example, textiles, sake-brewing, soy-sauce, oil, paper, iron, and china, which were mostly made by small enterprises, some of which have survived to the present day, such as Kikkoman, the largest producer of soy sauce (Fruin, 1983). Manufacturing activities based on Western technology, for instance, steel-making and weaponry, appeared toward the end of the era, financed by a few forward-looking feudal lords or merchants (see Chapter 7).

As the business prospered in merchant houses like Mitsui's, ownership and management became increasingly difficult. One of the reasons was the expansion of families. Since the founder, Mitsui Takatoshi, had a number of children, how to divide the wealth among them became a big issue. To ensure that Mitsui's assets remained integrated, Takatoshi left a will to the effect that Mitsui's business should be left as a partnership among eight Mitsui families, each led by Takatoshi's major sons and sons-in-law.

Another difficulty arose from the expanding business organization. Mitsui had business in drapery and finance, and had outlets in Edo, Kyoto, Osaka, and, Takatoshi's homeland, Matsuzaka near Nagoya. Maintaining efficiency in each business and in each outlet while co-ordinating them was a difficult task. As a solution, Mitsui, perhaps not surprisingly, adopted a sort of divisional organization. Mitsui's head-quarters controlled three divisions; drapery, finance, and the shop in Matsuzaka. The drapery division, for example, was responsible for the drapery business and had several outlets in Edo, Kyoto, and Osaka. These facts indicate that the combination of partnership and divisional form was used in Japan by 1700. Both the headquarters and the divisions usually had Mitsui family members as their heads; however, daily control was relegated to *banto*, the non-family managers who had been promoted internally. Among Mitsui families there were both executive and non-executive members. Both received fixed shares of the profits.

Accounting also became complicated as the business expanded. By the early eighteenth century, some of the big businesses, including Mitsui and Konoike, started adopting their own double accounting systems. Even though these systems may have been primitive in comparison to the European system that started two centuries earlier, their use during the Tokugawa Era made it easier for the Japanese businesses to adopt the Western accounting system in the Meiji Era (Sakudo, 1980).

There was some indication of the labour practices that later became the so-called 'Japanese' system. Employees were normally hired at the young age of 12–14, trained on the job, and gradually promoted. There were 15 ranks in Mitsui and it was common that they got their first promotion after 10–15 years of service, and then the second after 12–18 years. Most of the workers who were promoted thus far (or more) and were noted for their diligence and ability left the employer there-after, and started their·own businesses with the blessing of the former employer.

Although some people regard such a practice as an evidence of pa-ternalism in the Japanese management system, it should be noted that those who succeeded in either leaving the firm with the blessing or staying in the firm to be promoted to even higher positions were in fact the minority. According to Nakai (1966), among the 239 workers hired by Mitsui during 1696–1730, only thirty left the firm this way and thirteen were promoted to higher ranks. Among the 174 for whom

Nakai could find out the detail, they constituted only 17 and 7 per cent, respectively. By contrast, seventy-seven (44 per cent) of them were discharged by Mitsui while the others left employment due to death or illness. Therefore, it was by no means a *lifetime* employment system.

Seniority was the main criterion for promotion; yet, merits, such as ability and diligence, were also judged and their importance for promotion became more prominent in later periods.

Although we have mostly quoted the case of Mitsui to describe the management system during the Tokugawa Era, it was similar in other big businesses at the time. Because of Seclusionism, they had no chance of knowing the management system in the West and had to develop their own. Some of the practices were probably more Japanese, for example, the teaching of the Confucianistic work ethic to young workers. Also, they could not develop a system of joint-stock company. However, even here some cases were known of partnerships with some of the partners investing with limited liability. Similarities with the West were found in, for instance, the idea of double accounting, diversification, and on-the-job learning. These similarities are perhaps not surprising because they resulted from rational responses to economic forces. Whatever the cause, these similarities must have helped Japanese businesses to absorb the Western system rapidly after the Meiji Restoration of 1868.

4.2 THE EVOLUTION OF A CORPORATE SYSTEM AFTER THE MEIJI RESTORATION

4.2.1 The Start of Joint-Stock Companies

The start of free foreign trade and free geographical and occupational mobility in the mid- to late nineteenth century implied both competitive threat from abroad and business opportunities. However, those with risk-taking ambition and entrepreneurial talent often lacked capital, and those with money often lacked such talent. It was an urgent requirement that a business system be established to facilitate the flow of capital from the latter to the former.

The concept of the Western company had been introduced into Japan by Fukuzawa Yukichi and a few other people. Fukuzawa, who had at first studied Dutch at Tekijuku (see Section 1.7) and then English, went to the USA in 1860 as a member of the first delegate of the Tokugawa government. He learned the political, social, and economic systems of the West through this and other visits abroad and through books, and introduced them to Japan with his own books and at his own school, which later became Keio University. The concept of a joint-stock company was one of the systems he introduced into Japan.

However, private efforts alone had a limited effect and the government had to establish a legal framework to make the company system attractive to potential entrepreneurs. In 1872, the government issued the National Bank Act based on the recommendation of Ito Hirobumi (later to become the first Prime Minister) who had learned of the national banking system in the USA. The Act allowed the banks to issue transferable shares with limited liability and, hence, was considered to be the first governmental step in establishing a joint-stock company system. It also stipulated that the shareholders hold meetings in which they elect directors. At first, only four banks were established under this Act. However, after its revision in 1876 in which investors were allowed to raise the capital with bonds, as well as with cash, many entries took place, resulting in the establishment of 148 banks during the three-year period 1876–79. In order to explain why this revision made the business so attractive, we need to discuss a drastic policy that the government took at that time.

Under the Tokugawa feudal system, *daimyo* (feudal lords) were self-supporting, taxing the farmers in their *han* (fiefs or feudal domains) and paying salaries to *samurai*, who were their warriors and local government officials. Both daimyo and samurai were hereditary positions. When the Meiji government was established, it abolished the feudal system and deprived daimyo of their right to collect taxes. Instead, the central government had to assume the responsibility for supporting daimyo and samurai. It wished to eliminate a number of them, first because there were too many of them to employ in the government sector and, secondly, because the government intended to establish a new military system by means of conscription rather than by maintaining samurai, as in the Tokugawa Era. In the beginning, the government paid them all salaries but the financial burden was unbearable. The government finally decided to eliminate the salaries and instead give them lump-sum severance payments with government bonds equivalent to several years' salary. It was a drastic policy, in effect making some 320,000 people redundant. It is hardly surprising that several disputes and even a few civil wars were brought about by unhappy former samurai, though the government managed to defeat them.

It was intended that the revised National Bank Act would give former samurai, now called *shizoku*, an opportunity to invest their bonds. The result was the establishment of about 150 banks. Almost three-quarters of the capital was paid up with the bonds by *kazoku* (former daimyo and court nobles) and shizoku (Masaki, 1976). Many of these national banks prospered. After the government established the Bank of Japan in 1882 and forced the national banks (which could issue money) to convert to private banks (without a privilege to issue money), even more banks were established and the joint-stock company system became widely known.

Along with banks, many joint-stock companies were established in trading, textiles, paper, railroad, shipping, and marine insurance. The enactment of the Commercial Law in 1893 (revised in 1899) made joint-stock companies even more advantageous, by clearly stating the privilege of limited liability and free transferability of shares, and abolishing the requirement of a government licence to establish a joint-stock company. As a result, in 1900, there were 4,254 joint-stock companies, which accounted for about 50 per cent in terms of the number of companies and 90 per cent in terms of capital, even though many of them remained family-owned with limited dispersion of ownership (Masaki, 1976). It is also noted that the two biggest enterprises, Mitsui and Mitsubishi, were organized as partners: they adopted, however, several devices to limit the extent of liability.

By 1940, a year before the start of the Pacific War, the number of joint-stock companies increased nine-fold to 38,377, which accounted for about 40 per cent in terms of the number of companies and 90 per cent in terms of capital (Okazaki, 1993*a*).

4.2.2 The Accounting System

Fukuzawa also played a pioneering role in the introduction of the Western accounting system by publishing a Japanese translation of an American book on book-keeping in 1873. The government, in the same year, asked its British adviser to write a book on accounting. With the encouragement of the government to adopt the Western system of book-keeping and of depreciation accounting, the system started to be adopted in a number of businesses. Because the accounting system was first adopted by the national banks under the guidance of the Ministry of Finance, Takatera (1976) emphasizes the role the government played in introducing and spreading the concept of asset depreciation and other practices in the Western accounting system. He also notes the speed with which the businesses responded to the government initiative. The national bank was founded in 1872 and, after five years, started the depreciation calculation of its buildings. This experience may be compared to that of Canada where the national bank founded in 1875 started the depreciation calculation seven years later.

Yasuoka (1980), on the contrary, emphasizes the continuity from the Tokugawa Era, because, as discussed in the previous section, big merchant houses had used their own double-accounting systems. These businesses, as well as newly emerging businesses, were eager to learn the Western system. Fukuzawa's translation became popular and a number of book-keeping schools were established including Mitsui's school for employees. Actually, however, Mitsui did not adopt the Western system until 1893 owing to their familiarity with books written vertically in Chinese numbers. Mitsubishi adopted it earlier in 1876.

4.3   THE ENTREPRENEURS AND THE MANAGERS

Although Mitsui's was the case of an old merchant house surviving through the Restoration and prospering, it was exceptional. Most other big merchants of the Tokugawa Era collapsed during the political and economic turbulence around the Restoration. Their loans to daimyo became unrecoverable and they were heavily taxed by the new Meiji government, which was under a severe burden of deficits. The new era offered business opportunities but many of the old merchant houses were conservative. Furthermore, the inflation during the 1870s and 1880s drastically reduced the value of their assets.

Hence, Mitsui's success should be attributed to the rather rare talent and effort of the managers and not to monopolistic power or their accumulated wealth alone. These managers, furthermore, were not Mitsui's family members but hired managers, such as Minomura Rizaemon, Masuda Takashi, and Nakakamigawa Hikojiro. Neither were they traditional Mitsui managers in that they had not been internally promoted and their origins were low-class shizoku. These managers guided the business through the Restoration and the early industrialization period with foresight and risk-taking. Similarly, Iwasaki Yataro was a low-class shizoku who successfully laid the foundation for the Mitsubishi zaibatsu (see Section 4.4). These people had certain connections with the important figures in the Meiji government and used the information they got from these sources to their full advantage.

More generally, shizoku played an unproportionally large role as entrepreneurs and managers. According to the study by Ishikawa (1974), nearly a half of the managers in the Meiji Era (those born before 1869) were shizoku, who accounted for only 5 per cent of the population. Two facts seem to explain the prominence of shizoku as managers. One is the level of education they received during the pre-Restoration era in comparison to merchants and farmers. The other is their economic needs. Unlike farmers who could survive by harvesting crops from their farmlands, shizoku received government bonds as severance pay but lost jobs. They therefore struggled to find opportunities to earn income. This fact also explains why it was rather middle- to low-class shizoku who were keen to get into businesses.

Next to shizoku in the origin of the managers were merchants. Typically, they were local merchants who started modern industries, such as textiles and food processing, and newly emerging merchants who made money by trading with foreigners in Yokohama and other ports that were opened after the end of Seclusionism. By contrast, many of the former big merchants failed to survive.

Later, as more and more of the post-Restoration generation became managers, they became dominated by graduates from higher education institutions. Among national institutions, engineering schools, such as Kogakuryo (now the Engineering Department of University of Tokyo, see Section 2.4) and Tokyo Kogyo Gakko (now Tokyo Institute of Technology), and commerce schools, such as Tokyo Koto Shogyo Gakko (now Hitotsubashi University), were prominent. In addition, some private schools, most notably Fukuzawa's Keio, provided many graduates.

According to Ishikawa (ibid.), the proportion of managers who had studied at these institutions was 43 per cent among the managers born before 1840 and 52 per cent among those born during the 1840s, but increased to 81 per cent among those born during the 1860s. In particular, the proportion of those having studied at national institutions increased dramatically—from 5 per cent to 39 per cent.

Similarly, Morikawa (1973) found that 115 (68 per cent) of 170 professional managers of large firms in the Meiji Era received higher education. 'Professional managers', in his definition, are the full-time directors who did not have major share ownership at the time they joined the firm. Fifty-one graduated from Tokyo and its predecessors, and twenty-eight from Keio. Of those from Tokyo, twenty-four had studied law and twenty-one, engineering. He also found that the proportion of those who had studied science and engineering was lower in the companies affiliated to zaibatsu (mainly the 'Big Four' to be discussed soon) at 18.2 per cent, than in non-zaibatsu companies, 42.6 per cent.[1]

Clearly, the government's promotion of the education system was indispensable to Japan's business development. Particularly, in technology-oriented industries, many of the managers were graduates of Kogakuryo and other national engineering colleges, as will be shown in later chapters. Clearly, the national investment in education greatly contributed to Japan's accumulation of technological and managerial capabilities.

Morikawa also found that the proportion of professional managers was higher in zaibatsu companies but, even in non-zaibatsu companies, the proportion started to increase after 1900. The inter-firm mobility of these managers was high: about 70 per cent of professional managers taking a directorship by 1911 had experience of working in other companies. This proportion was somewhat lower, at 65 per cent, in zaibatsu companies than in non-zaibatsu companies (77 per cent). Gradually, it seems, owner-managers were replaced by non-owner professional managers and such moves took place faster among zaibatsu companies. Until the beginning of this century, however, talented, qualified, or experienced managers were scarce, and therefore 'poaching' did occur frequently. As companies expanded and became firmly established, they started to nurture professional managerial staff internally and the proportion of internal promotion started to rise.

According to Hirschmeier and Yui (1977), the general characteristics of entrepreneurs during the early Meiji Era may be summarized in four ways. First, many of them sought connections with the government. The reason is obvious. The government had the best knowledge both in technology and in managerial know-how. They had the best people. And they had money and regulatory power. Often, people moved from the public sector to the private sector. Ishikawa's (1974) study shows that 28 per cent of the managers born before 1869 had been, at one time or another, in the central government and, in addition, 10 per cent had been in local governments.

Shibusawa Eiichi, perhaps the most important businessman during the Meiji Era, is the best example. After resigning from the Ministry of Finance, he founded Daiichi Kokuritsu Ginko (First National Bank) in 1873. He subsequently started many businesses such as paper, textile, shipping, and others, with various partners. He was, in a sense, a pilot who guided the course of early industrialization. As we will discuss in the study of the textiles industry (see Chapter 6), his enterprise showed other entrepreneurs how to invest in the textiles business and make it sufficiently competitive against imports from the West. He also acted as a coordinator between the business community and the government, and as an adviser to other newer entrepreneurs. One such entrepreneur was Asano Soichiro who started his business with cement production and later diversified into coal-mining, shipping, and so forth, to become one of the industrial zaibatsu (to be discussed in the next section).

Secondly, as shown in this case of Shibusawa's, collaboration and cooperation among business people occurred in various ways. Joint investment was common. They often helped others in acquiring technology, procuring materials, and hiring good management and engineering staff. They established business organizations, such as Chambers of Commerce and Industry (with Shibusawa's initiative), which were often asked by the government to express their views on such matters as the patent, trademark, measurement, testing, and tariff systems. It should be noted, however, that such cooperation by no means implied a lack of competition. Mitsui and Mitsubishi, for instance, were fierce rivals in a number of industries yet they sometimes cooperated in exchanging information on practical business methods and participated, for instance, in jointly founding the Imperial Hotel in Tokyo, together with Shibusawa and other people.

Thirdly, most of the entrepreneurs were generalists and therefore took every opportunity to expand the business to whatever fields they considered promising, in a conglomerate-like fashion. Hirschmeier and Yui (1977: 135, my translation) argue that 'such generalistic and diversification-oriented activities of the entrepreneurs could be made because new entry into any modern industrial sector was feasible and the advice and encouragement from the government could be expected. Yet, new entry, however feasible, was quite challenging as most manufacturing industries, not to mention foreign trade and shipping, were under the control of foreign companies. Also, the government was under a severe constraint as regards finance and administrative capacity. Therefore, diversifying business activities had to be regarded as an indication of the abundance of entrepreneurship. Moreover, the diversification-oriented activities of entrepreneurs in the Meiji Era were not necessarily based on organic relationship in technology, products, or markets: rather, they were more of a conglomerate-style, to use the present terminology.'

Fourthly, because they lacked accumulated scientific and technological bases, they had to acquire the knowledge through various channels.

Some of them went abroad or read foreign books. Some sought advice from the government. Some hired foreign engineers, which was popular in the beginning but later became less common, partly because of the high salaries they demanded and partly because of the rise in nationalism. More commonly, they hired Japanese staff who had acquired technological or managerial skills abroad or at domestic higher education institutions, or sent the Japanese staff abroad to study the necessary technologies. Shibusawa, for instance, lacked technological knowledge of paper making and therefore hired Ohkawa Heizaburo and sent him to the USA as soon as he had established Oji Paper. He also asked Yamanobe Takeo, then living in England, to study textiles technology before going back to Japan to start a cotton-spinning factory (see Chapter 6).

There seems to be some over-simplification in these summaries by Hirschmeier and Yui in view of the industrial cases to be discussed in the latter half of this book. There were entrepreneurs who themselves had technical knowledge, either through accumulated indigenous knowledge or through education at newly established technical colleges. These entrepreneurs concentrated their efforts within the industries for which they had the technical knowledge, and they rarely diversified in a conglomerate fashion. See, for instance, the case of Toshiba in Chapter 8. Continuity from the pre-Meiji period, we believe, should not be disregarded.

4.4   THE DEVELOPMENT OF ZAIBATSU

Zaibatsu commonly refers to a giant group of firms that was diversified into a number of related or unrelated fields, and controlled by a holding company. Until the end of World War II, these zaibatsu were dominant in the Japanese economy. In 1937, the biggest four zaibatsu accounted for 10 per cent of total capital and five other zaibatsu accounted for an additional 5 per cent (Hadley, 1970). These proportions were further increased during the war because the government sought to control the economy through zaibatsu.

Many authors also raise family ownership and the connection with political parties, the government, the bureaucrats, or the military as other features of zaibatsu.

Two points should be noted, however. First, such business organizations were by no means unique to Japan but observed in many other countries at their developing stages, from German *Konzern* to Korean *Chaebol*. Secondly, those enterprises in Japan commonly regarded as zaibatsu vary in origin and organization to the extent that the single term 'zaibatsu' seems misleading. The following three categories of zaibatsu are in fact quite different.

4.4.1 'Big Four'

Enterprises considered to be representative of zaibatsu are the so-called Big Four—Mitsui, Mitsubishi, Sumitomo, and Yasuda—the first to develop into giant conglomerates. The origins of these four are diverse. As already discussed, Mitsui and Sumitomo started their businesses early during the seventeenth century. Mitsui started as a merchant and Sumitomo, as a copper miner. Both then entered into banking. Mitsubishi was established by Iwasaki Yataro in 1870, two years after the Meiji Restoration, with shipping as its core business. Yasuda Zenjiro, the founder of Yasuda Zaibatsu, was born into a poor family and started a small money exchange business in 1864, four years before the Restoration.

Therefore, chronologically, Mitsui and Sumitomo are on one side and Mitsubishi and Yasuda on the other. It is worth emphasizing again that Mitsui and Sumitomo could expand to become zaibatsu not simply because they were already big and rich at the start of modern industrial development. There were several others around the Restoration who were as big and yet collapsed. The Restoration and the start of modern industrial development offered both good business opportunities and acute business risk. Those with good managerial judgement and risk-taking capacity survived and prospered at the expense of those without. Even the House of Konoike, older and larger than Sumitomo, failed to grasp the opportunity to grow.[2] The House of Ono, equally powerful by the end of the Tokugawa Era, collapsed in 1874. By contrast, Mitsui and Sumitomo were led by non-family managers, most importantly Minomura Rizaemon of Mitsui and Hirose Saihei of Sumitomo, who guided the businesses by accurately forecasting the coming political and economic situations, by acquaintance with high-rank government officials or politicians, and bold investment.

In terms of the business composition, Mitsui and Yasuda were relatively similar, because both had finance at the core, while Mitsubishi and Sumitomo had shipping and mining, respectively, at the core. By the end of the nineteenth century and the early twentieth century, all four had diversified. In particular, all had banks and insurance businesses. Yasuda was least diversified and heavily dependent on the finance business. The other three were more diversified; for instance, all of them went into mining by purchasing mines from the government. They diversified both through internal investment and through acquisitions, though the importance of acquisitions was modest, particularly in comparison to the post-war conglomerates of the USA or the UK.

Moreover, their diversification was mostly into related fields. Mitsubishi's case is most illustrative. It entered into coal-mining to gain the coal needed for ships, bought a shipbuilding yard from the government to repair the ships it used, founded an iron mill to supply iron to the shipbuilding yard, started a marine insurance business to cater for its shipping business, and so forth. Later, the managerial resources and technological capabilities acquired through the operation of shipbuilding were utilized to expand the business further into the manufacture of aircraft and electrical equipment. Similarly, the experience of overseas shipping led the firm to enter into a trading business.

Mitsui's main businesses in the early period were drapery, finance, and trade, the first two being the businesses it inherited from the Tokugawa Era. It entered into mining partly because it acquired a mine as collateral for the loan it had made, and partly because it could buy a mine cheaply from the government. Mitsui then diversified to become the biggest business in pre-war Japan. The diversification was made mainly into related fields to take advantages of accumulated capabilities; for instance, the trading company entered into shipping and then shipbuilding, and the mining company entered into chemicals to attain forward integration. There were also businesses it acquired when the bank's loan could not be recovered. Shibaura Seisakusho (later to become Toshiba, see Chapter 8) is such an example.

Compared to Mitsui and Mitsubishi, Sumitomo and Yasuda were smaller and less diversified. Sumitomo entered into electric wire-making, copper-smelting, and iron-making as an extension of its copper mine business, in addition to the financial business it kept from the Tokugawa era. Yasuda Zenjiro, founder of the Yasuda Group, was no doubt one of the best financiers Japan had; however, he was not adventurous and hardly expanded the business beyond finance. Most of the industrial businesses associated with Yasuda were actually those that Asano Soichiro started, whom Yasuda trusted and provided loans to. More accurately, therefore, they belonged to Asano Zaibatsu and were merely affiliated to Yasuda Zaibatsu.

4.4.2 Industrial Zaibatsu

Asano Zaibatsu was one of industrial zaibatsu, which also included Kawasaki and Furukawa. Asano started with cement and expanded into coal-mining and shipping. Kawasaki started with shipbuilding and then expanded into shipping, rolling stock, motorcycles, aircraft, and steel-making. Furukawa started with copper-mining and then, as a joint venture with Germany's Siemens, established Fuji Electric. Therefore, unlike the Big Four, they were industrial-based and did not have a financial sector. This lack of financial business must have been a big factor in their failing to diversify as extensively as the Big Four.

Another factor was the lack of managerial resources. Whereas the Four, particularly Mitsui, knew that the family members had neither managerial nor technological capability to run the conglomerates and thus hired managers and engineers from universities, the founders of industrial zaibatsu had such a capability and, consequently, were reluctant to hire new people and delegate authority to them. This tendency put a constraint on their capacity to grow further. Industrial zaibatsu, as a result, remained rather secondary to the Big Four.

4.4.3 New Zaibatsu

After the turn of the century, a new breed of entrepreneurs appeared. They were educated at engineering colleges, and were extremely ambitious. The time was ripe for them because heavy manufacturing industries, such as chemicals and machinery, were expanding rapidly owing to the boom during World War I and then the military expansion. Also new technologies that were being developed worldwide became available.

Noguchi Shitagau (also called Noguchi Jun) was typical. He studied electrical engineering at the University of Tokyo and worked in several electric power companies as an engineer. He was then asked by mine owners in Kyushu to build and run a power plant to supply electricity to the mines. He complied with this request, building an 800 kW power plant. The capacity was in excess of the demand and Noguchi started to produce calcium carbide with the surplus electricity.

In 1906, two Germans, A. Frank and N. Caro, invented a new method to produce calcium cyanamide to be used as fertilizer. Noguchi learned of this invention in a newspaper and realized that the method could be used to utilize the calcium carbide that his plant produced. He sailed to

Germany to acquire the patent right. The negotiation was not easy because Mitsui and Furukawa were also aware of the invention and sent delegates to get the patent right. Compared to these two giants, Noguchi was unknown and had a difficult time persuading the patent owner. It was partly his enthusiasm and partly the fortune of his having a German acquaintance at Siemens who gave a supporting voice to the patent owner that made it possible for Noguchi to get the right, beating Mitsui and Furukawa.

With financial help from Mitsubishi, Noguchi established Nihon Chisso Hiryo (or Nitchitsu, meaning Japan Nitrogenous Fertilizer) in 1908 to produce with the Frank-Caro technology. However, acquiring a patent right by no means guaranteed commercial success. On the production side, Noguchi and his collaborator, Fujiyama Tsuneichi, found the product quality too poor and the production level too low when the original technology was used. Thus, it was necessary to fundamentally improve the technology. They finally developed a 'continuous method' of production to replace Frank and Caro's 'alternate method'. On the marketing side, nitrogenous fertilizer was unknown to the farmers, who therefore had to be educated. Yet, these farmers did not like the colour and smell and, moreover, the calcium carbide retained in the fertilizer was harmful to plants if given directly. Noguchi decided to produce ammonium sulphate out of the calcium cyanamide to sell to the farmers, because it was safer and better known.

Apparently, the importation of technology was an indispensable factor but not a sufficient one. It required Noguchi's and Fujiyama's talent and persistent efforts to make it commercially viable. In addition, the knowledge of electrical engineering they gained at universities was critical in their development effort.

After these improvements the business started to grow. In 1921, Noguchi bought new technology for synthetic ammonium from an Italian, L. Casale. It was still at the stage of a tiny pilot plant when he purchased the licence. Again, by their own effort, Nitchitsu succeeded in developing a commercially viable plant and selling ammonium sulphate cheaper than the rivals could, thereby dominating the market. It also diversified into the production of synthetic fibre (see Chapter 6), dynamite, and so forth.

A big breakthrough came in 1926 when Nitchitsu, with the collaboration of the Japanese Army occupying the Korean Peninsula, decided to move to Korea to start a huge electro-chemical complex. It developed Pujon and Chagjin Rivers in northern Korea to build a number of huge hydraulic power plants, and a number of chemical plants to utilize the electric power thus generated. The range of products was diverse, from fertilizer and explosives to soda and metals. By 1941, 659 million yen, 66 per cent of the fixed capital in the Nitchitsu Group, had been invested in Korea. Within Korea, 34 per cent of all the industrial production in 1939 was made by the group (Kobayashi, 1973).

The group lost momentum when Noguchi fell ill in 1940, and collapsed with Noguchi's death four years later and with the end of the war. Molony (1990) provides details of Noguchi and Nitchitsu for English-speaking readers.

Nitchitsu is one of the so-called New Zaibatsu. Nissan, even bigger than Nitchitsu, is another. It was started by Kuhara Fusanosuke with a mining business but it was his brother-in-law, Aikawa Yoshisuke, who expanded it to become a giant conglomerate. Aikawa studied machine engineering at the University of Tokyo and learned the techniques of malleable cast iron and steel pipe by working as a manual labourer in an American iron plant. He then established Tobata Imono (Tobata Casting) to produce malleable cast iron. In 1925, he was asked to take over Kuhara's businesses which, by then, were under financial difficulty. He reorganized the businesses under a parent company named Nihon Sangyo (or Nissan), and expanded them to include Nihon Kogyo (mining), Hitachi (electric machinery), Nissan Jidosha (automobile), Osaka Tekkosho (shipbuilding, now Hitachi Zosen), and other companies in steel, electric power, oil and fats, fishing, and so forth. Hitachi and Nissan will be discussed later in our case studies.

4.4.4 Old and New Zaibatsu: A Comparison

In comparison to older and established zaibatsu, such as the Big Four, New Zaibatsu such as Nitchitsu and Nissan share some distinctive characteristics. First, the owners were university-educated scientists or engineers, and were dominant in their groups as more or less autocratic managers. In contrast, delegation of authority from owner families to professional managers was common among established zaibatsu (even though the control of Mitsubishi by the Iwasaki family was stronger than that of Mitsui), and these managers were rarely engineers. More likely, they were educated in law, economics, or management.

Secondly, although these owners were the largest shareholders, the percentage they owned was much smaller than that of the family owners of the Big Four. Noguchi's shareholding of Nitchitsu, for example, was 27 per cent even in the early year of 1910. In 1938, it was 17 per cent including shareholding through a holding company. The share was publicly traded and the shareholders numbered more than 13,000, though the largest ten shareholders together accounted for 33 per cent (Udagawa, 1984). In contrast, the holding companies of the Big Four were private and totally or mostly owned by the family members.

Thirdly, the leaders of New Zaibatsu were more ambitious and less hesitant to take risks than those of the Big Four who tended to become risk-averse to avoid jeopardizing the family fortune. Perhaps for this reason and because of the different backgrounds of the leaders as mentioned above, New Zaibatsu were biased towards heavy manufacturing industries, taking advantages of opportunities created by the new technologies. They were keen observers of technological development within or outside the country, and made bold investment to materialize the potential gain from the new technologies. Often they endured costly and long-lasting struggles to adapt the technologies to their production processes and create markets for the products.

Fourthly, whereas the Big Four tended to maintain close relationship with politicians, New Zaibatsu tended to have similar relationship with the military, partly because the military influence on the economy became larger in the 1930s when New Zaibatsu expanded, and partly because the main customers of the heavy industries in which they specialized were the Army and Navy.

Therefore, even if one tends to associate zaibatsu with family ownership, it does not strictly apply to New Zaibatsu. Both the Big Four and New Zaibatsu took advantages of the opportunities created by the public sector, whether the government or military, which is hardly surprising in view of the large role the public sector plays in virtually every late-developing country. It is indeed misleading to draw a fixed image of zaibatsu from a single example, say, Mitsui, and discuss its peculiarity compared to other countries. The fact is that there are more similarities than differences between zaibatsu and big company groups in other countries, from Krupp and Siemens in Germany to Hyundai and Samsung in Korea. Even in the USA, Du Pont is known for family ownership, diversification, and the supply to the military (Chandler, 1990). The similarity is perhaps more evident with New Zaibatsu because Du Pont did not have a bank. Yet, Siemens invested in Deutsche Bank and Rockefeller invested in Citibank and Chase Manhattan Bank.

For our purpose, it is more useful to focus on the entrepreneurship of the founders or other leaders of zaibatsu. We have already given examples of innovation in retailing by Mitsui Takatoshi and innovation (with imported technology) in chemicals by Noguchi. We have also discussed the managerial talent and foresight of Minomura, Iwasaki, Yasuda, and others to guide the businesses through turbulent years. Even if they themselves lacked technological understanding, they understood its significance and hired engineers or provided finance to innovative entrepreneurs. More similar cases will be found later.

4.5 THE EVOLUTION OF AN INTERNAL LABOUR SYSTEM

The internal labour system, that is, the system of recruitment, job allocation, promotion, wage structure, employment adjustment, training, labour union, and so forth, of Japanese firms is often considered peculiarly 'Japanese'.[3] Some observers summarize it under the name of 'employer paternalism', or the so-called 'three pillars' of lifetime employment, seniority-based wage structure and promotion, and enterprise unionism. They commonly associate the system with the cultural and social background of Japanese people.

However, if one looks at the historical development closely, it becomes apparent that the system has gradually developed as a response to changing market conditions. How much of this response was 'rational' (in the sense that economists usually use) and how much was culture-bound is a moot question. For instance, among the three representative English books on the evolution of the internal system in Japan—Dore (1973), Hirschmeier and Yui (1975), and Taira (1970)—the first two recognize cultural influences (or the inheritance from the Tokugawa feudal period) whereas Taira virtually disregards them saying that 'paradoxical though it may seem, learning the rules of the labour market was the beginning of whatever meaning one now associates with "employer paternalism"'. (Taira, 1970: 119) To throw some light on this question, we shall briefly describe how the internal labour system evolved over the years.

As the economy grew and particularly as it boomed during and after the Sino-Japanese War (1894–5), the Russo-Japanese War (1904–5), and World War I (1914–18), labour shortage became a serious problem to the industries. In textiles, the leading industry during the last two decades of the nineteenth century, the required skill-level was low and the major workforce comprised unmarried females hired mostly from rural areas. These workers easily changed jobs for higher wages and the competition among employers to lure workers away from other companies was intense. In one factory, an annual separation ratio of 192 per cent was reported, about 80 per cent of which was caused by quits (Hazama, 1964: 277). In a sense, it was a very neoclassical labour market.

To employers, this instability in the labour force caused frequent labour shortages and high recruitment costs (such as the commission paid to recruiters). To solve this problem, many firms at first relied on coercive measures, for instance, hiring guards to prevent workers from escaping from the factories and dormitories, and severely punishing those who had tried to escape. Such measures, however effective in the short run, were destructive in the long run because reports of them and the poor working conditions (long hours, lack of holidays, poor bedding and food conditions at dormitories, etc.) spread and damaged the reputation of the employers, thereby making recruitment even more difficult. Many firms then decided to adopt more paternalistic policies ranging from better accommodation to schooling for those wishing to have a high-school education, courses in sewing, cooking, tea ceremony, and flower arrangements (considered to be a desirable qualification for marriage) for unmarried female employees, sport events or outings, and the sale of daily necessities at reduced prices in company shops. Many of them also started to offer financial benefits, such as insurance and company saving schemes at favourable conditions.

That the employers adopted these 'paternalistic' measures rather than simply increasing wages may be attributed to the socio-economic conditions in the rural areas from which most of the workers were recruited. In such areas, cooperation among farmers was a necessity: irrigation was essential in rice cropping as was the collection and allocation of water. They had to help each other when some were hit by flood or typhoon or when many hands were needed in rice-planting or harvesting. In addition, the Tokugawa government forced them to assume collective responsibility to prevent rioting. Thus rural people felt more secure living in a group of familiar people, and the employers tried to introduce a similar communal life into factories in order to settle the workers there.

It is noted that paternalism was by no means absent in American and European companies. In fact, Japanese firms borrowed many ideas from them. Muto Yamaji, the manager of Kanegafuchi Boseki (Kanegafuchi Spinning, now Kanebo), is known as a pioneer in adopting a number of paternalistic measures under the slogan of 'the firm as an extended family'. According to his autobiography, he learned of the practices in Krupp of Germany and National Cash Register of the USA, and applied many of them in his company. Another example is Furukawa Mining. Its plant manager adopted a paternalistic labour management system following the advice from Cadbury of the UK. (Hazama, 1964). As in science and technology, Japanese managers were eager to learn the advanced practices of the USA and Europe, and apply them in their firms with, if necessary, modification. Labour administration was no exception.

The shortage of labour was acute not only quantitatively but also qualitatively, that is, in terms of skills. Skill shortage was most serious in the machinery and metal industries where the level of required skills was high and was rising owing to the rapid technological progress in these fields.

In the beginning, subcontracting to *oyakata*, bosses with their own labour squads, was common. Oyakata took apprentices, boarded and fed them, gave them on-the-job training, and paid them out of whatever oyakata got from the company. These practices came from the tradition of master craftsmen in the Tokugawa era. However, the system became increasingly inappropriate as the technology progressed rapidly.

One should note here a difference from early developing countries, most notably England, where similar subcontracting to master craftsmen took place in the early period of the Industrial Revolution. Although subcontracting in England was gradually replaced by direct contracting between employers and workers, workers in the same occupation or craft could maintain an association regardless of their employer, thereby developing into craft unions.

In Japan, however, the change from indigenous craft skills to those skills required in modern factories took place much faster and in a less continuous fashion than in England, because the technology was advancing far more rapidly compared to that of England in the eighteenth century. As a result, the employers found the skills possessed by oyakata more and more obsolete and considered it urgent to train the workers themselves either within or outside the firms. Craftsmen sometimes tried to prevent this movement, establishing their own craft unions and controlling the flow of workers into the sector. However, changes in technology and in company labour practices were too rapid for them to maintain their control. The government hostility towards unionism did not help them either. Hence, the lack of craft unionism and the development of internal labour systems in Japan were very much the consequence of its being a late starter.

For companies in the metal and machinery industries, the big task was to maintain a stable workforce with sufficient skills. Thus, they started hiring young workers directly from schools (i.e., not through oyakata) and training them. Some firms established their own schools. For instance, Yawata Steel Works (now Nippon Steel) established a three-year (later two-year) course for 14 years-old boys in 1910, and Mitsubishi's Nagasaki Shipyard (now Mitsubishi Heavy Industries) started a five-year (later, three-year) course in 1932. Other firms, such as Shibaura Seisakusho (now Toshiba) and Ishikawajima Shipyard (now Ishikawajima-Harima Heavy Industries), sent their new employees to a one-year course at outside schools, such as Tokyo Furitsu Shokko Gakko (Tokyo Prefectural School for Workmen). In addition, systematic on-the-job training programmes were established in these and many other firms.

As one may easily imagine, the biggest problem for these firms was how to keep the workers thus trained from leaving for other employers. Around the turn of the century, the quit rate often exceeded 100 per cent per year and, in many metal, engineering, and shipbuilding factories, only about half of the blue-collar employees had been employed for a year or more (Hazama, 1964: 454). The situation was even worse at the national factories, such as Yawata Steel Works or the Naval Shipyard at Kure, because their training programmes were established earlier than those in private firms and many private firms lured workers away with the promise of higher wages.

To prevent such volatile movement of workers, major firms (occasionally including national factories) often agreed not to hire each other's workers; however, as in any cartel, such agreement was rarely effective or long-lasting. Thus, the only way for the firm to maintain their workers was to promise them a bright future upon their staying with the firm and, consequently, a system of seniority-based wages became common, where the worker was promised a higher wage the longer he stayed. Many firms also started using probationary periods for young employees. They would receive training during these periods on the condition that they would be promoted to the status of regular employee once they had finished the training successfully and stayed with the firm for a specified period. The firms also promised to make a maximum effort to maintain the regular workers even in recessions. Thus the spirit of lifetime employment was born, although by no means did it mean that redundancies were non-existent.

Two other factors that fostered the adoption of these labour practices and paternalism should be mentioned. One was the intensifying labour movement. Although the government tried to suppress it from time to time, the union movement became more and more widespread and was often violent. Strikes and other labour disputes numbered almost 500 in 1919 and caused many firms, including Yawata and the two largest private shipyards, Mitsubishi and Kawasaki, to suffer heavily. The adoption of more paternalistic attitudes and the promise of job security were a natural reaction by the employers.

The other factor pertains to the supply of an educated labour force. As discussed in Chapter 2, both elementary and higher education systems had been completed by, say, 1920 and had started to supply educated workers to industries. The higher education system, including universities and engineering institutions, supplied workers with technical knowledge that could be used for production control and labour management. As a consequence, the system of labour management became more organized, free from the discretion of oyakata. For instance, a rather complex wage schedule composed of basic seniority-related wages, incentive payments related to performance, allowances for specific needs, and welfare-related payments was introduced in many firms.

The principle of such an internal labour system—hiring workers from schools, training them at company expense, maintaining them for their lifetime (more or less as a norm but not necessarily as a reality), and paying them according to seniority as well as performance—was by no means established overnight. Some of the practices started to be adopted in a few factories, particularly national factories such as Yawata and Kure Shipyard during the Sino-Japanese War of 1884–5. Gradually they spread to other factories and more related measures were taken. In particular, the boom during and following World War I caused the firms to suffer from serious labour shortage and, in addition, because heavy industries, such as machinery and metals, had expanded more rapidly than other industries, the shortage of skilled workers was even more serious. This environment fostered the adoption of the internal labour system by most major firms. Therefore, the consensus among historians seems to be that the system was more of less established by the 1920s.

It should be noted, however, that the system, even after the 1920s, or even today for that matter, was applied only to a part of the workforce in the country. Primarily, it covered male employees in major private firms and the government or the semi-government sector. It was more prevalent in heavy industries than in light industries, for example, food and textiles. In addition, it was not applied to temporary workers that many firms started to employ to protect regular workers from business downturn.

4.6 THE WAR-TIME CONTROL

During the 1940s, as World War II approached and after it started, the government and the military intensified their control over industries. The flow of materials and products was controlled to increase the production of munitions and other war-related necessities. The government ordered many industries to establish associations for the purpose of allocating materials to member producers and coordinating the production plans. Across industries, the production plans were coordinated by the Ministry of Commerce and Industry (now MITI). Although these associations were disbanded after the war, many of them were reorganized on a smaller scale as voluntary trade associations. Their main activities are now limited to the promotion of public relations and exchange of information of a general kind.[4] Yet, Okazaki (1993c) argues that some of these associations cooperated in the priority-production policy and other industrial policies following the end of the war. He also argues that the current system, where, for instance, several trade association representatives become the members of government councils for economic planning, originates from the war-time experience.

The government also controlled the flow of funds, restricted the influence of shareholders on company decision-making, and controlled the allocation of the labour force.

In 1939, the government set an upper limit to the amount of dividend that companies could pay. Until then, the dividend ratio was fairly high in Japan. For instance, the average dividend as a ratio to profits was nearly 70 per cent among a sample of 20 large firms (Okazaki, 1993a). Stocks were thus attractive financial assets, making it possible and advantageous for companies to finance their investment by the sale of new shares rather than through indirect financing, that is, bank loans.

The government-imposed restriction on dividend caused many investors to switch their investment to bank deposits and, consequently, share prices fell. The firms now had to depend more on financing from banks. Although this fact seems in contradiction to the well-known Modigliani-Miller theorem of irrelevance of dividend policy, it is understandable that the stock market sensed general hostility in the government policy against shareholders. The banks, to deal with the increased demand for loans and to share default risk, started to form a loan syndicate for each borrower with one of the banks acting as the *main bank* to coordinate among the syndicate member banks. In 1944, the government in fact designated a main bank for every munitions producer.

In 1943, the government also restricted the right of shareholders by allowing the managers to make decisions without the approval of shareholder meetings. Instead they were put under control of the government or the industry associations.

As for the labour market, the government, to secure smooth production for military needs, not only banned unions but also restricted workers from changing jobs. It furthermore ordered the firms to increase in-company training and encouraged them to abolish the distinction between white-collar workers (*shokuin*) and blue-collar workers (*koin*) to enhance the morale of the latter.

These measures were all intended to increase the production and flow of war supplies. The basic view of the government (and the military) was that such a purpose would be best served by controlling the allocation of materials and labour, controlling the flow of funds, controlling company decision-making, and controlling the distribution of products. Whether the adoption of such a control system yielded the intended results or the results more desirable than those that would have been attained under the market-based free enterprise system with, if necessary, regulatory measures, is a formidable question.

Basically, all these government controls were repealed after the war. Not surprisingly, however, they left certain influences on how the industrial and managerial systems were formed in the post-war period.[5] We now turn to this topic.

5

Management in Post-War Japan and Today

In Chapter 3, we briefly discussed post-war reforms that were taken by the General Headquarters (GHQ) of the Allied Power under the name of the 'Economic Democratization Policy'. Here we will discuss some of these reforms in more detail, as their influence on the formation of the present Japanese management system cannot be ignored.

For GHQ, one of the major aims of the policy was to reduce concentration of economic power. Hadley (1970) documents this reform in detail. In addition to the enactment of the Act Concerning Prohibition of Private Monopoly and Maintenance of Fair Trade (usually abbreviated as the Antimonopoly Law) in 1947 and the creation of the Fair Trade Commission (FTC) to enforce the Law, GHQ ordered all zaibatsu to be dissolved and a number of large firms to be split.

Zaibatsu dissolution was mainly targeted at the Big Four and six New Zaibatsu although its effect extended to many other firms. Four measures were taken for this purpose. First, to sever the ownership ties, forty-two holding companies including, of course, the Big Four, were forced to liquidate and their shares confiscated by a special committee called the Holding Company Liquidation Commission (HCLC). The shares held by designated zaibatsu families were also confiscated with only nominal compensation paid. HCLC also ordered forty-one additional companies, including Japan Iron and Steel, Hitachi, Toshiba, and Kawasaki Heavy Industries, to dispose of their shareholdings.

Secondly, 1,575 executives from more than 400 companies (including, but not limited to, zaibatsu companies) were purged from their jobs and prohibited to take any managerial position.[1] Thirdly, Mitsui Bussan and Mitsubishi Shoji, the two largest trading companies (*sogo shosha*) and main members of, respectively, Mitsui and Mitsubishi Zaibatsu, were forced to be broken up into 220 and 130 companies, respectively.

Fourthly, the prohibition of the use of former zaibatsu names and trade-marks (i.e., Mitsui, Mitsubishi, and Sumitomo) was proposed, although, after all, the proposal never went through the National Diet.

As a consequence of these drastic measures, business groups such as Mitsui, Mitsubishi, and Sumitomo are essentially different today from pre-war zaibatsu. It is true that the group companies gradually started to acquire the shares of other member companies, and now 28 per cent of the shares of the member companies of these three groups on average are held by other companies of the same group (Fair Trade Commission, 1994). Yet there is no such central decision-making unit as the holding company of pre-war zaibatsu. In today's business groups, all the members are on equal terms and each member cooperates with others only as they wish. It is also true that the two trading companies, Mitsui Bussan (Mitsui & Co.) and Mitsubishi Shoji (Mitsubishi Corporation), were resurrected after a number of mergers and that many firms resumed the use of Mitsui, Mitsubishi, or Sumitomo names after temporarily adopting different names. Yet, the relative power of these trading companies has declined and the member companies of Mitsui and Mitsubishi do not necessarily use these trading companies as their partners for trade and joint ventures. Thus, it is more accurate to regard present business groups (*kigyo shudan*), as no more than loose federations of independent firms. See Goto (1982) and Odagiri (1992: ch. 7) for more details.

Another policy pursued by GHQ was to split companies with market power. Based on the Law for the Elimination of Excessive Concentrations of Economic Power (usually called the Deconcentration Law), GHQ at first made a list of 325 firms to be split but, with the resistance and opposition both in Japan and the USA, the list was eventually reduced to that of eleven firms. These included Japan Iron and Steel (to be discussed in Chapter 7), which was split into Yawata, Fuji, and two smaller firms, and Mitsubishi Heavy Industries (to be discussed in Chapters 9 and 10), which was split into three firms of roughly the same size. Both of these firms later re-merged. Others included Oji Paper, which was split into three companies, Oji (renamed New Oji after its merger with Kanzaki in 1993), Jujo (renamed Nippon Paper after its merger with Sanyo-Kokusaku Pulp in 1993), and Honshu, now competing with each other; and Dainippon Beer, which was split into Sapporo and Asahi, now competing with each other in one of the most concentrated industries in the country. In addition, seven firms were ordered to sell off their plant, which included Hitachi and Toshiba.

The eleven firms were designated by the Deconcentration Law because they were regarded as excessively monopolistic in view of market shares in excess of 70 per cent in respective markets. Exceptions were Mitsubishi Heavy Industries and three zaibatsu-owned mining companies which were designated irrespective of their smaller market shares because they were the integral components of respective zaibatsu.

The influence of these policies of zaibatsu dissolution and deconcentration was profound not only in terms of their effects on market competition but also of their effects on the ownership and managerial structure of the companies. We will discuss these effects further in the following sections.

With regard to the competition-promoting effect, we emphasize that the reform by itself was hardly sufficient to make the markets effectively competitive. It is true that in the steel industry, for instance, the break-up of the dominant market leader, Japan Iron and Steel, reduced mobility barriers and entry barriers, thereby making it easier for smaller firms to increase their shares and for new firms to enter. In fact, as we will discuss in Chapter 7, Nihon Kokan (now NKK), Kawasaki Steel, and Sumitomo Metal increased their shares to become viable competitors against Yawata and Fuji, which is why the FTC approved the merger of Yawata and Fuji in 1969.

Probably more important, however, was the presence of many opportunities for investment and entry in the post-war high-growth era, as well as the presence of entrepreneurs to take advantages of such opportunities. Very often, the firms most active in investment and innovation were newcomers, such as Tsuzuki Spinning (see Chapter 6), Sony and Sharp (see Chapter 8), and Honda (see Chapter 9), or secondary or fringe firms, such as Kawasaki Steel (see Chapter 7). These firms keenly sought new technologies, made their own research efforts, and utilized the new technologies thus acquired to develop new products and processes or to improve upon existing ones. The investment was often extremely risky and the government policy created obstacles as well as support. Notwithstanding these difficulties, many entrepreneurs did appear and expanded their businesses, thereby making the markets contestable. Were it not for these activities, the markets must have remained less competitive. That is, although a one-off reform such as the Deconcentration Law doubtlessly contributed to making markets less concentrated, it was by no means sufficient to sustain competition in markets.

The Antimonopoly Law, which took effect in 1947 and has been amended several times since, also contributed to the maintenance of competitive markets. Although we recommend the readers to refer to more specialized literature for details (e.g., Matsushita, 1990), let us give a very basic explanation of the law here. The law prohibits (i) private monopolization which is defined as meaning that 'any entrepreneur, individually or by combination or conspiracy with other entrepreneurs, or by in any other manner, excludes or controls the business activities of other entrepreneurs, thereby restraining, contrary to the public interest, substantially competition in any particular field' (the Law, Chapter 1, Section 2(5), as translated by Nakagawa 1984), (ii) unreasonable restraint of trade, that is, cartels and other anti-competitive collusion, and (iii) unfair trade practices, such as price discrimination, dumping, false advertising, exclusive dealing, tie-ins, resale price maintenance (with exemptions), and unjust use of a dominant bargaining position.

As an exception, certain cartels are permitted, which include depression cartels and rationalization cartels that FTC approves under certain conditions, and cartels permitted under other laws, such as those to protect small firms, those to enforce safety regulation, and those related to export and import. Although the number of these exempted cartels reached 1,079 (415 if cartels organized separately by prefecture in an industry are counted as one) in 1966, it has been declining since then and was just sixty-five in 1993. Among those in 1966, thirty were depression or rationalization cartels; since 1990, however, FTC has not approved any. Because the majority of the cartels have been made among mid-size and small firms, it seems rather difficult to argue that the legalization of these cartels has made significant impact on the market competition of major technology-oriented industries. Matsui (1989) even argues that depression cartels led to excessive capital investment and, consequently, enhanced the rivalry in the long run.

Prevention of the concentration of economic power is another aim of the law. To prevent the resurrection of zaibatsu, holding companies are banned. Mergers, acquisitions of shares or assets, and interlocking directorates are prohibited if they have the effect of restraining competition.[2] The law also sets limits to shareholdings by non-financial companies and financial institutions. In the beginning, shareholding by non-financial companies was totally prohibited excepting the shares of fully-owned subsidiaries, but this restriction was later relaxed. Shareholding by financial institutions (except insurance companies, for which the limit is higher) was limited to a maximum of 5 per cent of any company in the beginning, relaxed to 10 per cent in 1953, and tightened to 5 per cent again in 1977. The consequence of these restrictions on the pattern of share ownership will be discussed in the next section.

5.2   POST-WAR DEVELOPMENT

The post-war development of management systems in Japan took place in four major areas—ownership, finance, management, and labour. These will be discussed in turn.

5.2.1   Share Ownership

As discussed in the previous section, the shares of stock held by holding companies were confiscated and HCLC had to sell these shares. There were also other kinds of shares to be disposed of in the market: the Ministry of Finance had obtained a large amount of shares from zaibatsu families and others when in 1946 it allowed the heavy capital levy tax to be paid in kind. There were also shares of other companies held by closed institutions, mainly companies in the former colonized territories of Manchuria, Korea, and Taiwan. Finally, because of the restriction of shareholding in the original Antimonopoly Law as discussed above, financial and non-financial companies had to dispose of much of their shareholding. As a result, a hugh amount of shares had to be sold in the capital market. The total amount is estimated as 15 billion yen by Hadley (1970: 181) and as 25 billion yen by Teranishi (1993: 82). It is unclear why the two numbers differ so much. Also unclear is whether either figure includes the shares sold by companies without FTC's supervision to satisfy the antimonopoly restriction. Whichever is the right figure, the impact of the sales to the market must have been immense because the total amount of capital of Japanese corporations was 44 billion yen in book value in 1945 (Teranishi, 1993). As Hadley (1970: 185) puts it, 'in perspective it is difficult to understand how such a gigantic share disposal program could have been effected—but it was.'

In the disposal, employees were given a priority to purchase the shares of the company at a price approved by a special commission called the Securities Coordinating Liquidation Commission. In consequence, the proportion of total shares held by individuals (households)

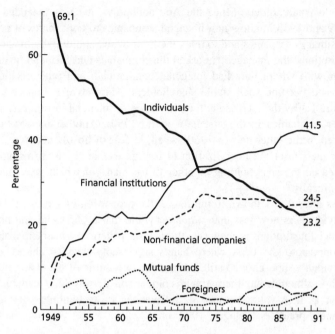

FIG. 5.1. Share ownership in Japan, by type of owner

increased from 24.6 per cent in 1945 to 69.1 per cent in 1949 and the number of household shareholders increased 2.5 times, from 1.7 million to 4.2 million. As shown in Figure 5.1, however, the proportion of individuals has been continuously declining since 1949 and is now less than a quarter. By contrast, shareholding by financial institutions and industrial companies has increased, jointly accounting for nearly two-thirds now. There are several reasons for this change.

The first was a collapse in the stock market after the Dodge Line in 1949 (see Chapter 3). Many individuals sold shares due to the prevailing pessimism, which lowered their proportion by more than ten percentage points by 1951. The Bank of Japan, to prevent further collapse, asked banks and other financial institutions to purchase shares.

The second were increasing attempts at hostile takeovers, including one against a former zaibatsu (i.e., Mitsui's) company, Taisho Marine Insurance. These attempts forced the management to recognize an urgent need to increase the shares of those whom they could trust to be 'stable' shareholders. Since the Antimonopoly Law was amended in 1949 and 1953 to allow non-financial companies to hold shares of non-subsidiary companies and to relax the limit of shareholding by financial institutions, the management asked the companies and financial institutions with whom they had financial, commercial, and other relationships to become such stable shareholders. This move is apparent in Figure 5.1 by the increase in the proportion of financial institutions and other companies in the first half of the 1950s. Another increase occurred in the latter half of 1960s when, in fear of hostile takeovers by foreigners after the liberalization of foreign exchange, the firms again increased the shareholding of other firms, many of which were made reciprocally.[3]

As a result, as shown in the figure, the proportion of shares held by individuals is now less than a quarter while that by financial and non-financial institutions is about two-thirds. This pattern of ownership makes a contrast to the USA where banks supposedly own no shares and individuals (households) still account for two-thirds of the share ownership, although an international comparison of this kind cannot be taken at face value because of differences in accounting rules and business practices (Odagiri, 1992: ch. 2).

5.2.2   Corporate Finance and the Main Bank System

The rising importance of financial institutions as shareholders coincided with their importance as suppliers of funds. As discussed already, indirect finance, especially bank loans, became the major source of finance during the war. This dependence on banks intensified after the war because the stock markets were closed until 1949 and soon afterwards the stock prices fell. It was thus not easy or advantageous for firms to finance through the stock market. Yet it was essential to maintain a smooth flow of funds for reconstruction and growth, particularly to those industries deemed essential to the economy. To support its priority production policy (see Chapter 3), the government set up a special fund, Reconstruction Finance Bank, which provided low-interest loans to, among others, the target industries of coal mining and steel. In 1947, the Bank provided finance almost equal to all the private banks (Kosai, 1988).

This bank was closed in two years and private banks became the major source of loans. To meet a large amount of loan request, banks often formed a syndicate for each borrower, as in the war period, with one of the banks, called the 'main bank', acting as a coordinator. To support this system of supplying funds through banks, the Bank of Japan started providing loans to banks when the latter fell short of funds to comply with loan demand. This was the so-called 'over-loan' system, which characterized the corporate financial system of post-war Japan, particularly during the high growth era of the 1950s and 1960s (Wallich and Wallich, 1976; Teranishi, 1993).

According to Corbett and Jenkinson (1994), banks provided 34.5 per cent of the finance for gross investment by Japanese firms during 1970–89, which compares to 18.0 per cent in Germany, 23.3 per cent in the UK, and 14.7 per cent in the USA. The proportion of internal finance was 40 per cent in Japan but 60 to 63 per cent in the other three countries. To finance net investment (net of deposits, equity purchases, bond purchases, and others), that is, to finance physical investment, Japanese firms depended on banks for 30.5 per cent of the necessary fund whereas the proportion was less than 20 per cent in the other countries.

But why has the dependence on banks persisted even after the post-war shortage of funds disappeared? Three explanations seem appropriate. One is the tax advantage of bank debts. As is well known, the Modigliani-Miller theorem implies that, under the corporate income tax scheme whereby interest payments can be deducted, debt financing is more advantageous than equity financing. In fact, the corporate tax rate has been much higher in Japan since the war.

The second is the pecking-order theory and the fast growth of Japanese firms. According to this theory, the management prefers financing internally, followed by bank financing, because of (1) asymmetric information where the management has better understanding of the environment and the probable consequence of investment, (2) transaction costs which tend to be higher with equity issues, and (3) the management's wish to minimize interference by outsiders. Thus in every country, the management tends to finance internally for the most part of investment and only if internal finance is insufficient do they rely on debt financing. This theory explains why the proportion of funds financed internally is the largest of any of the four countries studied by Corbett and Jenkinson. Furthermore, the higher proportion of debt financing in Japan can be understood in the light of the higher investment propensity and thereby the larger funds that Japanese firms needed to finance.

Some authors stress the monitoring function of the main banks (Hodder, 1988; Sheard, 1989). They argue that the main banks monitor the behaviour of the management and, if mismanagement is observed, will threaten to withdraw loans. That is, in Hirschman's (1970) terms, they 'voice' their dissatisfaction with the threat of 'exit'. In other instances, they help the management to get out of financial difficulty by giving advice, by sending in experienced managers, or by providing additional funds. Such an intermediate form of corporate governance, as these authors call it, has been beneficial to both the banks and the firms or, more precisely, the stakeholders of the firms including shareholders, managers, employees, suppliers, and customers. Consequently, debt financing may not have been as undesirable in Japan as it is believed to be in other countries.

The main bank, almost without exception, is one of the main shareholders, as are the several other banks providing loans to the firm; hence, another important function is the protection against hostile takeovers. That is, as stated above, they function as stable shareholders, though how stable they really are is not necessarily obvious. As a consequence, the main bank system has increased the discretionary power of the management, however large its monitoring function may be. We will come back to this topic later.

5.2.3 Management

The post-war reform had two consequences regarding top management. One was the increased spread of ownership and its separation from control: when the holding companies were dissolved, zaibatsu families lost a major part of the ownership, and the heavy capital levy tax and land reform caused many traditional capitalists to sell their shares. The other was the purge of quite a large number of top managers. The presidents and others senior directors of most major firms were ordered to leave their posts and were prohibited to take managerial positions. As a consequence, younger executives were promoted to the presidency of these companies.

Although the separation of ownership and management had already taken place in pre-war companies, including zaibatsu companies, and was further encouraged during the war, the post-war reform fostered this tendency even further, to the extent that it became a dominant fixture of Japanese management system. It is true that there have been a number of owner-managers, many of whom were also the founders, for instance, Matsushita Konosuke of Matsushita Electric, Hayakawa Tokuji of Sharp, Honda Soichiro of Honda, and Ishibashi Shojiro of

Bridgestone, or the descendants of founders, for instance, Toyoda Eiichi and Toyoda Shoichiro of Toyota and Matsuda Koji of Mazda. Even in these cases, however, the shares held by these managers were far short of majority and, except for a few cases, smaller than those of the main banks.

In subsidiary firms, the presidents are often sent from the parents. In firms with financial difficulties, the presidents may be sent from the main banks. In a few cases, former government officials may be recruited and made the presidents—the cases of the so-called *amakudari* or 'descent from heaven'. Except for these cases, it has been more or less a rule in established companies that the majority of directors are chosen internally by the top management and the presidents are selected from among these directors, most commonly by the nomination of retiring presidents.

Another consequence of the post-war purge was that the succeeding managers were younger. Very often they were more adventurous or had better knowledge of the new technologies and the techniques at the shop-floor. Probably the most typical is Nishiyama Yataro of Kawasaki Steel who led the company to invest in an innovative large-scale steel mill (see Chapter 7). It is perhaps not too far-fetched, therefore, to assume that, by introducing a new breed of managers, the purge contributed to fostering innovation and investment during the following high-growth era. In view of this fact, the relatively advanced years of top executives in many Japanese firms today appears to be something to worry about.[4]

5.2.4 Labour

GHQ legalized the formation of labour unions and, at least in the beginning, encouraged it. Consequently, the ratio of union participation among non-agricultural workers jumped to more than 50 per cent in 1949. Many unions became militant not only because the leaders tended to be communist-influenced but, more importantly, because a substantial part of the workforce was made redundant owing to insufficient demand, damaged equipment, lack of materials, and the excessive number of workers due to the expanded munitions production during the war. In addition, the workers suffered from severe inflation. Not surprisingly, labour disputes took place in many firms with the workers demanding that employers withdraw their redundancy plans and increase wages. Some of the disputes ran for months, thereby damaging the firms.

Although most of these disputes ended with the management's victory, they taught an important lesson: redundancies should be avoided and sympathetic employer–employee relationships should be fostered. In order to maintain jobs for the core of regular workers, the firms increasingly relied on temporary and seasonal workers, thereby maintaining flexibility in labour input. Secondly, many of the firms consciously increased the flow of information to the workers, and provided more welfare-related facilities and programmes, such as company housing, evening classes in the tea ceremony and English conversation, and company-wide sports meetings, to name but a few.

In the high-growth era of the 1950s and 1960s, the acute shortage of skills was unavoidable. The firms therefore increased their efforts in training, by establishing elaborate in-house educational programmes and encouraging on-the-job training. They also sought broad-ranging skills, to maintain flexibility. The combination of systematic job rotation and on-the-job training was used in many firms for this purpose.

These developments led us to the present internal labour system in Japan, details of which are discussed in, for instance, Koike (1988) and Odagiri (1992: ch. 3). It is thus the product of historical evolution in which the firms, the government, and the workers responded to the changing environment. The way they responded may have been culturally bound; yet, it has, for the most part, followed economic logic.

5.3   THE MANAGEMENT SYSTEM TODAY

Now that we have discussed how the Japanese management system was formed, it is time to discuss the present system, particularly its aspects relating to the innovation of Japanese firms.

5.3.1 *Motivations*

Decisions on how much to invest in research and development is inherently a dynamic one and depends on how much the firm is inclined to growth (i.e., long-term objectives) as opposed to short-term objectives. For several reasons, Japanese firms may be assumed to be more growth-oriented than American or European firms. The detail of this discussion is given in Odagiri (1994): we only give a brief sketch here.

On the ownership side, we have already stated that most of the shareholders are on friendly terms with the current management. Hostile takeovers are relatively few, partly because a block of shares is held by these friendly hands and partly because the internal labour system makes post-takeover restructuring by raiders, as well as takeovers themselves, more costly. Since the 'stable' shareholders are unlikely to interfere with the management unless the firm is in trouble, and since these shareholders are themselves controlled by sympathetic managers, the management is considered to possess significant discretional power.

Typically the managers are promoted from within the pool of those having worked with the company for, say, three decades who have gradually climbed up the promotion ladder. No wonder they feel closer to the employees with whom they have worked for many years. They would consider themselves, first and foremost, as representing the employees rather than the shareholders.

That managers tend to pursue growth more than the value of the firm has been put forward by many writers, most notably Marris (1964), for several reasons such as managers' pecuniary and non-pecuniary gains associated with growth. Add to this the managers' strong identification with the employees. The maintenance of employment has been given the highest priority by many Japanese employers, and the employer–employee relationship has been generally more stable in Japan than elsewhere in the past several decades.

Because employees are mostly concerned with the long-term survival and performance of the company, and the prospect of promotion which increases with the speed of organizational expansion, they are more growth-oriented than shareholders, and with the weak capital market constraint and the managers' identifying themselves with the employees, Japanese firms tend to be more growth-oriented. As a means for growth, they are bound to make a greater effort to the creation and acquisition of technological knowledge.

5.3.2 Managers' Background

We stated in the previous chapter that many of the pre-war entrepreneurs and managers had technological knowledge, and that the establishment of engineering schools at the higher level contributed to this tendency. This tendency is still present.

Take the case of Hitachi, which was established by Odaira Namihei in 1911. Until 1941, all eleven directors, including Odaira himself, had an engineering background and, except for one, were graduates of Tokyo's engineering department (Morikawa, 1975). A half century later, in 1991, Hitachi's board of directors was still dominated by those with an engineering background: of the 35 directors, 24 had graduated from engineering departments, including 9 from Tokyo. Not surprisingly, both the chairman and the president had graduated from Tokyo's engineering department.

More generally, among the presidents of 111 major Japanese manufacturing firms in 1991 for whom the educational background was known, 43 were graduates of engineering departments; 4, science; 41, economics, business, or commerce; 18, law; and 5, miscellaneous. In terms of the company department from which the directors were promoted, R&D and production accounted for 25 per cent among the 1,195 directors (all internally promoted and full-time) of 656 firms, even though these firms included financial and trading companies (Kono, 1984: 33). This percentage vied with marketing and export (26 per cent). Finance and accounting accounted for a mere 5 per cent.

By contrast, in the USA in 1991, a quarter of the top executives of the largest 1,000 companies started their career in finance or accounting, followed by 21 per cent in marketing. We should not overemphasize the Japan–USA difference because, even in the USA, engineering, technology, and production together account for nearly a quarter and there seems to be an increasing trend in the proportion of technology-based executive (Business Week 1991; 1993*b*). Nevertheless, it is important that more Japanese managers have their origins in production and technology and that this tendency has been a stable feature of Japanese management almost since the beginning of its industrialization.

The better knowledge and experience of Japanese managers in production and R&D provides them with a better understanding of the potential and limitation of R&D projects, more accurate evaluation of the outcome from R&D, and more favourable general attitudes towards R&D. Such managerial understanding must be particularly valuable in accumulating technological capabilities and adapting to a rapidly changing technological environment.

5.3.3 R&D–Production–Sales Links

It is known that the Japanese internal labour system is characterized not only by long-term attachment but also by a carefully organized training and rotation scheme (Koike, 1988). Many firms provide several months of well-programmed induction training, both for the acquisition of technical knowledge and skills and familiarization with the firm; and mid-career training every five years or so. In addition, rotation of workers from, say, R&D to production in the case of engineers, or from one shop-floor to another in the case of production workers, is more common than in other countries. These practices help to give the workers a company-wide view and acquire flexibility in a changing work environment.

Furthermore, long-term employment naturally leads to personal links across departments. If one has worked in R&D for many years, there will have been many opportunities to meet and talk with other people throughout the company, and to visit other departments and other plant to discuss mutual problems. Close human contacts are thus nurtured. Consequently, the R&D staff will be more familiar with the technological needs of the production and marketing departments, and the non-R&D departments will be more familiar with the developments in the laboratory, thus aiding more production-based and market-oriented R&D. The advantage is that the research will be more commercially relevant and the introduction of a new product into the production and marketing stages will be faster. The disadvantage, on the other hand, is that a truly original research idea may be either disregarded or more difficult to develop.

Another feature of Japanese firms that has made the internal links even more effective is a close contact with suppliers (or subcontractors). A stable buyer–supplier relationship with constant communication is usual in Japanese companies to the effect that an assembler (or any other type of buyer firm) and its suppliers tend to share the threat of market competition as well as the need for innovation.[5] Improvement in the product or production process by a supplier will be noted and rewarded by the assembler and, if possible, will be utilized in other firms in the group. On many occasions, cooperative R&D will be carried out between the assembler and the supplier(s). For instance, when an automobile assembler develops a new car model, it is essential that suitable components are developed simultaneously. Such development will be done by the supplier(s) in close communication with the assembler's developing team and often with the latter's technical advice. See Asanuma (1985) and Clark and Fujimoto (1991) for a detailed study of the automobile industry, and Imai et al. (1985) for a general discussion.

5.3.4 Introduction of New Technology

The invention of new processes or new products is not itself the ulti-
mate goal of the firm. They have to be introduced to factories or to
markets. And this introduction cannot be effectively made without
coordination between the R&D department and the production and sales
departments. For this purpose, many firms are adopting the organizational design whereby production or marketing staff participate in the
development team from an early stage. Such an organization can be
inefficient in terms of development itself but, since the views of the
production and marketing departments are reflected in the development of the final process or product, the transfer from development
to production and to the market is quicker, with little obstruction or
disruption.

In some firms the engineers in the development team are transferred
to the production department to work on applying the new technology
to production (Sakakibara and Westney, 1985). Such transfer may be
made intentionally because researchers' productivity tends to peak by
the age of, say, forty. Thereafter, their expertise may be better utilized
in administrative and managerial tasks. Obviously, the transfer not only
facilitates the introduction of a particular new technology that the engineer has developed, but also increases the technological capabilities
in general in the production department. It also fosters even tighter
personal links between R&D and production.

Even if the production manager is familiar with the new technology,
it cannot be smoothly transferred to production unless the workers are
skilled and flexible. The Japanese internal labour system helps this
transfer with workers' broad skills nurtured through off-the-job and on-
the-job training. It is important that the management has a free hand
in the reorganization of work. The prevalence of single and company-
wide unions in Japan is indispensable here. For instance, when automobile manufacturers introduced robots, most of the welding jobs were
eliminated, yet none of the Japanese firms dismissed their welders.
They were all retrained and transferred to other areas, such as metal-
work and assembly, resulting in no incidence of grievance or industrial
action being reported. If, on the contrary, workers in separate jobs are
organized into different unions, such transfers would have caused disputes and the introduction of new processes would have been resisted.
Good and integral labour relations are thus essential in carrying out
technological progress. It is for this reason that most Japanese firms

that set up abroad seek single-union representation (White and Trevor, 1983).

Furthermore, proposals from workers for improvements are encouraged by most firms. A good management–worker relationship is essential both to provide incentives for the workers' proposals and to ensure that good proposals are acted upon. Needless to say, workers must have high and broad capabilities if they are to analyse problems and provide solutions. The number of such proposals is surprisingly high in many factories and some of them have greatly contributed to improved productivity. The cases to be discussed of Kawasaki Steel (see Chapter 7) and Sony (see Chapter 8) will illustrate this fact.

5.3.5   *Internal and External Factors*

To sum up, four factors have contributed in making the Japanese companies a vigorous innovator. They are a bias to growth maximization, familiarity of management with research, production, and marketing, close R&D–production–sales links, and the smooth incorporation of technology into production. Behind these factors were the internal labour system and the ownership structure. Labour practices such as long-term worker–company attachment, internal training, and internal promotion have been conducive to the growth preference of managers and employees, inter-departmental personal contacts, and easy adaptability to new technology on the shop-floor.

These internal factors need to be accompanied by external factors, because an organization might survive without achieving its potential efficiency unless an external threat is posed. Competition and rapid changes in industrial structure play vital roles as such a threat. Competition among rival firms has been intensive in many industries in Japan even where the concentration ratio was not particularly low. Entry into growth industries has been fast and frequent. And shifts in industrial structure have been drastic in the past decades, with some of the once-glorious industries now fading into obscurity. These facts provide the firms with an acute awareness of potential crisis and motivation to be innovative.

This type of competition should not be seen as the 'perfect competition' as taught in standard microeconomics textbooks, where the number of competitors is so large that none affects the market. Rather it is an evolutionary one where only the fittest and the most efficient will survive. Such competition drives the firms into maximal efforts for innovation. The maintenance of such competitive markets must remain as one of the, if not *the*, most important policies for the government in quest of technical progress and economic growth. We will return to this topic in the concluding chapter.

5.4 OVERSEAS R&D ACTIVITIES

Japanese foreign direct investment (FDI) increased rapidly during the 1980s. It exceeded 1 billion dollars for the first time in 1972 and then gradually increased to the level of around 9 billion dollars during the first half of the 1980s. It then jumped to the peak level of 68 billion dollars in 1989. This surge in the latter half of the 1980s reflects a boom at the time in which profits were high with abundant liquidity, the costs of capital were low, and optimism prevailed, stimulating investment. Although the level of FDI then decreased to 34 billion dollars in 1992, following the collapse of the so-called 'bubble economy', many Japanese firms are now unmistakably multinational, with marketing, distribution, procurement, production, and even R&D subsidiaries in the USA, Europe, Asia, and other places.[6]

It is not that Japan had made little FDI before. In fact, as Wilkins (1990) states, certain investment was made even before the war, mostly to aid the export of products and the purchase of materials and machines. As we will discuss in the next chapter, general trading companies (*sogo shosha*) established overseas branch offices during the 1880s to import raw cotton and other products and later to export cotton products. Although these investments were confiscated during the war, Japan's FDI started to increase again after the war. Particularly active was the investment by the manufacturers to establish and expand the distribution network. In many industries, the extent of such investment exceeded investment by other countries and, as Williamson and Yamawaki (1991) claim, such 'investment in distribution has underpinned Japanese exporters' success'.

Although Japanese firms' investment in manufacturing abroad lagged significantly in comparison to that in distribution, or to that by American multinationals, the rising yen and the rising labour cost in Japan, as well as political factors such as the fear of import restriction (including voluntary export restraints) by American and other governments, gave the firms a strong incentive to transfer some of the manufacturing activities abroad. As a consequence, the ratio of sales by overseas subsidiaries of Japanese manufacturing firms to sales within Japan increased from 2.9 per cent in 1980 to 5.7 per cent in 1989. The ratio is especially high in transportation equipment and electrical equipment (including electronics) industries where the ratios in 1989 were, respectively, 14.3 per cent and 11.0 per cent. Among the firms possessing overseas subsidiaries, the ratio reached 22–3 per cent in these two industries.[7]

Japanese firms are also increasing their R&D efforts abroad. According to a survey by the Ministry of International Trade and Industry, Japanese overseas subsidiaries hired 6,975 researchers and spent 65 billion yen for R&D, which was 1.5 per cent of the total R&D expenditures of the parents (4,430 billion yen) surveyed.[8] The electrical equipment industry was most active, hiring 2,732 and spending 20 billion yen, followed by general machinery (605 researchers and 10 billion yen) and chemicals (707 researchers and 6 billion yen). Of the R&D expenditure, 66 per cent was expended in North America (55 per cent in the USA), 21 per cent in the EEC, and 9 per cent in Asia.

These overseas subsidiaries had 222 laboratories of which 170 were in manufacturing industries. Chemicals (including pharmaceuticals) were most active with 42 laboratories, followed by 36 in electrical equipment, and 27 in general machinery. Geographically, North America was dominant with 98 (95 in the USA), followed by 81 in Asia and 25 in the EEC.

MITI's survey also questioned firms about the main functions of R&D in their overseas subsidiaries (with or without laboratories), allowing them to choose a maximum of two, out of eleven, categories. The marketing-related categories, including 'the support of local sales activity', 'the adaptation and improvement of products exported to the host countries', and 'the development of products targeted at the host markets', were most popular, together accounting for 40 per cent. 'The support of local production' followed with 20 per cent. 'The collection and analysis of information' was similarly popular which, together with 'the maintenance of relationship with local universities and firms', accounted for another 20 per cent. By contrast, only 2.4 per cent cited basic research as the main function.

It thus seems that most overseas R&D facilities of Japanese firms are what Cordell (1973) called 'support laboratories', that is, their main function is to support the sales and marketing activities by developing products tailored to local markets, usually by modifying Japanese products, and provide technical services to the dealers and customers. They may also support the manufacturing activity by helping to transfer and, if necessary, adapt the production technology to the local plant, by attending to any unforeseeable technological problems, and by providing technical assistance to the suppliers.

Such a need to support local manufacturing activity may be particularly strong in Asia where many subsidiaries have been established. In fact, in the MITI survey, 'the support of local production' has a larger share of respondents in Asia (26 per cent), particularly in ASEAN countries (32 per cent), than elsewhere. By contrast, 'the collection and analysis of information' was the most common function raised by the subsidiaries in the USA (20 per cent), suggesting that they conduct R&D in the USA primarily to gain access to the rapidly progressing scientific and technological knowledge or to recruit high-quality researchers.[9]

Will Japanese firms evolve into truly multinational companies such as IBM and Phillips? Will they, for instance, build a network of interdependent laboratories on a substantial scale in the USA, Europe, and elsewhere, in addition to the one in Japan? Or will they rather concentrate their R&D resources in Japan? These are difficult questions to answer.

On the one hand, the large investment during the latter half of the 1980s clearly indicated the intensity of their efforts to catch up with American and European multinationals; hence, despite the setback in the early 1990s caused by the so-called 'post-bubble' depression, it appears fair to speculate that the long-term trend is towards globalization of R&D. A regression analysis indicates that the determinants of overseas R&D by Japanese firms are similar to those by American firms, suggesting nothing peculiarly 'Japanese' in their behaviour (Odagiri and Yasuda, 1994).

On the other hand, it may be especially advantageous for Japanese firms to concentrate their R&D resources within the country because the close link between R&D and manufacturing, including suppliers, has been the source of their technological strength. For instance, Business Week (1993a) illustrates the critical contribution of collaboration between R&D staff and production staff (from both Japan and the USA) in its article on the development of Honda's new car. Thus, most Japanese firms endeavour to retain at least the most advanced part of the manufacturing operation within Japan, in which prototypes are made and new processes are tested so that they can learn from the experience and seek the opinion of skilled workers. This is exactly why Toshiba, for instance, maintains a 'focal factory' (also called 'experimental factory' or 'mother factory') near Tokyo to promote the interaction between production and R&D (Fruin, 1992).

Two factors affect the decision of how much R&D to transfer abroad. Dispersion, which facilitates locally suitable R&D and interaction with local R&D resources, and concentration, which not only yields the gains from economies of scale and scope but also makes the interaction between R&D and core production facilities easier. The advantage of dispersion will undoubtedly increase as Japanese firms extend their marketing and manufacturing activities to many parts of the world. To take this advantage and yet maintain the advantages from concentration seems to be the one big challenge for Japanese firms in coming years.

5.5 CONCLUSION

In this and the preceding chapters, we have portrayed the development of the management system in Japan from the feudal Edo era to the present. Needless to say, full coverage of the development of such a drastically changing period would require more than this book can allow. Our treatise remains a sketchy one, with emphasis on matters related to the acquisition and accumulation of technologies. For a general discussion of the history of Japanese business in English, see, for instance, Hirschmeier and Yui (1975).

If we are to summarize Japan's experience in just two words, they would be change and continuity. Change was dramatic, particularly during the early Meiji era when the Western system of business was introduced; during World War II when economic control was tightened; and after World War II when a number of drastic reforms were implemented. Changes also took place, albeit more gradually, as industrialization progressed in the pre-war era; as the high speed of economic growth was maintained for several decades after the war; and as competition intensified on a global basis in recent years.

Yet, it is clearly misleading to argue that, for instance, post-war reforms completely changed the Japanese business system. Even though it is true that the separation of ownership from control became more common after zaibatsu dissolution, the delegation of a major part of authority to professional managers was observed in, say, Mitsui Zaibatsu before the war, or, to some extent, the House of Mitsui in the Edo era. Some of the features of the labour system, now commonly regarded as the Japanese system, started to be adopted in many firms during the 1910s.

It has always been the major task of Japanese industries to acquire technologies and accumulate their capabilities, because they were late-comers to industrialization. Organizational and other changes had to be made frequently. In addition, competition within and outside the country often gave impetus for change. Yet, changes can never be made independent of prevailing practices and customs. In any country, in any industry, and in any company, therefore, changes or evolution should and will take place, and yet are bound by the continuity of the past. Japan is no exception in this regard, except perhaps that the changes have been more rapid than in most other countries owing to rapid economic growth and the profound consequences of the war.

Such an evolutionary process is better understood by looking at the details of selected industries and companies, than by a general overview. We now proceed, therefore, to case studies.

6

Textiles

Textiles, particularly cotton spinning and weaving, was the first industry in Japan to successfully absorb the Western technology to establish modern large-scale operations. It is most appropriate, therefore, to start our series of case studies with this industry. The Japanese textiles industry, as will be presently shown, was at first dominated by less expensive and higher-quality imports from England and other countries, but started to catch up within two decades of the Meiji Restoration. By the early 1890s, the domestic production overwhelmed the import and, by the late 1890s, the export started to dominate the import. It was the most important Japanese export industry before World War II, replacing England during the 1930s as the largest producing country after the USA, and causing a number of trade frictions in many markets around the world—just as Japan's automobile and electronics industries now. The industry lost its dominance after the war, and it now imports more than it exports. Thus, just as it was the first industry to catch up with the West, it was also the first major industry to mature and then decline.

In this chapter, we will trace the history of this industry, mainly cotton-spinning, to see how the Japanese acquired and accumulated the necessary technologies and skills, and how they utilized them to establish and expand the industry. Throughout the discussion, we will see how entrepreneurship and technological capabilities interacted complementarily to foster entry, investment, and productivity increases.

6.1 THE THREE PIONEERING MILLS

A few years before Japan ended Seclusionism, Shimazu Nariakira, the lord (*daimyo*) of Satsuma Clan, who was known as one of the brightest and most open-minded of the lords, was given some woollen thread made in England.[1] He was impressed by the quality and became worried that the Japanese cotton industry might lose competition against imports. He immediately ordered Ishikawa Masatatsu of his clan to start research on Western cotton-spinning technology.

Nariakira's son, Tadayoshi, followed his father's wish and sent several of his young samurai to England to study technology and business, and buy spinning machines. These machines arrived in 1867 and, with the help of six engineers and skilled workers hired from England, Ishikawa started the first Western-style cotton mill in Kagoshima, the capital of Satsuma in Kyushu. It had 3,648 spindles and 100 power looms operated with hydraulic power. Three years later, Ishikawa built another cotton mill in Sakai near Osaka. Because of the small production scale and the competition against cheaper imports, it was not economically easy to maintain the mills. Kagoshima Mill was closed in 1897 when Tadayoshi, the constant supporter of the project, died, and Sakai Mill was purchased by the Meiji government.

In contrast with these two mills financed by a lord, the third mill was started as a purely private effort. Kashima Manpei, a cotton merchant, established a mill in Tokyo in 1868 with four spinning machines having 144 spindles each, bought from England. The operation met with difficulties in the beginning, particularly because the English machines were designed to process American-grown raw cotton, which had different characteristics from Japanese cotton. This problem was solved when one of the Japanese workers found that the best result could be gained by mixing raw cotton bought from the Mikawa area (now within Aichi Prefecture) with one from the Shimodate area (now within Ibaraki Prefecture), and by processing them through rollers spaced more widely than instructed by the English advisor.

Thereafter the operation became moderately successful and, when Kashima decided to add another machine, he manufactured one by imitation in a machinery shop he had set up within the mill. Although this in-house production proved to be several times more costly than the purchase of an imported machine, and required a long process of experiment and failure, it is worth noting that even at this early stage the machine could be made by reverse-engineering. It must have been a testimony to both Kashima's nationalistic passion and the technological capability of the people helping him.

These three pioneering mills, which started during the 1860s, were still tiny in comparison to those, say, in England, and all of them had to struggle against imports from England and other countries, which were generally cheaper and of a higher quality. There is no clear record of the profit performance of these mills, but it can be safely assumed that Kagoshima and Sakai Mills were losing money, except perhaps for a short period. Kashima Mill earned more than enough to cover variable costs; however, the profits do not appear to have been sufficiently large to cover the initial investment (Kinukawa, 1937: vol. 1). When other larger-scale mills were started, even Kashima had difficulty in competing against these rivals. Eventually, it was acquired by Amagasaki Boseki, to be discussed later (*Boseki* is a Japanese word for spinning).

6.2 THE GOVERNMENT POLICY DURING THE 1870S

The Meiji government, established in 1868, was keenly aware of the need to industrialize the nation. It was also aware that the textiles industry had to become one of the key industries along with mining, iron, communications, shipbuilding, and railroads. Thus, one of the first factories the government built was a silk-spinning factory in the town of Tomioka, with engineers and equipment imported from France. It started its operation in 1872. Gradually, the manual spinning method that had been traditionally employed by silk farmers was replaced by machine operation within larger mills, using either imported French or Italian machines or domestic machines manufactured after the Western technology. Silk thread and fabrics were Japan's main exportable products through the early Meiji era.

To support the cotton-spinning industry, the government adopted three policies during 1878–82. The first was to build two state mills, one in Aichi and the other in Hiroshima. The major machines were imported from England, and Ishikawa Masatatsu, mentioned earlier, designed the mills and helped the operation as chief engineer. The second was to import ten spinning machines and sell them to private entrepreneurs on credit, and the third was to provide loans to the entrepreneurs who bought imported machines.

All the mills built under these policies had the capacity of 2,000 spindles, operated with hydraulic power, and located in rural sites near cotton-growing areas. However, the hydraulic power was insufficient or unstable in many mills and the product quality was often poor. The production scale was not large enough and many of the entrepreneurs lacked firm financial resources to support the operation, particularly under the fluctuating product price influenced by imports. As a result, only a few of them prospered and managed to expand.

6.3 THE FIRST LARGE-SCALE OPERATION AS A PRIVATE EFFORT: OSAKA COTTON SPINNING COMPANY

During the late 1870s, Shibusawa Eiichi, who would later become the most influential banker and industrialist of the Meiji era and, at the time, was the manager of Daiichi Kokuritsu Ginko (First National Bank), became aware of the scale of the import of cotton products through the bank's foreign exchange business. Partly out of nationalistic concern to protect the domestic industry and partly out of his entrepreneurial instinct that the business should become viable if properly planned, he decided to start a cotton-spinning company.

He knew that the mill would not be able to compete against the import unless it was large enough to achieve the economies of scale and equipped with a modern production facility. Apparently, both financial and technological problems were there. His bank, though the largest at the time, was not yet secure enough to support the enterprise, and he had no intention of mixing the banking business with the textiles business. In seeking potential investors, he realized that the money collected from *kazoku* (former lords and nobles; see Chapter 4) in order to invest in the railroad business had not been used because of the government's reluctance to approve the expansion of the railroad network. Shibusawa succeeded in persuading these kazoku to invest in his cotton-spinning business instead. He also persuaded a number of cotton merchants, most of them in Osaka, to invest in the enterprise. In 1880 he established a company named Osaka Boseki (Osaka Cotton Spinning Co.) with these investors as the shareholders.[2]

Shibusawa also knew that one of the main reasons why the previous enterprises had only a limited success, if at all, was the lack of a technologically knowledgeable person who could design the mill, supervise the installation of the equipment, and take care of the operation. Apparently, however, there was no Japanese available who had studied Western textiles. He therefore sought a young, bright person who would be willing to study the technology. This he found in Yamanobe Takeo, who was then studying economics at the University of London and had been recommended to Shibusawa. Shibusawa sent him 150 pounds sterling and asked him to switch his subject to the study of textiles technology. Yamanobe, though surprised at the sudden offer, accepted it and moved to King's College to study mechanical engineering. He then went to Manchester, but none of the mill owners would accept him as an apprentice. Finally, he found a mill owner in Blackburn from whom he could learn the operation of the equipment as well as the management, such as the procurement of raw cotton and the sale of the product. He came back to Japan in 1880 and immediately started planning the mill.[3]

The first decision to be made was the location of the mill. At first, Yamanobe was planning to use hydraulic power, and so visited many rivers. However, he could not find anywhere suitable to provide enough power for the planned large-scale operation and sufficient space to build a large plant and a convenient transportation system to ship the products. He decided to use steam engines instead and chose a location near Osaka, the second largest city in the country, for ease in recruiting workers and shipping the product. He ordered steam engines and spinning machines from England. The total capacity was 10,500 spindles, several times larger than any of the previous mills in Japan.

An interesting episode illustrates the level of technological capability of Japanese engineers at the time. The spinning machines were bought from Platt Bros & Co., then the largest machine manufacturer in the world, and an engineer from Platt named Nield came to Osaka to supervise the assembly and installation. The steam engine was bought from another English company, Hargreaves, and Nield refused to (and probably could not) assemble the engine. Yamanobe, himself unfamiliar with the machine, asked the help of a foreign engineer at the Osaka Mint. This engineer, also unfamiliar with the technology, instead sent his Japanese subordinate, Saito Kozo, to the mill.

Saito, who had studied mechanical engineering at Kobu Daigakko (formerly Kogakuryo), tried to assemble the engine by following the manual, only to realize that, surprisingly, the engine ran in reverse. He examined the mechanism in detail and came to believe that one of the parts was made wrongly; he thus proposed to repair it. Nield insisted that there could be no such mistake in any machine made by a large English company, and refused Saito's proposal. Nield finally consented when Saito's foreign superior at the Mint came to inspect the problem and agreed with Saito's diagnosis. The repair was made and the engine started to run in the right direction.

Needless to say, it would be unfair to generalize this contrast between the two men, particularly because Nield was a man who had acquired his technological knowledge on the job through more than twenty years of work at Platt, whereas Saito was formally educated at a collage. Yet, Saito's ability to adapt his knowledge to the situation under investigation was remarkable. Not surprisingly, Yamanobe was so impressed by Saito that he would later recommended Saito as chief engineer at Mie Boseki.

The operation at Osaka Boseki started in 1883. It was a success owing to the large-scale modern production facility, and to the careful preparation led by Yamanobe, which included the dispatch of four college-educated workers to on-the-job training in other mills, and the search for the most suitable raw cotton in the country. The company could pay more than a satisfactory dividend from the beginning. Soon the company decided to add night shifts and became the first company to use electric light following the advice of Fujioka Ichisuke, a professor at Kobu Daigakko who would later found one of the predecessors to Toshiba (see Chapter 8). The firm expanded by adding the second mill in three years and the third in six years. The second mill was the first to adopt the more efficient ring-spinning machines instead of the mule machines that had been used in all the mills in the country. We will return to ring machines in Section 6.6. The company also became the first to integrate itself vertically into the weaving business, the first to use imported cotton from China and then India, and the first to export the product. In many ways, therefore, the company was a leading innovator in the early history of the Japanese cotton textiles industry.

6.4   ENTRY OF NEW FIRMS

The success of Osaka Boseki spurred many entrepreneurs to enter into the industry with similarly large-scale operations. Some of them had prior experience of the business but some had none. Among the first category was Kashima Manpei, who founded Tokyo Boseki in 1887 with about 9,000 spindles of both mule and ring types, and Ito Denhichi, who had earlier established a cotton-spinning mill in Mie with the 2,000 spindle machine purchased from the government, on credit, under the policy discussed in Section 6.2 above.

Despite Ito's enthusiasm, his mill continually suffered from the lack of technological knowledge, poor quality, and an unstable water supply. In fact, the profits were so poor that every year he had to request the government for postponement of the repayment of the debt. In 1886 he met Shibusawa who, following his experience with Osaka Boseki, advised Ito to start a large-scale, steam-powered mill and, furthermore, agreed to invest in the enterprise himself. This offer was a tremendous help to Ito not only because of the money provided by Shibusawa himself and the bank he was leading but, probably more important, because of the trust other people placed in Shibusawa's judgement.

Shibusawa's business acumen had been recognized by this time through his management of Daiichi Kokuritsu Bank and his initiative to start a number of successful new businesses including paper, marine insurance, shipping, and, of course, Osaka Boseki (which he never joined as a director but remained as an adviser until 1909). Thus, his commitment to Ito's enterprise had the other investors' trust in its future and led them to invest. This illustrates the critical role Shibusawa played in the early period of Japan's industrialization when many investors, including *kazoku* and local merchants, had little knowledge of Western-style manufacturing or of the future course the economy might take. This is why Shibusawa could establish so many new businesses despite his own investment being minor. In other words, he took full advantage of the joint-stock company system. Although some authors call the collection of firms established by Shibusawa by the name of 'Shibusawa Zaibatsu', it is misleading because, unlike, say, Mitsui, the ownership ties were limited. In fact, in any of the companies started by him or by someone else on his advice, the ownership was spread among a number of investors.

Shibusawa strongly advised Ito to hire an able and reliable Japanese engineer, because Shibusawa's experience at Osaka clearly taught him the indispensable role Yamanobe played in guiding the construction and operation of the mill, and also in mediating between the hired foreign engineers and Japanese workers. Ito asked the opinion of Yamanobe, who recommended Saito Kozo for the post. Saito, on request of Ito and Shibusawa, accepted the offer and went to England to buy the necessary machines and study the technology and trade. In England, he realized that ring spinning machines might be more suitable than the originally-planned mule machines and decided to buy ten ring machines with 3,440 spindles in total, in addition to ten mule machines with 7,000 spindles. The new company, named Mie Boseki (Mie Cotton Spinning), started its operation in 1888.

There were also many other entrants who had no earlier experience in modern textiles business. Most of the investors were merchants, financiers, and wealthy land-owners. A number of them were established in the vicinity of Osaka, obviously because the investors there were familiar with the success of Osaka Boseki and also because Osaka had a port that could be conveniently used both to bring coal and other materials, and to ship the product. Also it was the centre of one of the two largest markets (Tokyo is the other) and had abundant labour supply.

Among those in Osaka and its vicinity were Hirano Boseki, Amagasaki Boseki, and Settsu Boseki established during 1887–9 with 9,216 (Amagasaki) to 19,200 (Settsu) spindles. They also became aware of the need to have a knowledgeable Japanese engineer. Hirano Boseki begged Kikuchi Kyozo to join, who, like Saito, had studied mechanical engineering at Kobu Daigakko and succeeded Saito as an engineer at the Osaka Mint. Kikuchi accepted the offer on condition that the firm would provide a fund for him to spend a year in England to study cotton-spinning technology and business. It is worth noting that Yamanobe, Saito, and Kikuchi, called the 'three pioneers' in the industry (Nichibo Kabushiki Kaisha, 1966), all spent a year or so in England with company funds before starting their jobs in the company. That is to say, technology transfer was made by these Japanese engineers studying abroad as well as from the purchase of foreign-made machines and the advice of foreign engineers who were mainly hired to supervise the installation of these machines.

Kikuchi's knowledge and ability proved so valuable that both Amagasaki Boseki and Settsu Boseki asked for his help. Hirano Boseki accepted this request provided that the expense of Kikuchi's study in England be shared by them. Kikuchi, therefore, was the chief engineer and then the director of the three companies (and then the president of Amagasaki and Settsu) until they merged to establish a new company, Dainippon Boseki, with Kikuchi as the first president. This episode would indicate the indispensable role educated engineers played in the development of the industry as well as the limited supply of such people.

Another new entrant was Kanegafuchi Boseki, later to be renamed Kanebo, founded in Tokyo in 1886. The main investors were merchants in Tokyo, including Mitsui. The initial scale of 30,536 spindles far exceeded that of Osaka or any other firm. For several years, however, business was depressed and it survived only with a huge loan from Mitsui Bank. Mitsui sent in managers and put the firm under its control.

6.5 FROM AN IMPORTER TO AN EXPORTER

With these entries, the number of cotton-spinning firms increased. In 1887, there were 21 firms with 19 mills with a capacity of 77,000

TABLE 6.1 The pre-war production and demand of machine-made cotton yarn (thousand bales)

Year	Production		Import		Export		Demand
1887–8	58	(18)	269	(82)	0	(0)	328
1889–90	178	(42)	250	(58)	0	(0)	428
1891–2	374	(73)	140	(27)	0	(0)	513
1893–4	527	(82)	119	(18)	13	(2)	646
1895–6	812	(87)	117	(13)	54	(6)	930
1897–8	1,215	(92)	109	(8)	370	(28)	1,324
1899–00	1,433	(96)	59	(4)	550	(37)	1,492
1901–2	1,431	(98)	29	(2)	407	(28)	1,460
1903–4	1,497	(100)	5	(0)	565	(38)	1,502
1905–6	1,851	(99)	28	(1)	535	(28)	1,878
1907–8	1,862	(99)	11	(1)	394	(21)	1,873
1909–10	2,160	(100)	4	(0)	607	(28)	2,164
1911–12	2,481	(100)	4	(0)	660	(27)	2,485
1913–14	3,184	(100)	2	(0)	1,039	(33)	3,186

Note: Demand = Production + Import. Figures in parentheses are percentages of Demand.

Source: Abe (1990), Table 2(3)–1. The original source is N. Takamura (1971), *Nippon Boseki-Gyo Shi Josetsu*

spindles. Three years later in 1890, 30 mills with a capacity of 278,000 spindles were in operation, and by 1898 the capacity had exceeded a million spindles in 77 mills.[4] The consequence of such entry and investment is exhibited by the increase in production level in Table 6.1.

The table also indicates the speed of import substitution. In 1887–8, the import still dominated the market with the share of more than 80 per cent. The relative position turned around in six years, however. In 1893–4, the import accounted for only 18 per cent. After the turn of the century, the import was virtually negligible. Export of cotton yarn, on the other hand, was started in 1891 by Osaka Boseki and others, mainly to China. By 1897 the export dominated the import and Japan became a major exporting country. As shown in the table, more than a third of the cotton yarn produced domestically in 1903–04 was exported. Afterwards, this ratio declined, mainly because the spinners started to integrate vertically towards weaving, and export cloth instead of (or in addition to) yarn.

Such rapid expansion of the production level could not be sustained merely by the domestic supply of raw cotton. Import of raw cotton had begun earlier but the domestic cotton was still overwhelmingly used until 1886–7 when Mitsui Bussan (Mitsui Trading Company, now Mitsui & Co.) started importing from China, and Osaka Boseki sent its procurement officer to buy raw cotton in China. Two years later, the government and the spinners' association (*Boren*, to be discussed later in detail) sent four people to India to investigate the possibility of importing raw cotton from there. The import rapidly increased, first from China, then from India, and later from the USA. This increase was accelerated by the abolition in 1896 of tariff on imported raw cotton, which had been advocated by the association with strong opposition from the cotton farmers. In 1890, 70 per cent of the imported raw cotton came from China but after 1896 import from India started to dominate. Around 1905, about 50 per cent of the imported raw cotton came from India, 25 per cent from the USA, 20 per cent from China, and the rest from Egypt and elsewhere.[5] By this time, the domestic farming of raw cotton had nearly ceased except for a tiny market still operated by manual spinning and weaving in farm areas.

The rapid increase in the import of raw cotton had two important consequences. The first was the development of trading companies. Mitsui Bussan, established in 1876, had been prospering with the sale of woolen products to the Army, and the export of rice and coal. As stated above, it became one of the first to import raw cotton from China. Soon, it opened branch offices in China, India, and other places to become the largest importer. As will be discussed later, it was also a dominant importer of spinning and weaving machines.

Around 1890, two trading companies were newly established for the principal purpose of importing raw cotton, because foreign traders, still the major importers, often charged high prices to Japanese spinners. The new companies were Naigai and Nihon Menkwa (Japan Cotton Trading, now Nichimen), both based in Osaka. Naigai became the main importer for Osaka Boseki and Mie Boseki, and Nichimen for Amagasaki, Hirano, and Settsu, whereas Mitsui Bussan had a close relationship with Kanebo. As Japan became the exporter of cotton products, these trading companies also expanded by acting as the spinners' exporting agents. The relationship between the trading companies and the spinning companies became so close that the former sometimes played an important role in fostering mergers between the spinning companies (to be discussed later).

Another consequence is related to the different quality of raw cotton across countries. Japanese cotton had short staple but was good for dying, whereas Indian cotton had longer staple and American cotton had even longer staple with strength and elasticity. Thus, although Japanese cotton was suitable for the traditional manual spinning of low-count thick yarn, it was not suitable for machine spinning. Indian and American cotton were more suitable and, in particular, American cotton mixed with Indian and Chinese cotton was considered to be the best for the production of high-count fine yarn in high-speed spinning operations. Put differently, the spread of large-scale machine operations became feasible only with the availability of these imported raw cotton. This high-speed spinning was also achieved by the shift from mule-spinning machines to ring machines. As a consequence, the adoption of ring machines accelerated the import of raw cotton. We now turn to this topic.

6.6 FROM MULE TECHNOLOGY TO RING TECHNOLOGY

Probably the most prominent characteristic of the Japanese cotton-spinning industry was the extraordinarily rapid shift from mule techno-logy to ring technology for spinning machines. For details of these technologies see, for instance, Saxonhouse (1985) and Kandachi (1982). The ring-spinning technology was basically invented during the 1830s but mule spinning remained dominant until the 1870s when major im-provements in ring spinning were made with the introduction of the sawyer spindle. Since rings made the spinning and winding of yarn in one motion, the operation was simpler and could be made faster. As a result, around 1890, the productivity of rings outweighed that of mules by 10–15 per cent in making No. 20 to 30 count yarn (Kiyokawa, 1987: 87). The simplicity of the motion of rings also simplified the operation, making it possible for unskilled female workers to operate the ma-chines. The advantage of mules, on the other hand, only remained in either very low-count coarse yarn, say, less than No. 10, or for very high-count fine yarn, say, more than No. 60; however, the improvement in ring technology gradually made rings advantageous even in such high-count spinning.

The facts that most of the advances in ring technology were made in the USA, and that the USA was one of the first to adopt rings on an extensive scale, were clearly related to the fact that American raw cotton had long staple. By contrast, England, in which raw cotton had relatively short staple, and many experienced male workers had been employed, remained a mule-operating country for a long time after the USA and Japan converted to ring technology.

As discussed earlier, all the spinning machines installed at the first mill of Osaka Boseki and the mills built earlier by Satsuma Clan, the Meiji government, and others, were all mules. However, in 1886 when Osaka Boseki built the second mill, it already used rings in addition to mules, and the third mill built three years later was entirely equipped with rings. In 1892, the first and second mills were destroyed by fire and, in rebuilding them, the company completely switched to rings. Similarly, Mie completely switched to rings when its mill was similarly burned down.

Most of the companies that followed, such as Hirano, Amagasaki, and Settsu, built all-ring mills from the beginning. Kanebo at first used some mules but the majority were rings. As a result, the number of mules in operation reached its peak in 1890 at a little more than 100,000 spindles in capacity, whereas the capacity of rings exceeded that of mules in 1888 and reached a million spindles by 1897. Such a rapid adoption of the ring technology was incomparable to other countries. Even in the USA, the proportion of rings was 71 per cent in 1900: in the same year in Japan it was more than 90 per cent (Kiyokawa, 1987).

A number of reasons have been suggested to explain this rapid adoption of ring technology in Japan: see Kiyokawa (1973; 1987) and Saxonhouse (1974; 1985). These include (1) vertical integration of spinning and weaving, (2) the procurement of Indian cotton, (3) the use of cheaper female unskilled labour, (4) the sales activity of Mitsui Bussan, which acted as the sole representative to Platt who manufactured ring machines, and (5) the fast spread of technological information across Japanese companies either through the spinners' association (Boren, to be discussed later), through personal contacts among managers and engineers, or through the employment of foreign advisors (some from Platt) who tended to move from one company to another. As Kiyokawa (1987) argues, however, the adoption of ring technology generally preceded the increase in imported raw cotton as well as the increase in female workers, thereby suggesting that the causality was probably from the choice of ring technology to (2) and (3) than the other way round.

It is true that Platt was the dominant supplier of spinning machines. For instance, of the spinning machines bought in 1892 with the total capacity of some 218,000 spindles, 81 per cent was supplied by Platt, with Mitsui Bussan acting as the representative.[6] However, Platt had long been a mule manufacturer and it is difficult to argue that they had a stronger preference to sell rings.

More importantly, it must have been the initiative of Japanese engineers, such as Yamanobe, Saito, and Kikuchi mentioned earlier, who saw the advantage of ring technology. They could understand the technology by themselves or with the help of foreign advisors, owing to the formal education they received at Kobu Daigakko or elsewhere and/or to the training or study in England. Although their initial positions were as chief engineers of the respective firms, they were often involved in managerial decision-making and, in fact, all three would later become the presidents of their companies. Such assumption to top managerial positions by engineers was not uncommon during Japan's early industrialization period, as discussed in Chapter 4: we will find similar cases in the electrical equipment and automobile industries.[7]

It appears reasonable, therefore, to assume that such technological understanding of top management and its entrepreneurial attitude towards investment facilitated Japan's rapid adoption of ring technology, with the help of technological and other information made available through Boren, trading companies, foreign advisors, and, in the early period, the government. The capability of the management was also exhibited in its adapting the surrounding conditions, such as the procurement of raw cotton and labour employment, so that these conditions would fit the new technology. These capabilities and entrepreneurship were the major driving forces behind the rapid rise of the Japanese cotton textiles industry to become the major exporter.

6.7 THE PROGRESS OF MARKET CONCENTRATION

Table 6.1 indicated that the production of cotton yarn and cloth expanded through the late nineteenth century. Investment by both incumbent firms and new entrants was active, with the number of firms increasing to 79 by 1900. Then, a recession shook the industry, not only because the demand was depressed in the domestic market but also because the export to China declined for three reasons; the intensifying competition against Indian producers, the war in China, and the shift of Japan to the gold standard in 1897. This shift made Japanese exporters less competitive when the silver price went down in 1900, because China still used the silver standard.

TABLE 6.2 Concentration in production of cotton yarn: 1908–1931 (%)

1908		1919		1931	
Shares of top five firms:					
Mie	18.3	Toyobo	18.6	Toyobo	19.7
Kanebo	18.3	Dainippon	15.9	Dainippon	9.6
Settsu	12.8	Kanebo	15.2	Kanebo	7.7
Osaka Godo	7.7	Osaka Godo	7.1	Fuji Gasu	4.8
Kishiwada	6.6	Fuji Gasu	6.8	Fukushima	4.6
Accumulated shares:					
Top 3	49.4		49.7		37.0
Top 5	63.7		63.6		46.4
Top 8	77.8		79.7		57.6
Top 10	83.6		83.6		63.2

Note: Measured by the number of spindles in 1908, and by the volume of production in 1919 and 1931. Note that Toyobo was created in 1914 by the merger of Mie and Osaka; Dainippon was created in 1918 by the merger of Settsu and Amagasaki; and Toyobo acquired Osaka Godo in 1931. A number of small-scale acquisitions also occurred during this period.

Sources: Kajinishi (1964), Tables III-45 and IV-28. The original sources are Kurabo, *Kaiko 65 Nen Shi* for 1908, and the data compiled by Dainippon Boseki Rengo Kai for 1919 and 1931

The consequence was shown in Table 6.1 as the first drop, since the start of the industry, in both export and domestic demand in 1901–02. All the firms suffered badly. Osaka Boseki showed loss for the first time and few firms could pay dividend. According to Abe (1990), 37 firms disappeared around this period either through liquidation or acquisition, and the number of producers decreased to 49 by 1904. The result, needless to say, was market concentration in a number of well-managed firms. Mie Boseki was probably most active in acquiring smaller firms, acquiring no less than 8 firms during 1897–1907. Settsu Boseki acquired Hirano Boseki in 1902. Other firms, including Osaka Boseki and Kanebo, also made acquisitions.

In 1914, Osaka Boseki and Mie Boseki merged to become Toyo Boseki (Toyobo) and, in 1918, Amagasaki Boseki and Settsu Boseki merged to become Dainippon Boseki (later, Nichibo). Yamanobe was the first president of Toyobo and Kikuchi of Dainippon. The market shares of the top 5 firms in 1908, 1919 and 1931 are shown in Table 6.2. Toyobo, Dainippon, and Kanebo came to be called the 'Big Three' of the industry and the table shows that in 1908 and 1919 these three, or their predecessors, including Osaka Godo which was acquired by Toyobo in 1931, accounted for more than a half of the market.

Whether these major firms behaved competitively or cooperatively is difficult to say. There is evidence of cooperation among the producers. Most importantly, they organized *Boren* (short for Dai Nihon Boseki Rengo Kai or, in English, All Japan Cotton Spinners Association) in 1882, which became more active after 1888 when Yamanobe became its secretary. Their activity was diverse, including (1) lobbying towards the abolition of import tariff for raw cotton and export tariff for cotton yarn (which were abolished in 1896 and 1894, respectively), (2) the collection and publication of industry data, (3) the establishment of product standards and a testing institution, and (4) the spread of technological information. More dubious, at least from the equity viewpoint, was the exchange of information on labourers. In particular, they agreed not to hire any worker who had been discharged by any other firm on the grounds of their participation in strikes, although whether they really kept this agreement may be questioned because labour shortage was almost always an acute problem.

They also formed cartels in recessions, more than ten times during 1890–1937. In these cartels, member firms agreed to stop the operation of the entire capacity for a few days a month, or of a specified proportion of existing spindles for the duration of the cartels. Kiyokawa (1973), however, questions their anti-competition effect by arguing that, even without a cartel, 5–10 per cent of the machines remained idle, either awaiting repair or being obsolete. Moreover, he argues that, because the restriction of operation was made only to existing machines, cartels, in fact, had the effect of accelerating the speed of scrapping obsolete machines and replacing them with more productive new machines that were not subject to the restriction. Thus, the cartels did not seem to have had the effect of restricting competition but, rather, had the effect of intensifying oligopolistic competition among larger, aggressive firms. They also had the effect of raising productivity.

Another attempt at coordinating the activity of rival firms was the formation of an association for export to China and another association for export to Korea. These associations were formed under the mediation of Mitsui Bussan to deal with the extremely intense rivalry among Japanese producers. Since the trading companies imported raw cotton and sold cotton products on behalf of the spinning or weaving firms, their stake in these firms was high. Particularly, they sold imported raw cotton to the spinners on credit and, when the latter fell in financial difficulty, the trading companies intervened to secure the repayment. Mitsui Bussan, among other trading companies, was active in this regard partly because of its dominant position among trading companies but, probably more importantly, because, as discussed earlier, it sold spinning machines to nearly all the firms as Platt's sole representative. Thus, it could exert influence on failing companies, sometimes persuading the managers into acquisition.

More often, however, mergers were undertaken by the initiative of the managers themselves to achieve economies of scope (for instance, Amagasaki and Settsu were complementary because Amagasaki was mainly producing high-count yarns and Settsu, low-count yarns), to vertically integrate into weaving, to attain scale economies particularly in terms of distribution and marketing, and to acquire good managers, engineers, and skilled workers.

As the scale of the major firms expanded, more and more technological and managerial knowledge was required. All the firms started hiring graduates from technical colleges, such as those from the engineering departments of Tokyo and other national universities, and commerce colleges, such as Keio and Hitotsubashi.[8] This raising of the education level, in terms of both technical training among management staff and primary education among blue-collar workers, enhanced the productivity increase of the cotton spinning industry (Saxonhouse, 1977). As emphasized in Chapter 1, entrepreneurship and technological capabilities, which create a competitive environment, are the key factors in industrial development and, in this regard, the Japanese textiles industry provides a good example.

A brief word is also needed on the development of the domestic production of spinning machines and weaving machines. Of these two, import substitution took place earlier with weaving machines, as Toyoda Sakichi and others invented power looms. We will come back to this topic in Chapter 9 in relation to the entry into automobile production by Sakichi's son, Kiichiro, the founder of the present Toyota Motor. The proportion of domestic looms among the power looms in operation was 37 per cent in 1920 but increased to 80 per cent by 1930. In contrast, for spinning machines the proportion was still less than 1 per cent in 1925, even though domestic production of replacement parts had started much earlier (Otsuka, K., 1987).

6.8 MAN-MADE FIBRE: RAYON AND NYLON

Before proceeding to the discussion of wartime and the post-war cotton textiles industry, let us briefly discuss the development of regenerated man-made fibre such as rayon, and synthetic fibre such as nylon, in Japan.

Although the production of man-made fibre started in 1884 in France using the nitrocellulose process, the industry did not take off until 1892 when Cross, Bevan, and Beadle of the UK invented the viscose process, and 1904 when Courtaulds Ltd. succeeded in commercial production. Several other companies in Europe and the USA followed, and the world production expanded rapidly—more than ten times during the 15 years of 1910–25 and again more than ten times during the following 15 years. Courtaulds became one of the most profitable companies in the world before World War II. This profitability is partly due to the international cartel that they and others maintained during the inter-war period, and the protection of technology with patents.

Rayon, as Courtaulds called the product to avoid the negative impression the words '*artificial* silk' might give, started to be imported into Japan in 1905. The import expanded rapidly with about 40 per cent during 1912–25 coming from Courtaulds. Mitsui Bussan became the agent for Courtaulds in 1919 and between this year and 1923 the import increased thirteen times.[9]

The apparent profitability of Courtaulds's business, as well as the promising future of the market, attracted Japanese entrepreneurs into starting their own production of rayon. In addition, the idea of the artificial creation of fibre attracted the intellectual curiosity of engineers in colleges and industries. The first attempt by the nitrocellulose process was made in 1908 by an enterprise financed by Suzuki Shoten, Mitsubishi, and Iwai Shoten, but the company failed to produce a viable product and, after finding out that this process had been replaced by the viscose process in most European firms, the operation was closed down.

The next attempt started around 1909 by Hisamura Seita and Hata Itsuzo, graduates from the Engineering Department of the University of Tokyo reading applied chemistry, with the financial support of Suzuki Shoten. Suzuki Shoten (*shoten* is a Japanese word for shop or merchant), originally a rather small sugar merchant, started expanding after Japan colonized Taiwan in 1895 following Japan's victory in the

Sino-Japanese War. Its manager, Kaneko Naokichi, succeeded into monopolizing the profitable camphor business in Taiwan and then expanded the business aggressively by re-investing the profits. By 1917, it became comparable to Mitsui Bussan in size. Kaneko also invested heavily in manufacturing and shipping, including Kobe Seikosho (Kobe Steel), Nihon Seifun (Nippon Flour Mills), Nihon Cement, and more than seventy other companies, and formed a business group almost as large as Mitsui or Mitsubishi. Although the group collapsed in 1927 as a consequence of the financial panic after the Great Kanto Earthquake, Kaneko's achievement has been unparalleled and a number of companies he started remain to this day.

Teijin (originally, Teikoku Jinzo Kenshi or Imperial Artificial Silk Co.) is one such company which was established in 1918 based on the development efforts of Hisamura and Hata. As discussed above, Courtaulds and other companies tightly protected the technology with patents and, therefore, Hisamura and Hata could learn the basics of the rayon technology only through Cross's 1901 research paper, the last paper that had been made public, and a few brief news on patent applications. This situation forced them to experiment by themselves in making viscose and then thread. Although they came up with certain products, the quality was far from satisfactory. The strength, thickness, and density of the thread was uneven and it was hardly durable. In 1917, Hata went to Europe but, again because of the tight patent protection, he could hardly discover anything. Hisamura, who went to the USA in turn, found that a rayon factory was on sale in Cleveland and visited it as a potential buyer. Although he did not buy it after all, he obtained the list of machines installed there and this information helped him in building a plant in Japan and starting the operation. Nevertheless, the operation started to go smoothly and the product became sufficiently good only after he could finally buy a spinning machine from Germany in 1923. Clearly, the lag in technology was considerable and yet Japanese engineers and entrepreneurs had a strong will to pursue the technology to catch up with the Western rivals.

By contrast, when Noguchi Shitagau, the founder of Nitchitsu Zaibatsu (see Chapter 4), decided to enter into rayon production, he bought the whole technology from a German company, Glanzstoff, with the hefty price of 1 million yen because, by then, the international collusion on patent protection had been broken as a result of the defeat of Germany in World War I. Noguchi established Asahi Kasei (Asahi Chemical, initially called Asahi Kenshoku) whose Japanese engineers learned the technology from the advisors sent from the German company, and by visiting the company in Germany.

Mitsui Bussan, by acting as the representative for Courtaulds, was well aware of the future of the rayon market. Thus, it decided to start production on its own and established a company, Toyo Rayon (now Toray), in 1926. The fact that Mitsui did not allow the company to be named as a Mitsui company indicates their scepticism of the risk on the business. It approached Courtaulds and then Du Pont to buy the technology but, because the price was too high, it decided to buy equipment from a German engineering company and hire about twenty foreign engineers to start the operation. Toray's case is thus somewhere between Teijin, which basically developed the technology domestically, and Asahi Kasei, which basically acquired the technology by importation.

Following these three companies, a number of rayon firms were established, mostly as subsidiaries to cotton-spinning firms, including Nihon Rayon (Nippon Rayon, established by Dainippon Boseki), Showa Rayon (by Toyobo), and Kurashiki Rayon (by Kurashiki Boseki). All these bought the technology or equipment from foreign firms; in some cases, however, Japanese engineers played important roles in assimilating the technology or solving problems on imported technology. Teijin's Japanese engineers also succeeded in greatly improving its technology, often with the collaboration of equipment manufacturers, so that they achieved the same level of productivity and quality as those of rivals importing the technology.[10]

Let us turn to nylon. As is well known, Nylon 66 was invented in 1935 by Carothers of Du Pont, which was granted a patent right and started the production three years later. Toray immediately got hold of a sample product through the New York branch of Mitsui Bussan, and started research by dissolving this sample in sulphuric acid. Because of the patent protection, the company had to make its own effort to synthesize polyamide and make fibre out of it. The situation was similar to Teijin's earlier development of rayon. However, Japan's level of chemical research had been raised by that time. In addition, the government was eager to support the development effort because of the expected difficulty in importing raw cotton once the war with the USA and others had started.

In 1941, just three years after Du Pont's announcement of nylon, Toray completed the basic research on nylon and started building a small plant to produce Nylon 6. The operation started in 1943 and the product was sold, mainly to make fishing nets. In 1946, following the end of World War II, Du Pont requested an investigation by GHQ (the General Headquarters of Allied Powers) of Toray's infringement of Du Pont's nylon patents but GHQ found no evidence of infringement, certifying that Toray's nylon technology was of its own (Toyo Rayon Kabushiki Kaisha, 1954).

None the less, as discussed already in Chapter 3, Toray bought the patent in 1951. There were several reasons. First, although Toray had the basic technology, it wished to gain Du Pont's advanced technology on the production, weaving, and dyeing processes. In fact, quality improvement and cost saving were significant after the introduction of Du Pont's technology. Secondly, Toray wanted to procure equipment from American manufacturers, who would not sell them without Du Pont's approval. And thirdly, Toray feared that it might not be able to export its products to countries under different patent systems. Whatever the true motivation may have been behind these reasons cited by the company (Suzuki, 1991), the patent acquisition clearly benefitted the firm in expanding the production rapidly and making nylon its most profitable business.

Toray was not alone in the Japanese effort to develop synthetic fibre. In 1949, when the government selected the industry as one of the target industries in its 'nurturing policy', Kurashiki Rayon, which was making vinylon, was designated as another nylon producer. The policy, besides allocating precious foreign exchange to royalty payments, raised the rate of import tariff, allowed accelerated depreciation on the assets, and provided low-interest loans through the Japan Development Bank. In addition, the government encouraged the use of synthetic fibre for school uniforms, fishing nets, and so forth.

Even though there is no denying that such an industrial policy helped the industry to take off and become one of the major industries in the economy, it is worth noting again that the initial effort by Toray, as well as those of Kurashiki Rayon, Kanebo, and a few others, were undertaken with their own initiatives just as the efforts by Teijin and others to develop rayon were. It is equally worth noting that, despite Japan's substantial lag in scientific technology, particularly when rayon was introduced, Japanese engineers could succeed in developing the technology by themselves however poor its quality might have been in comparison to that of the pioneering nations, and in absorbing the advanced technology once it was imported. Such managerial attitudes and technological capabilities also resulted in entries by a number of firms, which advanced the industry through rivalry.

6.9 THE COTTON-SPINNING INDUSTRY DURING
AND AFTER WORLD WAR II

The cotton textiles industry was severely affected by World War II for the same reason that the synthetic fibre industry was supported by the government, that is, the shortage of raw cotton. The industry was heavily dependent on raw cotton imported from India and the USA, and the war meant the stoppage of this inflow. Under the wartime control economy, the government ordered the industry to reduce the number of firms to ten through integration, to organize an association that monopolistically supplied the product, to reduce the equipment so that the scrap metal could be used by the manufacturers of aircraft and munitions, to sell some of the plants and facilities to these manufacturers, and to start producing munitions in their factories. As a result, the capacity was drastically reduced to about 2 million spindles by 1945 from the peak of 13 million spindles in 1941–2 (Toyo Boseki Kabushiki Kaisha, 1953).

Post-war reconstruction of the industry was difficult. Many of the factories had been destroyed or damaged, the equipment was mostly obsolete, the investment that had been made in China and Korea was lost, and many of the top managers had been purged. Some companies were divested either to regain the pre-war independence, or to streamline the business composition. For instance, Kanebo divested its chemical business to establish Kanegafuchi Chemical, and Toyobo separated its synthetic rubber business into Toyo Rubber. In addition, some of the cotton-spinning firms that had to switch their businesses to, say, metal fabrication during the war, resumed the spinning business making competition even tougher in a market suffering from poor post-war demand.

What saved them from bankruptcy was, like many other industries, the Korean War, which boosted the demand through military procurement and macroeconomic recovery. Not only did existing firms invest to increase their capacity, but many new entries also took place. These entrants were called 'New Spinners' and 'New-New Spinners', and shares were increased rapidly. See Table 6.3 for the ranking of the top ten firms in 1949 onwards, together with concentration ratios. Although Toyobo, Nichibo (renamed from Dainippon Boseki, to be renamed Unitika in 1969 following the merger with its rayon-making subsidiary, Nippon Rayon), and Kanebo, namely, the pre-war Big Three, remained the top firms until the 1960s and were still among the top eleven in 1985 (with Kanebo being the eleventh), it is the rise of three New

TABLE 6.3 Concentration in production of cotton yarn: 1949–1985

	1949	1955	1964	1973	1985
Ranking of the top ten firms:					
1	Toyobo	Toyobo	Toyobo	Toyobo	Tsuzuki
2	Nichibo	Nichibo	Nichibo	Kondo	Kondo
3	Kureha	Nisshinbo	Kanebo	Nisshinbo	Toyobo
4	Kanebo	Kanebo	Nisshinbo	Kanebo	Nisshinbo
5	Shikibo	Kureha	Kondo	Unitika	Omikenshi
6	Daiwabo	Kurabo	Daiwabo	Tsuzuki	Daiwabo
7	Kurabo	Daiwabo	Fuji	Daiwabo	Kurabo
8	Fuji	Fuji	Kureha	Fuji	Shikibo
9	Nisshinbo	Kondo	Kurabo	Kurabo	Fuji
10	Kondo	Shikibo	Shikibo	Omikenshi	Unitika
Accumulated Market Share (%):					
Top 3	38.5	20.4	16.2	21.1	23.1
Top 5	57.2	31.9	25.7	31.4	35.9
Top 8	81.0	46.8	37.9	43.3	48.6
Top 10	93.7	54.6	45.1	49.7	54.8

Note: Measured in terms of volume of production. Company names are current ones. Nichibo was named Dainippon until 1963. In 1969, it merged with Nippon Rayon to become Unitika. Kureha Boseki was acquired by Toyobo in 1966. Fuji Boseki was named Fuji Gasu Boseki before the war. Shikibo (Shikishima Boseki) was created in 1944 by the merger of Fukushima Boseki and Asahi Boseki. Daiwabo and Nisshinbo, respectively, are also called Daiwa Boseki and Nisshin Boseki.

Sources: *Ranking*: Yonekawa (1991: Table 2–3)

Accumulated market shares: Fair Trade Commission. The 1949 data is published in *Nihon ni Okeru Keizai-ryoku Shuuchu no Jittai* (Tokyo: Jitsugyo-no-Nihon Sha, 1951), the 1955 data in *Nihon Sangyo Shuuchu no Jittai* (Tokyo: Toyo Keizai, 1957), the 1964 data in *Nihon no Sangyo Shuuchu* (Tokyo: Toyo Keizai, 1969), and the 1973 data in *Gendai Nihon no Sangyo Shuuchu* (Tokyo: Nihon Keizai Shimbun Sha, 1983). The 1985 data is unpublished

Spinners, Kondo, Tsuzuki, and Omikenshi, that is most striking. By the end of the 1960s, while nine older spinners (including the Big Three) had the capacity of about 3,160,000 spindles, which had slightly decreased from the 1949 level of 3,660,000 spindles, New and New-New Spinners had the capacity of 4,390,000 spindles of which Kondo, Tsuzuki, and Omikenshi had about 2 million (Yonekawa, 1991). Such a rapid rise of post-war entrants to top positions, in contrast to a rather stagnant move of incumbents from the pre-war period, is rare in other industries, and probably in any other country as well.

As for the entrants' advantages, Yonekawa (1991) lists (1) the larger wartime damages to spinning machines in comparison to those to weaving machines, which caused excess demand to yarns; (2) smaller labour costs of New Spinners owing to low unionization; (3) the loan provided by the American Export-Import Bank for the Japanese purchase of raw cotton; and (4) the higher productivity of post-war facilities. Even though these might explain the initial advantages of New Spinners, they need not explain why they persistently outperformed the older and larger rivals. Tsuzuki and Kondo have been (and still are) private firms, and Yonekawa notes the strong growth pursuit of their owner-managers through reinvestment of the profits. Tsuzuki has been keen to improve its technology and now owns a large number of patents, and its new spinning system is considered to be superior to those of rivals. Kondo, on the other hand, has been a shrewd investor, as well as a talented entrepreneur, and invested his returns from financial investment to acquire several rival firms.

Many of the larger firms, by contrast, have been busy expanding the scope of the business by vertically integrating into, for instance, apparel-making, by diversifying into related fields, such as synthetic fibre, and by diversifying into less related fields, such as pharmaceuticals, plastic, and automobile components. Kanebo, in particular, has been active in diversifying into several rather unrelated fields, often by means of acquisitions, such as food processing, housing, pharmaceuticals, and cosmetics. Its cosmetics business has been particularly successful, now having the second largest market share after Shiseido.

There were also firms which have been more or less concentrating their resources in cotton textiles, by investing in product and process improvement, and in new facilities. Nisshinbo, founded in 1907, has been such a firm, successfully maintaining its position as one of the dominant and high-quality producers.

Most of the post-war government policies towards the industry were targeted at the reduction of production capacity to eliminate the supposedly excess capacity. Such a policy started as early as 1956 and continued until 1983 through various legislations. It provided 52 billion yen of subsidies and 307 billion yen of low-interest loans to the industry over the twenty-seven-year period, for the purpose of scrapping 5 million spindles of spinning machines and 352,000 weaving machines (for both natural and man-made fibre) which, respectively, are about two-fifths and one-third of the capacity in 1966. About half of the subsidies and loans were provided during 1971–3 as a compensation to the industry's suffering from the Japan-US Textile Agreement in which the government restricted Japanese export to the USA, presumably as a political compromise associated with the return of Okinawa (Yamazawa, 1988).

Two points are appropriate regarding this adjustment policy. First, the policy was more extensively applied to the weaving sector than to the spinning sector, because of the presence of many small to medium-sized firms in the former. Secondly, whether the policy had the desirable effect has been questioned. When the policy was first announced in 1956, many firms rushed to invest and the capacity had actually increased by the time the policy started. Later, when the government required all the weaving machines to be purchased by the government be registered, the firms opted not to scrap their obsolete machines voluntarily while waiting for the government purchase. The result, therefore, may have been the prolongation, rather than shortening, of the excess capacity situation.

Clearly, those firms that made vigorous efforts to improve production processes to reduce costs, to develop high-quality products, and expand the operation to related fields to achieve economies of scope, such as those discussed above, would have done so with or without the help of the government. Whether the policies have helped or hampered their innovation effort is a moot question indeed.

6.10 SUMMARY AND CONCLUSION

Just as it was the first large-scale manufacturing industry to appear during the Industrial Revolution in England and in many other countries from the USA to India, cotton textiles was the first manufacturing industry to be firmly established in Japan with the Western technology and large-scale operations. Certainly, Japan's rapid rise as a textile-exporting country during the early period was helped by the availability of cheap labour, mostly female. Yet, this alone would not have been enough: otherwise, every late-developing country should have succeeded in achieving a similar position in the world market to that of Japan. Clearly, the building of technological capabilities was the key element.

Textiles is usually regarded as a *light* industry with a low technological content in contrast to the high-technology heavy industries, such as chemicals, machinery, electrical equipment, automobiles, and aircraft. None the less, to start a textiles business, one has to know the technology, even if it is not a science-based one like synthetic fibre. Technology is needed to determine which scale of operation to choose, which equipment to order, how to install, operate, and maintain it, how to empower the equipment, and which combination of raw cotton to use. In the early stage of industrial development, and particularly when, as in the early Meiji era, the Western scientific and technological information was not readily available, these questions were never easy to answer. Furthermore, under the yet-to-be-developed scientific and engineering education system, few in the country could provide answers to these questions. Thus, the entrepreneurs had to invest in the education of their engineers, who had to go to England or else learn the technology through formal education and/or practical training for an extensive period of time. Undoubtedly, they had to be capable of absorbing whatever was taught and whatever they observed, and adapt the knowledge thus obtained to the different technological and economic environment of Japan.

The discussion of the early history of the Japanese textile firms and industry, perhaps most typically in the case of Osaka Boseki, shows that there were indeed such entrepreneurs who understood the need to invest in technology and human resources, and that there were engineers who were capable and willing to absorb and adapt the technology. Initially, these engineers were supported by hired foreign engineers but, as they accumulated the experience and knowledge, they started to come up with many improvements of their own.

The role of the government in fostering the industry appears to have been more limited than in the steel or automobile industry to be discussed in the following chapters. The government made some of the first attempts at building Western-style mills; however, the choice of technology and the choice of operation scale were not appropriate, and they were soon overwhelmed by the investment effort of private entrepreneurs. The government also supported the industry by spreading information and conducting research in its laboratories; yet, the industrial association (Boren) was more active in these regards.

The principal finding from the textiles industry, then, is the presence of entrepreneurs and technologically capable people who together enhanced the technological capabilities further and maintained the competitiveness of the industry through rivalry and entry. Technological accumulation, which started with the assimilation of Western technology, resulted in many original innovations, and Japan still maintains an advantage in many high-technology, high-value-added, and high-fashion textiles products even after losing more traditional segments of the industry to Asian and other countries with lower labour costs. Textiles, in part, is now highly technology-oriented, as exemplified by the application of chemical knowledge to produce new kinds of fibre and the use of electronically controlled machines to produce fine products. In addition, its sensitivity to changing fashion requires the firms to maintain a flexible network for designing, manufacturing, and marketing. As a result, the intra-industrial trade has expanded with international rivalry taking place in a variety of ways. The need for further accumulation in technological and managerial innovation appears to be never diminishing.

7

Iron and Steel

Yawata Steel Works completed in 1901 was monumental for its size and for its representing modern Western technology. Supposedly, it epitomized two salient characteristics of Japan's modern industrial and technological development: first, the government played a large role in investing in (and supporting) industries and, secondly, the country heavily depended on imported technology. To be sure, Yawata Works was constructed by the government with the technology, equipment, and engineers imported from Germany. Still, the question remains: was it really the reason behind Yawata's success (if it should be called success at all)? Is the entire history of the Japanese iron and steel industry similarly characterized by such large involvement of the public sector and by such imitation or importation of foreign technology? A detailed inquiry will suggest that the reality is much more complicated.

7.1 THE FIRST WESTERN-STYLE FURNACE

The first attempt to make steel with Western technology was made during the 1850s, almost a half century before Yawata, still in the Tokugawa era, but after Seclusionism was abandoned. Before then, iron and steel had been made from iron sand and charcoal using an indigenous small-scale production method. However, under the military threat from Western countries, the Shogunate government and some of the powerful feudal lords considered it urgent to build strong cannons. Since quality steel was needed to make these cannons, they constructed reverberating furnaces copying the technology described in a Dutch book—an example of technological flow from the Dutch during the Tokugawa era—but entirely with Japanese hands. These furnaces produced wrought iron on a small scale out of pig iron made with indigenous technology.

One of the engineers who made these furnaces, Ohshima Takatou, proposed the building of a blast furnace to make pig iron using iron ore.

Ohshima was a samurai of Nambu Clan (now a part of Iwate Prefecture) in the north-eastern part of Honshu. Nambu had an iron mine and thus a history of iron making. Adding to this background, Ohshima went to Nagasaki to study Dutch and learned the steel- and cannon-making technology from the book mentioned earlier. He thus knew both indigenous and Western technologies, and, with the financial support of private investors, constructed a small blast furnace in Kamaishi, a city near an iron mine in Nambu. Although the production met with difficulties at first (in firebricks, ventilation, etc.), in about a year the production started to go smoothly.

Two facts are noteworthy in this Ohshima's enterprise. First, Ohshima did not merely copy Western technology. He combined the furnace built after the Dutch technology with the use of charcoal, wooden bellows, and water power, which had been common in the traditional Japanese iron-making method called *tatara*. Secondly, the enterprise was made as a private effort, with the lord of Nambu Clan giving a blessing but little funding. The presence of technological capabilities and entrepreneurship is thus obvious.

The business prospered by selling the product to Mito Clan to be used at the reverberating furnace that Ohshima had built there. Subsequently, nine more furnaces were built in the Kamaishi area, designed by Ohshima or his disciples. In 1858, however, the Mito Clan shut down the reverberating furnace, causing Ohshima's enterprise to suffer from insufficient demand. The operation, therefore, gradually ceased.

Probably the most important lesson from Ohshima's case is that the understanding of indigenous technology was essential in absorbing and adapting technologies developed overseas. This simple principle seems to have been neglected in the government investment, to be discussed in the next section.

7.2 KOBUSHO KAMAISHI WORKS

In 1874, Kobusho (the Ministry of Industries) decided to build a modern furnace in Kamaishi and hired Ohshima and a German engineer to make a plan. The German engineer proposed to build a large-scale mill (with a railway system to carry the product and iron ore) utilizing two imported 25-ton furnaces. Ohshima opposed this plan and instead proposed to build five relatively small furnaces and use a more modest transportation method.

The government, which never questioned the superiority of Western technology, rejected Ohshima's plan and imported furnaces, railway cars, and other equipment from Britain to construct the mill. It also hired British engineers to design the mill, supervise the construction, and teach Japanese workers how to operate it. The operation started in 1890 but immediately met with difficulties. The main problem was the use of charcoal as fuel. The scale of the operation required a large input of charcoal, requiring a vast area of wood to be cut down. After 97 days, a charcoal-making facility caught fire, forcing the mill to be shut down. The mill then built a coke oven and started using coke in addition to charcoal. However, 196 days after restarting the operation, it had to be shut down again. The reason was the poor quality of coke made from Japanese coal. The government finally gave up the operation. Records indicate that total sales during its operation, 175 thousand yen, failed to reach even one-tenth of the cost of construction (Shimokawa, 1989).

The Kamaishi case clearly tells us that technology cannot be free from natural, social, and economic conditions. Apparently, neither the European engineers nor the Meiji government was aware of this simple principle, blindly believing in the superiority of Western technology. By contrast, Ohshima, who knew the way iron had been made in Japan, was familiar with these conditions.

It is even more intriguing to know that, several years later, Kamaishi succeeded in restarting its operation, not through the government but by private entrepreneurship. Tanaka Chobei, a merchant and purveyor to the Military, rented the mill from the government and started to produce iron, not with the big furnace but with newly built, smaller (5–6 ton) furnaces following Ohshima's design, using charcoal as fuel. It was not easy. It took Tanaka and his people 22 months and 49 trial operations before they could finally produce the iron. Several months later in 1887, having been finally convinced that the enterprise could survive, Tanaka bought all the equipment from the government and established a private company, Kamaishi Kozan Tanaka Seitetsusho (Kamaishi Mine Tanaka Ironworks).

The company gradually improved the production process and product quality, and expanded the operation. In 1890, Osaka Arsenal, which had already started making steel from imported pig iron in order to make guns and bullets, compared the quality of bullets made from Kamaishi-made pig iron to that made from Italian-made pig iron, and concluded that the Kamaishi product was possibly superior. This announcement boosted the demand for Tanaka's product, thereby making the business even more sustainable. Finally, in 1894, Tanaka decided to restart the big furnaces that the government had built earlier. However, based on the earlier experience and the advice of Noro Kageyoshi, a professor of engineering at Imperial University (now University of Tokyo), and Kohmura Koroku, Noro's student who would later become the chief engineer at Tanaka Ironworks, Tanaka not only repaired but also redesigned the British-made furnaces and in 1894 succeeded in restarting them using coke as fuel.

Tanaka's experience provides several important lessons. As discussed above, the choice of technology cannot be (and should not be) free from the environment in which it is to be adopted. An efficient production facility in one country might not work well in another with differences in the quality of natural resources, climatic conditions, and levels of infrastructure. It can be inefficient due to differences between relative factor prices, labour systems, or skills accumulated by the workers. Therefore, imported technology, however modern and mechanically superior, had to be modified and adapted to local conditions before it could yield the expected contribution. Continuity with existing technologies played an important role because those technologies survived exactly because they fitted the local conditions. Some of the local conditions, in turn, are affected by these technologies. For instance, supply of certain resources may be strengthened, or transportation and distribution systems may be established.

A similar story was given by Rosenberg (1976: 183) about the USA, who argues that 'it is the combination of (1) this critical role of particular qualities of resource inputs as they determined their economic usefulness with (2) the specific locational matrix in which these resources were embedded, which accounted for the large American lag in the acquisition of new British iron technology.' He then went on to argue that 'the *selection* of a technology as appropriate in a particular context, and its *adaptation* and *modification* in order to enable it to function efficiently in an environment different from the one in which it originated, are activities which typically require a very high degree of technological sophistication' (ibid., 186, his emphases).

In addition to the physical environment Rosenberg has discussed, we emphasize the influence of the human and social environment. Perhaps most important of all, workers acquire skills and engineers learn technology on the job through their experience with adopted technologies. These skills and experience are more difficult to absorb the more distant the imported technology is from indigenous technologies. The success of Ohshima's enterprise, the failure of Kobusho Kamaishi Works, and the success of Tanaka Ironworks with smaller furnaces, all illustrate this fact. The workers in Kamaishi who had experience in indigenous iron-making method could work comfortably in Ohshima's mill because Ohshima adopted some of the technologies that had been long used in the Kamaishi area while learning how to operate the Western-style furnace that Ohshima had built. The skills thus learned could be utilized in Tanaka Ironworks because they built furnaces following Ohshima's design. By contrast, the skills required to operate the large-scale imported furnaces of the Kobusho Works were rather different.

Ohshima was in fact keenly aware of the importance of good working conditions for labourers. When Ohshima opposed the plan of a German engineer for Kobusho Works, the location of the plant was an important issue. In a proposal Ohshima submitted to the government, he gave five reasons for his choice of a site at Ootadagoe. The reason he regarded as most important was the good working condition: 'Ootadagoe, with mountains to the west, north, and east, and open view only to the south, has less rain, storm, and chill, thereby making the operation more bearable' (Ohshima's 1874 proposal to the government as cited in Iida (1979: 94), our translation). By contrast, in none of the seven reasons that the German engineer gave for the choice of Suzuko (which the government chose over Ootadagoe), were the working conditions mentioned.

We are not implying that continuity with past technologies is sufficient for a nation to advance its technological level. They have to be augmented by new technologies acquired from abroad or created within the country. That is, industrial development requires the nation's capabilities to understand and apply unfamiliar new technologies as well as capabilities in the indigenous or current technology. The Japanese iron industry was extremely fortunate to have had people like Ohshima and Noro, who had exactly these capabilities.

The Kamaishi case also provides valuable lessons concerning the role of the government. Apparently, the government was a poor selector of the technology. Not only did it neglect the supply conditions of fuel and skilled labour, among others, it also neglected the demand condition. Iida (1979) argues that the scale of the furnace was too large in comparison to the level of domestic demand for iron at the time.

None the less, Kobusho Works helped the operation of Tanaka Ironworks on two counts. The first, needless to say, was the capital equipment and unused materials. Without them Tanaka would not have started the enterprise. This need not imply that the government *de facto* gave subsidies to Tanaka. It is true that Tanaka only paid 12,600 yen to buy the works in which the government had invested 2,376,600 yen.[1] Yet, the works was losing money, implying that the value of the works, in terms of the present value of expected profit, must have been negative. Its property value was also limited. In fact, at first Tanaka thought of purchasing the works simply to sell the equipment second-hand or as scrap but having visited the site, gave up this idea because the revenue would not have been large enough to cover the cost of disassembly. He thus reluctantly decided to invest further and build new, smaller furnaces (Iida, 1982).

The importance of skill formation is again noted in this context. Some of the workers hired by Tanaka had worked at Kobusho Works, and this experience helped them in Tanaka's attempt with smaller furnaces and, later, the effort to restart the large furnaces. In turn, many years later, the skilled workers of Tanaka Ironworks would go to Yawata Works to help the workers there, until the latter could accumulate sufficient skills. The continuity and evolution in technology, including skills and experience, seem to have been maintained, without which the development of the industry would have been more difficult.

7.3   YAWATA WORKS

In steel making, more than in iron making, the role of the military was important. Around 1870, the government set up a few arsenals, most importantly in Osaka (the Army), Yokohama (the Navy), and Tokyo (the Navy), by taking over the military facilities that the Tokugawa government had built towards the end of its reign, with the equipment imported mostly from France and The Netherlands. Using these facilities and imported technologies on open hearth and other methods, the arsenals started making steel to be used in the production and repair of cannons, guns, and bullets. At first, they made steel from imported pig iron but, as discussed already, started using the iron made by Tanaka Ironworks, occasionally giving technical advice to the latter. Later, when private companies started steel production, some of them hired engineers from the arsenals: technological diffusion thus occurred, benefitting private enterprises.

As the demand for iron and steel increased, for both military and industrial uses, the import increased, accounting for nearly 80 per cent of the market. This dependence on imported iron was not only uneconomical but also risky from the national security viewpoint. Hence, the government decided to build an integrated steel mill in Yawata in Kyushu, the south-western part of Japan.

Ironically and unfortunately, the government repeated some of the misjudgment it made at Kamaishi.

When it decided to build a works in Yawata in 1897, the minister in charge was Enomoto Takeaki. Enomoto had studied technology in The Netherlands when he was still a young samurai of the Tokugawa government. He was thus exceptional among the Cabinet in his understanding of technology. Quite appropriately, he stated that 'very often a merely large-scale steel mill cannot have the expected productivity because of shortage in materials and skilled labour and, therefore, my policy for Yawata is to start on a small scale and then, as skills are accumulated and other conditions become ready, to expand the scale of operation gradually' (our abbreviated translation from Enomoto's Japanese statement cited in Iida (1979: 115)). His understanding of the very key factor of technological capability is clear in this statement, as well as his learning from the Kamaishi experience.

This view was shared by Noro Kageyoshi, who made a specific plan for Yawata utilizing three 60-ton furnaces. It should also be noted that Enomoto and Noro intended to nurture technology through learning by doing, without depending fully on imported technology. In addition, they accepted the public investment in Yawata only as an exceptional and temporary measure in the belief that such an enterprise should in principle be carried out by the private sector.

Unfortunately, both Enomoto and Noro had to resign, for unrelated and separate reasons, before the final plan was approved. Their successors changed the whole plan and decided to build a large-scale works with imported technology and equipment. Interestingly, the chief engineer making this proposal was Ohshima Takatou's son, Michitaro. Michitaro, who had studied in Germany, went there again to consult his professor and see some of the steel works, and proposed to built a mill with the German state-of-the-art technology, commissioning a German company to make a detailed plan, buying German equipment, and hiring German engineers for the top engineering posts. It had two 165-ton furnaces. Completed in 1901, it was a spectacularly modern and large plant by Japanese standards of the time.

The excitement, however, did not last long. Operational problems mounted and the mill was forced to shut after about a year. They restarted the operation about a year and a half later only to shut down again after seventeen days. There seemed to be only one person who could fix the problem—Noro, who had earlier resigned from all public posts. He accepted the invitation, made a thorough investigation, and found three problems: the inappropriate structure of the furnaces, the poor quality of coke, and insufficient work skills. The first two were mainly caused by German engineers' lack of understanding of the characteristics of Japanese coke. Yawata had been chosen as the site basically because there was a big coal mine nearby, and the mill used the coke produced with this coal. But the German engineers failed to understand its difference from German coal and, consequently, both the furnaces and coke-making facilities they had designed were inadequate. As emphasized earlier, the choice of technology must not be separated from environmental and social conditions because the 'state-of-the-art' technology might not be the best solution under certain circumstances. Apparently, neither the Japanese politicians (except Enomoto) nor the German engineers were aware of this simple truth. To make matters worse, the cost of construction exceeded the initial budget and, by the time they started constructing the coke-making facility, they were under a heavy budget constraint and had to settle for cheaper, obsolete equipment. Inevitably, the coke thus produced was poor in quality and made the steel production extremely difficult.

The other problem pertained to the human aspect. As Enomoto and Noro had suspected, the skills were generally insufficient due to the introduction of unfamiliar technology. In addition, hired German engineers and foremen were not much of a help, partly because some of them, engineers in particular, were not knowledgeable enough and partly because communication with Japanese workers was difficult owing to language difficulties or to an arrogant attitude in some of the Germans. Some of them were discharged before the conclusion of the contract.

The fact that it was Japanese not German engineers who could identify and resolve problems by, for instance, redesigning the furnace and installing new coke-making equipment, indicates that Japan already had a sufficiently high technological capability. In particular, Noro had a deep understanding of both Western technology and the environment surrounding the Japanese iron and steel industry. His former students at Yawata, such as Imaizumi Kaichiro, also helped.

The mill successfully restarted its operation in 1904 under Noro's leadership, and rapidly increased the production and improved on efficiency. For instance, the quantity of coke required per ton of iron decreased from 1.43 in 1904 to 1.02 in 1912 (Iida, 1979: 172). It also increased the capacity and remained the dominant producer in the market; for instance, in 1910, their share was 90 per cent in terms of domestic production and 30 per cent in terms of total supply, including the import.

Yawata was also active in improving firebricks, coke ovens, and such. It also started its own training programmes for the workers off the job, at its schools, and on the job. Since many of the workers and engineers thus trained moved to work for private enterprises, Yawata's role as the source of technological spillover continued to be important.

7.4   ENTRY BY PRIVATE PRODUCERS

Despite the dominance of the government-owned Yawata Works, entry by private enterprises was frequent, particularly into steel production. Tanaka's Kamaishi Works started making steel in 1903. Sumitomo started steel production in 1899, Kobe Seikosho (Kobe Steel) started in 1905, Kawasaki Zosen (Kawasaki Shipbuilding, now Kawasaki Heavy Industries, from which Kawasaki Steel was later hived off) started making steel in 1907, Nihon Seikosho (Japan Steel Works) financed by Mitsui and others started in 1907, and Nihon Kokan (now NKK) started in 1912. Nihon Kokan was founded by the initiative of Imaizumi Kaichiro, Noro's student, who had resigned from Yawata when his proposal to privatize Yawata was rejected. It was financially supported by industrial zaibatsu of Asano, Okura, and Shibusawa. Many more entered into the industry during the boom period of World War I. Most of these producers made steel out of domestic or imported pig iron (mainly from India but also from Europe and the USA), or scrap iron (mainly imported), depending on the relative prices.

Although entry into the production of pig iron was more difficult because of the required scale of investment, it was by no means absent. Wanishi Seitetsu started a 100-ton furnace in 1917 with the investment of Mitsui among others, Toyo Seitetsu started a 150-ton furnace in 1919, and Asano Zosen (Asano Shipbuilding) started a 150-ton furnace in 1927. In addition, Mitsubishi started one in colonized Korea. Hence private profit-seeking entry did take place actively. Still, Yawata maintained its dominant position with its own expansion.

In 1924, Yawata had a share of approximately 70 per cent in the domestic production of pig iron (with the total domestic production accounting for about two-thirds of domestic demand) and 55 per cent of steel, although the share varied among various steel products. For instance, Nihon Kokan was the leader in steel pipe with the market share of 75 per cent (Okazaki, 1993*b*).

In 1934, a partly state-owned company, Nihon Seitetsu (Japan Iron and Steel), was established to achieve a 'stable supply' of steel, which the Army considered was indispensable. Yawata was absorbed into this company and the government urged private companies to join. Kamaishi and most other iron producers and integrated steel producers complied with this request but Nihon Kokan, Sumitomo, Kawasaki, Kobe, Asano, and other non-integrated steel producers, kept their independence. There were probably three reasons. First, these non-integrated steel producers used to have a comparative advantage over the integrated producers because imported pig iron was cheaper. Although this advantage had been lost before the proposed merger by the depreciation of yen and the increase of tariff for imported pig iron, these producers remained less eager to be integrated. Secondly, the proposed formula for the re-evaluation of the assets of merging firms was more advantageous to integrated firms, such as Yawata. Thirdly, many of the private companies had a view that 'the merger may cause inefficiency to prevail, as typical of state-run companies, and this, together with the lack of competition, may hurt the healthy development of the industry,' as stated by the vice-president of Nihon Kokan at the time (Shimokawa, 1989: 117, our translation).

Despite the government's urging, therefore, the result was an incomplete integration. Apparently, the pursuit of independence by private enterprises helped to maintain a competitive market that was carried over to the post-war growth period.

The spread of technological knowledge across these companies took place frequently. As stated earlier, Yawata Works played an important role, as well as arsenals. Because they were state-run and because Yawata was a dominant leader in the industry, they did not hesitate to teach the knowledge they had accumulated. Technological spread across private companies also took place, albeit less frequently. An academic association, Nihon Tekkou Kyoukai (the Iron and Steel Institute of Japan) was established in 1915 under Noro's leadership. The members included engineers from companies and arsenals as well as researchers in universities and other research institutions. They exchanged technological information and discussed common problems through the Institute's journals and meetings. Research on steel also progressed in universities. The invention of KS steel by Honda Kotaro in 1917 showed that the Japanese scientific level had quickly caught up with that of the West, and a research institute was established within Tohoku University with Honda's initiative.

7.5 POST-WAR REORGANIZATION AND NEW INVESTMENT

When World War II ended in 1945, it was seriously doubted whether Japan could (and should) have an iron and steel industry, not only because some of the production facilities had been badly damaged during the war and the Occupation Force was expected to take punitive measures against the industry but, more importantly, because the lack of resources, iron ore and coal in particular, was expected to impose a serious constraint to the industry. Before and during the war, many of these resources had been brought to Japan from Manchuria, which now became subject to the communist rule. Instead, they had to be imported from Asian countries such as Indonesia or from the USA. If made domestically with these imported materials, however, the product was expected to cost more than the import from the USA. Also, India, with its abundant resources, was expected to become a formidable competitor. It was not groundless, therefore, that most of the industry people and policy-makers alike were pessimistic about the future of the industry. As Yonekura (1991) argues, it is far from the truth to assume, as many foreign observers do, that the Japanese government at the time had a clear vision of its steel industry as one of the target industries.

Yet, under the critical circumstances of deteriorating production in coal, steel, and electric power, the government adopted a 'priority production policy' in 1946 to encourage the production of steel, which would be allocated, with priority, into coal mining, which in turn would be allocated to steel production. For this purpose, the government provided these industries with subsidies, low-interest loans, and the application of a favourable exchange rate. These measures were abolished in 1949 under the Dodge Line discussed in Chapter 3. To the steel industry, the end of the subsidies caused a steep rise in production cost, which put the industry under a heavy competitive threat from cheaper imports. What saved the industry from this difficulty was the booming demand owing to the Korean War, and an increase in world iron and steel prices.[2]

As for the market structure, a drastic change took place when the Deconcentration Law was applied to Japan Iron and Steel, forcing it to split into Yawata Seitetsu (Yawata Steel), Fuji Seitetsu (Fuji Steel), and two other non-steel-making, smaller companies (see Chapter 5). In addition, these companies were fully privatized. The implication of this reorganization was twofold. On the one hand, the disappearance of the dominant leader resulted in a less concentrated industry, thereby improving the relative competitive position of other firms (see Table 7.1). On the other hand, whereas pre-war Japan Iron and Steel had put the stable supply of iron and steel ahead of profitability, the privatized companies would pursue profitability and might take more aggressive strategies. In particular, non-integrated steel producers who had depended on the pig iron supplied by Japan Iron and Steel (in addition to the imported iron) found themselves now vulnerable to any strategic moves Yawata and Fuji might make.

One such producer was Kawasaki Seitetsu (Kawasaki Steel), hived off from Kawasaki Heavy Industries in 1950. The president, Nishiyama Yataro, was keenly aware of this vulnerability and decided to enter into iron making. His plan for a new integrated plant to be built in Chiba surprised everyone. It intended to produce 350,000 tons a year of pig iron and 500,000 tons of crude steel, when nearly two-thirds of the existing furnaces in the country were idle because of insufficient demand. The investment cost was estimated at 16 billion yen (which actually cost 27 billion yen) when the company's equity capital was merely 0.5 billion yen. Not surprisingly, Nishiyama met heavy criticism from MITI and the Bank of Japan.

The real innovation of the plant was to be found in its location and layout. Whereas it was common to build an ironworks near a coal mine or an iron-ore mine, Nishiyama chose Chiba for its proximity to Tokyo, the largest market for the product. He also chose a seaside location so that ships could deliver iron ore and coal directly to a port within the plant. Furthermore, he made a careful plan of the layout of the facilities to minimize the movement of materials and half-made products. Nishiyama, a talented engineer, was awarded honour for his research paper on open hearth by the Iron and Steel Institute of Japan in 1933. He thus had a deep understanding of steel-making technology. To compensate for his lack of iron-making experience, he hired engineers who used to work for Showa Seikosho in Manchuria when they returned to Japan after the war.

The company therefore had technological capability. What it lacked

TABLE 7.1 Shares in iron and steel production

	1940	1945	1950	1955	1960	1965	1970	1975	1980	1985	1990
Pig Iron											
Nippon	73.5	85.7					44.0	39.3	38.8	84.1	83.7
Yawata			35.2	31.8	31.0	24.2					
Fuji			40.3	34.6	27.4	24.5					
NKK	16.6	7.3	20.3	18.1	14.3	13.4	16.0	16.1	16.4		
Kawasaki	0.0	0.0	0.0	6.3	8.9	13.6	14.3	14.9	14.5		
Sumitomo	0.0	0.0	0.0	2.8	5.0	12.4	13.4	15.7	15.3		
Kobe	0.0	0.0	0.0	3.1	8.2	6.3	7.3	9.4	9.3	9.2	9.5
Others	9.9	7.0	4.2	4.2	5.2	5.6	5.0	4.6	5.7	6.7	6.8
Crude Steel											
Nippon	43.9	52.0					35.9	31.8	29.2	27.1	26.0
Yawata			30.3	24.1	22.5	18.8					
Fuji			17.9	19.3	15.9	17.4					
NKK	13.9	4.6	13.6	12.3	10.1	10.3	13.7	14.3	12.4	11.6	11.0
Kawasaki	5.4	3.8	9.0	8.2	8.9	10.5	11.8	13.1	11.2	10.4	10.1
Sumitomo	2.9	2.1	4.3	6.4	5.8	10.1	12.0	13.1	11.2	10.4	10.1
Kobe	3.8	1.2	5.7	5.2	6.4	5.9	5.5	7.5	6.6	6.1	5.9
Others	30.0	36.3	19.1	24.5	30.4	27.1	21.3	20.2	29.4	34.3	36.8

Note: The figures for Kobe in 1955 and 1960 include those of Amagasaki Seitetsu which was merged to Kobe in 1965.

Sources: *1940–1970*: Yonekura (1983), Table 1
1975–1980: Toyo Keizai, *Toyo Keizai Toukei Geppo*
1985–1990: Fair Trade Commission, unpublished, for pig iron (the market shares of individual companies are not disclosed); Toyo Keizai, *Toyo Keizai Toukei Geppo*, for crude steel

was financial resources but Nishiyama decided to go ahead and managed to secure the necessary finance despite unsympathetic, if not hostile, attitudes of MITI and the Bank of Japan.

As repeatedly argued in this book, the combination of entrepreneurship with technological capabilities is the key factor in successful industrial development, and Kawasaki's case, like that of Ohshima Takatou almost a century before, provides a perfect example of this thesis.

The consequence was grave. The start of operation at Chiba immediately placed Kawasaki as one of the major iron producers behind Yawata, Fuji, and NKK (Nihon Kokan). Soon the other companies, such as Sumitomo and Kobe, followed suit, decreasing concentration and intensifying rivalry: see the changes in market shares from 1950 to 1965 in Table 7.1. As a result, the concentrated industry with a dominant state-run firm before the war was replaced by an oligopolistic industry with six rivalling major firms.

The competition was most prominent in the investment behaviour. MITI even worried of *over*-investment and adopted the policy of coordinating investment proposals, although whether the policy had the intended investment-reducing effect has been questioned (Yamawaki, 1988). The merger of Yawata and Fuji in 1970 to become the present Shin Nihon Seitetsu (Nippon Steel) was approved by the Fair Trade Commission exactly because the relative power of these two companies had been very much weakened by then, owing to the active investment behaviour of other companies.

Such active investment was pursued by all the firms, because new facilities embodied technical progress. Productivity increase resulted, not only from technological innovation but also managerial and operational innovation, as illustrated by the seaside ironworks and efficient layout pioneered by Kawasaki's Chiba plant, which others soon followed. As a consequence, constant pressure was exerted to invest in new, better, and larger production facilities and stay competitive. This active investment behaviour was supported by the rapid increase in demand, both in domestic and export markets, during the high growth era of the 1950s and 1960s. Productivity as a consequence increased tremendously; for instance, in 1973, between the two plants of Nippon Steel, the new one at Kimitsu had a labour productivity (steel production per worker) 2.5 times higher than the old one at Yawata, even though the latter's productivity itself had increased several times in the preceding thirty years (Iida, 1979).

Productivity also increased through constant effort to improve plant efficiency. Some were conspicuous, for instance, in the introduction of computers to control operations. Others were more subtle, such as the innovation made at shop-floor levels based on learning by doing and workers' proposals. As discuss in Chapter 5, Japanese firms have been relatively successful in attaining company-wide involvement in productivity improvement: the steel companies provide one of the best examples.

7.6 BASIC OXYGEN FURNACES AND CONTINUOUS CASTING

In terms of technological innovation, two developments had a significant impact. The first was the importation of basic oxygen furnace (BOF) technology from Austria and its improvement and adaptation to Japanese steel mills during the 1950s. The second was the introduction of the continuous casting method and strip mills during the 1950s and 1960s.

BOF, first developed for commercial use by an Austrian firm in 1952, is a brick-lined vessel that refines molten iron to make steel. However, unlike Thomas or Bessemer converters, which blow air from below, BOF blows pure oxygen from above. By that time, open hearth was a dominant steel-making method but it required a large input of scrap iron. Therefore, for the Japanese producers who were dependent on import scrap and were suffering from its fluctuating international price, BOF was an attractive alternative. In addition, BOF was expected to increase productivity if used in conjunction with an integrated iron–steel production process, which the major Japanese firms, like Kawasaki discussed above, were planning to build.

However, BOF had two problems. The first was that burning oxygen caused high heat which damaged the internal brickwork of the furnace and eventually it had to be relined. This took several days. The second problem was the high level of pollution emitted from the plant. It was for these reasons that American firms, some of which had introduced the technology earlier than Japanese firms, did not adopt the system extensively. Instead, Japanese firms solved these problems through their own innovation.

To solve the first problem, they developed, with the collaboration of brick producers, a new type of brick that could sustain the high heat. To solve the second problem, Yawata invented an oxygen converter gas recovery system (OG system) jointly with Yokoyama Kogyo, an equipment manufacturer. The OG system, by recycling the waste gas, not only prevented pollution but also reduced the energy use. As has been repeatedly argued, technology cannot be just imported and implemented: it has to be adapted or developed further. The BOF case illustrates this fact and it was these efforts of Japanese firms that made them the most efficient steel makers in the world. Furthermore, the innovations such as the OG system were adopted worldwide, making more in royalty fees than the amount paid to import the BOF technology.

Since Lynn (1982) provides a detailed account of the introduction of BOF, we will not discuss the case further, except for a brief discussion of the role that competition played in the adoption race and the role that MITI played as a coordinator.

The first firm to become aware of the new technology was NKK. At first, their management was not eager to invest in the importation of the technology, despite strong enthusiasm among a number of the engineers.[3] However, when they learned that Yawata had started to experiment with the technology, they accelerated their efforts. The two firms were thus going to compete in acquiring a licence from the Austrian firm. As discussed in Chapter 3, MITI, which became worried that this competition might raise the licence fee and prevent the industry-wide use of the technology, persuaded the two firms that the technology imported by NKK should be sub-licensed to other firms. The result was a licence fee much lower than that charged to American firms, although underestimation by the licensor of the growth of the Japanese steel production must have been another reason for this lower fee. It also enabled a rapid spread of the technology among Japanese steel makers. This is a very interesting case of interaction between competition and coordination.

Continuous casting (CC) is a method of producing slabs, billets, or blooms continuously and directly from molten steel. This technology made it possible to produce final products continuously through blast furnaces, BOFs, and casters, thereby enhancing efficiency and yield, and reducing energy use and labour input. However, when the method was first developed in Switzerland in the early 1950s, there were still a number of unsolved problems; for instance, the equipment was expensive, the maintenance was costly, and the quality of the product was not high. Thus, the technology at that time was not economical, and whether the firm should introduce it depended on how much confidence the management could place in its potential and their own ability to improve it.

According to Yonekura's (1986) case study of Armco of the USA and of Kawasaki Steel, there was a clear difference in this regard between the two. Armco first discussed the introduction of CC in 1965 but decided to postpone it, finally adopting the technology ten years later. Kawasaki learned of the technology while it was constructing a huge integrated works in Mizushima. It immediately built a test CC facility there and in 1967 built a full-scale plant. Why was there so clear a difference between the two companies? Yonekura suggests three reasons.

First, Armco's management, dominated by accountants, was most concerned with the uncertainty of the cost and efficiency of the technology. By contrast, Kawasaki's management was dominated by engineers, with Nishiyama still as the president, and had a view that no technology could be learned and improved until it was tried. In other words, they knew that they had a capability to understand the technology and learn by using it. Moreover, they knew they could never enhance their capability until they learned. Probably another way of comparing the two is to say that, while Armco had a rather static view, Kawasaki believed that technology evolves in a dynamic fashion. Kawasaki, furthermore, believed that this process of evolution could be fostered by their own initiatives.

Secondly, Kawasaki's management trusted the ability of the workers at the shop-floor level. When the engineer of the Swiss firm that made the equipment came to Kawasaki, he was astonished to find that Kawasaki showed every detail of the equipment to the workers and asked for their opinion and suggestions. The engineer opposed this policy at first, saying that the workers might damage the equipment. Here we find a very basic difference between Japan and the West in the management's attitude towards workers, particularly at the shop-floor level. In the end, the Swiss engineer became intrigued and impressed by the way the Japanese engineers took the workers' opinion seriously and utilized them to improve productivity (Yonekura, 1986).

As discussed in Chapter 5, such interaction between engineers and workers, and between R&D and manufacturing, has been the basic strength of Japanese firms. The workers not only accumulate skills through on-the-job learning but participate by making proposals for improvements in the production processes. The management takes these proposals seriously and encourages them, thereby creating a trusting relationship between the two.

Thirdly, there was an external force which more or less forced Kawasaki to adopt the new technology—competition. As discussed earlier, the industry was characterized by intense rivalry among six firms of similar size. Kawasaki knew at the time that Sumitomo Metal had already decided to adopt the technology. It also had a bitter memory of having been behind NKK and Yawata in the adoption of BOF, which put them at a competitive disadvantage. Not to be left behind the rivals, therefore, Kawasaki was eager to introduce better technology however premature and uncertain it might look. By contrast, American steel makers were rather diverse, in terms not only of size but also of the production system, product composition, and location. Furthermore, US Steel was there as a passive, though dominant, leader. Thus, competitive threat was much weaker against Armco.

These observations suggest that both internal and external factors played important roles in the early and widespread adoption of continuous casting process among Japanese firms. By 1980, the process had been adopted by 60 per cent of the Japanese plants but only 20 per cent of the American plants.

As a result of this and other innovation, Japan's productivity increase has outpaced that of other countries with companies starting to export technology and knowhow in plant construction and operation to many countries, including both developing countries, such as Brazil, and developed countries, such as Italy and the USA. In 1974 receipt of royalties exceeded payments for the first time among Japanese industries.

7.7 CONCLUSION

Both the pre-war and post-war experiences of the Japanese iron and steel industry teach us several important lessons. The role played by the government and the military in the development of the industry was obviously large, although whether it was unproportionally large in comparison to other countries may be questioned. Steel production is inseparable from the military's needs as illustrated by the fact that the first steel production using Western technology took place in order to make cannons.

The cases of Kamaishi and Yawata, however, imply that the government was less qualified than the private sector in the selection of technologies. In either case, the government placed too much confidence in Western technology as it was, and disregarded local conditions, such as the infrastructure and the accumulated indigenous technology. By contrast, Ohshima Takatou's and Tanaka's attempts at Kamaishi suggest that private enterprises were better suited for this purpose.

During the post-war period, MITI played important roles, sometimes as a supplier of subsidies and low-interest loans, sometimes as a coordinator among firms in capital investment or technology importation, and sometimes as a diffuser of knowledge. It is, however, a gross exaggeration to argue that the industrial policy was the main force behind the pre-war and post-war development of the industry. More often, it was a private initiative to start an enterprise, to invest in new plants, and to adopt or experiment with new technologies. Such investment was made even under very uncertain situations, in terms of market and/or technology, as the cases of Ohshima Takatou and Kawasaki's Nishiyama clearly implied. Such entrepreneurship was also present in the introduction of the continuous casting process by Kawasaki where entrepreneurship was exhibited, not by individuals, but by the organization.

The consequence of this entrepreneurial behaviour was a competitive market. Although the concentration ratio was modestly high, rivalry was intense among the firms and the entry threat was there. Competition must be taken more as a behavioral concept than a structural one and, as Schumpeter has argued forcefully, it is this behavioral concept of competition that drives the firms into innovation. Schumpeter's thesis is clearly consistent with the experience of the Japanese iron and steel industry.

The discussion in this chapter also provides important lessons on the nature of technology. First, the selection of the best technology cannot be made and should not be made without regard to the environmental, economic, and social conditions, as Rosenberg (1976) has also argued. Secondly, continuity with past and existing technologies should be respected, for the knowledge of existing technologies helps one to become aware of technological opportunity, to choose appropriate technology, to absorb new technology and adapt it if necessary, and to apply it at the production site. Thirdly, technologies progress in an evolutionary fashion: it is not only radical innovations that advance the technological level but, equally important, incremental innovations through learning have to be made. Fourthly, particularly for such incremental innovations, both the capability and willingness of the workers at the shop-floor level to learn from new technologies and improve them are indispensable, as well as close communication between workers and engineers, or even top management. Fifthly, top management has to have a clear understanding of the present capability of the firm and its technological requirements when making decisions about the selection, timing, and methods of introduction of new technologies.

In fact, as the continuous casting case illustrates, an introduction of one technology, e.g., BOF, may cause imbalance to the forward or backward process, fostering further innovations. As Yonekura (1994) puts it, 'innovation begets innovation'. The management failing to grasp the significance of this imbalance and remedy it will inevitably be left behind the competition.

8

Electrical and Communications Equipment

8.1 INTRODUCTION

Technology in the electrical and communications equipment industry is usually considered to be more science-based (that is, 'high-tech') and, hence, more distant from traditional crafts technology than textiles and iron. Nevertheless, the industry is another case where imported Western technology combined with Japan's indigenous technology as well as its own R&D efforts.

At least two factors explain why such a combination was effective when the industry started to develop in Japan. The first is the legacy of the Tokugawa era: sophisticated craft skills and technological knowledge in machine engineering that had been maintained prior to the Restoration (see Section 1.7) helped the Japanese to copy imported products and learn through reverse-engineering. In fact, one of the first Japanese to make a telegraph after the Western technology came exactly from this tradition, as we will show.

The second is the timing. Although, as in other industries, Japan was technologically behind America and Europe in the late nineteenth century when electrical and communications equipment started to be developed, the lag was not desperately large. Take the example of electric light. T. W. Swan invented an electric incandescent bulb in 1878 in the UK as did T. A. Edison in 1879 in the USA. Japan started its effort to produce these bulbs not long after. Similarly, the first telephone receiver was manufactured in Japan only two years after Bell's invention in 1876. Put differently, the mid- to late nineteenth century when Japan started to introduce Western technology following the Meiji Restoration, was also the time when several path-breaking innovations were made by Edison, Morse, Bell, and others in the use of electricity.

Thus, the technology was still rather primitive and could be learned by skilled Japanese craftsmen and engineers through reverse-engineering.

However, as the innovation efforts by American and European firms became more organized, as exemplified most typically by the activity in the Menlo Park Laboratory of Edison's, the still infant Japanese firms were left behind in technology. Many of them, therefore, could survive only by acquiring technologies and know-how from foreign firms, with the latter usually having equity stakes.

Although Japanese firms gradually narrowed the technological gap, partly through their own R&D efforts combined with imported technology, and partly through the military research activity, they had not yet really caught up with the West by the time World War II started. Thus the technological inferiority in radar and communications, among others, has been considered to be one of the reasons for Japan's defeat.

Two years after the war ended, the transistor was invented at Bell Laboratories, and the age of the semiconductor started. With few resources in finance, materials, and information readily available, the Japanese industry had to begin another effort to narrow the technological gap. The technological base accumulated before and during the war helped the catch-up process. Yet this was neither easy nor smooth. Even though MITI regarded the development of the industry as one of its priorities and assisted it in several measures, MITI was not always right and nor were the firms. Only through constant trial and error and the process of learning could they gradually accumulate technological capabilities and catch up with the USA. Intense competition with many entries also helped the development of the industry.

We purport to describe this development at some length in this chapter. Since the industry covers a wide range of fields, from heavy power generators to light household appliances, and from bulky mainframe computers of decades ago to tiny semiconductors, the discussion is bound to be selective. We will start by discussing the birth and development of several well-known firms and, for the post-war period, concentrate more or less on the field of semiconductors.

8.2   START OF THE INDUSTRY: THE STORY OF TOSHIBA

It is perhaps not far-fetched to assert that the history of the Japanese electrical equipment industry started in 1873 when Tanaka Hisashige came to Tokyo to make telegraphs. Born in 1799, Tanaka was one of the most original and productive inventor-engineers (*karakuri* masters, see Section 1.7) during the Tokugawa era. At the age of 14, he had already invented a loom. At 20 he made a karakuri doll with a hydraulic mechanism, earning popularity with its demonstration. The list of inventions and products he made during his active years (more than a half century) is surprisingly extensive—clocks, locks, torch lamps, furnaces, pumps, fire extinguishers, tobacco cutters, ice-makers, bicycles, oil-presses, rice-polishers, ships, dredgers, guns, and much more. He was also one of the first in the country to make a steam engine after the Western technology by the order of Nabeshima Kanso, the lord at Saga, Kyushu, near his home town, Kurume.

In 1873, six years after the Restoration, Tanaka, by then aged 74 and still energetic, was invited by Kobusho (the Ministry of Industries) to come to Tokyo to make telegraphs at the ministry's small factory. The Japanese first knew of telegraphs when USA Commodore Perry came to Japan in 1854, following his first visit of the previous year (that shook the Tokugawa Shogunate government, which had been maintaining Seclusionism). He demonstrated telegraphs and a miniature steam-driven train in order to impress the Japanese with the technological superiority of the West, thereby pressing the Shogunate government to accept a treaty with the USA. After that, a few Japanese experimented with telegraphs and many recognized the need to establish a telegraph network within the country. Such a need was particularly emphasized by those who visited the West, and by those who realized the advantage of fast communication during the civil wars caused by the Restoration.

In 1870, a European enterprise proposed to connect Nagasaki and several other Japanese ports with Shanghai and Vladivostok by cable. The Meiji government, in fear of the network being controlled by foreign interests, allowed them to connect the cable in Nagasaki only and instead rushed to build its own network between major domestic cities. It hired British engineers and imported most of the necessary equipment and materials from the UK. The construction met with many difficulties; for instance, most people could not comprehend the invisibility of electricity and, in fear of its 'supernatural' power, refused to allow the cable to go through their land. Furthermore, the budgetary conflicts within the government delayed the work. Finally, however, the Nagasaki–Tokyo line was completed in 1873.

Since all the equipment for the operation still had to be imported, Kobusho decided to promote the production and repair of telegraphs within the country, by hiring a German engineer and starting a factory within the ministry. Some of the Japanese employed by this factory had previously worked under Tanaka: they, therefore, entreated Tanaka to come to Tokyo, which he did. Upon his arrival, he immediately started a shop and made telegraphs by the order of the ministry. He soon established his own company, Tanaka Seisakusho, and made telegraphs, switches, and miscellaneous electrical and other equipment. For Tanaka, therefore, the technological development followed a more or less continuous path, and he must have felt little discontinuity between the indigenous technologies he grew up with and the Western ones.

Although Tanaka worked to make electrical and communications equipment in Tokyo for just eight years until his death in 1881, his contribution to the industry remains paramount to this day in two regards. First, Tanaka Seisakusho was inherited by his adopted son and later became half of the present Toshiba. Secondly, several people who worked at Tanaka Seisakusho or who received Tanaka's guidance at the Kobusho factory later became pioneers themselves. These included Miyoshi Shoichi who, as will be discussed, helped Fujioka to make the first power generator in Japan and to establish a company, Hakunetsusha, to make bulbs; Oki Kibataro, the founder of the present Oki Denki (Oki Electric); and Ishiguro Keizaburo, a co-founder of the present Anritsu.[1]

The other half of Toshiba came from an enterprise founded to manufacture incandescent light bulbs domestically. As stated earlier, Swan and Edison invented incandescent light in 1878 and 1879, respectively. Five years later, in 1884, it was first demonstrated in Japan. Not surprisingly, all the equipment used in this demonstration had been imported. However, in a similar demonstration in the following year, a domestically-manufactured generator was used which was designed by Fujioka Ichisuke, a young professor at Kogakuryo (the College of Engineering, now the Engineering Department of the University of Tokyo, as discussed in Chapter 2) who had studied with a British professor at the college, and manufactured by the aforementioned Miyoshi.

Fujioka had, in the previous year, been to the USA and visited Edison's company. He was now determined to make incandescent bulbs domestically. He quit the professorship to join Tokyo Dento (now Tokyo Electric Power Company), was sent by the company for another visit to America and Europe, bought bulb-manufacturing equipment in the UK, and came back in 1887. He started the development effort and, in 1890, in order to continue this effort independently from Tokyo Dento, established a new company, Hakunetsusha, with the collaboration of Miyoshi, who became the first president. Even with the equipment brought from the UK, the development met with many difficulties. For instance, following Swan's invention, his team first experimented with cotton yarn for filament but the result was unsatisfactory, and it took some time before they learned about Edison's use of Japanese bamboo and did the same. Hakunetsusha started selling the bulbs in 1890. Thus, although America was unquestionably earlier in innovation and was a dominant producing country by the time Hakunetsusha started, it is worth noting that the Japanese started the industry with the delay of only about a decade.

Since Japan did not have a means to protect the domestic industries owing to the Unequal Treaty (see Chapter 2), Hakunetsusha met with fierce competition from imports. Its bulb cost about 60 per cent more than the imports and the quality was poorer. The company, even though it managed to survive with the booms after the Sino-Japanese war of 1894–5 and the Russo-Japanese war of 1904–5, and also owing to the international price increase caused by an electric bulb cartel of European manufacturers in 1903, was in an extremely precarious financial condition in the early years of the twentieth century.

In 1905, the company, having been renamed Tokyo Denki (Tokyo Electric) by this time, asked for financial and technological assistance from General Electric (GE) of the USA. General Electric acquired a 51 per cent share of the ownership, sent a vice president, and provided the technology for bulb-making. Production equipment was bought from GE, and GE's budgetary and accounting systems were introduced. Tokyo Denki soon started selling the products with GE's trademark. With these measures, the product quality improved and the production cost decreased significantly. For instance, the use of tungsten filament invented at GE in 1910 was soon adopted by Tokyo Denki. Later it started its own research efforts and, by 1929, the number of laboratory staff had increased to 100. Two critical innovations, a dual filament bulb and a frosted bulb, were completed at this laboratory and were copied worldwide (Tokyo Denki Kabushiki Kaisha, 1940).

Around the same time, Tanaka Seisakusho also became partly owned by GE. As stated above, after the death of Tanaka Hisashige in 1881, his adopted son took over the company. At first, he succeeded in expanding the company with the production of torpedoes and mines at the request of the Navy, to make it one of the largest manufacturing companies of the time. However, as the Navy started to use competitive bids and then built its own works, the demand decreased substantially and the company started to lose money. The main creditor to the company, Mitsui Bank, took over the insolvent company in 1893 and renamed it Shibaura Seisakusho (Shibaura Engineering Works). The company's main products were steam engines, power generators, and other heavy electrical equipment.

Even though Shibaura had developed its own generators (after copying imported ones), it found its technology still lagging behind that of the USA. Thus, in 1910, it formed a tie-up with GE of America. GE acquired about a quarter of the share and allowed Shibaura to acquire GE's technology by, for instance, sending the engineers to learn at GE.

Consequently, GE had its investment in both Tokyo Denki and Shibaura Seisakusho. Since the main business of the first was light-weight electrical equipment and appliances while that of the latter was biased towards heavy equipment, the two were considered complementary and, with GE's support, they merged in 1939 to become Tokyo Shibaura Denki (Tokyo Shibaura Electric, now Toshiba). General Electric owned 33 per cent of the share, and Mitsui 15 per cent. The relation with GE continued until the beginning of the war and, after the war, resumed in 1953 with GE's 24 per cent shareholding. This percentage, however, has decreased substantially since then.

Before discussing the communications equipment producers, let us briefly discuss Toshiba's main rival, Hitachi. It was established in 1911 by Odaira Namihei, a graduate of the University of Tokyo's Engineering Department, as a plant affiliated to Hitachi Kozan (Hitachi Mine), and became independent nine years later. It started with the production of generators, blowers, transformers, and other heavy electrical equipment to be used in the mine, but soon began selling the products to other customers and expanded the business to industrial machines and lighter electrical equipment. Although Hitachi grew in the boom during World War I, Shibaura Seisakusho remained dominant until the mid-1920s.

Hitachi is rather unique among the Japanese producers in its reliance on its own R&D efforts (together with reverse-engineering) and the absence of any tie-up with foreign companies until the end of World War II. By contrast, most others had such tie-ups to gain technological knowledge: in addition to Toshiba's tie-up with GE, Mitsubishi Denki (Mitsubishi Electric), separated from Mitsubishi Zosen (Mitsubishi Shipbuilding, now Mitsubishi Heavy Industries; see Chapter 10) in 1921, tied up with Westinghouse (with 10 per cent share ownership) in 1923; and Fuji Denki (Fuji Electric) started in 1923 as a joint venture between Siemens (30 per cent ownership) and Furukawa Kogyo (Furukawa Mine). That Hitachi could survive and expand against the competition of these firms, without the benefit of formal technological importation, is a testimony to the capability of its Japanese engineers to learn through reverse-engineering.

It must also be noted that even the companies with foreign affiliations made a significant amount of their own R&D efforts. The two predecessors of Toshiba, Tokyo Electric and Shibaura Engineering, established their laboratories in 1918 and 1921, respectively, while affiliated with GE. Hitachi established its laboratory in 1934, though it started an independent R&D section much earlier in 1918.

8.3 MANUFACTURERS OF COMMUNICATIONS EQUIPMENT

Let us turn to communications equipment. We have already discussed the start of the telegraph in Japan. In 1877, only a year after Bell's invention, Kobusho experimented with the first telephone in Japan using American equipment. The engineers at the Kobusho factory started an effort to make telephone receivers by reverse-engineering and, in the following year, came up with the first prototype. One of the engineers, Oki Kibataro, felt that a bright future lay ahead in the business and left Kobusho to start his own company, named Meikosha (later Oki). The telephone business itself was not established until 1890 partly because of scepticism (for instance, hiring a messenger was thought to be a cheaper and more reliable means of conveying information) and partly because of the controversy within the government as to whether the service should be provided by the government or the private sector. Immediately following the introduction of the service (as a government business), however, the public was easily convinced of its convenience, and demand rose. Both imported and domestic equipment (receivers, switchboards, wire, etc.) was used and, as the sole domestic producer, Meikosha prospered.

Western Electric (WE) of the USA saw a growing market in Japan and wished to enter by means of a joint venture. At first, it approached Meikosha but the prospering Oki proposed conditions too severe for WE to accept. It finally decided to team with Iwadare Kunihiko, who had been WE's sales agent in Japan, and established Nihon Denki (Nippon Electric Co., now NEC) in 1898, with WE owning 54 per cent of the share, and Iwadare 33 per cent. To start the business, NEC bought the land and plant of Miyoshi Shoichi, who had one of the largest manufacturing factories at the time but was on the brink of bankruptcy as a consequence of too rapid expansion and the depression at the time. As mentioned earlier, Miyoshi was another Tanaka disciple at the Kobusho factory and also Fujioka's collaborator in establishing Hakunetsusha. Hence, one can see a historical connection from Tanaka, the master of pre-Meiji technology, to not only Oki but also NEC, in addition to Toshiba.

Iwadare's career illustrates another (and newer) type of engineer at the time. He studied electrical engineering at Kogakuryo (the College of Engineering) one year after Fujioka, worked at Kobusho for four years, went to the USA and got a job at GE, came back to Japan to be the engineering manager of Osaka Dento (Osaka Electric Lamp Company), and, after eight years, quit this post to start his own business as an agent for GE and WE. Thus, his career, like Fujioka's, may be said to be more 'Western' than Oki's or Miyoshi's in that he studied engineering in a modern university planned and taught by Europeans, was employed as an engineer in large companies and then changed jobs, and had the experience of going abroad.

In the beginning, NEC not only produced telephones and other communications equipment with WE's technology, but also copied WE's management methods (including the accounting system and work management) and bought WE's supplies, ranging from machines and materials to notepaper. Gradually, however, it replaced them with their own or with products procured domestically. With the expansion of the telephone network, the company expanded rapidly and competed against Oki as well as new entrants such as Toshiba, Hitachi and Fuji (whose communication equipment business was later hived off as Fujitsu). NEC started its R&D department in 1926, which was expanded into a separate laboratory in 1939. From just assimilating WE's technology at first, it gradually increased its own R&D efforts and started producing innovations that often surpassed WE's (Nihon Denki Kabushiki Kaisha, 1972).

8.4 GOVERNMENT AND MILITARY RESEARCH INSTITUTES

Two national research institutes, among others, contributed to the technological development of the industry—Denki Shikensho (Electric Laboratory) and Kaigun Gijutsu Kenkyusho (Naval Research Institute).

In 1875, while the government was extending the telegraph cable line, it established a small laboratory, Gaishi Shikensho (Insulator Laboratory), within Kobusho (the Ministry of Industry), to test the insulators it procured. At first, it had only three workers under the supervision of a British engineer, but started to expand gradually. In particular, Shida Rinzaburo, one of the first graduates from Kogakuryo (two years ahead of Fujioka), joined the laboratory in 1879 and started conducting research on telecommunications in addition to its original role of testing the procured equipment. In 1885, Teishinsho (the Ministry of Telecommunication) was set up to operate the telegraph and telephone services and the laboratory was transferred to this ministry from Kobusho. In 1891 it became Denki Shikensho, and expanded its research to include that on the generation and application of electric power.

Earlier work at the laboratory included the design (and the supervision of the construction) of a cable network, including the submarine telegraph to colonized Taiwan, research on relays and batteries to improve the quality of the telephone service, experiments with wireless communications, improvement on power transmission, and, later, the study of vacuum tubes. However, the technological level was generally behind that of the USA and Europe; for instance, the study on vacuum tubes relied on supplies from Tokyo Denki (later Toshiba), which produced them with GE's technology (Nihon Denshin Denwa Kosha, 1960).

Between and during the two world wars, the research at the laboratory also included that on wireless radio, facsimile, television, and high-frequency waves, some of which was done in collaboration with the military. After Japan's defeat, the laboratory was reorganized in 1948 and the research on communications was separated from that on electricity. The first part became Denki Tsushin Kenkyusho (Electrical Communications Laboratories; ECL) as a research institute within Nihon Denshin Denwa Kosha (Nippon Telegraph and Telephone Public Corporation), a national company detached from the ministry under the order of the Allied Powers and, later in 1985, privatized as Nihon Denshin Denwa Kabushiki Kaisha (Nippon Telegraph and Telephone Co.; NTT). The remaining part of the laboratory was transferred to the Ministry of International Trade and Industry to become an institute within its Kogyo Gijustu In (Agency for Industrial Science and Technology; AIST). The latter was called Denki Shikensho at first, but was renamed Denshi Gijutsu Sogo Kenkyusho (Densoken or Electro-Technical Laboratory; ETL). As we will show, ETL would play a significant role in the development of semiconductors in Japan.

Before and during World War II, the Army and Navy had several laboratories, many of which belonged to arsenals and naval shipyards. For our discussion here, Kaigun Gijutsu Kenkyusho (Naval Research Institute; NRI) is probably the most important. It was established in 1923 to integrate several laboratories within the Navy. It had eight departments: physical science, chemistry, electricity, radio, shipbuilding, materials, sound, and experimental psychology.

One of the main themes in the electricity and radio departments was the development of radar. When Germany, the USA, and the UK started using radar, Japan had no knowledge of it and, when World War II started, NRI increased the development efforts. By the time Japan had developed the first radar using meter waves, the other countries had already developed microwave radar. NRI intensified its development effort with certain technological help from Germany (Japan's ally during the war) and the collaboration of suppliers and a few other research institutes. However, the lack of knowledge, the constraint on budget, and the lack of understanding within the Navy, where spiritualism dominated scientific thinking, all hindered the efforts of the NRI researchers. Quite likely, the technological inferiority that resulted was one of the causes of Japan's defeat.[2]

None the less, NRI's role in Japan's technological development cannot be overlooked, because many of the researchers went into private businesses when it was disbanded after the war and played significant roles in the development of Japan's electrical equipment and electronics industry. These included Ohuchi Atsuyoshi, who would lead R&D at NEC and become the vice-chairman, and Kiyomiya Hiroshi, who would become the chairman at Fujitsu. At its peak of activity, NRI also asked for the participation of outside researchers including several professors, such as Watanabe Yasushi of Tohoku University, who would later help Denki Shikensho to start research on the transistor, and Asada Tsunesaburo of Osaka University, who would recommend his student, Morita Akio, to join NRI; and several researchers from other institutes, such as Takayanagi Kenjiro of the research institute at Nihon Hoso Kyokai (NHK or Japan Broadcasting Corporation), who had been one of the world pioneers of television. Takayanagi and several members of his research team later moved to Nihon Victor (Victor Company of Japan; JVC) and played a significant role in developing television technology and later VHS video-cassette recorders. Takayanagi himself later became JVC's vice-president. One of his staff who moved to JVC, Shinji Ichiro, became the chairman.

One of the suppliers to the Army and Navy was a company named Nihon Sokuteiki (Japan Measuring Instruments). Its director, Ibuka Masaru, was known as an inventor of relays and other electrical equipment, and often participated in NRI's research seminars. After the war, Ibuka started his own company, and some of the people who knew Ibuka at NRI, most notably Morita, joined him in this enterprise. The company, named Tokyo Tsushin Kogyo in the beginning, aimed at developing electronic products for consumers and succeeded in developing two new products—tape recorders and transistor radios— commercially as well as technologically. The popularity of these products put the company onto a course for rapid expansion. Its brand name became known worldwide, later being adopted as the company name as well. This of course was the start of Sony.[3] Their use of transistors for consumer appliances was a novel idea and may have been one of the key factors in Japan's rapid technical progress in semiconductors. In the next section, therefore, we will discuss the development of transistor technology and then, in Section 8.6, we will come back to Sony's story.

8.5 THE START OF RESEARCH ON SEMICONDUCTORS[4]

As is well known, the transistor was invented in December 1947 by William Shockley, John Bardeen, and Walter Bratten of Bell Laboratories and was reported in a rather obscure article in *Time* in the 12 July issue of the following year. A few people in Japan learned of this invention from this article or from an American engineer at the General Headquarters (GHQ) of the Allied Powers, who had been connected with Bell Labs. ETL, still called Denki Shikensho, organized a study group. The aforementioned Watanabe of Tohoku University acted as an advisor, in addition to conducting his own research at his university with his student, Nishizawa Jun'ichi, who would later make important inventions in semiconductor technology. The central members were two ETL researchers, Hatoyama Michio, who joined ETL after working with the Institute of Physical and Chemical Research (Riken; see Chapter 2) and NRI, and Kikuchi Makoto.[5] There were also members from other universities and firms, such as Toshiba, NEC and Hitachi.[6] The main source of information was *Physical Review* and other American literature which was only available at GHQ's library. With the copying machine being as yet unavailable, they made copies of any related articles by typing or handwriting and tried to analyse them at the monthly meetings.

Kikuchi soon started an experiment on the transistor. According to Kikuchi's (1992) own account, Hatoyama ordered Kikuchi to start an experiment knowing only that amplification had taken place at Bell Labs when two needles were put very close together onto the surface of a geranium or silicon crystal. Kikuchi bought a piece of silicon and tried to put two tungsten needles onto it as closely as possible. After two months of repeated experiments, which resulted in failure, he learned that the Americans had used 99.9999999 per cent pure (the so-called nine-nine) silicon while he could only get 90 per cent pure silicon (that is, silicon too impure to make a transistor). He thus had to begin an effort to purify silicon; however, the lack of high-quality materials and equipment was a big obstacle. As Kikuchi (1992: 74, our translation) puts in, 'in order to achieve something in technology, it is absolutely necessary that the technological levels in several related key fields be sufficiently enhanced as well.' The Japanese technology level in such fields was still far below that in the USA, and the researchers had to struggle to devise ways to produce the necessary materials and equipment themselves, have the suppliers produce them, or find other ways to circumvent the problems.

It is from this experience that Kikuchi (1992: 78) argues that 'some people say that the transistor was just a borrowed technology. I would like to say from my own experience that the transistor is a kind of thing that, if you can copy it, it in itself is a spectacular achievement.' This statement clearly indicates that reverse-engineering is by no means an easy task: a country has to possess a high level of technological capabilities to be able to replicate foreign advanced products and learn by reverse-engineering. As we have been repeatedly arguing in this book, such capabilities were present in Japan. Even more important, there were people willing to take hardship and risk to accumulate such capabilities, which, we believe, have been the single most important factor for Japan's success in catching-up.

In 1955, Kikuchi and his team finally succeeded in making a transistor and, around the same time, a few others, including those at ECL and NEC, also succeeded. The technology was still far from practical and, when Western Electric (WE) started to sell the basic technology, many Japanese firms bought it and, since WE did not sell the production know-how, they had to buy it from GE, RCA, or Westinghouse. It should be noted, nevertheless, that, in absorbing the licensed technology and starting production, the previous experience of making a transistor by themselves certainly helped these firms.

8.6   MASS PRODUCTION OF TRANSISTORS: THE CASE OF SONY

Probably the most noteworthy case of a firm importing a technology and developing it further was Sony. In 1952, when Sony had already made a success in developing and marketing tape recorders, but was still insecure and small with about 120 employees, Ibuka went to the USA to investigate the possibility of selling his tape recorders. While he was in New York, he learned that WE had started selling the transistor patent. Ibuka, who was determined to make Sony a producer of innovative consumer appliances, thought of making portable radios with transistors and went to WE to buy the patent. Western Electric advised against Ibuka's plan because the production of transistors was as yet extremely unsteady, and was considered unsuitable for civil uses that would require the price to stay below a marketable level, as opposed to selling to military and other public users who would scarcely mind paying a high price. Yet, Ibuka was determined.

The problem for Sony, however, was to get an approval from MITI. As stated in Chapter 2, foreign exchanges were still controlled by the government and Sony had to obtain MITI's approval to import the technology from WE. To MITI officials, the transistor technology hardly appeared to be promising and, moreover, they did not consider the tiny new company sufficiently capable of absorbing the imported technology. It took Ibuka about six months of visits and persuasion before he finally got the approval.[7] It is thus no wonder that Morita (1986: 66), Ibuka's partner at Sony, insists that 'MITI has not been the great benefactor of the Japanese electronics industry that some critics seem to think it has.'

Acquiring WE's patent and MITI's approval was, in fact, merely a small first step. After all, as stated above, WE itself had advised them not to use transistors for radios because the quality was so poor and production so difficult. Sony started the development effort by sending Iwama Kazuo (previously at NRI; later to become Sony's president) to WE. Western Electric sold Sony the basic technology but not production know-how; so, although they allowed Iwama to visit the factory and answered his questions, they gave no written instructions and prohibited his making notes or taking pictures at the factory. Iwama tried his best to understand the production process, made drawings of the equipment from memory, and sent detailed notes to the engineers in Tokyo with which they started making the equipment and experimenting with production. They decided to try the so-called 'grown-type' transistors even though the 'alloy-type' was more common in the USA and was considered easier to make, because the former, Sony assumed, had characteristics more desirable for radios and was presumably more suitable for mass production.

In 1954, after making hundreds of transistors without success and spending 100 million yen (0.3 million dollars), which was pushing Sony to the brink of bankruptcy, it finally came up with a product. Yet, the production was so unstable that the yield could not achieve more than 5 per cent; that is, only five transistors in every hundred were good enough to make radios. Yet Ibuka decided to go ahead in the belief that 'even if the yield rate is so poor, there is a chance for improvement if we try hard and, if it can be improved to the level of, say, 50 per cent, the cost should become one tenth and we will be able to make huge profits' (Nakagawa, 1981: 64, our translation). Such a spirit to challenge the risk and technological problems, and the belief in its own capability must be the very basic factors of entrepreneurship as discussed in Chapter 1.

Although the product was at first considered a flop because of the poor sound quality, young consumers liked the portability and the small consumption of batteries. It gradually started to sell well and became a hit product. This boom, however, caused two problems for Sony. First, owing to the still poor yield rate, the production could not catch up with the demand. And secondly, larger rival firms started to make their own transistor radios, making alloy-type transistors with the know-how of RCA and other US firms. This rapid imitation and entry activity would illustrate the extent of competition in the Japanese industry.

The only solution was to reduce defects. According to Ibuka, it was the instinct and insistence of a female production worker to scrutinize all the processes to find out the causes of defects. Following her suggestions, the engineers started the cumbersome task of testing every product at every point of the process and came to the conclusion that the use of antimony caused the problem. After several trials, they started using phosphorus instead and the yield rate greatly improved (Aida, 1991: vol. 1).[8] This innovation helped Sony to solve both of the problems above and put the company in a far more advantageous position in its competition against other larger rivals. With this success, Sony became a household name and started its growth towards becoming a multinational.

This case illustrates the willingness of production workers to participate in improving the product and the production process. Although it can be misleading to generalize this observation to other companies or other industries, one cannot fail noting its similarity to the often observed participation of Japanese shop-floor workers in improving the production process, a practice called *kaizen* (a Japanese word for 'improvement'). The similarity is also apparent with the experience of Kawasaki Steel discussed in Section 7.6.

From the policy viewpoint, one notes the difference between the US firms, which had by this time accumulated technologies in various related fields and had stable and generous customers in the Defense Department and other government agencies, and the Japanese firms, which could rely neither on such related technologies nor on the defence market and therefore had to develop the consumer market to achieve growth. It is true that, as noted earlier, MITI's ETL contributed by providing information and research manpower; however, none of Sony's engineers had attended the ETL's study meetings and MITI in fact tried to discourage Sony from acquiring the foreign technology. Sony struggled to solve the technological problems, because it was determined to (and it had no choice but to) develop innovative products that would appeal to consumers. As an afterthought, one may be tempted to conclude that the lack of military and space procurement in Japan was fortunate for its industrial development. No doubt, however, it was a hard struggle for growth and not many countries in a similar situation would have succeeded.

The crucial role that the consumer market played in the development of the Japanese electronics industry can be studied in yet another case— calculators. We now turn to this.

8.7 ICS, LSIS, MICROPROCESSORS, AND THE DEVELOPMENT OF CALCULATORS

It is well known that integrated circuits (ICs) became a practical device around 1959 with the invention of solid-state circuits by Jack Kilby of Texas Instruments (TI), and the introduction of planar processing to interconnect circuit elements by Robert Noyce and others at Fairchild

Semiconductors. Noyce soon came to Japan to invest in the production of planar transistors and ICs in Japan but the plan met resistance from MITI. He thus had no choice but to sell the planar technology. It was bought by NEC on the condition that it would pay 4.5 per cent of the sales as royalties and become the sole licensee in Japan. The last clause implied that other Japanese firms wishing to use the technology had to pay royalties to NEC. To avoid this payment, some of the other companies made large R&D efforts so that they could bypass the planar patent. For instance, Hitachi and Toshiba came up with what they called, respectively, the low-temperature passivation method and the perfect crystal technology method.

Texas Instruments similarly planned to invest in Japan in 1964 and applied for approval to start a wholly-owned subsidiary. Again, MITI, fearing that Japanese firms would be kept from the use of the Kilby patent, sabotaged this application. The Japanese government was then pressurised by TI through the White House. In the meantime, NEC, which, as stated above, had the sole right to Fairchild's planar technology in Japan, started to argue that TI's technology infringed Fairchild's patent. Finally, after a long political and legal fight, MITI in 1968 approved TI's plan to set up a subsidiary as a joint venture with Sony. Texas Instruments agreed to let any Japanese party use its technology with the royalty rate at 3.5 per cent, except NEC, which would pay TI a lump sum but no other royalties and instead would not object to TI's use of planar technology.

The development of the semiconductor technology in the USA was mostly carried out by private enterprises, besides Bell Labs, but the research funds provided by the government played a significant role. According to Uenohara et al. (1984: 23), 'in the United States, the Department of Defense was quick to recognize the potential importance of the transistor and invested large amounts of money in its development. In the year 1954 alone, Department of Defense R&D funding for semiconductor technology was greater than the total amount of funding given the Japanese industry by MITI up to 1974.' Although the Japanese and American authors in this article disagree about the extent to which this support by the US government helped the American industry, it would be wrong to regard the Japanese industry as being supported and protected by MITI in contrast to the presumably *laissez-faire* American system.

In addition, a major portion of the American products was bought by the military as well as the computer industry. More than 95 per cent of

US IC production was supplied to the government in 1964 (Uenohara et al., 1984: 22). In Japan, although the procurement by Nippon Telegraph and Telephone (NTT) played an important role, the demand came predominantly from the private sector for civilian use. The demand from calculator producers was particularly conducive to the development of semiconductor technology in Japan.

The first electronic calculator, which still used vacuum bulbs and therefore was bulky and costly, was invented by a British company in 1962. Two years later, Sharp developed the world's first transistor calculator, which was priced at 535,000 yen (US$1,400). It took Sharp several years to develop the product as they had no experience in making computing devices and, therefore, the engineers had to start with a study of the logic of digital computing. Hence, the news of a British company inventing a calculator ahead of them was a disappointment but, in making the final product, the technology learned from this British product helped them.[9] Three other companies, including Sony, also developed calculators through reverse-engineering of the British one.

Encouraged by the commercial success of the product, Sharp started a development effort for an IC-based calculator. Since Sharp did not make ICs at the time, Sasaki Tadashi, who was leading Sharp's development team, visited several IC producers, and tried to persuade them to develop an IC for calculators and to supply Sharp at a low cost. Sasaki emphasized the advantage of scale economies with the promise of buying a large quantity. The IC producers were reluctant to accept Sharp's offer because ICs had been basically used for computers and hence the producers were not familiar with mass production. Mitsubishi Electric, being a latecomer in the production of ICs, took the chance and, in 1966, Sharp introduced its first IC calculator using 145 Mitsubishi-made bipolar ICs, priced at 350,000 yen (a little less than $1,000).[10]

Sasaki, however, realized the limitation of bipolar technology in increasing the density and thereby reducing the size of the calculator. Thus, in the following year, he introduced a calculator using fifty-six MOS (metal oxide semiconductor) ICs. Although MOS technology had been known to be superior for its capacity to increase the density of circuits, there were still many problems to be solved. In particular, the yield in production remained surprisingly low until the real cause was eventually found to be the contamination of the production process by alkaline ions, salt sodium in particular. Thus, Mitsubishi, Hitachi, and NEC, which supplied MOS ICs to Sharp by Sasaki's persuasion, and several other firms, turned down Sasaki's next request to produce MOS LSIs for calculators.[11] He then went to the USA and visited Fairchild, TI, Motorola, RCA, and others, but none of them accepted Sasaki's offer. As a last resort, Sasaki visited Rockwell, which at first turned down the offer but changed its mind the following day and managed to inform Sasaki of the news just as he was to board a flight to Japan.

Apparently, the main reason for rejecting Sasaki's offer differed between the Japanese firms and the US firms (Aida, 1991; Nakagawa, 1981). For the Japanese firms, the instability in MOS technology was the main concern. The American firms were more advanced techno-logy-wise and at least some of them had partially solved the instability problem. What worried them was the large volume and the low unit price Sharp offered—3 million units at $10 each. For US firms used to supplying a small amount of high-margin semiconductors to computer makers and the government, Sharp's offer was beyond imagination and must have appeared extraordinarily risky.

Sharp introduced the first LSI calculator into the market in 1969. It was the first pocketable calculator and the first with a price less than 100,000 yen (less than $300). It immediately became a hit and brought huge profits to Sharp and Rockwell. In addition, the experience that Sharp's engineers gained through working with Rockwell gave invalu-able expertise as Rockwell's LSI technology was far more advanced.

The use of LSIs, however, made market entry easier. Many Japanese firms in fact bought LSIs from US producers and started selling their own calculators, which included Canon who bought TI's calculator technology,[12] and Sharp's main rival, Casio. In 1971, there were thirty-three firms (including several foreign firms) selling 210 different calcu-lators. Naturally, the price fell rapidly and Casio caused a sensation in 1972 by selling the 'Casio-Mini', which had only a six-digit display but was priced at a mere 12,800 yen ($36), a surprising drop from the 535,000 yen, the price of the first transistor calculator Sharp introduced only eight years before.

This so-called 'Calculator War' did not last long. Smaller firms, some of which made calculators in a tiny factory with, say, twenty workers, could not follow the rapid technical change and were forced to close. Many US firms set up their plants for semiconductors and/or calculators in South-east Asia to take advantages of the low wage costs and many Asian firms entered as well. However, due to the poor quality control in these plants, many defects occurred, causing some of the

Japanese firms buying from them to suffer and go bankrupt, and some of the others to switch to Japanese suppliers. The Japanese suppliers had by then established LSI technology and their reliability in quality and delivery helped them to regain a position as the main suppliers of semiconductors to calculator producers.[13]

The calculator war eventually ended leaving only two survivors, Sharp and Casio. One of the last to leave was a company named Nippon Calculating Machine Sales (usually called Busicom after its brand name), which played a significant role in Intel's development of microprocessors. Busicom was planning to develop a calculator that could calculate according to stored programs, as computers do. The first product—introduced in 1967—could handle twenty different calculations, from solving simultaneous system of equations to calculating interest, according to the cards inserted into the attached card-reader. The company then planned using read-only memories (ROMs) to store the programs. In this calculator, they wanted to use LSIs but, because Busicom was also making other products, such as cash registers and scientific calculators, they wanted to have LSIs that could be used for different purposes and controlled by appropriate programs stored in the ROMs. It asked Intel to develop such LSIs because Kojima Yoshio, the president, was impressed by Robert Noyce, who had just started Intel and visited Japan to sell the random-access memories (RAMs) it had developed.

Busicom's engineer, Shima Masatoshi, went to Intel and perplexed the engineers there by requesting the development of non-custom LSIs. Ted Hoff of Intel struggled for two months to find a way to comply with Busicom's request in a simplified way and came up with the idea of the microprocessor, a one-chip computer. Shima helped Intel's engineers in designing the logic, and the first microprocessor, Intel 4004, came into the world in 1971. Busicom soon introduced microprocessor-driven calculators into the market, which did not sell as well as Busicom hoped it would, because of the severe competition by the aforementioned low-cost calculators developed by Casio and Sharp. The company went bankrupt in a few years and Kojima now regrets not having applied for a patent on the microprocessor jointly with Intel (Aida, 1991).

In the meantime, Intel realized the wide applicability of the microprocessor and, in two years, it enhanced the capacity by developing an 8-bit microprocessor, Intel 8080, again with Shima's collaboration (Intel 4004 was a 4-bit microprocessor). This microprocessor, as is well-known, triggered the PC (personal computer) revolution.

8.8   CONCLUSION WITH REMARKS ON THE ROLE OF POST-WAR GOVERNMENT POLICIES

In this chapter, we discussed how the electrical and communications equipment industry accumulated their technologies. The industry is too vast and diverse to be discussed in its entirety in a short chapter, and we have necessarily confined our discussion to that of the start of the industry during the Meiji era and that of the development of semiconductors in the post-war period, in particular, its relation to consumer products, such as radios and calculators.

From the first discussion, we identified the following characteristics, some of which, we note, are also commonly found in other industries. First, when the Japanese industry started, it was technologically behind the USA and Europe but the lag was tolerable—a marked difference from the current developing countries. Secondly, as a consequence, imported technologies were not entirely unrelated to the indigenous technologies, and some of the entrepreneurs and engineers could utilize the skills and knowledge they accumulated in the pre-Meiji period. Thirdly, at the same time, those engineers educated at colleges and other institutions established by the Meiji government and taught initially by foreign professors, greatly contributed to the Japanese industry's assimilating the Western technologies.

Fourthly, foreign technologies were actively imported through joint ventures, technology contracts, reverse-engineering, and so forth. The Japanese had the capability to absorb or adapt the imported technologies, and the ability to run joint ventures successfully. In addition, many of them had a strong desire to become independent of foreign dominance of technology—one may call it nationalism—as illustrated most clearly by Hitachi's Odaira.

Finally, the government played an important role in establishing science and engineering education systems, establishing telegraph and telephone networks with equipment procured mainly from domestic producers, guaranteeing demand through military procurement, and sponsoring research at government institutions, such as Electric Laboratory, and the Army and Navy, including Naval Research Institute. Such policies, together with active entrepreneurship in the private sector and efforts to raise technological and managerial capabilities, must be responsible for Japanese industrial development.

When World War II ended, Japanese firms had to resume the

catch-up process. The situation may have been even worse than that of the early Meiji era, owing to the technological gap which had widened as the USA did active research during the war, and also to the post-war prohibition of defence research and military procurement. Thus, almost all the firms resumed their relationship with US or European firms in order to import technology. Even firms like Hitachi, which had remained independent prior to the war, entered into contracts to import technologies from such companies as RCA, GE, Phillips, and Western Electric. As a consequence, royalty payments by the industry greatly exceeded the receipts. They still do. Yet, with continuous innovation by Japanese firms, the receipts have increased much faster than the payments: during the 20-year period of 1971–90, the receipts increased 28 times while the payments increased 4 times. The payment : receipt ratio has declined as a consequence from 12.2 to 1.6.[14]

Lacking defence-related procurement, Japanese firms had to rely on the consumer market, besides NTT's procurement. We have already shown that, in the mid-1960s, nearly all the ICs produced in the USA were bought by the government. By 1982, this proportion had decreased to 17.5 per cent, with the remaining 72.4 per cent bought for industrial uses and 10.5 per cent for consumer uses. In comparison, in Japan in the same year, the majority, 55.4 per cent, were bought for consumer uses including calculators (Itami, 1988: 115).

This dependence on consumer markets and the presence of strong market rivalry, as shown in the cases of transistor radios and calculators, forced the firms to reduce costs by mass production and reduced defects, developing marketable products, and raising productivity in assembling. Together with NTT's strict quality regulation, the firms had to be aware of the need to improve the products and process (*kaizen*) and to maintain clean and organized shop-floors (*seiri seiton*). They encouraged the workers to be conscious in such practices and, with the help of the statistical quality control technique taught by William Deming (who came to Japan on GHQ's invitation) and others, improved the quality and productivity gradually.

We do not wish to imply that the government played no role at all. In fact, they did. Although much discussion of the post-war government policies has been made in Chapter 3, let us summarize their roles in the post-war development of the electrical equipment and electronics industry. First, the government maintained a large market for Japanese firms by protecting the industry from imports and direct investment before the trade and capital liberalization of the late 1960s. Such protection was most conspicuous in the case of computers and components, and also in telephone equipment that NTT bought exclusively from Japanese producers. The classical infant industry argument may be applied to this protection and nurturing policy. The restriction of direct foreign investment into Japan left foreign firms with few choices other than undertaking joint ventures with Japanese partners or licensing technologies to Japanese firms. Either way, they could not stop the flow of technologies to Japanese firms.

Secondly, the government controlled technology importation until the capital liberalization of 1967. The effect was twofold. On the one hand, this control guaranteed the allocation of dollars to be paid as royalties to importing firms. On some occasions, it also prevented Japanese firms from competing against each other in the race to buy patents and know-how, so as not to weaken their bargaining position. On the other hand, as shown in the case of Sony, it often caused a substantial delay in the firms' acquisition of technologies, thereby raising an entry barrier.

Thirdly, the government research institutes, in particular MITI's ETL and NTT's ECL, benefited the firms both in terms of the spillover of research outcome and the supply of researchers. For instance, ETL played a significant role in experimenting with transistors and diffusing the information to the private sector. Often it also acted as a coordinator in research associations. However, as the firms accumulated technological knowledge and increased their research budgets, the role of ETL as a technological pioneer and a disseminator of technological knowledge diminished.

ECL often collaborated with the so-called NTT family firms, primarily NEC, Fujitsu, Hitachi, Toshiba, and Oki, in the development of telecommunications equipment and computers. Such a relationship, Fransman (1994) argues, is somewhere between that of AT&T, which vertically integrated the manufacture of equipment, and that of British Telecom, which basically kept equipment manufacturers at arm's length. It helped NTT to maintain competition among suppliers and yet achieve collaboration in development. The relationship is clearly parallel to the assembler–supplier relationship in, for instance, the automobile industry (Odagiri, 1992: ch. 6). The disadvantage, on the other hand, was difficulty for NTT in accumulating manufacturing know-how that was needed for better design, and to aid procurement from outside suppliers.

Fourthly, the government subsidized R&D activity of the firms through various means. Quantitatively, such subsidy was not large. The ratio to the industry R&D funds was declining and was much smaller than that of the USA, where a large amount of subsidies had been granted by the US government mainly through defence contracts. The proportion of government funds in the R&D expenditures of electronics and communications equipment industry was 42.3 per cent in the USA in 1979 whereas the same proportion for the Japanese semiconductor industry was 12.8 per cent in the same year (Wakasugi, 1984). The proportion in Japan was largest in 1977 at 35.1 per cent when the research at the Very Large-Scale Integrated Circuits Research Association (VLSI RA) was at its peak; still, it was lower than that in the USA and it has been generally declining since then.

Among MITI's subsidies to the semiconductor and computer industry, nearly half were allocated through research associations (JRA) as discussed in Section 3.6. The case of VLSI RA is particularly well known and, in view of the large number of patents granted (more than 1,000) and of papers published (about 460), it has been regarded as a success. Uenohara et al. (1984: 20) argued, for instance, that 'clearly, the VLSI project was a remarkable organizational innovation that essentially succeeded in engendering a new breadth of capability in the Japanese semiconductor industry.' While we do not intend to deny the contribution of the project to technological accumulation of not only the JRA member firms but also equipment manufactures such as Nikon, which became the world's leading manufacturer of wafer-steppers, and the suppliers of various materials and equipment, it is difficult to assert that the participating firms genuinely collaborated with each other and shared all their information (Fransman, 1990). In other words, it is questionable whether the industry would have failed to achieve a similar technical progress without the JRA.

For other JRAs, it is even more difficult to evaluate the performance. In terms of the number of patents per unit of R&D expenditures, JRAs have been generally less productive than individual companies, although the adequacy of the productivity measure may be debated. For futuristic and costly research projects with uncertain outcomes, JRAs can be an appropriate structure because of the public-goods characteristics of such projects. Yet incentives are usually higher for firms doing individual research, because of the competitive pressure and the chance of monopolizing the fruits of the research. In addition, the cost of co-ordinating the participating firms with different cultures may be costly. The aforementioned lower productivity of JRAs may have been caused by these factors.[15]

To conclude, the government policies helped the development of the industry through procurement, protection, national laboratories, engineering education, and subsidies. Yet it remains a moot question whether the Japanese government was particularly active in this respect if compared internationally. Moreover, such policies may well have failed to have the desired effects were it not for the willingness and capability of the private sector to take the opportunities provided. Japanese enterprises in fact had such willingness and were keen in accumulating technological capabilities. Entries were made vigorously and those failing to develop high-quality, marketable products at reasonable costs had to disappear. More than anything else, it was this behaviour of Japanese firms and the resulting evolutionary process of market competition that contributed to the development of the Japanese electrical equipment industry.

9

Automobiles

The history of the Japanese automobile industry is characterized by the initial dominance of foreign producers with scale advantages and superior technology; technology acquisition by Japanese pioneers through reverse-engineering and/or technological tie-ups and then R&D and learning by doing; and plentiful entrepreneurship that resulted in numerous entry attempts and intensive investment under extremely risky circumstances. The government also played an important role in its development through financial incentives, standard setting, procurement by the military and the transportation authority, and protection from foreign competitors. After more than half a century of struggle, Japanese car manufacturers have now caught up with the European and US rivals technologically, and are surpassing them in certain areas. No book on the technology and industrial development of Japan would be complete without a discussion of this industry.[1]

9.1 THE EARLY PERIOD

The first automobile driven in Japan is considered to be a steam-engine car imported from Europe by a foreign trader in 1897, when automobiles were still a novelty, even in Europe. An American established a company in 1901 to import steam-engine cars from a US manufacturer called Locomotive, and sold about ten units to curious Japanese. Yet, until 1903, when two cars, one steam-driven and the other electric-driven, were used as buses in a large exposition, few Japanese had seen automobiles. One of the visitors to this exposition, Yamabane Torao, was impressed and started an effort to make an automobile domestically. This effort produced one steam-driven car but it had so many troubles, particularly with the durability of tyres, that Yamabane gave up any commercial application. Four years later, domestic production of gasoline-driven cars started with the main parts (including engines, it seems) imported at first but gradually replaced by domestic production.

This effort also collapsed after selling 10 units, 8 of which were bought by the police to add to its stock of 41 European cars and 11 US cars. Similar efforts had been made by more than ten entrepreneurs by the end of Meiji Era in 1910: all failed.

The first significant and persistent effort for automobile production was made by Hashimoto Masujiro. Hashimoto studied at Tokyo College of Engineering (now Tokyo Institute of Technology) and, after two years of working in a mining company, went to the USA for three years with a scholarship from the Japanese government to learn engineering in a steam-engine manufacturing company. In 1911, after returning from the USA and working for a few Japanese companies, he established a company named Kaishinsha, with the goal of manufacturing and selling automobiles. Because of limited capital the enterprise was tiny, employing only seven workers. Hashimoto, therefore, had to support himself by importing and repairing British cars, through which he learned the British technology.

The development was by no means easy: the first product was a failure for lack of the casting technology needed to make a sufficiently durable engine. He struggled for a few more years before finally producing a viable product. It had a 2-cylinder engine with 10 horsepower, carrying four passengers. Although he had to rely on imports for some components including tyres, wheels, spark-plugs, and ball-bearings, he managed to use domestic products for the majority of the components. He named the car 'Dat' after the initials of the three outside investors in Kaishinsha. The car was received favourably in a national exposition in 1914. After developing a 4-cylinder version of Dat, he expanded Kaishinsha into a joint stock company to produce and sell the product. However, the competition with Ford, GM, and other imports as severe, and Kaishinsha could sell only seven Dats by 1917, far lower than the commercially viable level.

Import of foreign cars (passenger cars, trucks, buses, etc.) increased in the meantime and completely dominated the market: more than 200 cars had been imported by 1910 and 6,800 by 1920. The Great Earthquake in Tokyo of 1923 increased this trend further because all the train services had been disrupted and automobiles were urgently needed to deliver food, medicine, and other necessities. For instance, the City of Tokyo at once imported 800 Model T trucks from Ford to be used as buses and, in 1924 alone, more than 4,000 cars were imported. Naturally, Ford found the Japanese market promising and decided to establish a Japanese subsidiary with an assembly plant in Yokohama. It imported all the production equipment from the USA and, in 1925, started knock-down production with the capacity of 200 cars a day. General Motors followed two years later with a plant in Osaka having the capacity of 130 cars a day. In addition, a Japanese company, Kyoritsu, had a tie-up with Chrysler for knock-down production, though the production level was much smaller in comparison to Japan Ford and Japan GM. Apparently, local production was advantageous to the American car makers because of saving in freight cost, lower wage rates in Japan, and the lower tariff rates the Japanese government set for components compared with complete cars. With their cost advantages and quality, the market became dominated by the US producers (see Table 9.1).

Direct investment by Ford and GM made a significant impact on the Japanese automobile industry, not only by their huge investment but also by a number of innovations they brought to the country. First, the conveyor-operated, mass-production system pioneered by Henry Ford was introduced into Japan for the first time, setting examples for Nissan and Toyota to assimilate when they started their own mass production later. Secondly, though all the components were at first imported from the USA, they were gradually procured domestically under pressure from the Japanese government worried by the increasing trade imbalance. Japanese firms had just started production of most of the components, such as batteries, glass, wheels, tyres, and other rubber products, and, finding their technological level still low, Ford and GM had to assist many of them, fostering technology transfer. They also taught Japanese producers the concept of quality control. Thirdly, Ford and GM made huge investments to create the chain of 70–80 dealers each across the country. To emphasize after-sale service, these dealers were required to have repair and service shops and keep stocks of replacement parts. They also provided monthly instalment plans, and Ford and GM provided the necessary finances to the dealers.

Needless to say, since the presence of these foreign firms with the advantages in scale, cost, and quality created barriers for Japanese potential entrants, it is difficult to assess whether they fostered or hindered the development of the Japanese domestic industry. As will be discussed in the next section, the policies taken by the Japanese government, which was desperate to encourage the production by domestic firms for economic as well as defence reasons, were in effect to help domestic producers to overcome these entry barriers.

TABLE 9.1 The supply of automobiles before World War II

Year	Domestic	Import	Knock-down			
			Ford	GM	Kyoritsu	Total
1922		752				
1923		1,938				
1924	about 740	4,063				
1925	by 1925	1,765	3,437			3,437
1926	245	2,381	8,677			8,677
1927	302	3,895	7,033	5,635		12,668
1928	347	7,883	8,850	15,491		24,341
1929	437	5,018	10,674	15,745	1,251	29,338
1930	458	2,591	10,620	8,049	1,015	19,678
1931	436	1,887	11,505	7,478	1,201	20,199
1932	880	997	7,448	5,893	760	14,087
1933	1,681	491	8,156	5,942	998	15,082
1934	2,247	896	17,244	12,322	2,574	33,458
1935	5,094	934	14,865	12,492	3,612	30,787
1936	12,186	1,117				30,997
1937	18,055	1,100				31,000
1938	24,388	500				20,000
1939	34,514					
1940	46,041					
1941	46,498					
1942	37,188					
1943	25,879					
1944	21,762					
1945	6,726					

Note: The numbers of Ford, GM, and Kyoritsu may not add up to the total because of different data sources.

Source: Nihon Jidosha Kaigi Sho, *Nihon Jidosha Sangyo no Hensen to Shorai no Arikata*. Cited from Nihon Jidosha Kogyo Kai (1988: 16)

9.2 EARLY GOVERNMENT POLICIES

The experience during the Russo-Japanese War (1904–5) taught the Army that they could not rely on horses to transport soldiers, munitions, and other necessities to the vast Chinese and Siberian Continent. Thus, they bought a few trucks from America and Europe, tested them, learned the technology, and even manufactured two trucks in their arsenal in 1911. The news that trucks and tanks were extensively used in

Europe during World War I further convinced the Army of an immediate need to nurture car production by domestic firms.

In 1918, after surveying the military procurement policy in Britain, France and Germany, the government enacted the Military Motor Vehicle Subsidy Law (*Gun-yo Jidosha Hojo Ho*) to subsidize production of trucks and buses by Japanese-owned companies and the civilian purchase of these vehicles, on condition that the purchased vehicles might be requisitioned by the Army in times of war. The subsidies of 1,500 yen to the producer, 1,000 yen to the purchaser, and 300 yen for maintenance in the case of one ton to one and a half ton trucks must have been significant in view of the fact that the first Datsun, a 500 cc passenger car introduced in 1931 (to be discussed), was priced at 1,200 yen (Nissan Jidosha Kabushiki Kaisha, 1965). Although restrictive clauses in the subsidy programme, such as the prohibition of design change and cumbersome paper submission reduced the merit of the subsidies, the policy gave an expectation of increased procurement and thereby attracted three companies to start production.

The first was Tokyo Gasu Denki (Tokyo Gas Electric; TGE) established in 1910 to manufacture gas equipment.[2] It inherited the trial truck production of the arsenal and became the first company to meet the Army's standard in 1919. The second was Kaishinsha who, observing the difficulty in the passenger car market, decided to enter into the production of trucks and, after some difficulties in meeting the Army's standard, was accepted in 1924. The third was Ishikawajima Zosensho (Ishikawajima Shipyard, now Ishikawajima-Harima Heavy Industries; see Chapter 10) which, with the profits from shipbuilding during the boom in World War I, entered into the production of passenger cars and then trucks, first by disassembling a Fiat car to learn the technology and then by buying technology from Wolseley, a major British company at the time.

In addition, several others, including Mitsubishi Shipbuilding (now Mitsubishi Heavy Industries; see Chapter 10), Daihatsu (3-wheel car producer), and other less-known companies, started their efforts to develop qualified vehicles; however, they all failed for technological reasons. As a consequence, despite the Army's efforts, the domestic production under the law was by no means large. During 1918–24, the three companies together produced 160 cars with the subsidy, about 30 per cent of the total car production by Japanese companies. As shown in Table 9.1 above, the market (including trucks and buses) was totally dominated by Ford, GM, and the imports.

The next government initiative occurred in 1930 when the Ministry of Railways made a detailed open test of the three domestic producers, and then in 1931 when the Ministry of Commerce and Industry (MCI, the predecessor to MITI) set up the Survey Committee for the Establishment of the Automobile Industry that included two professors from University of Tokyo, the Presidents of Ishikawajima, TGE, and Dat Jidosha (to be discussed), and government officials from not only MCI but also the Ministry of Railways, the Ministry of Army, and others. In 1932 the committee recommended supporting the mass production of standardized trucks and buses, and integrating the production among the three producers. In this integration plan, like a similar one in the steel industry, one can see the government's belief in scale economies with disregard of individualism and rivalry. This belief, one may be tempted to say, has been the trademark of the Japanese industrial policy: we will later see that similar policy initiatives were taken after World War II.

Although the three companies were reluctant to collaborate, they had no way to oppose the government plan because they were dominated by Ford and GM in the private market and were surviving only with the government procurement and military vehicle subsidy. A joint venture to develop a standardized car started with Ishikawajima working on engines, Dat on transmission, TGE on axles, and the Ministry of Railways on frames. The product, named *Isuzu*, was introduced into the market in 1932. The government gave a subsidy of 500 yen per car, which was later reduced. At the same time, it increased the tariff rate for imported engines and other components to make it equal to that of complete cars in order to encourage Ford and GM to purchase components from domestic suppliers.

Despite these measures, the joint venture lasted for only two years with the production of 750 cars, which were mostly bought by the Army and the Ministry of Railways; however, the experience resulted in a reorganization of the industry and the start of the current Isuzu Jidosha (Isuzu Motors).

The three companies were not the only entrants into the industry. In fact, the number of entry attempts around this time was surprisingly large. Mitsubishi and Kawasaki made some efforts with trucks. More than ten entries were made into motorcycles and three-wheel cars, which were well received by the public for their cheapness and easy handling on narrow Japanese roads. Only two of them, Daihatsu and Mazda, survived to this day. A number of efforts were also made in the passenger car market, including that by Mitsui Shipbuilding, but most were small-scale non-zaibatsu companies. Most failed but Nissan and Toyota were important exceptions. Two facts deserve emphasis. The first is the frequency of entry attempts, clearly indicating the presence of strong entrepreneurship as well as the capability to challenge new technologies. Secondly, the role of established zaibatsu was limited. In fact, they gave up rather early. By contrast, independent entrepreneurs like Aikawa (Nissan), Toyoda (Toyota), and Matsuda (Mazda), not to mention Hashimoto and others in the early period, were more persistent.

9.3 THE START OF NISSAN

William R. Gorham, an American who had studied at the Heald Engineering College in San Francisco, came to Japan in 1918 to sell his design of an aircraft engine but, failing to do so, developed a 2-passenger, 3-wheel car powered by a Harley–Davidson engine. This attempt became known to Kubota Gonshiro, the founder of the present Kubota, the top maker of agricultural machinery and cast iron pipes. He established Jitsuyo Jidosha in Osaka in 1919 and hired Gorham as its chief engineer. Gorham designed the plant, ordered the equipment and some components from the USA, and hired two more Americans to guide inexperienced Japanese workers. Although the plant had the capacity of 50 units per month, the company could sell only 150 units in about a year. Gorham then designed a 4-wheel model but, against the competition of foreign models, the company could sell only about 100 units. The model was re-designed in 1923 by a Japanese engineer, Goto Takayoshi, who had learned with Gorham: he adopted, for instance, a wheel rather than a stick for steering. Gorham had already quit Jitsuyo Jidosha and started working with Tobata Casting. The new model sold about 200 units during 1923–6.

The experience clearly indicated to Kubota that the competition in passenger car market against foreign firms was too keen. In fact, Jitsuyo Jidosha was surviving only by accepting car repair work and subcontracting to the parent Kubota company and, later, to GM. Kubota thus sought to enter into the production of military trucks to gain subsidies, which led to a merger between Kubota's Jitsuyo Jidosha and Hashimoto's Kaishinsha (reorganized as Dat Jidosha Shokai by this time) in 1926 because the latter had a licence to produce military trucks and yet was suffering from losses. Although the new company adopted the name of

Dat Jidosha Seizo and Hashimoto remained as the managing director, it was actually the acquisition of Dat by Jitsuyo. Five years later, this company was acquired by Tobata Imono (Tobata Casting) founded by Aikawa (also spelled Ayukawa) Yoshisuke.

Aikawa, a graduate of the Engineering Department of the University of Tokyo, learned the technology of black-hearted iron casting by working as an apprentice in factories in the USA. He returned and in 1910 founded Tobata Casting to manufacture cast-iron tubing and other products using this technology. Because the products were suitable as components for cars, the company started supplying to Ishikawajima, Dat, and then Ford and GM, thereby accumulating knowledge of the automobile industry.

Aikawa's talent as a manager was so evident that, when the business conglomerate of his brother-in-law, Kuhara Fusanosuke, collapsed, Kuhara asked Aikawa to take over. Kuhara had made a huge success by mining copper at the town of Hitachi, some 200 km north of Tokyo, and then investing the profits into booming but rather unrelated fields, such as shipping, steel, shipbuilding, and trade. Although his conglomerate also included Hitachi Manufacturing, this was established under the leadership of his subordinate, Odaira Namihei, with Kuhara being reluctant to invest (see Chapter 8). The failure in speculative trading by Kuhara Trading and the collapse of the international copper price after World War I caused huge losses to Kuhara, forcing him to ask Aikawa to step in.

Aikawa reorganized Kuhara's businesses as well as his own under the newly established holding company, Nihon Sangyo (abbreviated as Nissan), and, after managing to get Kuhara's business out of crisis, gradually expanded his business to include mining, shipbuilding, electrical equipment (Hitachi), chemicals, cable, construction, fishing, fats, and fire and marine insurance. He also invested heavily in Manchuria and, by the start of World War II, the paid-up capital of Aikawa's Nissan Group was third largest after Mitsui and Mitsubishi. It was the largest among the so-called New Zaibatsu (see Chapter 4). For our purpose here, however, we confine our discussion to the case of Nissan Jidosha (Nissan Motor, simply called Nissan in this chapter).

Dat Jidosha, acquired by Aikawa, had two factories: one in Tokyo, inherited from Kaishinsha and mostly producing military trucks, and the other in Osaka, inherited from Jitsuyo Jidosha and mostly producing passenger cars. Aikawa, who had the dream of selling small passenger cars to the Japanese public, decided to sell a new model of passenger car. Gorham, who had earlier quit Jitsuyo Jidosha to join Tobata Casting, guided Goto at the Osaka plant into developing a new model with a 495 cc engine and two seats. The model was first called 'Datson', meaning the son of Dat, but then renamed to 'Datsun' because the Japanese pronunciation of 'son' meant 'loss' and was considered ominous. It was priced at 1,200 yen when an imported Austin was priced at 1,600 yen. It sold only 150 units in 1932 but the sales increased to 880 units two years later.

In the meantime, the truck production by Dat, Ishikawajima, and TGE increased owing to the demand created by the Manchurian Incident. These companies were reluctant to cooperate with each other in producing the standardized car and the government had to accept their producing separate models. Not being happy with this situation, the government and the Army pressed the companies to merge. Aikawa did not object because he was eager to concentrate on the production of passenger cars. In consequence, the truck business of Dat merged with Ishikawajima and TGE, and became Tokyo Jidosha Kogyo, to be renamed Isuzu Motors after World War II, whereas the passenger car business was at first absorbed into Tobata Casting and then, in 1933, separated as Nissan Jidosha (Nissan Motor) as a subsidiary of Nihon Sangyo holding company and Tobata Casting.

For Aikawa, the objective of Nissan was the mass production and mass sales of passenger cars, in competition with Ford and GM. For this purpose, he built a plant in Yokohama of a scale ten times larger than the previous Osaka plant, and even larger than Japan Ford and Japan GM. He bought the whole production equipment including jigs and tools as well as technology from the Graham-Paige Company in Detroit, and shipped them to Japan. Graham-Paige was the fourteenth largest producer in the USA but was planning to liquidate because of financial difficulties. Gorham acted as the technical adviser, leading the design and other technological planning associated with plant construction as well as the design of improved Datsun models. In addition, several engineers were hired from the USA to cooperate with Gorham.

As a consequence, Nissan's technology was essentially a direct import from the USA, even though its root may be traced to the Japanese pioneer, Hashimoto. Such a course was taken partly because of the availability of Gorham as an adviser and partly because of Aikawa's dream of following Henry Ford in the mass production of inexpensive passenger cars to sell to the Japanese public. Obviously, the technology importation made it possible for Nissan to start production faster and witfi less risk. Nissan, in fact, repeated technology importation after World War II when it formed a tie-up with Austin. This strategy makes a good contrast to Toyota, which essentially chose to accumulate technological capabilities through reverse-engineering.

9.4   THE START OF TOYOTA

Toyoda Sakichi was a typical inventor and entrepreneur of pre-war Japan, much like Thomas Edison, though in a different field. Born in 1867 into a poor carpenter's family, in 1890 he invented the first loom, wooden-made and hand-operated, after several years of struggle. He started selling the looms and making cloth with them, but the business did not prosper. The struggle continued until he invented automatic looms in 1897. This time the business was a success, with a strong demand both for the looms and for the high-quality cloth made with them. He worked further to improve the loom, so that a wider cloth could be made faster and more efficiently. His company, Toyoda Jido Shokki (Toyoda Automatic Loom, now Toyota Automatic Loom), started exporting. The quality of his loom was confirmed when in 1929 the world's largest loom manufacturer, Platt (UK), bought the technology for the price of 100,000 pounds. It is worth noting that Sakichi's development effort over his lifetime was a purely private and independent enterprise. Although Mitsui Bussan (the largest trading company at the time, now Mitsui & Co.; see Chapter 6) from time to time gave financial support or helped Toyoda to sell his products, the relation was not smooth because Sakichi was too independent-minded and technology-oriented in comparison to the more conservative and finance-oriented Mitsui.

Sakichi saw a bright future in automobiles when he visited the USA in 1910: Ford had already started to produce Model T in large quantities. While he was occupied with automatic looms, he encouraged Kiichiro, his son, to enter into automobile production. Kiichiro, who had studied mechanical engineering at the University of Tokyo, joined his father's company in 1920 to help his father develop new looms. Although he waited until 1933 to establish an automobile division within Toyoda Automatic Loom, he prepared gradually for entry into car production. In addition to his accumulating experience and know-how in mechanical engineering through the development of looms, he bought high-quality machines, in fact of too high a quality to be used just for the production of looms, so that the workers could get used to their operation. He was finally convinced that he would be able to make automobiles and invested the fee from Platt and the accumulated profits from loom sales into the newly established automobile division.

The way he organized his development team and collected information shows his talent in creating and utilizing a network of informed people. First, he hired a number of engineers from outside in such fields as steel, tools, and three-wheel cars. He had known some of them at his high school and university, but he came to know others, such as the technicians in the companies supplying to Toyoda Automatic Loom, while working in the loom business. These included an engineer, Suga Takatoshi, who was involved in an earlier effort to produce a car in Nagoya, almost at the centre of Japan's main Honshu island, where Toyoda's loom business was also located. Suga would become an executive director and Kiichiro's chief engineer. In addition, Kiichiro succeeded in hiring Kamiya Shotaro from Japan GM who would establish a chain of dealers and lead Toyota's sales division for nearly half a century.

Secondly, he sought technological and other advice from a number of professors. Many of them were his classmates at the University of Tokyo's Engineering Department. For instance, Kumabe Kazuo, with whom Kiichiro had written a thesis, was an associate professor at the University of Tokyo, and helped Kiichiro to make engines. Kumabe's association with Toyota was consistent and, after World War II, he joined Toyota as an executive director. Kiichiro also gained invaluable information on, say, government policies from his former classmates then working in the Ministry of Railways and the Ministry of Commerce and Industry. In addition, he visited Honda Kotaro, a professor at Tohoku University and world-renowned for his research in steel (see Chapter 7), who encouraged Kiichiro to build a mill to manufacture steel of sufficiently high quality to be used in automobiles.[3]

Since the USA was clearly ahead of other countries in terms of car-manufacturing technology, Suga was sent there and stayed for seven months at Ford and other plants to learn, for instance, the process and facilities in the plant, and the materials used for components. He also purchased necessary machines. On his return, he started to disassemble a Chevrolet engine and copy it in an experimental plant built within Toyoda Automatic Loom. As in the previous experience by Kaishinsha, casting was a problem. Although Toyoda had the casting technology to manufacture looms, they needed a more complex and finer technology to produce an engine. After a year of seemingly endless process of trial and error, and some modification to Chevrolet's original design, they finally developed an engine with sufficient power. To save time, they decided to use many of Chevrolet's and Ford's parts and also buy many materials and components from outside suppliers including Tobata Casting and other part producers around Nagoya. This was the origin of Toyota's supplier system. The first viable product, a truck, was introduced into the market in 1935 at the price of 3,200 yen, 200 yen cheaper than Ford and Chevrolet and below cost. A passenger car followed in 1936.

The automobile division was separated from Toyoda Automatic Loom in 1937 as Toyota Jidosha (Toyota Motor), so named because they believed that 'Toyota' sounds lighter than 'Toyoda' and would be preferred by the public. At the same time, they sought a place to build a plant with full production line. They bought a huge piece of land, almost ten times larger than that of Nissan's Yokohama Plant, in a town of Koromo (now renamed Toyota City), 20 km east of Nagoya. The plant was completed in 1938 with a capacity of 1,500 cars a month. Kiichiro's aim was to have an integrated production system with all the components produced domestically—internally or by associated suppliers nearby. Of course, it would take many years before this aim was to be achieved. It is also noteworthy that, even during this initial period, he used the words 'just-in-time' in a message to the employees to commemorate the completion of the plant.

His emphasis on research and development should be also noted. The first laboratory was built as early as 1936 and became the R&D division of Toyota Motor in 1938. It had physics and chemistry divisions to do research on materials, rubber, paint, fuel, and so forth, and invited seven professors as advisers, including the aforementioned Kumabe. Others were specialists in materials, thermodynamics, gears, and art. It was expanded in 1940 as the independent Toyoda Institute of Physical and Chemical Research with the annual budget of 270,000 yen provided by the Toyoda family, Toyoda Automatic Loom, and Toyota Motor. The significance of this amount can be seen by comparing it to the profits of Toyota Motor, which was 323,000 yen in its first year ending in September 1938, 1,500,000 yen in the second year, and 2,375,000 yen in the third year (Toyota Jidosha Kabushiki Kaisha, 1967).

Nissan did not have a similar research division before the war.

9.5 THE AUTOMOBILE MANUFACTURING
ENTERPRISE LAW

It would have been difficult for either Nissan or Toyota to compete against Ford and GM were it not for the government policy taken in 1936 to foster domestic car production. In the Automobile Manufacturing Enterprise Law (*Jidosha Seizo Jigyo Ho*), the government required any automobile-producing company to have a government licence unless the annual production was less than 3,000 units, and to be majority-owned by Japanese citizens. In return, licensed companies were exempted from paying corporate income tax and tariff for imported materials and equipment. The law also stipulated that any existing business could maintain its operation only within the level attained in 1935. This latter clause was clearly targeted at Japan Ford and Japan GM, and banned them from increasing annual production above the levels of 12,360 units (Ford) and 9,470 units (GM). The government also increased the tariff rate from 50 to 70 per cent for complete cars and from 35 to 60 per cent for engines, making it even more difficult for these American companies to maintain operation. Finally, with the soaring cost of importing parts caused by the rapid depreciation of the yen after 1937 and the worsening Japan–USA relationship, the two exited from the Japanese market in 1939.

The government encouraged established zaibatsu, such as Mitsui, Mitsubishi, and Kawasaki, as well as Isuzu, to apply for a licence, but they all declined, assuming that the production of more than 3,000 units a year was too risky, whereas the two new companies, Toyota and Nissan, took chances and applied for the licences in 1936. With the licences, they increased their production. In 1938, the production level of Toyota and Nissan combined was 6,568 for non-military sales against 12,441 of Ford and GM. For military sales, Toyota and Nissan together produced 5,930 and Ford and GM 5,999, showing the Army's willingness to support the domestic producers. After the exit of Ford and GM, the production level of Toyota and Nissan increased further, each exceeding 15,000 around 1941, with Isuzu, which obtained the licence in 1941, following with about half the production level of Toyota or Nissan. By this time, the government had virtually prohibited the production of passenger cars in order to secure supply to the Army, which mostly required trucks.

Without question, the determination of the government and the Army

to procure from domestic producers played a decisive role in supporting the Japanese automobile industry. Still, as the unwillingness of
zaibatsu to comply with the government's invitation indicates, such
determination alone would not have attained the purpose. It also required the determination of private entrepreneurs, such as Hashimoto,
Kubota, Aikawa, and Toyoda, who were willing to take risks and had
certain technological capabilities, for the industry to take off from the
infant stage.

In addition, two remarks are appropriate. First, despite the Army's
continual purchase of domestically produced cars before and during
World War II, the quality of these cars seems to have never caught up
with that of Ford and GM. Complaints of breakdowns were frequent,
including broken shafts, water dripping out of radiators, and the early
wear of moving parts (Ohshima and Yamaoka, 1987). Secondly, because it was Aikawa's and Toyoda's dream to mass-produce passenger
cars at a price affordable to the general public, neither was happy about
the ban on the production of passenger cars, even though the truck sales
to the Army guaranteed profits. The inability to accumulate know-how
to produce inexpensive but reliable and comfortable passenger cars
proved to be a handicap when the Japanese companies shifted their
weight towards the production of passenger cars after the war and,
particularly, when they started to compete against foreign cars in export
markets.

It is also noted that the pre-war presence of Ford and GM with their
formidable financial and technological clout remained in the minds of
Japanese car makers. After the war, their potential threat, together with
the knowledge that trade liberalization was inevitable, prompted Toyota,
Nissan, and other Japanese manufacturers to struggle to improve their
competitiveness in cost and quality. Fujimoto and Tidd (1993) compare
this experience to that in the UK and argue that, perhaps ironically, the
pre-war dominance of British mass producers, such as Morris and Austin
in the UK market, and Ford's failure to penetrate there, may have
caused the delay in the British producers' introduction of a full-scale,
mass-production, US system when international competition intensified
after the war. Japanese producers, by contrast, had strong memories of
Ford as a competitor with superior technology, Toyota, for instance,
desperately tried to learn from the mass-production system of Ford and
other car producers, and even from those of other industries, most
notably of textiles, to come up with its own system, which is now
called the Toyota production system.

9.6 POST-WAR TRANSITION

The Japanese automobile industry after the end of World War II was, to say the least, in turmoil. The General Headquarters (GHQ) of the Allied Powers prohibited the production of passenger cars until June 1947 because the general economic and distribution activities were so damaged that the GHQ saw the need for trucks and buses as urgent. The production of trucks met severe difficulties, however. The production facilities were either destroyed or obsolete, materials and components were of poor quality, if they could be obtained at all, electricity supply was erratic, and transportation among plants was not easy. In 1946, the production level was at 14,154 units, only 32 per cent of the previous peak of 1941. Since the number of workers had increased as the companies accepted those returning from battlefields or from plants in Manchuria and Korea, the production level per worker was a mere 0.66, in comparison to the pre-war peak of 2.28 (Nihon Jidosha Kogyo Kai, 1988: 61).

Furthermore, trade unions were formed in 1946 following their legalization and, with the high rate of inflation at the time, they demanded wage increases. The situation was aggravated by a very severe deflationary policy of Dodge Line that was adopted in order to balance the government budget and reduce the inflation rate (see Chapter 3). The firms had no choice but to reduce the labour force even if it meant confrontation with the unions. During 1949–50, Toyota, Nissan, Isuzu, and other manufacturers made 6,248 redundancies; 24 per cent of the labour force. All these firms suffered from strikes but the 1953 strike at Nissan that lasted for more than three months had the most profound impact as it ended with the industry-based union being replaced by company-based unions supported by the management.[4]

Another noteworthy organizational change that took place around this time was the separation of part-making divisions and sales divisions from the main firms. This separation was most conspicuous in Toyota. The sales division was separated in 1950 to reduce Toyota's financial difficulty caused by the large inventory. It would not be re-merged into Toyota until 1982. Nippondenso, founded as a parts factory within Toyota in 1936, was hived off in 1949. At first, Toyota completely owned it but, with Nippondenso's rapid growth (1.5 million yen in 1949 to 85 billion yen in 1992 in terms of paid-up capital), Toyota's share declined to 24 per cent beside the 7 per cent ownership by Toyota Automatic Loom. It is now the second-largest electric parts producer in the world. Similarly, Toyota Auto Body, Aishin Seiki, Aichi Horo, and a few others were hived off around the same time.

Toyota started its suppliers' association in 1939 with about twenty members. The major reason was that, with such a relationship, it was easier for smaller suppliers to persuade the Army to obtain scarce materials under the war-time control system. As Fruin (1992: 266) puts it, 'the Association was more akin to that of a black market clearing-house than a management improvement association.' After the war, Toyota decided to coordinate parts supply more comprehensively and more systematically, and, in addition to expanding the association membership to the suppliers around the main plant in the city of Toyota, it established similar associations in Tokyo and Osaka. These associations, named Tokai Kyohokai (mainly in Toyota City), Kanto Kyohokai (Tokyo), and Kansai Kyohokai (Osaka), include both those suppliers that were originally independent, like Koito, and those hived off from Toyota, like Nippondenso. This so-called *keiretsu* supply system expanded as Toyota expanded, because they were busy expanding the assembly operation and had decided to utilize and nurture a closely-knit supplier system. Following the example of Toyota, other firms also started similar associations.[5]

Even with these measures of streamlining workers and corporate organizations, the firms might not have survived were it not for the increased demand created by the Korean War. The US Army ordered about 12,000 units of trucks and other vehicles from Japanese producers during the latter half of 1950 and early 1951, when the annual production level of the industry was still around 30,000. In addition, they bought a substantial amount of repair parts and services. Also, the general economic upswing caused by the war contributed to an increase in demand. Although these conditions enabled the firms to earn profits which they invested in the modernization of production facilities, they were still under a severe threat from imported cars. During 1951–3, the number of domestically produced passenger cars, 17,237, was over-whelmed by the supply of foreign cars at 30,463 units, of which about two-thirds were the used cars sold by the occupation force and its personnel (Nihon Jidosha Kogyo Kai, 1988).

9.7   PROTECTION, TIE-UPS, AND THE ACCUMULATION OF TECHNOLOGICAL CAPABILITIES

A heated controversy took place within the Japanese government: should Japan protect and nurture domestic producers, or import cheaper and better-quality cars from abroad? The first view, which was based on the infant industry theory, was taken mostly by MITI and the auto producers themselves, whereas the latter, which was based on the static comparative advantage theory, was taken by the Ministry of Transport, the Bank of Japan, users such as taxi companies, and dealers of imported cars. The government settled on the first position not necessarily to promote domestic production but, more importantly, to save scarce foreign currency under the very tight balance of payments. The specific policies the government adopted were well documented in Genther (1990) and Muto (1988). They included (1) restriction on the use of foreign currency to import cars, (2) high tariff rates, (3) higher rates of commodity tax applied to big cars for which foreign producers had a relative advantage, (4) *de facto* prohibition of foreign companies from investing in Japan, (5) low-interest loans to domestic producers by Japan Development Bank, (6) special depreciation allowances to designated machines and equipment, and (7) subsidies to the Automobile Technology Association, which analysed the performance and efficiency of imported foreign cars.

Direct financial incentives included in (5) to (7) were modest, however. The subsidies were only 369 million yen during the nine year period of 1951–9 when Toyota's profits in 1959 alone were in excess of 9 billion yen. The loan provided by Japan Development Bank in 1951–6 accounted for only 4 per cent of the industry's investment.

In comparison, the first four measures, aimed at protecting the market against foreign producers and guaranteeing a growing market to domestic producers, may have played a significant role: they gave the producers a chance to lower costs and improve quality through the adoption of mass production, learning by doing, and imported technology. Because the foreign firms could neither export to Japan nor set up production facilities within Japan, the only way they could gain from their technological superiority was to sell the technology to Japanese producers. As a result, Austin (UK, now Rover), Rootes (UK, producer of Hillman, later acquired by Chrysler and then Peugeot), Renault (France), and Willys-Overland (USA, producer of jeep, later acquired

by American Motors and then Chrysler) consented to sell their technologies to, respectively, Nissan, Isuzu, Hino, and Shin Mitsubishi
Jukogyo (now a part of Mitsubishi Heavy Industry, from which
Mitsubishi Motors was hived off in 1970) when the Japanese firms
approached them with MITI's guarantee of royalty payments.

In these tie-ups, which began in 1952–3, they initially imported most
of the parts including engines, but gradually replaced them with domestically produced ones, succeeding in complete domestic production within
five years. The foreign partners not only provided components, designs,
and some equipment, but also sent their engineers to help Japanese
partners acquire the technology and test the quality of domestically
procured components. In return, Nissan, for instance, paid 3.5 per cent
(none in the first year and 2 per cent in the second year) of the price
for each Austin it sold. During 1953–9, the cars produced under these
tie-ups (excluding Jeeps) accounted for 30 per cent of car production,
thereby increasing domestic competition and also enabling the Japanese
firms to acquire know-how through learning by doing. They incorp-
orated the technology thus learned into the development of their own
models, such as Datsun, and terminated the contracts by 1962.

The difference between Toyota and other producers, Nissan in particular, is worth emphasizing in terms of their attitudes towards technology. We earlier explained that, when they entered the industry,
Nissan's Aikawa chose to hire American engineers and buy all the
production equipment from an existing American plant, whereas Toyota's
Toyoda Kiichiro decided to acquire technology basically through
reverse-engineering. This difference parallels their difference after the
war when Nissan formed a tie-up with Austin while Toyota pursued its
own development effort.

Actually, it is not that Toyota never sought a tie-up. In 1939, it
approached Ford to form a tie-up, which collapsed through the Japanese Army's objection. In the same year, a joint venture between Ford,
Toyota, and Nissan was discussed but again collapsed. Toyota also
approached Ford after the war for a tie-up but the two could not agree,
partly because the US government regulated the dispatch of American
engineers after the Korean War had broken out. Yet there seems to
have been a friendly relationship between the two because Ford had
Toyoda Eiji (Kiichiro's cousin, later Toyota's president and chairman)
stay at its plants for three months in 1950, just as it had Suga Takatoshi
stay and learn its technology in 1933.

Another difference between Toyota and Nissan pertains to the

research and development activity. As discussed earlier, Toyota had a
research division almost from its start, which was separated as Toyoda
Institute of Physical and Chemical Research during the war. Nissan, by
contrast, started a research division only in 1958. Cusumano argues
that:

the case of Toyota suggests that a firm relying on indirect technology transfer,
when supported by in-house research and development efforts focused on the
analysis of foreign products, gained several benefits denied to firms relying
mainly on tie-ups. First, indirect technology transfer enabled Toyota engineers
to copy proven technology selectively from different manufacturers and to
incorporate advanced features before Nissan or other Japanese automakers introduced these through foreign assistance. Tie-ups, on the other hand, locked
Nissan into designs that, while adequate, were not always the most advanced
in the industry or suited to local market conditions. Second, indirect technology
transfer provided experience in designing vehicles and solving engineering
problems that Toyota found useful for developing new products or improving
existing models. Third, relying on in-house engineers prevented Toyota from
acquiring a bias toward manufacturing techniques on equipment better suited to
larger markets in the US or Europe.   (Cusumano, 1985: 375)

It is also noted that many Japanese automobile producers, including
Toyota and Nissan, benefited from aircraft technologies accumulated
during the war. Since production and research of aircraft were prohibited by GHQ immediately following the end of the war (see Chapter
10), the aircraft engineers had to find jobs in which they could utilize
their knowledge. The most natural choice was automobiles because the
technologies had a number of similarities; for instance, combustion
engines were used in both aircraft and automobiles, and aerodynamics
was important in designing the bodies of both. Furthermore, a growing
civil demand was expected for automobiles.

Among a number of engineers who moved to existing automobile
firms were Hasegawa Tatsuo, who had been designing a high-altitude
fighter at Tachikawa Hikoki (Tachikawa Aircraft) and was hired by
Toyota; and Nakamura Yoshio, who had been an engine engineer at
Nakajima Hikoki (Nakajima Aircraft), then had a job at a rather small
tricycle manufacturer, Kurogane, and when they went bankrupt, got a
job at the emerging Honda Motor. Some started their own automobile
firms. A new company, Prince Jidosha (Prince Motors), was established
by the engineers of Nakajima Hikoki and Tachikawa Hikoki, including
Nakagawa Ryoichi who had designed engines for Zero fighters at
Nakajima Hikoki. It was financially supported by Ishibashi Shoichiro,

the founder of Bridgestone Tyres. Also the main part of Nakajima Hikoki was re-established as Fuji Juko (Fuji Heavy Industries), which later developed Subaru cars. Shin Mitsubishi Jukogyo, one of the three companies created by the partition of pre-war Mitsubishi Heavy Industries under the Deconcentration Law (see Chapter 5), started the production of automobiles by applying its own aircraft technology. The automobile division was later hived off from the re-merged Mitsubishi Heavy Industries as Mitsubishi Jidosha (Mitsubishi Motors).

These engineers became some of the main sources of technological development in the industry. Hasegawa, for instance, as the project team leader later developed Toyota Corolla. Nakagawa was the main engineer in the development of Prince Skyline cars, which captured the imagination of young drivers by winning many of the automobile races in Japan during the early 1960s. After Prince was acquired by Nissan (to be discussed), he became the leader of its R&D department. Naka-mura designed engines for Honda's racing cars and led the Honda team to its victory at Formula One motor races (Maema, 1993).

In the previous chapter we have shown that some of the researchers at the Naval Research Institute and other military-related organizations made significant inputs into the development of electronics. We have also shown that the post-war Japanese firms had to concentrate on the civilian market owing to the lack of military procurement. The automobile case indicates a very similar experience. The firms had to rely on the consumer market to survive, unlike the war period when military demand supported a significant proportion of their sales. Thus, they had to develop products that would satisfy consumers' needs and tastes, and would be affordable to most consumers. The engineers who had lost military-related R&D jobs were re-allocated for these purposes and were given opportunities to apply their technological knowledge to other related purposes. It is worth remembering that this re-allocation was not at all a consequence of deliberate calculation and planning by the firms or by the government. It was, as a matter of fact, the only way the engineers could survive. None the less, two of the Japanese industries that have grown most rapidly since the end of the war, and, for that matter, two of the German industries that did the same, were the industries that must have inherited the technological base accumulated during the war period.

We also note, however, that the success in these industries would not have been achieved by the demise of the munitions industry alone. Post-Communist Russian experience in the 1990s testifies to this fact and, as in the electronics industry, the mechanism of market competition played an indispensable role in the development of the automobile industry. We now turn to this topic.

9.8   MITI'S INTEGRATION PLANS AND MARKET ENTRIES

To understand the role of market competition in the post-war development of the industry, there seems no better example than the cases of MITI's two major structural policies called the 'people's car' project and the 'three-group' concept, both of which were proposed to achieve economies of scale by concentrating the production activity. In either case, however, the consequence was quite contrary to MITI's intention.

In 1955, MITI proposed that firms develop what was called a 'people's car' with four seats, a 350–500 cc engine, and a 100 km-per-hour maximum speed. Two thousand units were to be produced monthly (at the time when Toyota's or Nissan's monthly production of passenger cars was less than 1,000) priced at 250,000 yen (when Nissan's Datsun with 722 cc engine was sold at 800,000 yen). MITI's plan was to have the producers submit their proposals based on this specification, choose the best among them, give it a subsidy, and have it produced on a large scale.

The industry opposed this plan on the grounds that not only was it technically and economically implausible but also that the selection by the government of a single manufacturer would violate the principle of free competition. That is, the firms wished to pursue independent efforts to develop the sort of cars the market demanded. The project was finally dropped for want of MITI's power to maintain the policy against the industry's objection, indicating a clear difference from its pre-war experience.

Despite the failure, the project yielded two consequences. First, it aroused an interest in mini-cars by those who would be able to afford the proposed low price. Secondly, it gave an idea to potential entrants of what kind of car they should develop and introduce into the market. The most likely entrants would be the producers of two-wheel vehicles (motorcycles) and three-wheel cars, partly because they had the related technology and partly because these markets had been saturated or were declining. As a consequence, Suzuki, a motorcycle producer, entered into the market in 1955 with its own four-wheel car named

Suzulight; Fuji Heavy Industry, a scooter producer, with Subaru in 1958; and Mazda, a three-wheel car producer, with Mazda Coupé in 1960. They all had 360 cc engines and were priced at 300,000–425,000 yen. In addition, Mitsubishi entered with a model with a 500 cc engine, priced at 390,000 yen. The result, very clearly, was not a concentrated industry as MITI had envisaged but, on the contrary, an industry with a larger number of producers.

The three-group concept was proposed to classify each auto producer into one of the three groups: a group of producers of mass-produced conventional cars, a group of producers of speciality cars including luxury cars and sports cars, and a group of mini-car producers. Each group was to have two or three producers only, thus fostering concentration. For the first group of conventional car producers, the plan required a monthly production of 7,000 units, which could be cleared only by Toyota and Nissan. In effect, therefore, the plan tried to concentrate the production of conventional cars to these two producers only. The plan also proposed that any new entry should need MITI's approval. It was to be included in the Special Measures Law for the Promotion of Designated Industries (*Tokutei Sangyo Shinko Rinji Ho*, abbreviated as *Tokushin Ho*), which was proposed to the Diet in 1963 but failed to pass owing to the opposition of the business leaders. Clearly, the industries were not eager to be subject to MITI's control. The opposition parties also opposed it from the anti-trust viewpoint.

One of the most vocal opponents to MITI's plan was Honda Soichiro who, at the time, was planning to enter into the production of passenger cars. Honda was born in 1906 and, during the war, manufactured piston rings in his small company to supply to Toyota and others. He sold this company to Toyota in 1945 and, in the following year, established Honda Gijutsu Kenkyusho (Honda Technical Research Institute), later to be renamed Honda Giken, which is now translated as Honda Motor. The name of the company itself indicates Honda's emphasis on technology. Indeed, Honda spent most of his time on the shop-floor working on improving engines and developing new products that ranged from small engines to be attached to bicycles to 125 cc, 250 cc and 350 cc motorcycles that won the races in the Isle of Man. He scarcely attended managerial meetings, even board meetings, until his retirement in 1973, leaving all the financial, organizational, and marketing aspects of the business to his close ally, Fujisawa Takeo.

Fujisawa, too, was an innovator in the Schumpeterian sense. He organized the chain of dealers in a novel way, for instance, by inviting bicycle shops to join. He led Honda to become international by exporting motorcycles to the US market as the first Japanese vehicle producer, and setting up a manufacturing subsidiary in Belgium as the first Japanese manufacturer to have a factory in the USA or Europe (Pascale, 1984; Sakiya, 1982). Honda also led the industry (except for Toyota's Research Institute during the war) in hiving off its R&D division in 1957 as an autonomous organization, named Honda Gijutsu Kenkyusho (Honda R&D Co.), to create a non-pyramidal structure better to promote independent and original research efforts. It was also the first to set up R&D facilities in the USA and Europe. Such emphasis on technology resulted in a number of innovations, for instance, high-speed, high-power engines for Formula One races, which were then applied to the models targeted at general markets, and CVCC, the first engine that met the 1975 standard set forth by the US Clean Air Act.

In 1961 when the three-group concept was first suggested, Honda was planning to enter into the four-wheel car market in addition to its successful motorcycle business. Naturally, he was furious that his entry might be blocked by the three-group concept. He hastened to put his first products, S360 sports cars and T360 lightweight trucks, both with 360 cc engines, into the market to establish his presence, and at the same time strongly criticized the policy saying that 'we have a right to manufacture what we want to!' (Genther, 1990: 142). He even confronted a MITI high official who tried to persuade him not to enter. Although MITI's administrative guidance (*gyosei shido*) is, at least formally, no more than guidance without legal power, one may worry about the negative consequence of disobeying it; for instance, the bank may become less eager to provide loans.

Honda, however, decided to go ahead and in 1969 marketed its first non-mini, non-sports car, the Honda 1300, which was targeted at the largest segment of the market. Again, therefore, we find the case of entry *despite* the government's intention towards restricting entry and attaining a more concentrated industry. There is no question at all that the competitive structure thus created played a very critical role in the development of the industry.

Although Tokushin Ho was scrapped, MITI kept encouraging reorganization (namely, an increased concentration) of the industry on the grounds that forthcoming trade and capital liberalization would have US and European large firms, such as GM whose sales were 26 times larger than Toyota in 1965, dominate the fragmented Japanese industry. This guidance by MITI bore some fruit, such as the Nissan–Prince merger in 1966 and the Toyota-Hino-Daihatsu alliance in 1966–7. As a consequence, market concentration to these two groups increased but the entry of independents like Honda kept the market highly competitive, which, together with the increasing threat of international competition, contributed to maintaining and even intensifying the innovation efforts.

Finally, two additional remarks. First, although Suzuki, Mazda, Subaru, Mitsubishi, Daihatsu, and Honda were the only entrants to survive to date, there were many more attempts, amounting to nearly thirty between 1945 and 1960, including those into three-wheel car production. They were diverse, including ex-zaibatsu companies like Mitsubishi, re-entrants like Mazda and Daihatsu, former aircraft manufacturers like Prince and Subaru, and former machinery manufacturers like Suzuki. The majority were non-zaibatsu, newly emerged independents, with Honda providing the best example. Except for the above-mentioned companies, hardly any of them survived for more than five years.

Secondly, the strength of the post-war Japanese automobile industry is probably most evident in the fields of production management and human resource management, including training programmes and the TQC (total quality control) movement. Toyota's *kanban* and just-in-time production system and *keiretsu* supplier system are well-known. Since these have been well documented elsewhere, we will not pursue them further.[6]

9.9 CONCLUSION

The experience of the Japanese car industry throws light on some key issues. How could Japan succeed in establishing its own car industry in the presence (in the pre-war period) of the technologically far-advanced companies, Ford and GM? Two factors appear to be most significant. One is the presence of entrepreneurs, such as Toyoda and Aikawa, who were willing to take risks and sustain efforts under adversity. The other is the capability of engineers to absorb foreign technology and the capability of workers to absorb new production processes. Needless to say, the education system discussed earlier contributed to this effect. Also, the emphasis on engineering education in universities helped not only in supplying educated engineers but also in providing technical assistance to the industry, as most typically shown by Toyoda's episode of visiting professors.

As in any late-developing country, reverse-engineering was the first source of foreign technology. The visiting of advanced foreign factories, the hiring of foreign engineers, and the purchasing of foreign technologies were other important means of acquiring the technology.

The government's role may have been more important here than in other industries (except, of course, shipbuilding and aircraft to be discussed in the next chapter). Probably the most effective of the policies were procurement by the Army and other ministries, and protection against foreign rivals. These policies guaranteed demand to domestic manufacturers, thereby encouraging investment in capital and in research and development, although R&D *was* mostly development, particularly in the early period. By contrast, several policies adopted (or proposed) by the government before and after the war to concentrate the industry into one or two large-scale manufacturers in pursuit of scale economies met with reluctance or even outright objection, attaining only limited results.

Entrepreneurial enthusiasm for entering into risky and challenging but promising markets and for pursuing independent development efforts outweighed the government's desire to control the industry, resulting in a lower concentration than in any other country. It must have been this highly competitive environment that drove the firms into intensive innovation efforts, not only in product development but also in production process, human management, marketing, and international activity, and resulted in high growth and competitiveness in a market that increases its internationalism.

10

Shipbuilding and Aircraft

In this chapter, we discuss shipbuilding and aircraft manufacturing together, mainly because most of the major aircraft manufacturers were originally shipbuilders. Currently, these manufacturers include Mitsubishi Jukogyo (Mitsubishi Heavy Industries, abbreviated as MHI), Kawasaki Jukogyo (Kawasaki Heavy Industries, KHI), and Ishikawajima-Harima Jukogyo (Ishikawajima-Harima Heavy Industries, IHI), all of which started as shipbuilding companies.

Therefore, we begin by discussing the early history of shipbuilding in Japan, and then proceed to the discussion of the aircraft industry. The discussion of the shipbuilding industry is rather brief and confined to the pre-war period. We discuss the aircraft industry in more detail, mostly because the Japanese aircraft industry has a unique history of rapidly catching up with the West to become one of the major producing countries and, then, following defeat in World War II, of being banned from production. It then resumed production but, unlike steel, electrical and electronic equipment, and automobiles, the world market remains dominated by US firms. It must be of interest to find out why.

Another reason is that a number of studies of the shipbuilding industry have been recently published in English, such as Chida and Davies (1990) and Fukasaku (1992). The latter is particularly complementary to ours because, through a detailed case study of Mitsubishi's shipyard, it discusses how the pre-war Japanese shipbuilding industry developed. The former, by contrast, provides a detailed discussion of government policies for the shipping industry, which affected the demand for shipbuilders, and for the shipbuilding industry itself, both before and after the war. Yonezawa (1988) also discusses the post-war government policies for the industry.

The pre-war development of the shipbuilding industry, like that of the automobile industry, was very much affected by government policies, including military procurement. Unlike automobiles, however, the technological level had more or less caught up with the West by the time World War II started. The earlier start of shipbuilding in comparison to automobiles is one apparent reason. We begin, therefore, by discussing how the industry started.

10.1 THE START OF MODERN SHIPBUILDING

The Tokugawa Shogunate government prohibited the construction of large ships, except for commercial navigation along the coast and rivers, to maintain its seclusionist policy and to restrict the military capacity of feudal lords (*daimyo*). Consequently, for almost 200 years before the mid-nineteenth century, the only large ships produced within the country were wooden, keel-less, flat-bottomed sailing boats, called *Yamato*-style boats, which were unsuitable for ocean navigation. The arrival of a fleet of steel-made steamships led by US Commodore Perry in 1853 was thus quite a shock, not only to the Shogunate government but to all Japanese citizens, from both the defence and the technological viewpoint. The government soon lifted the ban and constructed its own shipyard in Uraga, some 52 km south-west of Tokyo. However, the lack of technical knowledge on the Western-style ship was a big obstacle.

An opportunity to learn the Western shipbuilding technology came in an unexpected manner. In 1854, while a Russian warship was visiting Japan, a strong earthquake occurred, destroying the ship. To replace it, the Russians decided to build two schooners, employing Japanese carpenters under the leadership of a Russian technician. These carpenters thus learned how to build Western-style ships. In addition, the Russians left their drawings and other technological documents behind, as well as their tools. Consequently, the Japanese carpenters could build several more schooners by themselves for the Shogunate government.

In the following year, the government started a school in Nagasaki with the help of the Dutch, in which the operation of vessels was taught. A shipyard was also built so that the students could study maintainance and repair. Several feudal lords also started their own shipyards, most of which were soon abandoned as they realized that importing ships was much cheaper. One exception was the shipyard the Mito Clan built in Ishikawajima in the seaside area of Edo (Tokyo), which was subsequently acquired by the Shogunate government. Some of the aforementioned carpenters who had worked with the Russians were invited to this shipyard.

This Ishikawajima Shipyard became the first privately run shipyard in the country. In 1866, the Shogunate government decided to build a larger shipyard in Yokosuka, 50 km south-west of Tokyo, with technical and financial assistance from France, which was completed after the Meiji Restoration and later became the largest shipyard of the Japanese Navy. The government transferred the equipment in Ishikawajima to Yokosuka and closed down the Ishikawajima Shipyard. Hirano Tomiji, who had earlier worked at Nagasaki Shipyard, bought the land and buildings from the government in 1876 and re-started the shipyard as a private business. This is the origin of the present Ishikawajima-Harima Heavy Industries (IHI).

Nagasaki Shipyard was taken over by the Meiji government after the Restoration and employed British and French engineers. The operation suffered from continuous loss and, in 1887, the government sold it to Mitsubishi, which had been operating a small experimental shipyard in Yokohama. Similarly, the shipyard in Hyogo (now a part of the City of Kobe), which had been acquired by the Tokugawa government from the Kanazawa Clan, was sold to Kawasaki Shozo. Therefore, three of the largest shipbuilding firms, MHI, KHI, and IHI, all started during the 1870s and 1880s by inheriting the initiatives of the Tokugawa government and some of the feudal lords.

By no means were they the only enterprises, however. Some of the traditional shipbuilders started to build Western ships, including Fujinagata Shipyard in Osaka, which had been established during the seventeenth century. It invited German engineers in 1869 to learn the Western shipbuilding technology. After World War II, the company was acquired by Mitsui Zosen (Mitsui Engineering and Shipbuilding). Several new shipyards were also started as private enterprises. Some were established by foreigners, for example, Osaka Tekkosho was established by a British engineer, E. H. Hunter, which was later (in 1934) acquired by the Nissan group and became the present Hitachi Zosen.

With such active entries, the number of shipyards reached 153 by 1900, which was further increased to 350 by 1920 (Kaneko, 1964: 148). However, the market, particularly for steam vessels, was dominated by imports. During the ten-year period of 1878–87, 244 steam vessels were domestically produced with the total gross tonnage (Gt.) of 17,764, while 51 were imported with the total of 28,911 Gt. (Chida and Davies, 1990). The dominance of imports among large steam vessels is apparent.

10.2   THE DEVELOPMENT OF THE SHIPBUILDING
INDUSTRY

Figure 10.1 shows the growth in value of shipbuilding production (Western-style ships only) from 1870, three years after the Restoration, to 1920, two years after the end of World War I. Clearly, there are three periods when production increased rapidly. The first is 1874–80 when several civil wars, such as the Seinan War, took place. The second is 1896–1900 when the laws to promote navigation and shipbuilding were enacted. And the third is 1914–20 when the outbreak of World War I in Europe caused a jump in demand for Japanese shipbuilding. Each of these three occasions warrants further discussion.

At the beginning of the Meiji era, both coastal navigation and ocean navigation around Japan were dominated by Western companies, in particular, Pacific Mail of the USA. When the war with Taiwan broke out in 1874, followed by a few civil wars caused by former samurai who were dissatisfied with the policy of the Meiji government, it became crucial to have a shipping service run by the Japanese so that their ships could be requisitioned to carry soldiers, munitions, food, and other supplies in case of wars. The government imported 13 steam vessels and had them operated by the company that Iwasaki Yataro had established a few years earlier with the ships he bought from his former employer, the lord of Tosa Clan. The company, named Mitsubishi, expanded rapidly thanks to Iwasaki's business acumen, beating Pacific Mail. It soon started ocean services in addition to coastal services. The competition among domestic and foreign shipping rivals was intense, reducing fares, which, together with the expanding volume of trade, increased the demand for ships, as shown in the first steep rise in Figure 10.1.

Mitsubishi's shipping business became Nihon Yusen Kaisha (NYK) after the merger with Kyodo Unyu, and became only indirectly related to the Mitsubishi group, whose main business became the shipbuilding at Nagasaki. The government financially supported NYK and subsequent entrants, such as Osaka Shosen Kaisha (OSK, now Mitsui OSK after the merger with Mitsui Senpaku) and Toyo Kisen (later acquired by Showa Kaiun), to reduce dependence on foreign shipping companies. Yet, during 1883–97, the share of Japanese imports and exports delivered by Japanese ships remained only around 10 per cent (Inoue, 1990).

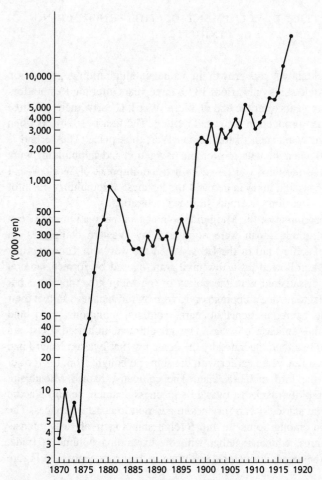

FIG. 10.1. The growth of shipbuilding production, 1870–1920

Note: The vertical axis shows the value of production in 1930 prices (in '000 yen). It includes both steamships and sailing ships, but not warships or ships made in the traditional Japanese style.

Source: Otsuka, M., 1987: Fig. 8.1. The original data source is *Chouki Keizai Toukei* [Estimates of Long-term Economic Statistics of Japan], vol. 3, edited by Ohkawa Kazushi, Ishiwatari Shigeru, Yamada Saburo, and Ishi Hiromitsu (Tokyo: Toyo Keizai, 1966).

To promote the industry further, the government enacted the Navigation Promotion Law (*Kokai Shorei Ho*) and the Shipbuilding Promotion Law (*Zosen Shorei Ho*) in 1896. The former gave subsidies for the purchase of ships by Japanese shipping companies, while the latter gave subsidies for the production of ships in excess of 700 Gt. to Japanese shipbuilding companies. The former had a more profound effect as the total subsidy given under this law was nearly ten times larger than the total subsidy under the latter law. The subsidy to the shipping companies was substantial: at NYK and OSK, the amount of subsidy was nearly as large as their profits during 1896–1903. It thus increased the incentive for shipping companies to increase their fleet, thereby increasing the demand for shipbuilding, as shown in the second steep rise in Figure 10.1.

Since the subsidy was also given for imported ships and since they were of a higher quality, while the domestic shipbuilders could barely match the import price with the aid of the subsidy given under the Shipbuilding Promotion Law, many shipping companies preferred to purchase from abroad. The Law was amended in 1899 to the effect that the subsidy given for imported ships was reduced to half of that given for domestic ships. In addition, tariffs started to be charged on import ships in 1897 at the rate of 5 per cent, which was raised to 15 per cent in 1911 following the revision of the Commercial Treaty (the Unequal Treaty discussed in Chapter 2) with the USA, the UK, and other Western nations. These policies made domestic shipbuilding more advantageous, supporting the shipbuilding industry.

The start of World War I in 1914 greatly increased the demand for domestic shipbuilding for three reasons. First, it increased the Japanese export to Europe, where the production capacity has declined owing to the war, and to Asia, to which the formerly dominant European exporters could no longer fully supply. This export boom caused a sharp increase in the demand for shipping services. Secondly, European and US shipping companies could not maintain their services to Japan and Asia because their fleet had been transferred to Europe to fulfil war-related shipping needs. The result was a sharp rise in shipping fares, which in turn increased the incentive of Japanese shippers to order more ships. Thirdly, foreign shipbuilders could not increase their supply to Japan because they were occupied with the orders within their own countries, including those from their navies. As a result, the shipping companies rushed to Japanese shipbuilding companies to buy ships.

In 1914, the domestic shipbuilders supplied ships of 59,000 Gt. in total, which accounted for about two-thirds of the market, with the remaining third accounted for by the import. In 1918, when the war ended, the domestic supply was 636,000 Gt. while the import was virtually nil (Inoue, 1990). This increase in production is shown in Figure 10.1 by the steep rise after 1914. Japan was, by then, the third largest shipbuilding country after the USA and the UK. In 1912, the UK was clearly the world leader in shipbuilding, producing about 30 times more ships in Gt. than Japan. Six years later, the UK production was only 3 times larger than that of Japan, and the USA was producing more than the UK (Kaneko, 1964).

Another factor in the development of Japanese shipbuilding was the expansion of the Japanese Navy. Since the Sino-Japanese War (1894–5) and the Russo-Japanese War (1904–5), the Japanese military found it strategically necessary to have a large fleet of warships to maintain its influence over the Asian Continent. Some of these ships were built at the Naval Shipyards in Yokosuka, Kure, Sasebo, and Maizuru but, as the technological level of private shipbuilding companies rose and as the Naval Shipyards became occupied with the repair of existing warships, more and more orders were given to private companies, particularly Mitsubishi and Kawasaki. In 1884–1903, 88 per cent of the Navy's vessels were imported. In 1922–8, only 10 per cent were imported, while 65 per cent were built at private shipyards with the remaining 25 per cent built at Naval Shipyards (Fukasaku, 1992).

The experience therefore suggests that, if the government policies were conducive at all to the development of the shipbuilding industry, they were mainly the policies of supporting the demand, such as the policy of subsidizing shipping companies that encouraged them to order vessels from Japanese shipbuilding companies, and the procurement by the Navy. By contrast, the subsidy programme to shipbuilding companies themselves appears to have been less effective. This fact is quite similar to the automobile case discussed in the previous chapter.

It is also similar to the industry's post-World War II experience, where the provision of subsidies or low-interest loans to shipping companies, according to the Programmed Shipbuilding Scheme (*Keikaku Zosen*), supported the demand for shipbuilding. Both Chida and Davies (1990) and Mizota (1991) argue that this scheme was instrumental in the industry's early recovery from the wartime destruction and the postwar depression. Its effectiveness since the 1960s has been questioned, however (Yonezawa, 1988).

Similarity is also evident with the Japan–USA difference in the post-war development of the aircraft industry, where the US industry greatly benefited from the expansion of the US Air Force while the Japanese industry could not because of the very limited presence of the Air Self Defense Force. We will return to this topic later in this chapter.

10.3 BUILDING TECHNOLOGICAL CAPABILITIES IN SHIPBUILDING

As discussed above, the UK was a dominant leader in shipbuilding up to World War I. There, the construction of steel-made steamships was a natural development because the complementary activities of steel-making and machine-manufacturing had been gradually developed. Steel-making technology had been mostly developed in the UK as had turbine technology. Suppliers of these and other materials and components were present.

The situation was quite different when Japan started building steam-ships. As discussed in Chapter 7, Tanaka's steel-making enterprise in Kamaishi did not start until 1887 and Yawata Works started to operate smoothly only in 1904. Japan lacked knowledge of steam engines. Furthermore, Japan had been making ships of a completely different structure.

The consequence was not only that shipbuilders lacked essential technology when they started, but also that they lacked the support of complementary suppliers. Therefore, they had to either import materials, machines, and other parts, or make them. This fact should be remembered because their efforts to make them internally provided a basis for their diversification.

To acquire the technology, all the major shipbuilders hired British engineers. For instance, most of the technical staff of Mitsubishi's Nagasaki Shipyard in 1887 were British, including the manager who came to Japan after working with a shipbuilder in Glasgow (Inoue, 1990: 123). In 1880, Kobu Daigakko (the successor to Kogakuryo and the predecessor to the University of Tokyo; see Chapter 2) started a department on shipbuilding technology with both Japanese and British professors, and the graduates started to be employed by Mitsubishi, Kawasaki, and other shipbuilders. Many of these graduates were sent to the UK to learn the technologies.

Technological capability was thus gradually accumulated through the hired British engineers and the Japanese engineers who had been educated at Kobu Daigakko and/or learned in the UK. Still, in 1898 when 'Hitachi-Maru', the first ship over 5,000 Gt. ever made in Japan, was built at Mitsubishi Nagasaki Shipyard at NYK's order, it depended on British technology. In fact, NYK ordered several vessels from a British shipbuilder and only experimentally asked Mitsubishi if they would build a ship with the same design at the same price. Mitsubishi accepted it, and sent several of their Japanese engineers to the British shipbuilder to learn the technology and to buy the necessary tools and equipment. They bought the designs of the hull, the turbine, the boiler, and so on from British companies, hired a British engineer, and expanded the dock.

It was a huge and risky investment for Mitsubishi, and the production cost far exceeded the sales revenue; yet, it gave an indispensable experience with which they could enhance their capability.

Ten years later, when a much larger 'Tenyo-Maru' (13,454 Gt.) was built by Mitsubishi, most of the technology was their own, although the turbine was still imported. The following year, Mitsubishi built 'Sakura-Maru' (3,205 Gt.) with the turbine made internally with imported technology. Clearly, therefore, the industry gradually accumulated their technological capability, and the catch-up with the Western technology was accelerated in the first two decades of the twentieth century.

Mitsubishi had started a small chemical laboratory in the foundry shop in 1904 to make chemical analyses of metals. During the 1910s, it was expanded into a research institute with more than 150 staff, doing research in the field of metal and machinery. It also started providing training programmes to its workers, although the frequent loss of the workers thus trained to other companies, including the rival shipbuilders, was a big concern. To encourage the workers to stay with the company, they gradually adopted such policies as the seniority-based wage system and miscellaneous welfare programmes, as discussed in Chapter 4.

Since the technological development at Mitsubishi Nagasaki Shipyard is well documented in Fukasaku (1992), we will not discuss it further except to say that other companies, such as Kawasaki, Osaka Tekkosho, and Ishikawajima, also gradually raised their capabilities. The process of learning was not at all a passive activity: it involved active involvement by the engineers and workers. According to Fukasaku (1992: 147), 'imported technologies underwent considerable improvements after initial importing through the accumulation of minor technological changes' and these improvements resulted in innovation in both product engineering and production engineering. Furthermore, they increased their own research efforts as the technological gap with the advanced nations narrowed. Learning and innovation were thus continuous and complementary means of gaining technological capabilities, and the involvement of the whole body of the enterprise, from the researchers and engineers to the labourers, was essential to the rapid technological catch-up.

As discussed earlier, the Japanese shipbuilders had to provide most of the materials and machines themselves and, hence, technologies had to be accumulated in a rather wide range. These technologies were gradually utilized in their diversification efforts. Some of them started making steel, such as Kawasaki and Asano Zosen (Asano Shipbuilding, later acquired a by Nihon Kokan), as discussed in Chapter 7. Mitsubishi started a steel mill in Korea. Mitsubishi also started making electrical equipment to be used for ships. In 1921, this division was hived off as Mitsubishi Electric (see Chapter 8). Some companies also started making automobiles, including Mitsubishi and Kawasaki, both of which gave up their efforts early. As discussed in Chapter 9, Ishikawajima's effort was more persistent, which continues in the present Isuzu Motor.

Mitsubishi (MHI), Kawasaki (KHI), and Ishikawajima (IHI) also entered into the production of aircraft.

10.4 THE START OF THE AIRCRAFT INDUSTRY[1]

In 1910, seven years after the Wright brothers made the world's first flight, the first flight over the Japanese sky was made with an aircraft imported from France and piloted by a Japanese. In the previous year, the Army, the Navy, and the University of Tokyo had jointly organized a study group named Temporary Research Committee on Military Balloon (*Rinji Gunyo Kikyu Kenkyu Kai*). Despite the name 'balloon', which was inherited from an organization established within the Army in 1905 to conduct aerial reconnaissance with manned balloons, the major aim of the Temporary Research Committee was to conduct research on aircraft which had already started to be used for various purposes in Europe and the USA. The Army officers were sent to Europe to learn how to fly and came back with two airplanes, one French-made and the other German-made, to conduct the historic flight mentioned above.

Even before this government effort, a few inventors dreamed of flying. The most well-known is Ninomiya Chuhachi, who designed a flying machine with three engines earlier than the Wright brothers, even though his plane failed to take off. Yet, the real development effort started only with the establishment of the Temporary Research Committee. For 35 years, from then to the end of World War II, the Japanese aircraft industry rapidly accumulated their capabilities to design and manufacture aircraft, at first by technology importation and learning, and eventually succeeding in the development of unique world-class aircraft during the 1930s.

This fast catch-up was helped by two factors. First, the military made a major effort to strengthen the industry's capabilities by providing various resources and by purchasing the products. Secondly, Japan had by then established technological and manufacturing bases in related industries, most notably shipbuilding, which could be utilized in aircraft research and production.

Even though the Temporary Research Committee was organized as a collaborative effort of the Army and the Navy, the relation between the two was strained and the Navy soon split off from the Committee to form its own. Seven navy officers and engineers were sent abroad, and brought back two Farman planes from France and two Curtis planes from the USA.

In addition to these efforts to learn from imported aircraft, the military took several measures in the early 1910s to prepare the ground for domestic aircraft production. The first airfield was built near Tokyo by the Army in 1911. The Navy opened a base for seaplanes in a port near Tokyo, because they were commonly used at the time. Also, the Navy converted one of its ships into a carrier, which carried six Farman planes to Tsingtao, China, when Japan fought against Germany during World War I. This fight gave Japanese pilots their first combat experience.

In 1911, an army arsenal made an engine, after a French model, by reverse-engineering. Three years later, they made an engine, after Renault's, and fitted it to an imported Farman airframe, succeeding in flight. Similarly, a navy arsenal started test production of engines and aircraft in 1915.

World War I had a major impact on Japan's aircraft industry in three ways. First, when Japan fought against the Germans in China, it used aircraft for the first time for reconnaissance and bombing, however limited the operation was. Secondly, the post-war worldwide disarmament agreement mainly targeted battleships; hence, the relative focus shifted towards the use of aircraft. Thirdly, perhaps most importantly, the war in Europe convinced Japan of the importance of developing its own aircraft industry.

Consequently, several efforts started in the latter half of the 1910s. The Army established Air Corps in 1915, followed by a similar move by the Navy in the following year. Both the Army and Navy created organizations to oversee the research and production of aircraft. Not only did they manufacture foreign-designed aircraft and engines, and conduct research internally, they also contracted out the production of engines and aircraft to private companies, as will be discussed presently.

In 1918, Aviation Laboratory (*Kouku Kenkyu Sho*) and an aviation course was established within the Engineering Department of the University of Tokyo, and started supplying many aviation engineers. For instance, Horikoshi Jiro, the chief engineer in the design of 'Zero' fighters at Mitsubishi, graduated from this course in 1927. So did other major engineers, such as Doi Takeo of Kawasaki, who developed many engines. After studying at the University of Tokyo, these engineers typically worked under foreign engineers hired by the companies and then became the chief engineers in charge of the development of new aircraft or new engines. They were usually promoted at a very young age, say, in their late twenties, reflecting the rapid development of the industry and the shortage of educated engineers.

Several private companies started the production of aircraft and engines around 1920. Nakajima Hikoki (Nakajima Aircraft) and Mitsubishi Heavy Industries were the largest two, followed by Kawanishi Koukuki (Kawanishi Aircraft), Kawasaki Koukuki (Kawasaki Aircraft), Aichi Koukuki (Aichi Aircraft), Tokyo Gas Electric (TGE, see Chapter 9; later joined the Hitachi group and renamed Hitachi Aircraft), Kyushu Hikoki (Kyushu Aircraft), and Tachikawa Hikoki (Tachikawa Aircraft). These eight companies were established or started the production of engines or aircraft between 1917 and 1925, and a few more were established later. Nakajima, Mitsubishi, Kawasaki, Aichi, and Hitachi manufactured both aircraft and engines.

These companies underwent a series of organizational changes and divestitures, which makes it difficult to determine the exact years of their establishment. Nakajima Aircraft was established in 1918 as Nihon Hikoki (Nippon Aircraft) by a joint venture between a navy engineer, Nakajima Chikuhei, and a textiles manufacturer, Kawanishi Seibei. In the following year, the two founders split and Nakajima bought out Nihon Aircraft's factory with tacit help from the Army and renamed the company Nakajima Aircraft. Kawanishi started his own company, Kawanishi Kikai (Kawanishi Machinery) in 1920 in Kobe, from which the aircraft division was hived off as Kawanishi Aircraft in 1928.

Mitsubishi, Kawasaki, and Tachikawa had their origins in ship-building. Kawasaki Hikoki was established as KHI's subsidiary and Tachikawa Aircraft was originally established as Ishikawajima Hikoki (Ishikawajima Aircraft) as a subsidiary to IHI. Mitsubishi started an internal combustion section within its Kobe shipyard in 1916, and started research on both automobiles and aircraft. It sent three workers to the naval arsenal for training where engines were being manufactured. In 1920, Mitsubishi Nainenki (Mitsubishi Internal Combustion) was established in Nagoya and the operation in Kobe became a part of this new company. Eight years later, Mitsubishi Internal Combustion changed its name to Mitsubishi Aircraft, and finally in 1934, it merged with Mitsubishi Shipbuilding to become Mitsubishi Jukogyo (Mitsubishi Heavy Industries; MHI).

Entry by these shipbuilding companies into the aircraft industry was a natural development because of, first, technological complementarity, that is, the ease in utilizing their technological capabilities and worker skills in mechanical engineering; secondly, financial resources; and, thirdly, their close relationship with the Army and Navy. Some of the later entrants were textiles manufacturers. Another interesting case is Aichi Aircraft, which was originally named Aichi Clock and Electric Machinery. As the name indicates, it was a manufacturer of clocks, along with gramophones and ordnance: with the prodding and support of the Navy, it started making seaplanes by importing the technology from Short Brothers of the UK.

The Army and Navy gradually shifted their aircraft procurement policy from the production at their own arsenals towards the purchase from emerging private manufacturers, because the military budget was re-duced during the post-war, arms-reduction period, and the private sec-tor tended to be more cost effective. The military thus decided to promote the private manufacturers and increased the procurement from them, though the Navy maintained a large facility and staff to conduct re-search in advanced and special aircraft. In 1924, the production in the private sector exceeded that of military arsenals for the first time.

In the procurement, the Army (or the Navy) normally announced the required specification and had the companies make and submit a prototype. It tested them and awarded the contract to the best one. Competition was thus maintained among companies, although most companies had their strong fields or niches and, therefore, not all of them made a bid at every opportunity.

The actual size of production was still very small. Mitsubishi, one of the largest manufacturers, produced only 69 aircraft and 70 engines in as late as 1926. Since the number of manufacturers was large despite the limited amount of military budget, some of them even made furniture and musical instruments to survive and support workers.

Nevertheless, all the manufacturers sought advanced technologies in expectation of the growth of the market, so as to win in the procurement competition. A number of missions were sent abroad and a number of them were invited from abroad. The Army invited a team of French pilots and engineers in 1919 and the Navy followed by inviting a British team. Some of them stayed for several months to teach Japanese manufacturers every aspect of aviation. All the major Japanese manufacturers imported designs and other critical technologies extensively through licensing from French, British, and other foreign companies in the late 1910s through 1920s.

In addition, Japan imported technology from Germany which, until 1926, was banned from research and production of military aircraft following its defeat in World War I. German manufacturers sought ties with Japan to utilize their technological resources and also to maintain these resources intact through the prohibition period. For Japan, the German technologies were of course welcome, particularly because they had the leading technology in metal-framed aircraft. Mitsubishi signed a technology agreement with Junkers in 1925; Aichi, with Heinkel in 1924; and Kawasaki, with Dornier in 1924. Many German engineers came to Japan under these and other arrangements.

In a paper on the transfer of aircraft technology from Germany to Japan, Caspary (1995) reports an interesting episode. Heinkel received an order from Aichi, on the Navy's behalf, to design a small aircraft. At the time, a team from the League of Nations occasionally visited German aircraft manufacturers to monitor the ban on military aircraft research and production. A Japanese military attaché who was a member of the monitoring team let Heinkel know, confidentially and in advance, of the planned visit. Heinkel thus succeeded in continuing, without being spotted, its design on the aircraft ordered by Aichi Aircraft.

During the inter-war period, therefore, Japan could and did actively import aircraft technology from the UK, France, the USA, as well as from Germany, until Japan went into alliance with Germany and Italy in 1940, which left Germany as practically the only source of technology importation.[2]

10.5 WORLD WAR II AND THE EXPANSION OF AIRCRAFT PRODUCTION

When the 1930s began and as Japan accelerated its military build-up, the aircraft industry started to grow. The Army invaded Manchuria in 1931 and established a puppet state, Manchukuo, in 1932. The Shanghai Incident occurred in the same year. These events gradually led to the war against China and the start of Pacific War four years later. The annual production of aircraft increased rapidly from approximately 400 in 1931 to 4,800 in 1941 and peaked at 24,000 in 1944.

As the production level started to rise, it became increasingly necessary to develop airframe and engines with Japan's own technology. By this time, most of the aircraft manufactured in Japan had been designed by foreign engineers, manufactured under license agreements, or made by imitating foreign models. Like the other industries, technological capabilities had to be now enhanced by own R&D efforts, in addition to learning from imported technologies. The Army and Navy naturally encouraged these efforts for national security reasons and took various policy measures, such as financial assistance, to promote the new technologies.

In 1932, the Navy founded Naval Aviation Arsenal by consolidating its various sections and laboratories related to aviation. It became the centre for research and testing of aviation in Japan. In the same year, the Navy launched a three-year programme to have the manufacturers develop certain types of aircraft under competition. Most important of them were '96-Shiki' (96-Type) fighters and bombers developed by Mitsubishi with engines made by Nakajima. Introduced in 1936, it had the maximum hourly speed of 450 km, clearly showing that the technological level of these Japanese manufacturers had finally reached that of the world leaders.

With the outbreak of war against China in 1937, the Japanese economy moved to a wartime control system (see also Chapter 4). In 1938, the National Total Mobilization Law (*Kokka So Doin Ho*) was enacted, which gave the government the power to control every aspect of the economy without approval of the Diet. In the same year, the Aircraft

Manufacturing Enterprise Law (*Kouku Seizou Jigyo Ho*) was enacted to promote and control the production of aircraft for military uses. Preceding this law, several companies had entered into the production of aircraft and/or engines in anticipation of the growing demand for military aircraft, in the second wave of entry (the first was in 1918–25). For instance, Ishikawajima had started engine production. The law tried to discourage further entry, increase the production level, and upgrade the technology level of existing manufactures by providing tax breaks, other financial incentives, and preferential access to materials.

Under the law, the government abolished the competitive procurement system and instead adopted a system whereby the military designated a specific firm to develop a certain model, the production of which was to be shared by other manufacturers. Although this system had the effect of lessening competitive pressure on the manufacturers, it reduced inter-firm variance in work-load, which was especially beneficial to smaller firms that tended to suffer from an unpredictable flow of orders. In addition, the system facilitated and even forced the inter-firm transfer of technology, which used to be hindered by the rivalry between the Navy and the Army.

As World War II broke out in Europe in 1939, technology importation became virtually impossible. Communications with Germany, Japan's ally that had an advanced aviation technology, became difficult, although some information was nevertheless brought in by submarine. Efforts were intensified to nurture and upgrade technologies and to increase production levels. These efforts bore fruit. In particular, the 'Zero' fighter was developed and manufactured by Mitsubishi based on the '96-Shiki' fighter mentioned earlier, and became world famous. It had a maximum speed of more than 500 km per hour, with high manoeuvrability. Also well-known was the '100-Shiki' reconnaissance plane with a maximum speed of 540 km per hour. The production of these and other models expanded rapidly.

In 1945, however, the amount of aircraft production dropped to 5,130, and engine production to 10,281, barely a quarter of the respective figures in the previous year. The whole economy was suffering from the shortage of materials, energy, and skilled workers, and the breakdown of production flow caused by bombing. Even the aircraft industry suffered badly despite the government's giving priority to the industry in the allocation of resources. The effort to develop faster aircraft continued. For instance, a jet engine was developed with the help of German technology. The test flight being made successfully in 1945. The research on rockets, infra-red homing bombs, and missiles was started. There was no time left, however, and all the efforts were terminated in August 1945 when Japan surrendered.

How shall we evaluate the achievement of the pre-war Japanese aircraft manufacturing industry? The answer perhaps depends on whether it should be compared over time or across countries. Over time, it was a remarkable achievement despite the short period of 35 years. After intensive learning from the West, it succeeded in developing world-class small aircraft such as 'Zero' and small engines such as 'Homare' and 'Sakae'. The 'A-26' long-range plane set the world distance record at the time. It was one of the three countries that succeeded in flying a jet plane before the end of World War II, along with Germany and Britain. The Japanese industry was fourth largest in the world in terms of the number of aircraft produced, after the US, the UK, and Germany. The cumulative amount of production was about 100,000 planes and 150,000 engines by the end of the war.

When compared to the best practices in the world, the industry still had a long way to go. However successful it might have been in developing small aircraft and small engines, it failed to develop good large aircraft and large engines. Quality control and production management were hardly satisfactory, particularly in comparison to the USA. In a study of the adoption of gauge and industrial standards in Japan, Baba, Kuroda, and Yoshiki (1996) observed that standardization of such basic components as thread was delayed and interchangeability of parts was hardly achieved. The production depended heavily on the input of massive manpower and craftsmanship rather than scientific production and management control. Even discounting the fact that the industry had to make do with limited resources and limited time, product quality was always the problem.

Therefore, despite the impressive progress of the Japanese aircraft industry, it may have never caught up with that of the advanced Western nations: in fact, the technology gap with the USA and Germany might have widened by the end of war. Karasawa (1986) argues, for instance, that during the five-year war period, the horsepower of Zero fighters could be increased only by 20 per cent whereas Americans and Germans more than doubled the horsepower of their fighters, thereby surpassing Zero fighters by the end of war. This technological gap, together with similar gaps in electronics (see Chapter 8) and automobiles (see Chapter 9), was arguably at least partly responsible for Japan's defeat.

10.6   POST-WAR RECONSTRUCTION OF THE AIRCRAFT INDUSTRY

After the end of the war, all aircraft-related activities were banned. The manufacturing equipment and facilities were designated as assets to be seized for reparations, and the facilities for research, development, and testing were destroyed. In addition, the major airframe manufacturers, including Mitsubishi, Nakajima, and Kawasaki, were divided into several smaller firms under the Economic Democratization Policies of the Allied Powers.

To survive, these firms started producing various merchandise, such as scooters, bus bodies, auto parts, and farm equipment, during the seven years of prohibition. Since the aircraft industry had expanded to be one of the major industries during the war and, at one time, employed nearly 700,000 workers, it was a massive conversion from military-related production to civilian production, somewhat similar to events in several countries after the end of the Cold War.

The damage was most severe at Nakajima because it was one of the two largest aircraft manufacturers, together with Mitsubishi Heavy Industries and, furthermore, it was not as diversified as MHI, which had shipbuilding and general machinery businesses. The company was dissolved and a number of spin-off companies were started by the former managers, engineers, and workers. In 1953, several of them got together to form Fuji Heavy Industries, which succeeded in entering the automobile market with Subaru cars and, eventually, in resuming aircraft production. Another spin-off company merged with a company formed by some of the former workers of Tachikawa Aircraft to start Prince Motors, which was later acquired by Nissan. As discussed in Chapter 4, MHI was split into three firms under the Deconcentration Law but re-merged in 1964. Its aircraft engineers started making automobiles, and Mitsubishi Motors was later established as a subsidiary.

In addition, quite a few aircraft engineers joined automobile firms, such as Toyota, Honda, and Nissan (see Chapter 9). As we saw earlier, the shipbuilding industry played a major role in the birth of the Japanese aircraft industry: now, the aircraft industry played a major role in the post-war development of the automobile industry.

Some of the aircraft engineers joined Nihon Kokuyu Tetsudo (Japan National Railway) and played an important role in developing the famous *Shinkansen* bullet train. Kawanishi Aircraft became Shin Meiwa

Kogyo (ShinMaywa Industries) and essentially remained in the aircraft business.

The aircraft manufacturing industry was allowed to resume its activity after the Peace Treaty of San Francisco went into effect in 1952. However, the technology in aircraft manufacturing had advanced drastically during the seven-year period of the production ban, particularly in two regards. The first was the development of jet planes. The switch from reciprocating engines to jet engines not only made the enormous increase in travel speed possible but also caused a drastic change in the design of aircraft, especially of wings, and required new materials that were resistant to high heat. The second was the progress in radar technology, which caused a radical change in aviation control. Consequently, when the Japanese aircraft industry resumed its activity, it found itself lagging far behind the best practice of the world. The process of learning and catch-up started again.

Four firms started to develop and manufacture light planes. They were training planes and sports planes, but all the plans were abandoned after a few prototypes were made. An exception was a new entrant, Toyo Aircraft, which succeeded in exporting its aircraft: it soon went bankrupt, however.

The main activity of the industry in the early 1950s was the production of parts and repair work for the US Air Force, which was involved in the Korean War. The amount of production was worth 3.4 billion yen and the amount of repair work 2.6 billion yen during the 1952–4 period. About three-quarters of the production and almost all of the repair work was for the US Air Force. However, the sales to the US Air Force declined rapidly after the cease-fire agreement in 1953.

In 1952, the Aircraft Manufacturing Law (*Koukuki Seizo Ho*) was enacted and the Aircraft Division was created within the Ministry of International Trade and Industry (MITI). The law required aircraft manufacturers to be registered so that their technological level was kept high enough to maintain the safety of the products. Thirty-nine firms registered and about another 30 firms showed interest. The law was amended in 1954 to become the Aircraft Manufacturing Enterprise Law (*Koukuki Seizo Jigyo Ho*), which stipulated that only the firms with 'excellent technology and healthy management' would be approved for aircraft production.

The policy to promote the industry started. MITI's advisory board, the Aircraft Production Council, published a recommendation which encouraged the promotion of the industry on four grounds: (1) the demand for aircraft would increase, (2) the industry would be suitable for Japan and could become a promising export industry, (3) Japan should move up the ladder ahead as the developing countries were catching up, (4) technological spill-over to other industries would take place.

In 1954, Japan Defence Agency (hereafter JDA) was established and Japan started to arm itself gradually with the help of the USA under the intensifying strain of the Cold War. Accordingly, the industry started to manufacture military aircraft for JDA under license agreements with US manufacturers.

Two big projects started in 1955: F86F fighter planes and T33A trainers. A number of engineers and managers were sent by North American, the licensor of F86F, to Shin Mitsubishi (later MHI), the licensee and main contractor. Similarly, engineers were sent from Lockheed, the licensor of T33A, to Kawasaki. Japanese engineers also visited factories in the USA. Transfer of knowledge took place in terms not only of production technology but also of know-how concerning inventory control, labour management, and quality control. Tools, jigs, and fixtures were developed and the production facilities of parts and equipment suppliers were modernized. Strict quality control was emphasized not only to maintain the quality of the aircraft but also to maintain interchangeability of parts between Japanese and American military aircraft.

As the learning proceeded, the proportion of domestic contents increased. The first 70 F86F planes were entirely made by knockdown production, with all the components and parts, as well as jigs and tools, imported from the USA. However, the domestic content ratio rose to 32.4 per cent in terms of value in the next 77 planes and to 48.0 per cent in the last 120. Similarly, the production of T33A planes proceeded from simple knockdown production of the first 30 planes to 43.1 per cent domestic content of the last 30 (Adachi, 1981). The technological capabilities were thus accumulated through learning.

Even after production of the T33A ended in 1959 and that of the F86F in 1960, production under license agreements with US manufacturers continued. The aircraft thus produced included the P2V7 (Lockheed), the F104J (Lockheed), the F-4 (McDonnell Douglas), the F-15 (McDonnell Douglas) and other smaller planes and helicopters. The names of the licensors are in parentheses. Hall and Johnson (1970) describe in detail how Japanese manufacturers of airframes, engines, and components learned the technology through these projects. Samuels

(1994) argues that Japanese manufacturers benefited from these licensing agreements and that the aircraft technology thus learned was used in other fields as well.

In 1955, when the need for a new jet trainer was emphasized by JDA, a heated controversy took place between JDA and the Ministry of Finance on the one hand and MITI on the other. The former two insisted on licensed production because of expected reliability, fast delivery, and cost saving, whereas MITI insisted on domestic development to promote the industry (Samuels, 1994). MITI won and a design competition was held, with Fuji Heavy Industries (FHI) winning the contract. They started delivering the jet trainer, T-1, in 1958 and, in total, 66 T-1 planes were built. It thus became the first mass-produced jet aircraft in Japan. At first it was fitted with a British jet engine but, two years later, began to use a J-3 jet engine developed by the consortium of Japanese manufacturers including IHI, FHI, MHI, and Fuji Seimitsu (later Prince Motors, which would merge with Nissan). The consortium eventually dissolved after transferring the production of J-3 to IHI (Ministry of International Trade and Industry, 1985).

10.7 THE FIRST COMMERCIAL AIRCRAFT, THE YS-11

T-1 was not the only project to develop aircraft domestically and several others were undertaken during the 1960s and 1970s. Among these, the YS-11, a short-range, 60-seat, turboprop airliner, deserves more discussion because it was the first (and, to this day, the only) commercial aircraft that Japan has developed, manufactured, and sold worldwide.

The basic research and design for the YS-11 started with the establishment in 1957 of Yusoki Sekkei Kenkyu Kyokai (Association for the Research on Transport Airplane), an umbrella organization of airframe manufacturers and researchers. This association developed into a semigovernmental corporation, Nihon Koukuki Seizo (Nippon Aircraft Manufacturing Co.; NAM), established under the Aircraft Manufacturing Promotion Law (*Koukuki Kogyo Shinko Ho*). Of the initial capitalization of 500 million yen, 300 million was funded by the government and 200 by private firms, including MHI, KHI, FHI, and ShinMaywa. NAM was responsible for the detailed design and manufacture of the prototype, while the actual manufacturing was subcontracted to airframe manufacturers on a cost basis. This arrangement was similar to the one JDA used in its procurement.

The development effort started at NAM in 1959 with 125 members, seventy of whom were in the design department. These people were all seconded from the participating firms. The chief design engineer was Tojo Teruo of MHI. Tojo had, before the war, worked under the afore-mentioned Horikoshi Jiro in the development of Zero fighters. Horikoshi himself served as an advisor for NAM as did Doi Takeo who had developed several engines at pre-war KHI. Therefore, the technological capability accumulated before and during the war did contribute to the development of the YS-11. Yet, the technology had tremendously advanced in the meantime and they found the required design, attributes, and performance of commercial aircraft to be often quite different from those of military aircraft. This difficulty caused the development cost of the YS-11 to exceed the original estimate and reach 5.7 billion yen, of which the government provided 3 billion. NAM financed its production cost mostly through loans from banks and participating aircraft manufacturers, which the government guaranteed.

The first flight was made in 1962, three years after the start of the development. However, there were several severe problems, such as poor steering, vibration, and noise, and it took another two years to solve them. Finally, in 1964, the US Federal Aviation Authority issued a licence to YS-11 and full-scale production began. At first, demand came from Japanese airlines only. Yet, as the performance and passenger comfort of the YS-11 were gradually improved, and as its merits, particularly easy landing and take-off on short runways became known, it started to be sold overseas. In total, 182 planes were manufactured and 82 planes were exported to 15 countries. An American airline, Piedmont, was the largest customer with the purchase of 21 planes. Today they are still used in various parts of the world.[3]

Production of the YS-11 was terminated in 1971 with the total loss of 36 billion yen, of which 16 per cent was shouldered by participating firms. This financial failure may be explained by the following four factors. First, NAM's marketing capacity was insufficient because the YS-11 was the first commercial aircraft ever produced in Japan and, consequently, skills and resources necessary for marketing had not been accumulated. In contrast to the military demand, on which the industry had been dependent both before and after the war, marketing is crucially important in the commercial aircraft business not only for the sales activity itself but also for collecting information on the airlines' needs, as well as for maintenance and repair services. The lack of marketing skills and of connections with airlines thus turned out to be a serious handicap.

Secondly, the demand for turboprop planes did not grow as much as expected, because large jet planes started to dominate the world market. In this relatively small market, the YS-11 faced stiff competition against other turboprops, such as the Fokker F27 and the Hughes HS748.

Thirdly, as already mentioned, the production of the YS-11 was contracted out to several airframe manufacturers. They had little incentive to reduce costs because NAM compensated on a cost basis. Consequently, the production cost decreased only marginally, even after production entered the mass-production stage. Clearly, the slope of the learning curve depends on the effectiveness of incentive mechanisms, and the lack of market competition and of a performance-based compensation scheme failed to solicit the efforts of manufacturers to achieve effective learning. Such a lack made it extremely difficult for NAM to compete, in a competitive world market for commercial aircraft.

Fourthly, the appreciation of the yen in 1971 caused the loss of nearly 15 billion yen, because the planes had been sold on a dollar basis.

Despite the financial failure, the YS-11 project, some argue, was successful from a technological viewpoint. The performance of the plane stabilized and improved greatly in later products; the airframe manufacturers acquired the technology for development, design, and production; and the suppliers accumulated capabilities to develop parts and equipment. In addition, even though NAM suffered from a huge loss and the participating firms shouldered part of it, they were paid for their work as subcontractors on a cost basis, and they could maintain the workload at a time when defence demand was low because of the transition from the Second Defense Procurement Program to the Third Program. Thus, the manufacturers benefited in several ways.

It is, therefore, difficult to make a total evaluation of the YS-11 project. The money spent was enormous but it left technological knowledge and skills, and many lessons. With these lessons, it might have been possible to proceed to the next stage of the development of commercial aircraft with more efficient organizational arrangements and financial support from the government, similarly perhaps to the Airbus project in Europe. As was the case with the Airbus, however, it was debatable whether such a project would have increased the net economic welfare.

10.8 DEVELOPMENT AFTER THE YS-11

In addition to the YS-11, a few commercial attempts were made in the late 1960s and early 1970s. MHI introduced MU-2 turboprop business aircraft into the market in 1965 and succeeded in selling 757 planes by 1985, mainly in North America through Mitsubishi Aircraft International, Inc., a final-assembly and marketing subsidiary in Texas. Its successor, the MU-300, was introduced in 1979 as the first business jet developed in Japan. MHI sold 101 planes by the end of 1985. FHI introduced the FA-200 light plane, 299 units of which were manufactured (Nihon Kouku Uchu Kogyo Kai, 1994).

In the decade 1965–75, eight new models of aircraft were developed by the Japanese manufacturers, including the T-2, the first supersonic trainer, which made Japan the sixth nation to design and manufacture supersonic aircraft, after the US, the USSR, the UK, France, and Sweden (Samuels, 1994). The production of these eight models combined reached 1,952 by the end of the 1970s. The sales of the aircraft industry exceeded 100 billion yen in 1972 and 200 billion yen in 1975. It was still a small industry compared to other major manufacturing industries such as automobiles, electric machinery, and steel, or to the aircraft industry in other developed countries. Yet, it had been growing rapidly and the technological capabilities were accumulated.

Arguably, the next plausible step was to develop a larger transport plane as a follow-up to the YS-11, and to develop more military aircraft for JDA, while continuing the licenced production of advanced military aircraft. For the first purpose, the YX Development Division was set up within NAM in 1968. Various plans were investigated including the development of 90-seat, 110-to-149-seat, 150-to-180-seat, and 200-to-250-seat aircraft. However, while these plans were discussed, it became increasingly apparent that, in any of these market segments, the fierce competition would make profitable survival extremely difficult. Moreover, the Japanese manufacturers, which were used to relatively risk-free defence procurement business, were reluctant to commit themselves in the risky worldwide civilian aircraft market. Finally, the plan was merged with the 7X7 project of Boeing and materialized as the Boeing 767 in 1981. The Japanese firms participated in this international venture as 'risk-sharing subcontractors' together with an Italian firm. With it, the dream vanished of the Japanese aircraft industry accumulating sufficient design technology and marketing know-how to become one of the world's leading manufacturers.

The truth, however, is that it is increasingly difficult for a firm, even a firm as big and advanced as Boeing, to develop large commercial aircraft alone because of the accelerating development cost. In addition, international collaboration makes it easier for the partners to penetrate their home markets, and to gain subsidies from their governments. And the rising technological level of partners in various countries makes it possible to purchase quality components at low cost from these countries. Hence, international collaboration is and will be used extensively, with Boeing playing the central role. The Japanese aircraft industry may be able to increase their share in development and production in such international consortia, and may be able to get access to design technology and marketing know-how. For instance, in the Boeing 777 project started in 1990, the Japanese manufacturers became the 'program partners' and were allowed to have ceratin access to design technology.

The domestic development of advanced military aircraft met similar difficulties. Partly because the US military budget has been cut as the Cold War ended and partly because the USA is increasingly concerned with the mounting trade deficit against Japan, the USA has been pressing the Japanese government so as to secure the large Japanese defence market for American manufacturers. The result was a setback in Japan's plan to develop FS-X fighters domestically in the late 1980s. Instead, Japan and the USA agreed to upgrade the F-16 of General Dynamics jointly. See Samuels (1994) for more details.

The USA has also been concerned with the 'boomerang effect', fearing that the technology transfer to Japan might eventually create strong competitor in the world aircraft market that the USA has been dominating. As a result, technology transfer through licensing agreements between Japanese and American manufacturers is increasingly restricted.

10.9 THE JAPANESE AIRCRAFT INDUSTRY TODAY

In 1992, sales of the Japanese aerospace industry were worth 1.2 trillion yen, which is smaller than those of not only the USA (17.5 trillion yen) but also the UK (2.1 trillion yen), France (2.5 trillion yen), and Germany (1.8 trillion yen). It was also much smaller than those of other major Japanese manufacturing industries, for instance, automobiles (44.1 trillion yen), general machinery (35.4 trillion yen), steel (18.6 trillion yen), and electric appliances (15.1 trillion yen). Thus, despite its gradual development since the re-start in 1952, it is still a small industry.[4]

The industry is heavily dependent on defence demand. In 1992, 74 per cent of the demand came from Japan Defence Agency. This percentage fell to 52 in 1968 when the production of the YS-11 was at its peak: afterwards, it exceeded 70 per cent persistently.

There are five airframe manufacturers currently in operation, suggesting that, relative to the small size of the industry, the number of firms is not small. These manufacturers are all divisions within diversified firms and, in these firms, the ratio of aircraft sales to total sales was only 12 per cent in 1992. This makes a good contrast to Boeing and McDonnell Douglas where the same ratio was more than 80 per cent. One may be tempted to compare this with the case of the semiconductor industry where diversified firms are dominating in Japan, but specialists such as Texas Instruments, Motorola, and Intel, are active in the USA. Some authors, such as Kimura (1996), has argued that this diversification in the Japanese semiconductor producers has been the source of their strength.

The profit rate of the Japanese aircraft industry has been low. The ratio of before-tax profit to sales in the 1970s was a mere 1–2 per cent as an average of the aircraft divisions of twenty-five firms. In 1980, the industry recorded losses of 3.5 billion yen, which increased to 10.2 billion yen in 1981. It has been recording profits since 1983, but the profit rate remains low. In 1991–2, the before-tax profit rate on sales was 1.2 per cent while that of all firms having aircraft divisions was 2.7 per cent.

It is difficult to expect a rapid expansion of demand in the domestic market. As mentioned earlier, the industry is heavily dependent on defence demand. However, the growth in defence demand is constrained for two reasons. The first is the limited size of Japan's defence spending. Although Japan has increased defence spending in the 1980s, the end of the Cold War and the tight government budget has reversed this trend. The second is the policy of the Japanese Government not to allow the export of military hardware. For instance, the Japanese airframe manufacturers are prohibited from exporting fighter planes.

The prospect for domestic demand in commercial planes is also dim. Since Japan is geographically a small country, a network of ground transportation is well developed and the high land price has made the construction cost of airports extremely high. Therefore, the rapid growth of demand for air travel and for airplanes are unlikely to materialize. This fact makes a contrast to the experience of the automobile industry where the presence of a large and expanding domestic market was vital for the industry at an early stage of its development. Through the realization of scale economy and learning effects, together with fierce competition in the consumer market, the automobile industry could develop an efficient production process that enabled the manufacturers to reduce costs. This efficiency had them compete effectively in the world market. In the aircraft industry, by contrast, the limited size of the domestic market has made it difficult for the manufacturers to accumulate experience and increase the productivity through learning and improvement.

It also makes a contrast with the US aircraft industry where the manufacturers have been enjoying a large defence market, as well as a large civilian market, which enabled them to accumulate technologies in development, design, and manufacturing.

The Japanese manufacturers are facing difficulties in the export market as well, for three reasons. First, as mentioned earlier, their marketing capacity is limited. This weakness comes partly from the fact that they are newcomers in the world market and, therefore, marketing channels and brand names are not well established. Perhaps more importantly, however, they have not been making persistent marketing efforts because of their dependence on defence demand. This lack of marketing capacity caused not only the difficulty in sales but also the difficulty in gaining information on the customers' needs. This feedback of information on user needs is vital in developing new aircraft and in introducing the variations of original models.

Secondly, the Japanese aircraft industry is said to be less cost-conscious than their counterparts in the USA or other Japanese industries, say, the automobile industry, largely because of their heavy dependence on defence demand. This fact is partly responsible for the demise of the YS-11, Japan's first mid-sized civilian transport.

Thirdly, since, as repeatedly argued, the Japanese industry has been producing military aircraft under the license agreements with US firms, as well as small aircraft, it has lacked the experience and capability in developing large-scale commercial aircraft. Again, this lack was one of the causes of the failure of the YS-11 project.

Perhaps the gap between Japan and the USA regarding process technology and product-embodied technology has been narrowing. However, Japan still lags far behind the USA in management technology and design technology, which are now regarded as the most important factors for the past and present dominance of US commercial aircraft producers. The Japanese manufacturers are now finding it extremely difficult to acquire the design technology necessary for developing large aircraft, either through accumulation of their own experience or through technology transfer from abroad.

To sum up, the aircraft industry differs from other manufacturing industries in its dependence on military demand. It has been a rather small industry and its prospect of becoming a leading industry appears bleak despite several government policies, unlike the automobile or electronics industry. None the less, it has learned and accumulated advanced technologies. Some of the component manufacturers are considered to be at the frontier of technology development. In addition, as Samuels (1994) emphasizes, there has been significant spillover of aircraft technology, a large part of which was imported from the USA, to related industries and other divisions within the diversified aircraft manufacturers. To this extent, the true contribution of the aircraft industry can never be evaluated by looking at the performance of this industry alone.

10.10   CONCLUSION

In the industries studied here, shipbuilding and aircraft, the role of the government was larger than in any other industry studied in this book, apparently owing to their strong military connection. Such strong connection did (and does) exist in virtually any nation, where the government support was similarly large. Yet, the support may have been more conspicuous in Japan (and perhaps Germany) than, say, in the UK because of the late start in Japan's industrialization and military build-up.

The government support was given in terms of financial support (e.g., subsidies), technical support (e.g., the provision of technical information by the arsenals and naval shipyards), and the support of demand through procurement. Although it is impossible to compare the contribution of these means quantitatively, we note the importance of demand support in particular. In the shipbuilding industry, subsidies given to shipping companies for the purchase of domestically built ships appear to have been more effective than the subsidies given directly to shipbuilding companies. Such subsidies to shipping companies were given both in the pre-war period through the Navigation Promotion Law and in the post-war period through the Programmed Shipbuilding

Scheme. Moreover, the Navy procured preferentially from domestic shipbuilders despite the initial high cost and poor quality of warship.

In the aircraft industry, virtually all the aircraft produced before and during World War II was purchased by the military, which urged the industry to develop faster and more reliable aircraft. The post-war production was also supported by the Japan Defence Army, which encouraged the firms to import technology through licensing from American manufacturers. The technological capability thus accumulated helped the post-war effort to develop the YS-11, the first commercial aircraft. However, the dependence on military demand had the firms become less cost-conscious and less familiar with the business of commercial aircraft, which turned out to be a significant handicap in the development, manufacture, and marketing of the YS-11.

As in other industries, technological capabilities started to be accumulated through copying and reverse-engineering foreign advanced products, and importing technology by licensing agreements, followed by learning from production experience and then R&D efforts. Unlike most other industries, however, the aircraft industry has not really caught up with the world's technological frontier and, hence, has been (and still is, to a significant extent) relying on imported technology. In this process, the government support of demand helped the manufacturers to accumulate production experience and thereby learn from it. Even though the YS-11 project was a failure financially, the case also indicated the importance of learning from experience. In fact, from the experience of developing and manufacturing the YS-11, the industry has accumulated so much capability that, had the government further supported the domestic development of the next commercial aircraft, the industry might have been able to develop a more attractive product with which, some argue, it could compete against Boeing and Airbus.

However, the worldwide commercial aircraft market is limited in size and the presence of huge development and start-up costs causes significant scale economies. Hence, the advantage of pioneering producers, such as Boeing, is substantial and a huge sunk cost would have been required for the Japanese firms to accumulate sufficiently large production experience to reduce costs to the competitive level. Now that Japan has abandoned (at least for the moment) an independent effort to develop major commercial aircraft in favour of participation to Boeing-led international consortium, the big question is whether it should maintain and hopefully enhance the technological capability that would be needed to develop at least small-scale passenger planes, or remain merely as a subcontractor to Boeing and others. The first view is held by the believers of the infant industry theory and those who believe that an economy of Japan's size should have a portfolio of industries to benefit from inter-industry technological and other spillovers, whereas the second view is held by the believers of international division of labour.

Inter-industry technological spillover has been significant. Such spillover took place from the shipbuilding industry to the electrical equipment industry, the automobile industry, and the aircraft industry among others, and from the aircraft industry to the automobile industry, the metals industry, the precision instrument industry, and so forth. The channel for this spillover was diverse. In part it accompanied the diversification of firms, for instance, the diversification of Mitsubishi Shipbuilding to the electrical equipment business (to be hived off as Mitsubishi Electric), aircraft business, and machinery business. It also accompanied the move of managers, engineers, and workers when they changed jobs in response to changing industrial structures. The case of former aircraft engineers moving to the post-war automobile industry was typical. It also accompanied the purchase of materials and components. Thus, the introduction of British technology in shipbuilding also brought technology regarding the electrical parts to be fitted to ships, and the post-war introduction of US technology in aircraft also brought technology to the instruments to be fitted to military planes, thereby enhancing the technological capability of the suppliers of these parts and instruments.

Such spillover, however, takes place neither instantaneously nor automatically. It may take decades, because industrial structure changes slowly, except for the turbulent periods following, say, the Meiji Restoration or the defeat in World War II. This observation casts doubt on the relevance of a number of empirical studies in which the extent of inter-industry R&D spillover is measured by the effect of R&D by other industries to the productivity (or other measures of R&D output) of the industry in the same year or, at most, a few years later. After surveying these studies, Griliches (1992: S41) warned that 'the usual procedure . . . ignores the possibility that spillovers take more time than "own" effects, both because of secrecy and the time it may take for them to be expressed in new products and processes and diffused throughout the relevant industrial structure.' According to our case studies, this lag may actually be much larger than Griliches perhaps had in mind. To this extent, all the existing empirical findings must have underestimated the real significance of inter-industry technological spillover. Quite likely, this spillover was one of the critical sources of industrial development and industrial re-structuring in Japan.

Neither is spillover automatic. The technology would not spread from industry A to industry B unless A makes a conscious effort to spread it outside or B makes a conscious effort to acquire it by copying or learning. B must have a capability to find out which technology is available, to select which technology should be adopted, and to adapt in-coming technology to utilize it fully for its own purpose. Such adaptation, furthermore, may entail a major investment. If the spillover is to be made within a diversified firm, division A has to be aware of the technologies available in the other division B, and a collaborative effort by the engineers of A and B may be required; therefore, in addition to technological capabilities, a suitable organizational arrangement is needed to foster the collaboration. We have suggested that the Japanese management system has been conducive to such collaboration (see Chapter 5) and that the general technological capability has been raised by education, learning by doing, and innovation efforts. Were it not for these managerial and technological efforts and innovation, Japan's industrial development would have been much slower.

11

Pharmaceuticals

The history of the pharmaceutical industry in Japan may be separated roughly into six stages: Stage I (up to the Meiji Restoration, 1868) when the firms sold various herb medicines of Japanese, Chinese, and Korean origin; Stage II (from the Restoration to World War I) when the firms imported Western medicines; Stage III (between the two world wars) when the firms started producing medicines to substitute imports; Stage IV (from the end of World War II to around 1960) when the firms imported technology through license agreements with Western firms; and Stage V (the 1960s onwards) when the firms have been intensifying their original R&D efforts.

There are now some 1,500 pharmaceutical producers in Japan. Most are small, with only 12 per cent of them employing 300 or more workers. The origins of these companies are diverse. Some of them, including the industry leader, Takeda, have a history that goes back to Stage I. Others have a much shorter history. For example, Eisai, which is currently one of the top ten, started in 1936, i.e., around the end of Stage III. This diversity has resulted from the downfall of many old firms that could not cope with the changing economic conditions, and active entries of new firms.

11.1 THE EARLY PERIOD

Although the history of the Japanese pharmaceutical industry has been basically that of catching up with the West, the technological gap should not be over-emphasized. Even in Europe, modern medical science is considered to have started in the mid- to late nineteenth century when Pasteur (1822–95) of France, and Koch (1843–1910) of Germany discovered bacteria and their relation to diseases. Therefore, even though Seclusionism during the Tokugawa era caused a delay in Japan's learning of the Western medical method, the delay was not as large as one might think.

During the Tokugawa era, medical knowledge came from China. The Chinese method used various kinds of herb medicines and, therefore, these medicines had to be supplied. Later, knowledge of Western medical science was brought by Dutch doctors living in Nagasaki, the only city in which the Shogunate government allowed Dutchmen to live (see Section 1.7). The most important of them was von Siebold (a German doctor employed by the Dutch government) who lived there from 1823 to 1828 and taught a number of Japanese doctors. He taught, for example, pathological anatomy, which was not only unfamiliar to the Japanese doctors at the time but considered to be sacrilegious to the deceased. It was still before Pasteur, and the medicine he used was of botanical, zoological, or mineral (that is, non-synthetic) origin, such as herb medicines.

Another technology brought by von Siebold was vaccination, which had been developed by Jenner a few decades earlier. Von Siebold taught the method to Japanese students, but it was another twenty years before an effective vaccine was brought to Japan. A number of Japanese doctors who had learned from von Siebold or his disciples made efforts to spread vaccination among the population. One of them was Ogata Koan, who established a private school, Tekijuku (see Section 1.7), and, in his later years, was invited by the Shogun to become his chief doctor and, at the same time, to head a school which would later develop into the Medical School of the University of Tokyo, as will be presently discussed.

Therefore, although the knowledge of Western medicine came to Japan late, the delay was in the order of, say, a few decades. None the less, doctors with such knowledge were very few compared to the majority of doctors who practised according to the Chinese method. As a result, the demand was overwhelmingly towards Chinese-style medicines.

The main trading centre for these medicines was an area in Osaka called Doshomachi. In the seventeenth century, many wholesalers and brokers of medicines started to gather here. In 1722, the government allowed 124 of them to form a Guild (*Kabu Nakama*), which basically continued until the Meiji Restoration. This Guild formed a market to which Japanese herbs were collected, and imported ones brought via the port of Nagasaki. They were then sold all over the country either as raw medicines or as mixed medicines with brand names.

These wholesalers played several roles.[1] The first and most obvious was the distribution to local areas around the country. The second was risk-bearing, because the price they had to pay to the Chinese, Korean, and Dutch traders, and the price they could charge to local retailers fluctuated according to separate market conditions. The third was the assurance of quality. Guild members' seals on merchandise were taken by the buyers as the assurance of quality and, being aware of this effect, the sellers carefully appraised the quality to avoid selling defective goods and to maintain their reputation. The fourth was the maintenance of commercial order. For instance, they carefully watched lest illegal imports, direct sales from producers to retailers bypassing the Guild, or any other wrongdoing (as they saw it) should take place. Needless to say, it is a moot question whether the maintenance of such 'order' was beneficial to the public or harmful through the restriction of free trade. Apparently, it had a certain price-maintenance effect.

The Guild membership was hereditary but could be sold to others under certain conditions. The purchase of the membership occurred in two ways. The first was the case of the second or younger sons of proprietors. Because of the right of primogeniture, these younger sons had to either work for eldest brothers or start their own businesses. The other was the case of former employees starting their own businesses. The former employers, as a reward for their long and diligent services, usually supported them by providing part of the initial investment or allowing them to take a number of customers with them. As discussed in Chapter 4, such a practice was commonly adopted to provide work incentives to the employees.

Since the number of such people wishing to join the Guild almost always exceeded the number of vacancies, the price of membership soared. A second-tier group of traders was also created to accommodate those who could not get the Guild membership immediately.

Although some of the present pharmaceutical companies started as members of the Guild, their number is surprisingly small compared to the size of the Guild (124 members, later expanded to 129), indicating that it was only the adventurous and well-managed members who survived through the turbulent years following the Meiji Restoration, by first becoming import traders and then manufacturers.

Probably the oldest among the present major pharmaceutical companies is Tanabe. It started in 1678 before the Guild was formed, when Tanabe Gohei started a wholesale business at Doshomachi. His business prospered as he sold medicine, a mix of herbs, under the brand name 'Tanabe-ya Kusuri' (Tanabe Store Medicine). The present market leader, Takeda, was also a big member of the Guild, founded in 1781 when Takeda Chobei started his own business after nineteen years of service with an established wholesaler. Similarly, Ono started when Ono Ichibei became independent in 1717.

Among the top thirty or so companies today, these three seem to be the only cases of former Guild members. Therefore, the percentage of Guild members surviving till today is very small indeed. In addition, when the Guild was forced to disband after the Meiji Restoration, two companies among the present top ten started their businesses as wholesalers in Doshomachi. They were Shionogi, founded in 1878, and Fujisawa, founded in 1894.

11.2   THE SPREAD OF WESTERN MEDICINE AND THE START OF PHARMACEUTICAL PRODUCTION

The start of trade with Westerners (besides the Dutch) in 1859, together with the first appointment of a doctor practising the Western method to serve the Tokugawa Shogun, signalled both an increasing supply of imported medicines and an increasing demand for Western medicines. The distribution of these medicines could no longer be monopolized by the Guild in Doshomachi because many entrepreneurs started buying from the USA, the UK, Germany, and France in newly-opened ports, Yokohama in particular because of its proximity to Tokyo. Moreover, four years after the Meiji Restoration of 1868, the new government ordered the Guild to disband to encourage freer economic activity. These developments created much confusion and uncertainty in Doshomachi. For entrepreneurs with foresight, the situation presented a big opportunity. For most of the former Guild members, however, the risk was too large to bear. Not surprisingly, all those who survived to this day belong to the former category, such as Tanabe and Takeda.

The shift to the Western medical method was accelerated by the conscientious efforts of the Meiji government. Immediately after the Restoration, the government, which placed a high priority on education (see Chapter 2), expanded the Western-style medical school that the Tokugawa government had founded seven years earlier. In 1877 this school was merged with an arts and science school (also started by the Tokugawa government in 1855) to become the University of Tokyo. The medical school was further expanded and became the Department of Medical Science of this university. The department had a Division of Medicine. The faculty included a Japanese professor, Shibata Shokei, and a few foreign teachers. Shibata had been to Berlin as one of the first students sent abroad by the government. Among other such students was Nagai Nagayoshi, later to play an important role in the development of the pharmaceutical industry.

The government also hurried to provide a regulatory framework for medical services. In 1874, it opened a drug-testing facility in Tokyo and Osaka. Besides testing, this facility provided information on drug-making technology and first-stage pharmacology. The government also required the producers and traders of medicines to be licensed. Finally, in 1896, the government published the first Japanese Pharmacopoeia to set a standard for drugs.

The person who contributed to this development was Nagayo Sensai, who had studied at Ogata's private school, Tekijuku, and then with a Dutch doctor, J. L. C. Pompe van Meerdervoort, invited by the Tokugawa government. Nagayo, in charge of health and sanitation problems in the Meiji government, not only set a regulatory framework for medical services but also pursued the domestic production of Western drugs. Thus, he persuaded a number of investors to start producing drugs. This effort resulted in the establishment of Dainippon Seiyaku (Dainippon Pharmaceutical), a wholly private company invested by a number of people in Tokyo and Osaka, with the land and buildings let by the government.

In starting the operation at Dainippon, the most difficult task was to find a person who could advise on the technological aspect of the business, since there were very few in the country who were familiar with the production of Western drugs. Shibata and Nagai, who had both studied in Germany, were probably the only candidates. The company therefore entreated Nagai to take the job. Since he was staying in Germany at the time to continue his research and was making progress (and furthermore was engaged to a German woman), it must have been his nationalistic passion that made him decide to comply with the request to come back and take up the position of technical chief of the company (and simultaneously a professorship at the University of Tokyo).

The company started its operation in 1885 with equipment imported from Germany. The main products were tincture and other rather simple drugs listed in the Pharmacopoeia. In 1893, however, Nagai left the company and the business started to make a loss. In 1898 it was acquired by Osaka Seiyaku (Osaka Pharmaceutical) and continues to the present as Dainippon Pharmaceutical, which is currently the fourteenth largest pharmaceutical company in Japan in terms of sales.

Osaka Pharmaceutical was founded in 1896 with the investment of a number of former merchants in Doshomachi, many of whom were former Guild members. These included Tanabe, Takeda, and Shiono Gisaburo (the founder of Shionogi). Nagai again advised the company though he declined to join as a full-time member, and instead Hori Yuzo, one of the early graduates from the University of Tokyo, joined as technical chief. Their products included alcohol, tincture, and sodium benzoate. The company also had a quality-testing facility which was used to test not only its own products but also other drugs. Fees from this service contributed to the survival of the company.

Dainippon and Osaka were not the only entrants into drug production. In 1880, drug-making licenses were granted to 424 persons, many of whom started small-scale production efforts (Takeda Yakuhin Kogyo Kabushiki Kaisha, 1983). Not many of them survived for long although a few did, and grew into the main pharmaceutical companies of today. These included Tanabe (1877), Uchibayashi (1887), Ono (1887), Shionogi (1892), and Fujisawa (1899), the first year of production being in parentheses. Uchibayashi's products were sold by Takeda and these two merged into the present Takeda in 1918.

11.3 CATCHING-UP

Until the turn of the century, production by Japanese pharmaceutical firms was primitive. Most products were simple, such as alcohol, ammonia, caffeine, and camphor. None of the drugs had been invented in Japan, and many of the materials were imported. By contrast, in Germany, dyestuffs manufacturers, Bayer and Hoechst, started laboratories for chemical and pharmaceutical research by 1890 and, in the USA, Smith Kline started a laboratory and Parke Davis started collaborating with the University of Michigan during the 1890s (Liebenau, 1984).

Due to this lag in the technological level, Japan started a catch-up effort. Early efforts were made by a few Japanese scientists doing research abroad. The aforementioned Nagai, for instance, had invented an anti-asthma drug, Ephedrine, in 1885, which was introduced into the market by Dainippon.

Similarly, a digestive named Takadiastase was invented by Takamine Jokichi who, after studying at Kobu Daigakko (the successor to

Kogakuryo; see Chapter 2) and then in England, was continuing his research in the USA. Takamine gave the exclusive production right to Parke Davis, one of the largest US pharmaceutical companies at the time. He then gave the exclusive right to import and market the drug in Japan to Shiobara Matasaku, a young silk trader. Shiobara established a company named Sankyo for this purpose which, thanks to the popularity of Takadiastase, grew rapidly. Takamine's next important discovery was Adrenalin, which again was made by Parke Davis and imported by Sankyo. The invention of Takadiastase happened in 1894 and that of Adrenalin in 1900. Takamine's relationship with Sankyo became so close that, when Sankyo was reorganized in 1912 as a joint-stock company and started domestic production of Takadiastase and other drugs, Takamine became the first president, even though Shiobara was in charge of the daily management. The technology and equipment needed for production were imported from the USA.

Nagai and Takamine were not the only Japanese whose contribution to the discovery of new drugs was noted worldwide. In 1908, Hata Sahachiro invented an anti-syphilitic drug, Salvarsan (arsphenamine), together with Paul Ehrlich of Germany. In 1910, Suzuki Umetaro, who had studied in Switzerland and Germany and was teaching at the University of Tokyo, found a way to extract a nutritive element, the lack of which caused beriberi. He named it Oryzanin. This was one of the first discoveries of a vitamin.

If one recalls the fact that modern pharmacology did not really start until the latter half of the nineteenth century in any part of the world, it is surprising that in just a few decades after the establishment of a modern government and the official approval of Western medical practice, Japan could produce a few scientists whose impact was comparable to that of Europeans and Americans. This ability to absorb new knowledge quickly and fully, and to develop it further has been imperative for Japan's development, as has been discussed in many chapters of this book.

The start of World War I in 1914 created a new climate, because Germany, the main exporter to Japan, became Japan's enemy. Consequently, supply was drastically reduced and drug prices rose sharply. Of course, the traders desperately sought other suppliers in allied countries, most importantly, the USA, but their market was also tight because of war-related demand, both in the domestic and European markets. As a result, the price of phenol, for instance, increased 15–20 times during the eighteen-month period of July 1914 to January 1916 (Takeda

Yakuhin Kogyo Kabushiki Kaisha, 1983). Needless to say, this gave domestic producers a big incentive to boost their production.

The government made a few policies to reduce the price increase, such as export restriction in 1914 and the encouragement of production through subsidies in 1915, though with only limited success. In 1917, the government enforced the Wartime Law on Industrial Property (*Kogyo Shoyuken Senji Ho*), which declared that any patents owned by the nationals of countries in a state of war with Japan no longer had effect. The impact was both immense and lasting because the majority of drugs had been invented in Germany and this law meant that Japanese companies could now produce them without worrying about patent infringement.

In response to this new climate, the major companies not only increased the range of products and the output level but also started their own research efforts. Takeda, Shionogi, and Sankyo started their own R&D laboratories in 1915, and Tanabe and Fujisawa started experimental sections within their factories around the same time. Statistics show that the number of new drugs in 1914 was 658 of which 103, or 16 per cent, were developed domestically. By 1928, the number increased 2.6 times to 1,705 and the proportion of domestic development increased to 46 per cent. Further, by 1936, the number of new drugs increased to 2,402 of which more than half, 57 per cent, were developed domestically (Hasegawa, 1986). Although if they are really 'new' drugs is questionable because the full regulation on new drugs began only after World War II, the figures show the impressive speed of Japan's technological catch-up.

In some of these company laboratories, a close relationship was sought with university faculties. For instance, Shionogi's laboratory was supervised by Kondo Heizaburo, a professor of the University of Tokyo, and Sankyo's laboratory, named Takamine Laboratory, had a close relationship with Takamine's American laboratory. In addition, all the company laboratories were eager to employ graduates who had studied pharmacology at universities.

11.4 WORLD WAR II AND AFTERWARDS

During World War II, as a part of the wartime control discussed in Chapter 4, the government enforced tight controls over the supply of materials and the distribution of drugs. The war also caused the stoppage of scientific and technological flow from the USA and its allies; consequently, the technological level lagged badly behind that of the USA, which was by then the world leader. A typical example is penicillin, discovered by Fleming in 1928 and manufactured in the USA in 1942. Japan learned of penicillin only after the war when the Allied Powers brought the information.

Despite the damaged production facilities and limited availability of materials, the firms were determined to recover the pre-war production levels and introduce new technologies in order to meet a large demand created by post-war malnutrition and insanitary living conditions. For example, the production approval for penicillin was sought by seventy-nine firms in 1946 and 1947, including not only pharmaceutical companies but also many other entry-seekers, such as confectioners, brewers, sake producers, soysauce producers, dairy companies, chemical companies, and even construction companies (Hasegawa, 1986). Similar stories followed concerning streptomycin, tetracycline, and other antibiotics, which were discovered during and after the war, mostly in the USA.

After the first wave of catch-up and after the firms became confident of business conditions, they started increasing their R&D efforts. All the major companies started or reopened their laboratories, both to test licensed drugs and to develop new drugs. During the 1950s and 1960s, the R&D efforts of Japanese firms were particularly strong in the field of antibiotics. The number of new antibiotics discovered in Japan was second largest in the world after the USA.

The regulatory framework was also organized. The Drugs, Cosmetics and Medical Instruments Law (*Yakuji Ho*) was revised in 1948 after the American model, and then further revised in 1961. The law now required governmental approval for new drugs and the procedure for application was formalized. Ethical drugs and over-the-counter drugs were formally separated.

The national health insurance system had already started before the war in 1923, but was expanded in 1961 so that every citizen would be covered by one of several insurance schemes. These insurances, mostly set up by the employers or the government, together form a fund which reimburses the hospitals and doctors. When a patient visits a doctor, he (or she) pays 10 to 20 per cent of the cost while the rest is reimbursed to the doctor by the fund upon the doctor's application. About a quarter of the insurance cost is supported by the government, with the rest paid roughly equally by the insured and the employers.

Dispensation of medicines in Japan is seldom separated from medical practice. Thus, the majority of the doctors, particularly those at clinics, prescribe drugs, dispense them, buy them from wholesalers, and are reimbursed by the insurance fund for the main part of the cost of dispensation.

Although patients are the consumers of the drugs, they are hardly concerned about the prices because the insurance picks up the major part of the bill. Moreover, their knowledge on the availability and quality of alternative drugs is limited. As a result, doctors have substantial discretion in selecting drugs to maximize their own interests.

The fund reimburses the doctors for the dispensed drugs based on the prices (*yakka* or list prices) set by the Ministry of Health and Welfare (MHW). Hence, if the doctors buy drugs at prices below the list prices, they can gain the difference. Such 'doctor's margins' (*yakka saeki*) were estimated by MHW to be 1.3 trillion yen in 1987, which was nearly a quarter of the total payments by the patients and the Fund for the drugs prescribed by the doctors and hospitals.

The presence of doctor's margins has three consequences. First, even though MHW has been fostering the separation of dispensation from prescription, doctors have been sabotaging it because the margins are an important source of their income; as a result, only about 10 per cent of ethical drugs are dispensed by independent pharmacists with doctors' prescriptions. Secondly, doctors have an incentive to dispense large amounts of drugs to increase their income from the margins; as a result, over-prescription has been a serious problem. Thirdly, doctors and hospitals have a strong incentive to press the pharmaceutical producers and dealers to lower the purchase prices (relative to the list prices).

The system has been also advantageous to the pharmaceutical industry, because it contributed to the firms maintaining a large and growing domestic demand. Even if their selling prices, namely, the doctors' purchase prices, were lower than the list prices, the industry could gain healthy profits as long as the list prices were set at reasonably high levels. The list prices have been regularly revised downwards following the market prices. Yet, the price reduction had been modest until the late 1970s. Since then, however, the reduction has been significant, mainly because, under the worsening budgetary constraint, the Ministry of Finance started pressing MHW to contain the ever-increasing medical costs.

The adjustment of list prices to market levels, together with doctors' insistence on price discounts, implies a constant spiralling downward pressure on list and market prices. As a result, between 1978–88, the list prices fell by 51 per cent. According to an international comparison conducted by Nihon Seiyaku Kogyo Kai (Japan Pharmaceutical Manufacturers Association, hereafter JPMA, 1987), the drug prices fell on average by 39 per cent in Japan during 1982–8 but increased in seven US and European countries, for instance, by 40 per cent in the USA. As a result, even though the average drug prices may have been higher in Japan than in Europe until the early 1980s (Reich, 1990), the prices of many drugs in 1985 were lower in Japan than in the USA and West Germany (JPMA, 1987). It needs to be noted, however, that an international comparison of this sort is vulnerable to exchange-rate fluctuation and that the result tends to differ widely according to the particular drugs chosen for comparison.

The consequence of this pharmaceutical pricing scheme on company R&D seems to have been twofold. On the one hand, as the industry people have been arguing, the constant reduction in prices may have decreased the profits and thereby made R&D funding more difficult. Also it may have reduced the returns to new drugs. Like other countries, however, the profit rates of pharmaceutical companies have been among the highest of all industries and the rate of return to pharmaceutical R&D has not been low (Odagiri and Murakami, 1992).

There is also an R&D-promoting effect. Because the market prices fall more rapidly when generic alternatives become available and because the list prices are revised downward following the fall in market prices, the companies have a strong incentive to develop new drugs that can be protected from generic competition. The result has been an increasingly intensive R&D. The R&D : sales ratio increased from 3.0 per cent in 1964 to 4.4 in 1974, 6.5 in 1984, and 8.0 in 1990. The ratio is still smaller than that in the USA, yet it is largest among the Japanese industries. The major pharmaceutical firms expend an even higher proportion of their sales to R&D: 12.0 per cent for the average of the 79 JPMA members (JPMA, 1991).

The number of new drugs has been impressive. Among the list of 15,024 drugs in 1985, only 1,482, namely a little less than 10 per cent, existed in 1950, the rest being newly introduced to the market during the thirty-five-year interval. The number of newly approved chemical entities during 1975–90 was 570, of which slightly less than half were invented domestically. The rest were introduced from abroad with licenses (JPMA, 1991).

Despite these efforts, truly innovative new drugs have rarely been invented by Japanese companies. Maurer (1988: 41), a representative in Japan of the American Pharmaceutical Manufacturing Association, suggests this tendency referring to the fact that 'over the period 1970 through 1985, original products discovered in Japan represented 25.7 per cent of total drug sales in Japan but only 4.4 per cent of total drug sales in the US.' Thus he argues that 'these Japanese originals were pushed in Japan by strong marketing, but were not competitive on the US market.' It should be also noted, however, that these market shares have been increasing: during 1975–89, drugs discovered in Japan accounted for 33.8 per cent of Japanese sales and 5.9 per cent of US sales.

Whether the increasing R&D intensity of Japanese pharmaceutical firms will bring them the inventiveness and originality comparable to US and European firms depends on the extent of economies of scale and scope in pharmaceutical research. It may be argued that these economies are larger in basic research than in applied research and development because of the greater uncertainty, financial burden, and the need for interdisciplinary interaction. Thus, given that pharmaceutical research is more inclined to the basic end of research than in other industries, the smaller size of Japanese firms may become a disadvantage. In 1992, the largest company in Japan, Takeda, ranked at sixteenth in the world in terms of pharmaceutical sales. The world leader, Glaxo, had 2.2 times more pharmaceutical sales than Takeda. Although the subsequent appreciation of the yen must have narrowed the gap between Japanese firms and their overseas rivals, a significant difference remains in size between the average Japanese firm and US and European firms, and this difference may remain as a handicap for Japanese firms conducting basic research.

Needless to say, this scale difference had Japanese firms worrying about the impact of capital liberalization, when it took place in 1970. Since then, most of the large foreign firms have invested in Japan, some through acquisitions of Japanese companies, for instance, that in 1983 of Banyu Seiyaku (Banyu Pharmaceutical, founded in 1915) by Merck, or joint ventures with Japanese firms, but also through the establishment of their own subsidiaries. Usually, they started with marketing their drugs, either imported from abroad or produced in Japan. Many of them found marketing in Japan difficult and time-consuming, because roughly a thousand representatives are needed to cover the entire country, and it takes time for them to create a good relationship with the doctors and hospitals. Still, their combined market share has been gradually rising and is currently estimated to be around 20 per cent. Most of them now have production facilities in addition to marketing offices. Furthermore, many of them are active in R&D in Japan. According to JPMA's survey (1993), 19 of the 22 foreign-owned subsidiaries had 28 research laboratories in Japan.

The move for the globalization of research is mutual and many Japanese firms have also started R&D abroad. As discussed in Chapter 5, the establishment of overseas laboratories by Japanese firms has increased and the pharmaceutical industry is most active in this regard together with the electronics and automobile industries. According to the same JPMA survey (1993), 38 among the sample of 66 Japanese pharmaceutical firms were conducting R&D overseas; 30 of them conducting research at the stage of search; 14, pre-clinical study; 25, clinical tests; and 16, application. For example, Takeda, Tanabe, Fujisawa, Yamanouchi, Eisai, and Otsuka now have research laboratories in the USA and/or Europe, some of which are conducting research at the basic level and/or with the collaboration of the universities in the area.

11.5 CONCLUSION

We can draw a number of conclusions from this exposition of the Japanese pharmaceutical industry. First, only the firms capable of adapting to the changes in social and economic environment, by transforming themselves first from being wholesale merchants to import traders, and then to manufacturers, could survive. For instance, the current market leader, Takeda, was one of the traditional merchants and an exclusive member of the Guild in the Tokugawa Era. Yet, it was neither the largest nor the oldest. It survived and developed because it started to deal with Western medicines when there still was a much larger and stable market for Chinese and Japanese medicines, and trading with unknown American and European merchants was risky and cumbersome (just consider the language barrier!), and because it entered into manufacturing when the technology was hardly known to the Japanese. The story of hardship abounds in the beginning, such as inexperienced handling of materials causing deadly explosions.

Secondly, the government provided an infrastructure, and a legal and regulatory framework. They also provided certain initiatives to aid industrialization. However, it was overwhelmingly the private efforts that fostered developments. There were numerous entry efforts, some of which developed into the major companies of today. These included, in addition to Sankyo discussed above, Yamanouchi, Eisai, Daiichi, Taisho, and Kyowa Hakko of the current top ten. In addition, entries by Shionogi and Fujisawa took place after the Meiji Restoration, although they initially chose to enter into the wholesale business rather than manufacturing, in contrast to the above six companies which manufactured from the beginning. This leaves only Takeda and Tanabe as survivors from the Tokugawa Era. As shown also in other chapters, the entry activity was vigorous during the course of Japan's economic development, and the pharmaceutical industry was no exception.

Thirdly, although most technologies were imported in the beginning, Japan gradually caught up. Yet, there are at least two differences between this and the other industries. One is the role played by the universities. Both in terms of the scientific and technical advice given by the faculty members and the supply of scientists employed in company laboratories, the role seems to have been larger here. The obvious reason is that pharmaceutical research is more connected to academic research than research in the assembly industries.[2]

The other is that patent protection was more vigorous. Consequently, the free use of German patents during World War I helped Japanese firms to develop their technological capabilities. After World War II, the restriction of foreign direct investment into Japan until the mid 1960s probably had the effect of protecting Japanese producers because, otherwise, technologically superior US and European firms would have refused to sell the licenses to Japanese firms.[3]

Unlike the steel, electronics, automobile, and shipbuilding industries (but somewhat like the aircraft industry) the technological level of the Japanese pharmaceutical industry has not yet surpassed the US and European level with Japan still a net importer of medicines. The reason may be closely related to these characteristics of pharmaceuticals. As discussed in Chapter 5, the internal organization of Japanese firms has contributed to innovation where the interaction between R&D and manufacturing and between R&D and sales is effective in finding the seeds of technology and the needs of the market with which the desirable research orientation can be grasped. In pharmaceuticals, however, the research is more academic and basic. It is more closely related to the research done in universities than to the manufacturing stage. Linkages among intra-company functions may not be important, therefore.

Furthermore, Japanese universities are hardly at the world forefront of research. As we will discuss in more detail in the concluding chapter, research budgets allocated to universities are far below those in the USA, and many of the research facilities are outdated. Neither has Japan a large national research institution like the US National Institutes of Health.

Still, the technological level of the Japanese pharmaceutical industry has been steadily rising. Whereas Japanese import of pharmaceutical technology outweighed its export by more than four times in 1975, the export has dominated the import since 1986. During 1975–90, the export increased by 21.6 per cent annually while the import increased by 9.5 per cent. In 1990, the export was 25.0 billion yen and the import, 22.5 billion yen.[4] The number of cases of export was 385 and that of import, 247; hence, receipts per export are still lower than the payments per import, which may indicate that the value (and, therefore, the originality) of new Japanese drugs is still behind that of drugs invented elsewhere. Nevertheless, there is no denying the fact that the Japanese industry has increased its capabilities needed to develop new drugs marketable not only in Japan but worldwide.

It seems appropriate to say that the industry is still in the process of learning in regard to conducting research of a more basic nature, and to making a global business activity. As Reich (1990: 145) argued, 'the Japanese government has provided few direct positive measures to assist the pharmaceutical industry in globalization. The overseas achievements by the Japanese pharmaceutical industry have proceeded mainly by trial-and-error business strategy, as the industry has moved up the international learning curve.' The history of this and other industries in Japan seems to teach us that the Japanese have been adept at learning from imported knowledge and from experience.

The same author concluded his paper, entitled 'Why the Japanese Don't Export More Pharmaceuticals', by saying that 'we are unlikely to pop Japanese drugs as avidly as we now drive Japanese cars; at least not before the 21st century' (Reich, 1990: 146). Who knows what it will be like in the 21st century?

12

What Can We Learn from the Past?

12.1 THE NATURE OF TECHNOLOGY

The discussion of technological and industrial development in this book provides us with several important observations and lessons. As a way of concluding the book, these will be now discussed. We begin by discussing them in relation to economic theories.

It has been more than three decades since Nelson (1959) and Arrow (1962) elucidated the peculiarities of technology (or, more broadly, information) as economic goods. Most importantly, they emphasized the presence of non-rivalry in consumption and the difficulty in fully appropriating the returns. Arrow (1962: 618) also discussed the 'interdependence of inventive activities, which reinforces the difficulties in achieving an optimal allocation of the results. Information is not only the product of inventive activity, it is also an input—in some sense, the major input apart from the talent of the inventor.' This last observation implies that the interdependence of inventive activity takes place both spatially and intertemporally, because it should be the information accumulated up to now that would be utilized as an input into the current inventive activity.

This intertemporal interdependence is exactly what we found to be the conspicuous nature of science and technology. How much technology a nation can absorb and how much it can generate are dependent in a crucial way upon the accumulated quantity and quality of technological capabilities. Some of these capabilities may be consciously created through innovation and education, while some may be acquired rather by chance, as the adoption of the QWERTY keyboard layout illustrates (David, 1985). Consequently, the process of technological progress and economic change is *path-dependent*. The presence of sunk investment reinforces this dependence. For instance, getting used to typing on a QWERTY keyboard is a sunk investment. Switching costs, that is, the costs of switching to other keyboards, are therefore substantial, and the future course of technological development is constrained by this fact.

A very important consequence of this path-dependence, shown in many of our case studies, is that technology is not just something to be imported and implemented. In order to make full use of imported technologies, a high level of capabilities is needed. It is not just the so-called 'absorptive' capacity, that is, the capacity to *absorb* and *assimilate* the imported technology, that is needed. Certainly, making a product based on an imported blueprint or copying an imported product is difficult enough, as suggested by Toyota's effort to reverse-engineer imported cars, or Sony's and others' efforts to make a transistor, because not only scientific and technological understanding but also a sufficient level of know-how in production management and labour skills are needed. The supply of materials and components can be another obstacle; for instance, as discussed in Chapter 8, the lack of sufficiently pure silicon (or even the lack of knowledge that silicon can be made so pure) impeded the Japanese effort to make transistors.

Still, copying foreign technologies is only a first step. One has to *adapt* and *modify* them, just as Noro had to re-design the furnaces imported from Europe, and Sony had to invent a way to mass-produce transistors for use in radios. Usually, technologies have to be adapted in order for them to be effective in an environment physically or socially different from that of the country that originated them. Such adaptation requires a high level of technological capabilities on the part of the nation that imports them.

A similarly high level of capability is needed even to *select* appropriate technologies, because the right selection can only be made with a sufficient understanding of both the technologies themselves and the environment in which they are to be utilized.

Without first having such capabilities, one would never be able to proceed further to the stage of creating capabilities to *invent* new technologies. A corollary to this thesis is that a discontinuous jump in technological level is difficult to achieve, even if the country receives advanced technologies and finance. Unless it has sufficient capabilities, as well as a strong will to absorb and adapt the granted technology, it will never be able to utilize the technology fully efficiently. Although we are not denying the contribution that foreign technological and economic aid can bring to developing countries, such aid has to be made carefully, with their level of technological capabilities and other conditions taken into account. Such aid would be able to raise technological capabilities only gradually.

Technological capabilities are accumulated partly through conscious efforts, such as education and training. In the main, however, they can be gained only through the process of trial and error, and learning-by-doing. For, unless one experiences the technology in all its aspects, including the drawbacks, one would never really understand its potential as well as its limitations. This learning process can and must take place at every level of the firm from managers and engineers to shop-floor workers. Managers, in other words, have to provide the workers with opportunities to learn from the new technology. It can be risky, particularly if the new technology has to be used at the site of actual production rather than within laboratories. Such risk-taking is an important function of entrepreneurship. Some of the cases in this book, such as Kawasaki Steel's introduction of continuous casting and Sony's development of a transistor production system, indicate that such a function was indeed fulfilled by Japanese entrepreneurs and managers.

The steel case also illustrates another important aspect of technology: a new technology often calls for yet more new technology. To be more precise, the adoption of a new technology may create a disequilibrium which begets an opportunity or a need for more new technology. The adoption of basic oxygen furnaces, for instance, created a need to re-cycle the waste gas, thereby forcing Yawata with a supplier to develop a new gas recovery system. BOF also made continuous casting more advantageous, accelerating the development effort. Furthermore, the adoption of BOF and continuous casting in a large-scale integrated steel mill necessitated a computer-aided central control system to coordinate the activities. The development of such a system was accelerated as a result.

Similar cases can be found in many other industries. In computers, the development of faster CPUs (central processing units) necessitated the development of faster storage devices and, in aircraft and automobiles, the development of faster engines necessitated a chassis and parts that could sustain the increased pressure.

The presence of such complementarity in technologies also implies that timing can be very important. A new technology may function effectively only when complementary technological and other conditions are met. More broadly, a new technology can be fully assimilated only when sufficient capabilities have been developed. Japan was fortunate in this regard because, when it started the development effort, it already had certain technological capabilities, partly as a legacy of indigenous technology and partly as a product of education. At the same time, the technologies imported from the West, although they were no doubt more advanced, were still not as sophisticated as those of today. Thus, as the various cases indicate, Japanese scientists and engineers in the early Meiji period could absorb and adapt the imported technologies within a few years. It must be much more difficult for current developing countries to do the same, because the great majority of current state-of-the-art technologies are based on sophisticated scientific knowledge.

The development since World War II again shows that historical timing and chance can be influential. The defeat forced the industries to concentrate on civilian demand and the engineers previously employed in the military-related sector to move to other sectors. As the automobile case illustrated, such engineers played a significant role in post-war product development activities.

The process of technological development is neither a smooth one nor the consequence of well-calculated planning. It may accelerate in certain periods and in certain industries, and stagnate in others. The development may take place in an unforeseen direction. An obscure and forgotten technology may become prominent when the surrounding conditions change.

The nature of technology itself is hardly stationary. Many technologies have become more science-based, illustrated most typically by pharmaceutical research. On the other hand, learning through experience may appear to have become less and less important. So, will the past accumulation of technological capabilities become less relevant? We do not think so. In many industries, learning through experience is still important and will remain so. Even in science-based sectors, accumulated scientific knowledge and the know-how in doing research are imperative. Therefore, the process of technological development will never cease to be path-dependent.

12.2 THE PROCESS OF ECONOMIC DEVELOPMENT

We started this book by referring to three recent theories, including the endogenous growth theory and the evolutionary theory. The endogenous growth theory is quite correct in emphasizing that the speed of technical progress is determined endogenously within the economic system. The theory, such as Grossman and Helpman's (1990) and Romer's (1990), is also correct in assuming that the amount of new technologies generated by R&D depends on the accumulated level of technology.

They are incorrect, however, in assuming that the process of technical progress can be approximated by a deterministic and monotonically increasing function of the number of human resources allocated to the R&D sector. In fact, as stated above, technology develops not only as a result of calculated R&D activity but, equally important, as a result of trial and error. Consequently, the process is a probabilistic and bumpy one. In this regard, we sympathize with the evolutionary theory of Nelson and Winter (1982), in which R&D activity is modelled in terms of a probability distribution for coming up with different new techniques. Yet, we do not share their assumption that the consequence of R&D is depicted as a sampling from a distribution of existing techniques, because truly new technologies may emerge out of R&D.

We have also found that this sampling is not entirely a chance event. In fact, the higher the level of technological capabilities one has accumulated, the higher the probability that one selects a better technology. Such intertemporal dependence is not taken into account in the simulation model of Nelson and Winter. In addition, quality and style of management can affect the probability distribution. We have suggested in Chapter 5 and in some of the industrial cases that the Japanese management system, such as the managers' career background in favour of technology and marketing, and the close communication among managers, engineers, and workers (which sustains trust among them) must have contributed in this regard.

The process of economic development entails changes in the structure and organization both between and within industries. Some industries grow while some decline. The pattern of life cycle is observable—from an infant phase to growing, maturity, and then declining phases—although not all the industries follow this simplistic pattern and the length of each phase varies considerably across industries.

Among the industries studied in this book, textiles was the first to reach the maturity phase, followed by iron and steel, and shipbuilding, although one cannot say if they have already reached the declining phase. The automobile and electrical and communications equipment industries appear to be nearing the maturity phase, while in the pharmaceutical industry the maturity phase seems still to come. Yet, within each of these industries, there is quite a diversity. In the textiles industry, although the production level in cotton spinning has clearly declined, Japan still enjoys comparative advantage in some of the high value-added new textiles products. In the electrical equipment and electronics industry, many of the production bases for low-price house-hold appliances have already moved out of the country but not the high-tech products.

It therefore does not appear fruitful to depict the development of any industry in a deterministic model of product life cycle. An industry reaching a certain phase may revert to an earlier phase under changing conditions. Some of these conditions are exogenous, such as changes in international comparative advantages caused by, for instance, changing factor prices and changing resource endowments, but some are endogenous, such as the development of new products, and the development of new ways of production, distribution, and marketing.

As a result, the path of economic development has not been, and will never be that of a *balanced* or *steady-state* growth as envisaged by most of the growth theories, including the endogenous growth theory, in which all the sectors grow in a common and constant rate. In reality, the shift across industries and across products takes place continuously, if slowly. To model such a growth process, in association with (endogenous and exogenous) changes in technologies and factor prices, must remain a task of growth theorists.

Within industries, some firms gain market shares while others lose, and entries and exits take place. The growth process has to be accompanied by market competition, and a loss of such competitive forces would inevitably hinder industrial development. Such competition, furthermore, has never been the sort portrayed in the microeconomic theory as *perfect competition*.

12.3 THE THEORY OF THE FIRM AND INDUSTRIAL ORGANIZATION

In the traditional theory of industrial organization, market structure variables, represented by concentration ratios, have been the centre of attention. Our study seems to suggest that these static variables are unimportant because, first, they do not necessarily indicate the real strength of market competition and, secondly, they are the consequences, more than the determinants, of an evolutionary competitive process.

As is well known, many empirical studies have been made to confirm the correlation between market concentration and profitability, and have suggested that firms in concentrated industries possess market power (Scherer and Ross, 1990: ch. 11). Criticizing this interpretation,

Demsetz (1973: 1) argued that 'under the pressure of competitive rivalry, and in the apparent absence of effective barriers to entry, it would seem that the concentration of an industry's output in a few firms could only derive from their superiority in producing and marketing products or in the superiority of a structure of industry in which there are only a few firms.'

This superiority depends on a number of factors including, but not limited to, superior technology. As suggested in our industrial cases, firms that succeeded in establishing better technology could enter the market successfully and expand their market shares, while others who failed to do so lost their shares. Toshiba could become a dominant seller of electric bulbs owing to Fujioka's and others' struggle to develop commercially viable products and, afterwards, maintain continuous efforts to improve them. Sony became a leader in transistor radios and other appliances after its innovation efforts.

Innovation in this context should be taken as a broad concept. As Schumpeter (1942: 84) has forcefully argued, 'it is not that kind of competition [i.e., competition within a rigid pattern of invariant conditions, methods of production and forms of industrial organization in particular] that counts but the competition from the new commodity, the new technology, the new source of supply, the new type of organization (the largest-scale unit of control for instance)—competition which commands a decisive cost or quality advantage and which strikes not at the margins of the profits and the outputs of the existing firms but at their foundations and their very lives.'

Schumpeterian innovation, therefore, is not confined to production and product technologies. It should include all those activities that are made to enhance what Penrose (1959: 24) called 'productive resources' of the firm or what Chandler (1990) called 'organizational capabilities'. In addition to technological capabilities, which we have repeatedly discussed, they would include capabilities for domestic and overseas marketing, capabilities for securing supplies, capabilities for human and financial management, and capabilities for making strategic decisions and reorganizing the firm to fulfil these decisions. Recent management scientists, for instance, Prahalad and Hamel (1990), emphasize the need for the firm to find out its 'core competence' among these capabilities, nurture it, and apply it in its growth strategy.

Are the firms profit-maximizers? Some of the cases discussed in this book seem to suggest that they are not always so. In cases like Ohshima's investment in blast furnaces at Kamaishi, Fujioka's development of electric bulbs, Odaira's establishment of Hitachi, Ibuka's challenge to transistor radios, and Toyoda's and Honda's entry into automobiles, it is rather difficult to assume that they made rational calculations. More likely, they have been driven by scientific and technological curiosity and nationalistic passion to make Japan independent of foreign technological dominance. They may simply have had 'animal spirits', as Keynes suggested: 'most, probably, of our decisions to do something positive, the full consequences of which will be drawn out over many days to come, can only be taken as a result of *animal spirits*—of a spontaneous urge to action rather than inaction, and not as the outcome of a weighted average of quantitative benefits multiplied by quantitative probabilities' (Keynes, 1936: 161, our emphasis).

The word, *entrepreneurship*, is probably more widely accepted among economists to indicate these spirits, which include both the quest for innovation, as Schumpeter emphasized, and the willingness to take risks, as Knight emphasized. The presence of such entrepreneurship was a necessary, if not sufficient, factor for Japan's success in industrial development, particularly during the Meiji-period modernization efforts and the post-war, high-growth era.

It is extremely difficult to analyse such entrepreneurship in a formal economic model. The growth-maximization hypothesis, pioneered by Marris (1964) and modelled more formally by Odagiri (1981), assumes that the manager opts to pursue growth beyond the level the owners would prefer, which may approximate what Keynes called 'a spontaneous urge to action'. The problem of risk-bearing, as well as that of the discontinuous nature of innovation, is abstracted in this theory, however.

Does this argument imply that profits are unimportant? Hardly so, because profits remain as a necessity for survival. Any firm that fails to secure positive profits will be forced out of business and only the firms that have succeeded in accumulating the necessary capabilities and adapting to a changing environment would generate sufficient profits to survive and expand. Here is a process of *natural selection* and, as Alchian (1950: 213–14) has argued, 'among all competitors, those whose particular conditions happen to be the most appropriate of those offered to the economic system for testing and adoption will be "selected" to survive.'

However, as Alchian (1950: 211) has also argued, 'adaptive, imitative, and trial-and-error behavior in the pursuit of "positive profits" is utilized rather than its sharp contrast, the pursuit of "maximized profits".'

Furthermore, the long-run equilibrium in a natural selection system is consistent not only with profit maximization but also with satisficing behaviour as modelled by Winter (1971) and Nelson and Winter (1982), or with the growth-maximization behaviour discussed above.

The implication of this argument is twofold. First, the profit-maximization hypothesis may be a poor approximation of the real behaviour of the firm, and neither may it be a theoretical necessity. We are not suggesting that it is useless. We are aware that many economic theories based on the profit-maximization hypothesis have proved useful. We are also aware that a number of business decisions discussed in our industrial cases are probably consistent with the hypothesis. Yet, there appears room to establish a more realistic theory(ies) of the firm.

Secondly, the process of market competition is better considered in a dynamic setting. Market structure is never stationary and it should not be so. A stationary market structure implies either that innovation is not taking place or that innovative firms cannot enter the market. Whichever is the case, the engine of industrial development is lost and natural selection as a competitive mechanism is not at work.

Japan's experience suggests that this was not the case. Strong entry activities were there and market shares of individual firms were rarely stable, with the exception, perhaps, of the steel industry after the Yawata–Fuji merger. There were some cases of government intervention in the direction of maintaining a stable and concentrated market structure; yet, fortunately (at least to these authors), such intervention was not successful owing to entrepreneurial entry attempts. In the pre-war period, there were a number of entries into steel production, despite the presence of the dominant Yawata, and the entries by non-zaibatsu-affiliated Nissan and Toyota into automobile production can be cited as examples. In the post-war period, entries by Sony and Honda, despite MITI's objection, provide perfect examples.

In suggesting that the extent of entry barrier is probably more important than the static concept of concentration ratios, we share the view of the contestable market theory, such as Baumol et al. (1982). The barrier may arise from technological conditions, such as the presence of sunk cost, or from strategic moves by incumbent firms, as discussed in Tirole (1988, ch. 8). Such strategic moves, it seems, were not a decisive hindrance to the entry into, say, the electronics or automobile industry, probably because the growth potential was large enough to attract new entrants. By contrast, in industries at a maturity or declining phase, say, iron and steel since the Oil Crisis, it appears more difficult to assert that the move by a dominant firm, such as Nippon Steel, has not really deterred entries.

To sum up, entrepreneurial innovation and investment are the keys for dynamic evolution of industries. Such behaviour may not be characterized by profit maximization but, probably more likely, by growth maximization and a Schumpeterian quest for innovation, subject to positive profits. Innovation is an activity to enhance technological and other capabilities of the firm, and only those firms succeeding in innovation and adapting to changing conditions, technological or otherwise, will be able to survive. Market entries and the shift of market shares necessarily take place as a consequence, changing the market structure incessantly. The development of an industry, therefore, is always accompanied by a shift across industries and across firms, unlike the picture depicted by the theory of balanced growth.

If this evolutionary process of natural selection begins to fail because of the loss of entrepreneurship or, say, government regulation, the economy is doomed to stagnation. Two big questions to Japan now are: Does it still have the capacity to adapt itself to changing conditions? Is there not a possibility that government activities are hindering the adaptation? We now turn to this topic.

12.4   GOVERNMENT POLICIES: INFRASTRUCTURE AND INDUSTRIAL POLICY

In its popular report on the 'East Asian Miracle', the World Bank (1933: 5) asked 'what caused East Asia's success?' and argued that 'in large measure the high-performing Asian economies achieved high growth by getting the basics right.'

The same can be probably said of Japan, because the government policies that contributed most were those of 'getting the basics right.' These included, first of all, the provision of infrastructure, ranging from transportation, communications, and utilities to the legal system, including the commercial code and the patent law. The government also established standards, such as the metric system, and eliminated many obstacles against mobility—geographical as well as occupational—that existed during the Tokugawa feudal system.

The role of education may have been especially important in two regards. First, elementary education spread across the country within a short period of time. Consequently, illiteracy virtually vanished by the turn of the century, which raised the average quality of the workers, at least to the level needed to follow instructions. This rapid educational achievement, however, would not have been possible by government investment alone. There was, as we have noted, a strong demand for education as well: parents were eager to send the children to schools and many children were eager to learn. Without such eagerness, the government effort might have ended in vain.

Secondly, at least in the beginning, practical education, such as commerce and engineering, was emphasized at the level of higher education. This education yielded numerous engineers, administrators, and accountants, who helped many industries in the acquisition of sufficient technological and managerial capabilities. Most of the engineer-turned entrepreneurs of the pioneering firms discussed in this book were, in fact, graduates from Kogakuryo (later, the Engineering Department of University of Tokyo) and similar educational institutions. The priority of practical education above purely scientific education appears to have been useful in the catch-up process during the Meiji era and the post-war period. Whether the same will be true in coming years, when a large part of research in Japan will need to be re-targeted into more original areas, is a moot question, to which we will return later.

In addition to these policies of 'getting the basics right', the Japanese government played a more active role in some industries and at certain periods.

For instance, the government supported demand for growing industries, not only through its macro-economic policy, but also through procurement by the Army and Navy, the Ministry of Telecommunications (later Nippon Telephone and Telegraph), and the Ministry of Railways or Transport. These agencies had an incentive to buy from domestic suppliers, for defence and other reasons, despite the initial low quality and high cost in comparison to the imports. Such support provided the domestic firms with an opportunity to accumulate production experience and learn from trial and error. In addition, these agencies often insisted on high quality and punctual delivery, with occasional technological assistance, which forced the firms to be quality conscious.

At certain stages, the government supported the demand for domestic producers by excluding foreign suppliers through tariff or non-tariff import restrictions, and restrictions on direct investment. Among the industries studied in this book, the automobile industry probably benefited most significantly by this policy. The restriction on the activity of Ford and GM before the war gave an advantage to Toyota and

Nissan. The post-war protection policy not only guaranteed the growing domestic market to Japanese producers but also encouraged foreign producers to sell their technologies, because they could not take advantage of their technological superiority by exporting into, or investing in, Japan.

The traditional infant industry theory may apply in these cases. An infant industry is an industry where, although the industry cannot be self-sustained because of the higher costs than those of foreign competitors, once entered, the firms would in the long run decrease their costs through learning, and thereby the present value of social surplus would improve (Negishi, 1968; Odagiri, 1986). Even though it may be doubted that cost reductions through learning was accurately predicted in advance by the Japanese policy-makers, such cost reductions were significant and therefore the policy may have increased the national welfare through larger profits and lower product prices.

However, three reservations are in order. First, such protection could not be made during the early Meiji period, because of the Unequal Treaty with the USA and European countries, which could not be revised until 1911. Thus, some of the industries, including textiles, iron, and electric bulbs, were at one time dominated by imports, with the domestic suppliers barely managing to survive. The fact that the textiles industry became competitive and started to export even under such conditions clearly indicates that one cannot attribute Japan's success to the protection policy alone.

Secondly, it seems critically important that the firms understood that protection could not go on forever. The post-war Japanese firms were aware that, once trade and foreign exchange were liberalized, severe competition would be inevitable against technologically superior foreign rivals, which was exactly the reason for striving hard to catch up with them. The cases of automobiles and computers are typical and, as discussed by Fujimoto and Tidd (1993), the memory of pre-war market dominance by Ford and GM was a clear reminder to manufacturers of the need to raise productivity and develop high-quality products to stay competitive after the expected trade liberalization. In addition, some firms had started exporting the products before the liberalization, thus being exposed to international competition.

And thirdly, one may ask if the government had sufficient information and capacity to determine whether a particular industry was qualified as an infant industry as defined above. It is true that several target industries achieved growth as much as (or more than) expected by the government; for instance, automobiles and electronics. There were other industries, however, that failed to meet the government's expectation. The post-war aircraft industry discussed in Chapter 10 is an example. On the energy policy, the government kept supporting coal mining for some time, without realizing that it would be replaced by cheaper oil.

The contribution of financial incentives to industries, such as subsidies, tax concessions, and low-interest loans, has been over-evaluated. Even in the well-advertised nurturing policy towards the post-war computer industry, R&D and other investment was paid overwhelmingly by the firms themselves, and the share in the industry R&D expenditure of government subsidies and other financial incentives remained far below 10 per cent except during 1973–6 (Wakasugi, 1988).

More importantly, these incentives may have functioned as a signal to the private sector that the industries were promising and that the government intended to nurture them. Like a pump-primer, they encouraged private financial institutions to provide loans to the firms, which was particularly helpful because the capital market during the post-war, high-growth era was persistently under excess demand because of the low-interest 'over-loan' policy (see Section 5.2).

Another signalling was made with the announcement of economic plans and visions, such as the 'Vision for Trade and Industrial Policy in the 1980s'. In this vision, for instance, the Ministry of International Trade and Industry (MITI) suggested that knowledge-intensive industries were to be promoted, with emphasis on biotechnology, new material technologies, and new energy technologies. According to Komiya and Yokobori (1991: 1), '[the visions] are not of the nature of directives. For the private business executives, they are perceived as one of future scenarios which reflect views of wide ranging experts. For industrial policy planners, they serve as guidelines in formulating specific policy measures such as tax and financial incentives.'

These plans and visions were deliberated by specifically organized councils (*Shingi-kai*) represented by business people, academics, former government officials, journalists, and trade union and consumer group representatives. Komiya (1988) suggest that these councils fostered the communication between industries and the government, and coordinated the interests among conflicting industries.

This system, however, may have also worked to increase the influence of industries and other interest groups, which tried (and are still trying) to amend government regulations and industrial policies in their favour. Since these interest groups, or 'distributional coalitions' as Olson called them, act mainly to protect existing interests, 'distributional coalitions slow down a society's capacity to adopt new technologies and to reallocate resources in response to changing conditions, and thereby reduce the rate of economic growth' (Olson, 1982: 65). The resistance on de-regulation is evident in many parts of the economy, from agriculture and energy to telecommunications and transportation, and there seems no question that the protection of existing interests by interest groups, as well as the government bureaucracy, is causing it. The result is a deterrent to the adjustment, both among industries and within industries, that is needed to achieve future growth.

Another obstacle to de-regulation and to efficient policy-making has been the split among ministerial interests (*tatewari gyosei*). For instance, planning for the development of information technology has not always been easy because MITI is in charge of the computer industry, whereas telecommunication is controlled by the Ministry of Posts and Telecommunications (MPT). As a consequence, MITI and MPT occasionally develop very similar policies simultaneously but separately, with MITI's policy targeted at computer makers and MPT's policy at Nippon Telegraph and Telephone (NTT) and others, when the policy would have been more effective were a collaborative approach taken. Similarly, the policy on biotechnology has been advocated both by the Ministry of Health and Welfare (MHW), which oversees the pharmaceutical industry, and MITI, which oversees the chemical and other industries. Each ministry tended to pay more attention to the protection of its authority than to making policies from a national viewpoint. The elimination of ministerial conflict through, for instance, increased interministerial mobility of government officials, must remain one of the policy priorities in coming years.

12.5 GOVERNMENT POLICIES: COMPETITION POLICY

Has the competition policy contributed to Japan's industrial development? Surely, the post-war reform has had a strong influence by dissolving dominant *zaibatsu* and breaking up Japan Iron and Steel, and other dominant market leaders. As discussed in Chapter 7, this breakup encouraged investment and innovation by the fringe firms at the time, such as Kawasaki Steel.

Since then, the Antimonopoly Law has prevented the emergence of strong market leaders by, for instance, discouraging the re-merger of three paper companies, which had ben divested from the pre-war Oji Paper by the post-war reform (Odagiri, 1994). Thus, the law must have contributed to the maintenance of competitive and contestable markets; yet, it is difficult to say how many of the entries were facilitated by the market structure the antimonopoly policy helped to create, and how many were prompted simply by the prospect of growth opportunities and entrepreneurship. The competition these entries caused, in turn, fostered innovation and productivity increase, thereby supporting the growth of the industry. The cycle of growth through competition, and competition through growth, has been sustained in this way, as Odagiri's book title (1992) implied.

The experience in the pre-war period is suggestive, because there was no Antimonopoly Law and the government in fact favoured market concentration and the formation of cartels. Clearly, our study indicated that, even during this period, entries did take place in many industries, including such concentrated industries as steel and textiles. Although there is no way of knowing how different the situation would have been were the Antimonopoly Law in effect at the time, we can perhaps say that if there was any harmful collusive or entry-deterring behaviour at all, it was neutralized, at least to a certain extent, by active entrepreneurship that existed at the time. There seems a strong possibility that, were it not for such entrepreneurship, the presence of dominant incumbents in some industries might have hampered entry efforts.

The situation might also have been different were the industry in a different phase of its product life cycle. Most of the discussion in this book pertained to the start-up and growth phases of the life cycle, in which the incentive for market entry tended to be higher. In the maturity and declining phases, by contrast, entry would be more difficult owing to the lack of growth opportunity and the difficulty in developing a new product or a new cost-saving process with which the firm would enter the market; hence, a dominant market position of the incumbents was unlikely to be challenged and the collusive behaviour might have been sustained.[1]

It is true that, as shown by the case of 'New (and New-New) Spinners' in the post-war cotton-spinning industry, entry by innovative entrepreneurs was feasible, even into a mature industry, contributing to the industry regaining dynamism. However, in the steel industry since the Yawata-Fuji merger, no larger-scale innovation has been made and the relative market shares among five major steel producers have been surprisingly stable. Although this fact alone need not imply a lack of competition, it is a worrying sign, particularly because more and more manufacturing industries in Japan are entering into the maturity and declining phases of their life cycles. Accordingly, the role of competition policy may become more critical.

Finally, a word is needed on the government's role as an R&D-conducting agency and a disseminator of scientific and technological knowledge. We have shown that some of the government research institutions, such as research sections within arsenals, Naval Research Institute, and Electric Laboratory (and its descendants, ECL and ETL), initiated experiments on, for instance, steel-making, automobiles, aircraft, wireless radio, and transistors, and passed the information to the private sector. Some of the researchers in these institutions later went to the private sector.

Universities and their predecessors, such as Kogakuryo, not only supplied graduates but also introduced Western technologies and ideas into the country. As shown in the cases of Noro in steel, Fujioka in electrical equipment, Kumabe in automobiles, and Nagai in pharmaceuticals, a number of university professors were actively involved in giving technological advice to industries, in doing joint research with companies, or even in establishing their own companies. In some cases, the university laboratory acted as a hub of informational network as well as being the supplier of educated engineers (Odagiri, 1993).

Their role, apart from that of education, was important, particularly in introducing advanced knowledge from abroad and spreading it to the private sector. Such a role was much appreciated when the country was trying to catch up with the West, and when the private sector still lacked financial and human resources for research, Now that the situation has changed in both of these regards, the focus of research activity in universities and government institutions in Japan has to shift to more basic, original research. The question is: are they capable of such research? This is one of the questions we ask in the next and final section.

12.6 JAPAN IN THE COMING YEARS

Compared to the period mainly discussed in this book, namely, from the mid-nineteenth century to the high-growth era of the 1960s, three major changes have taken, or are taking, place in Japan today. First, catch-up with US and European technologies is complete in most industries, with Japan at the forefront of the world-wide technical race. Secondly, the financial and informational superiority of the public sector, including universities, has been lost as the private sector has accumulated sufficient capabilities. And thirdly, Japan is now firmly locked into the world economy through trade, as well as direct investment. The consequences of these changes are grave.

We have just stated that the major focus of universities and government research institutions has to shift to basic and original research. The fact, however, is that most universities are suffering from obsolete equipment, poor funding, and the loss of talented researchers to companies. In fact, in 1990, 27 per cent of researchers in Japan belonged to universities, but they spent only 12 per cent of the nation's R&D expenditure, which is a significant decline from the 18 per cent of twenty years earlier.[2] As a consequence, real R&D expenditure per university researcher has stayed nearly unchanged during the twenty-year period, despite the increase from 1.59 to 2.77 in the percentage of national R&D expenditure to GNP, and almost twofold increase in real GNP.

This trend contrasts with that of industries, whose proportion of R&D expenditures has been increasing from 69 per cent to 77 per cent. Not surprisingly, major companies now have much better research facilities, for instance, state-of-the-art equipment for computing and experimentation, whereas many university researchers are struggling with obsolete equipment and lack of space.

According to a survey conducted by the Science and Technology Agency (1991), 51 per cent of university researchers in Japan stated that their research facilities were poorer than those in Europe and North America, while the percentage was lower, at 23 per cent, among the researchers in companies. The shortage of research-support staff is particularly problematic: the number of such staff per researcher is only 0.26 in Japanese universities in comparison to 1.06 in the UK and 0.83 in Germany.

The inflow of research funds from the private sector to universities, in the form of joint research, subcontracting of research, or grants, has increased more than five times during 1981–91, reflecting the change in the relative financial situation of the two sectors. In 1991, it was 57 billion yen to national universities and slightly outweighed the amount of Grants-in-Aid for Scientific Research provided by the Ministry of Education (equivalent, more or less, to the grants by the US National

Science Foundation).[3] Such an increase can be beneficial in fostering industry–university collaboration. Yet, if the increase is the result of university researchers desperately seeking industry funds to compensate for the shortage of government funds, one may worry whether truly basic research can be maintained.

In addition, the inflexibility in both the financial and personnel aspects of Japanese universities is limiting the merit of external research funds. These funds cannot be used to buy teaching time of faculty members or to hire research staff, except on a part-time basis. Neither can they be used for indirect costs, for instance, electricity charges. It can occur, therefore, that, when a faculty member gets external funding, indirect costs have to be paid from his other funds or from the university's general fund. Such inflexibility in the use of external funds, imposed by the Ministry of Education to national universities in particular, has been reducing the attractiveness and effectiveness of external funds.[4]

The hiring restriction is related to the employment system in Japanese universities. Basically, all the faculty members in Japan get tenure upon appointment, making it extremely difficult for the university to hire someone on a temporary basis. Whereas, as noted in Chapter 5, lifetime employment has never been guaranteed and redundancies can take place in industries, it is still strictly applied in the government sector and universities. More flexibility in the administration of universities is strongly called for to facilitate the effective use of external funds and the flexibility of research organization in response to changing needs; for instance, the emergence of new scientific fields.

By contrast, in the private sector, lifetime employment appears to be getting less and less of a reality, with the 'post-bubble' depression since 1990 accelerating this trend. Although many firms still try to maintain employment of at least core members, they have been reducing employment through the voluntary early retirement scheme, the permanent transfer to subsidiaries, and the reduction of non-core members, such as part-timers and temporary workers. These changes should not be exaggerated, since lifetime employment has not been strictly observed in the past, and much of the current move may have been caused by temporary factors. If the trend nevertheless continues, the consequence will be twofold.

On the one hand, as discussed in Chapter 5, the loss of long-term, company-employee attachment may result in weaker growth pursuit by the firms (and a stronger pursuit of short-term financial gains), weaker interdepartmental linkage, and less emphasis on the skills accumulated on the job, which may threaten the intensity and efficiency of innovation activity. On the other hand, with the increased mobility of researchers and workers, collaboration may become easier among researchers with diverse job experiences and diverse fields, and talented researchers may find it easier to start new businesses of their own, in the manner of venture businesses in the USA in, for instance, biotechnology and electronics, such as Fairchild and Intel discussed in Chapter 8. It is much too early to discuss which of these two scenarios will dominate, particularly because the long-term employment system is still deeply rooted in the Japanese corporate system, and change is slow.

A related move is the transfer of production and other activities, including some R&D, to overseas as discussed in Chapter 5. In some industries, this transfer has been so rapid that the loss of manufacturing technologies is worrying. Such loss, some people argue, may occur at two levels: in medium to small firms, and in large firms. Imai (1984) argued that the accumulation of medium and small firms in certain areas, such as Ohta Ward in Tokyo, particularly in the fields of metal products, machinery, and instruments, resulted in a network for exchanging technological information and achieving division of work among them. The skill level was high and each firm had an advantage in a certain area. With the frequent exchange of information and trust among the firms, they, as a whole, attained a high technological level and a high level of flexibility to accommodate unforeseen orders.

Some of these firms are now either exiting altogether or moving out to developing countries, because of the ageing of owner-managers and workers, high land prices, and the rapid appreciation of the yen, which made imports much cheaper. If this trend continues, it might become more difficult to maintain the network and the merits of agglomeration may be lost.

The overseas transfer of plants and factories is more prominent among large firms. If such transfer is accelerated, the linkage between production and R&D discussed in Chapter 5 may be lost. In fact, many firms are aware of this danger and have maintained some of the factories deliberately within Japan, usually those specialized in high-technology and high-value-added products, called 'mother factories' or 'focal factories' (Fruin, 1992). These factories are located near laboratories and maintain close relationship with R&D departments by making prototypes or test-running new processes for the development teams.

Whether or not such overseas transfer of companies and factories is going to hamper the technological development of Japan, it seems beyond doubt that Japan is now so enmeshed in the interdependent economic system of the world that it is hardly meaningful to discuss the consequences from a national viewpoint alone. The transfer may be both necessary and inevitable to foster the division of labour among countries, in particular, the East Asian countries. Helping these countries to acquire technologies and achieve economic growth will eventually benefit Japan, through an increased demand for high-technology Japanese products and the supply of cheaper and yet reliable products to Japanese consumers.

As one of the technological and economic leaders of the world, Japan is now expected to make an international contribution to the scientific and technological front as well. Its contribution has been increasing in education and in the training of foreigners, the provision of research funds to universities and research institutions overseas, the establishment of overseas laboratories, research collaboration with foreign companies, and the publication of scientific papers. For instance, in the Fifth Generation Computer Systems (FGCS) Project, the most recent MITI-sponsored joint R&D project, the emphasis has been not on the enhancement of Japan's industrial competitiveness but on the support of basic research to benefit the international community (Nakamura and Shibuya, 1995).

The trend would, and should, go on and the public policy should aim at easing this process. Some reforms have already been made, for instance, encouraging foreign firms to join research associations (including FGCS), and making it easier for national universities and research institutions to hire foreign staff. Many of the problems that still remain are embedded in the Japanese social system, and may take a long time to be resolved. The hiring system of universities, discussed above, is one such problem. The preference of more secure jobs by university graduates, which has been making recruitment by foreign firms in Japan (including their laboratories) difficult, may be another.

Japan has gradually built its capabilities through importing technological and other knowledge from overseas, adapting them to its own advantage, learning from trial and error, and, increasingly, making its own innovation efforts. These efforts will, in the long run, help other countries to enhance their capabilities and Japan's capabilities will, in turn, be enhanced by the efforts and capabilities of others, through international technological, economic, and social interaction.

Notes

NOTES TO CHAPTER 1

1. The first use of the word 'entrepreneur' is attributed to Cantillon (1755) whose English original is believed to have been destroyed in a fire that killed him; thus, only the French translation was left in which the French word 'entrepreneur' was used. Although he seems to have regarded the prime function of entrepreneurs as that of undertakers who profits by taking advantages of price differentials between markets or between producers and consumers, he also indicated that '[Inhabitants of a State] can be divided into two classes, Undertakers and Hired people; and that all the Undertakers are as it were on unfixed wages and the others on wages fixed so long as they receive them though their functions and ranks may be very unequal' (Cantillon, 1755; Higgs' English translation, p. 55) where, needless to say, the word 'undertakers' is the English translation of 'entrepreneurs'. This statement is surprisingly similar to Knight's distinction between entrepreneurs and labourers: 'the entrepreneurs also guarantee to those who furnish productive services a fixed remuneration' (Knight, 1921: 271), which led him to his distinction between wages, which are contractual, and profits, which are residual.
2. That the Japanese made rice-polishing machines while the West made mills reflects the difference in eating habit. Some authors suggest that this difference caused the Japanese to be good at machines having reciprocating motion but behind the West with those having rotary motion.

NOTES TO CHAPTER 2

1. The readers are advised to see, for instance, Reischauer (1974) for the exposition of the general Japanese history in English.
2. For the discussion of the start of the telegraph and telephone services, see Chapter 8.
3. For details on Kogakuryo, see Miyoshi (1979).
4. However, at least one college in Britain had a similar programme. It was Marshall who introduced this programme—he was aware of Dyer's achievement: 'A good plan is that of spending the six winter months of several years after leaving school in learning science in College, and the six summer months as articled pupils in large workshops. The present writer introduced this plan several years ago at University College, Bristol. It has also been adopted in Japan' (Marshall, 1898: 290).
5. The list of these laboratories is translated into English by Fukasaku (1992: 88–9).

6. The role of Takamine in the development of the Japanese pharmaceutical industry will be discussed in Chapter 11.
7. The data here is from *Kogyo Chosa Shuho*, 2(2), 1924, reprinted in *Nihon Kagaku Gijutsushi Taikei* (1967).
8. A survey conducted by the Resources Bureau of the Government, quoted in Hiroshige (1973: 115).
9. A survey conducted by the Technology Agency of the Cabinet, quoted in the Agency of Industrial Science and Technology (1964: 125).

NOTES TO CHAPTER 3

1. The discussion on technology importation in this chapter depends heavily on Goto (1993).
2. Ekonomisuto (1984). Many of the cases of technology importation in this chapter are taken from this book.
3. For a theoretical treatment of these two roles of R&D, see Cohen and Levinthal (1989).
4. The figures in this paragraph are taken from the Ministry of International Trade and Industry, *Gaikoku Gijutsu Donyu Nenpo* [Annual Report on the Importation of Foreign Technology], various years.
5. Some authors, such as Saxonhouse (1988), emphasized the information-disseminating role of cooperative research. It is difficult to estimate how important this role was. It has been reported that, in the much publicized case of VLSI Research Association mentioned earlier, it took a considerable talent and effort (and drinks!) of the director to bring together the scientists from different companies (Sakakibara, 1995). Since, as discussed earlier, this RA was exceptional in having a common laboratory and a dedicated director from a third party (namely, a government research institution and not companies), we imagine that communication among scientists from different companies must have been infrequent in most of other RAs.
6. The data on education is from Mombusho (Ministry of Education), *Gakko Kihon Chosa Houkokusho (Basic Research Report on Schools)*.

NOTES TO CHAPTER 4

1. Similar studies on the educational background of managers in the Meiji era were made by Mannari (1974) and Yonekawa (1984).
2. Konoike survived to become part of the present Sanwa Bank.
3. Abegglen (1958) is most often cited in this connection. It is noteworthy, however, that Abegglen's warning in this book that 'the difference between the [Japanese and American] systems is not, of course, absolute, but one of degree' seems to have been overlooked by most of the readers and that his more recent books, such as Abegglen and Stalk (1985), puts less emphasis on the, say, Japanese-ness of the internal labour system.
4. Needless to say, the Japanese Antimonopoly Law prohibits trade associations to engage in any anti-competitive acts or to restrict the membership.

5. The views stressing the influence of war-time control on the post-war period are expressed most comprehensively in Okazaki and Okuno (1993).

NOTES TO CHAPTER 5

1. Hadley (1970). Some other authors quote even larger numbers of purged executives: 2,132 (Okazaki, 1993) and more than 3,600 (Nakagawa, Morikawa and Yui, 1979).

2. See Odagiri (1994) for more discussion of the Japanese antimonopoly policies concerning mergers and acquisitions.

3. Kester (1991) shows that hostile takeovers have not been absent in Japan, many of which aimed at greenmailing rather than taking real control of management.

4. Both Kato and Rockel (1992) and Kaplan (1994) found the average age of the top executives of major Japanese corporations in the 1980s to be higher than that of American corporations.

5. The case of the automobile industry is well known. As we will discuss in Chapter 9, close relationships between assemblers and suppliers in this industry is partly a result of historical development.

6. The statistics on FDI is taken from the Ministry of Finance, *Taigai Chokusetsu Toushi no Kyoka Todokede Jisseki.*

7. The Ministry of International Trade and Industry, *Dai 4 Kai Kaigai Toushi Toukei Souran,* 1990.

8. The Ministry of International Trade and Industry, *Dai 4 Kai Kaigai Toushi Toukei Souran,* 1990. In this survey, the ministry obtained responses from 1,563 parent firms (47 per cent response rate) and 6,362 overseas subsidiaries (72 per cent response rate).

9. For a more detailed comparison of Japanese R&D in Asia and in the USA (and Europe) by means of regression analyses of the determinants, see Odagiri and Yasuda (1994).

NOTES TO CHAPTER 6

1. Together with Choshu, Satsuma later became the central force in the coup against the Tokugawa Shogunate government, which eventually led to the Meiji Restoration.

2. Shibusawa used another part of this kazoku's fund to establish a marine insurance company, which grew into the present Tokio Marine and Fire Insurance Company. Eventually, kazoku did invest in railroad as well, after the government changed its policy in favour of a nation-wide railroad network.

3. The details on Yamanobe and Osaka Boseki as discussed here and in the following are from Kinukawa (1937), vol. 2, and Toyo Boseki Kabushiki Kaisha (1953). For English readers, Yasumuro (1993) gives some detail.

4. Kajinishi (1964: 174); the original sources are *Naigai Mengyo Nenkan* and *No-Shomu Toukei Hyo.*

5. Kajinishi (1964: 176 and 270). The original sources are *Nihon Boeki Toukei* for the figures up to 1900 and *Dainippon Boseki Rengo Kai Chosa* for those after 1904.
6. Kajinishi (1964: 176); the original source is *Tokyo Nichi Nichi Shimbun*.
7. Yasumuro (1993) also emphasizes this fact.
8. Yonekawa (1984) provides a case study of Kanebo concerning the educational background of the managers.
9. The figures on world production and import are from Toyo Rayon Kabushiki Kaisha (1954). The original source for world production is *Textile Organon*.
10. For more details, see Kajinishi (1964: ch. 5), Toyo Rayon Kabushiki Kaisha (1954), and Uchida (1983). In addition, Uchida notes that all the pioneering engineers of rayon had been taught at University of Tokyo and Osaka Koto Kogyo (now the Engineering Department of Osaka University), emphasizing the role of these institutions both in providing basic scientific and engineering knowledge and in introducing them to the companies in need of them.

NOTES TO CHAPTER 7

1. A simplistic comparison of these two numbers is misleading because the amount of government investment includes the cost for the railway system, which the government transferred to other places before selling the Works to Tanaka.
2. See Kosai (1988) for the details of this post-war industrial policy in general and Yonekura (1991) for that of the steel industry.
3. That NKK should have been the first firm to become interested in BOF was more than a coincidence. Even in the pre-war era when open hearth was the dominant technology, Imaizumi, one of the founders of NKK, and Noro's disciple as mentioned earlier, experimented with the Thomas converter method. Thus, although the technological and economic conditions forced NKK to adopt mostly open hearth, it had a certain accumulation of knowledge on the converter which, technologically, is a predecessor to BOF.

NOTES TO CHAPTER 8

1. Our discussion of Tanaka's activities and the development of the telegraph in Japan benefited from Imatsu´(1992) and Shibaura Seisakusho (1940). Incidentally, *Giemon* in the title of Imatsu's book refers to Tanaka Hisashige's *nom de plume*.
2. It is also noted, however, that the scientific capability of the researchers at NRI was high. For instance, there was even some discussion on the idea of atomic bombs. See Nakagawa (1987) for the details of NRI.
3. For the early history of Sony, see Morita's autobiography (1986) and Nakagawa (1981; 1987).
4. The factual account of the Japanese semiconductor industry in this and the following sections relies mainly on two documentary books, Nakagawa

(1987) and Aida (1991). For a Japan–USA comparison, see Okimoto et al. (1984).

5. Incidentally, Hatoyama later became the first director of Sony's Central Laboratory, and Kikuchi the fourth.

6. Interestingly, these companies did not believe in the future of transistor technology and therefore the researchers had to go to the study meetings without the support of the company. When a researcher from NEC started experimenting with the transistor, the company refused to give him any research budget. See Nakagawa (1981).

7. Trezise and Suzuki (1976) argued that Sony was delayed by nearly two years until they could get the approval to import the technology. However, Aida's (1991) interview with Ibuka indicates that the delay was six months, shorter than two years but still substantial. Lynn's (1994) study also supports this interview.

8. As a by-product of this experiment, Esaki Leona, then a researcher at Sony and now the president of the University of Tsukuba (where, incidentally, one of the authors teaches), found the tunnel diode principle which, some argue, has been the only truly original invention by the Japanese in the field of the semiconductor.

9. However, an engineer at Sharp, working on the calculator at the time, insists that 'we studied the British calculator in a number of ways but, technologically, it was not so helpful because we were aiming at high speed, portability, and high reliability, which could not be attained with a vacuum-tube calculator. Nevertheless, it convinced us that our direction for product development was right' (Aida, 1991, vol. 3: 156, our translation).

10. In the USA around the same time, Texas Instruments also developed an IC calculator. However, it was not introduced into the market because of a negative market research report, giving an interesting contrast to Sharp and other Japanese calculator producers who successively introduced new products into the market with little market research. Entrepreneurship, or what Keynes (1936) called 'animal spirits' (see Chapter 12) seems to apply to such behaviour of Japanese firms rather than 'rational behaviour' as taught in business schools.

11. LSI stands for large-scale integrated circuits. To be more precise, what Sharp used at this stage may have been SSI (small-scale integrated circuits) or MSI (medium-scale integrated circuits) but we ignore this distinction.

12. See note 10 above.

13. Hewlett-Packard in the late 1970s conducted a test of approximately 300,000 memory chips which they bought from American and Japanese suppliers. They found that 'none of the Japanese lots was rejected because of failures, whereas failure rates for lots from the U.S. companies ranged from 0.11 to 0.19 per cent' (Weinstein et al., 1984: 53).

14. Management and Coordination Agency, *Kagaku Gijutsu Kenkyu Chosa*

Houkoku (Report on the Survey of Research and Development), various years.

15. The study of the productivity of JRAs was done by Fujishiro (1988) and cited in detail in Odagiri (1992, ch. 11). For government policies in general regarding the computer industry, see Fransman (1990) and Shinjo (1988).

NOTES TO CHAPTER 9

1. The discussion in this chapter depends on a number of sources, in particular, Nihon Jidosha Kogyo Kai (1988), Nissan Jidosha Kabushiki Kaisha (1965), Toyota Jidosha Kabushiki Kaisha (1967), Ohshima and Yamaoka (1987) and, among those in English, Cusumano (1985) and Genther (1990).

2. TGE later joined the Hitachi group to become Hitachi Aircraft, see Chapter 10. After World War II, the company joined the Komatsu group and is now part of Komatsu Zenoah.

3. Toyota Jidosha Kabushiki Kaisha (1967). For English-speaking readers, Cusumano (1985, 63–4) gives some detail of the people from whom Kiichiro sought advice, or whom he hired.

4. Cusumano (1985, ch. 3) and Halberstam (1987) give a detailed account of the Nissan strike.

5. For more details on the historical formation of supplier system, see Cusumano (1985); Fruin (1992); Smitka (1991). Odagiri (1992, ch. 6) discusses the competitive aspect of the current supplier system.

6. See Cusumano (1985). Toyota's kanban production system is discussed in Monden (1983); its use of interfirm networks in Fruin (1992), and its relation to product development in Clark and Fujimoto (1991).

NOTES TO CHAPTER 10

1. The discussion of the pre-war aircraft industry in this section and the next benefited from Ministry of International Trade and Industry (1976), Okamura et al., (1976), Samuels (1994), and Toyo Keizai (1950). The figures cited without reference are taken from Toyo Keizai (1950).

2. According to Maema (1993), however, an American engineer from Curtis stayed at Nakajima's Musashi Plant until several months before the start of World War II. This fact suggests both that technology transfer from the USA to Japan did take place to a certain extent even after the political relationship between the two countries turned sour, and that the USA might have been aware of the technology of Zero fighters because Musashi plant made 'Sakae' engines mounted in Zero fighters.

3. For the detail of the YS-11 project, see Maema (1994) and the Ministry of International Trade and Industry (1985), from which the figures in the text are cited.

4. Most of the figures cited in this section are taken from Nihon Kouku Uchu Kogyo Kai (1994).

NOTES TO CHAPTER 11

1. In Japanese, these businesses were called *nakagai* or, literally translated, brokers. There were also *ton-ya* or wholesalers. However, *ton-ya* acted only as intermediaries, taking a fixed percentage of their trade as fees. It was *nakagai* who played a more substantial role as described in the text, and in the usual sense would better be called wholesalers. Therefore, we translate *nakagai* as wholesalers.
2. The role of universities was large in the American and German pharmaceutical industries as well: see Liebenau (1984).
3. In addition, MHW's drug approval policy may have discriminated against foreign firms until the mid 1980s: see Reich (1990).
4. Management and Coordination Agency, *Kagaku Gijutsu Kenkyu Chosa Houkoku* [Report on the Survey of Research and Development], various years. The technology export is measured by the receipts of royalties and the import, the payments of royalties.

NOTES TO CHAPTER 12

1. For the analyses of how the number of firms tends to vary along product life cycles, see Gort and Klepper (1982) and Klepper and Graddy (1990).
2. Management and Coordination Agency, *Kagaku Gijutsu Kenkyu Chosa Houkoku* [Report on the Survey of Research and Development], 1991.
3. An unpublished interim report of Kokuritsu Daigaku Kyokai (the Association of National Universities).
4. The extent of university–industry cooperation in Japan is documented by Hicks (1994). She suggests that such cooperation is more widespread than the figures indicate and that some of the forms of cooperation are closely related to the recruitment of graduates.

APPENDIX
A Brief Chronology of Japan's History

660 B.C.	Traditional date of accession of first emperor, Jimmu
593–620	Regency of Prince Shotoku
607	First embassy to Sui dynasty of China
710–784	NARA ERA
710	Founding of Heijo Capital (Nara)
794–1185	HEIAN ERA
794	Founding of Heian Capital (Kyoto)
866–1160	Rule by the Family of Fujiwara as Regent or Chancellor
1160–1185	Rule by the Family of Taira as Prime Minister
1180–1185	War between the Minamoto and Taira (Gempei Wars)
1192–1333	KAMAKURA ERA
1192	Assumption of title of *Shogun* by Minamoto Yoritomo (d. 1199) Start of Shogunate government (*Bakufu*) in Kamakura
1333	Destruction of Kamakura by Nitta Yoshisada
1333–1392	NANBOKUCHO ERA (ERA OF THE NORTHERN AND SOUTHERN COURTS)
1333–1335	Rule by Emperor Godaigo (d. 1339)
1338–1573	ASHIKAGA (or MUROMACHI) ERA
1338	Assumption of title of *Shogun* by Ashikaga Takauji (d. 1358) Start of Shogunate government (*Bakufu*) in Muromachi, Kyoto
1467–1477	Onin Wars
1477–1590	Wars among *daimyo* (SENGOKU ERA)
1568	Seizure of Kyoto by Oda Nobunaga
1573	Deposition of Ashikaga Yoshiaki by Oda Nobunaga
1576–1600	AZUCHI–MOMOYAMA ERA
1577–1582	Rule by Oda Nobunaga (d. 1582) as Minister at Azuchi
1585–1598	Rule by Toyotomi Hideyoshi (d. 1598) as Chancellor at Osaka and, later, Momoyama
1592, 1597	Invasion of Korea
1600	Victory of Tokugawa Ieyasu at Battle of Sekigahara
1600–1867	TOKUGAWA (or EDO) ERA
1603	Assumption of title of *Shogun* by Tokugawa Ieyasu (d. 1616) Start of Shogunate government (*Bakufu*) in Edo (Tokyo)
1639	Expulsion of Portuguese: Start of Seclusionism (*Sakoku*)

1853 Arrival of Commodore Perry from the USA
1854 Treaty of Kanagawa with the US: End of Seclusionism
1858 Commercial Treaty ('Unequal Treaty') with the USA, The Netherlands, Russia, the UK, and France
1867 Return of power by Tokugawa Yoshinobu to Emperor Meiji: Meiji Restoration (*Meiji Ishin*)

1867–1912 MEIJI ERA
1868 Establishment of Tokyo (formerly Edo) as new capital
1871 Substitution of prefectures (*ken*) for fiefs (*han*)
1877 Civil War caused by Satsuma Rebellion (Seinan War)
1882 Founding of Bank of Japan
1885 Adoption of cabinet system with Ito Hirobumi as first Prime Minister
1889 Promulgation of Constitution
1890 First general election for Diet
1894–1895 Sino-Japanese (*Nisshin*) War
1904–1905 Russo-Japanese (*Nichiro*) War
1910 Annexation of Korea
1911 Revision of Commercial Treaty with the USA, the UK, and Germany
1912 Death of Emperor Meiji and succession of Yoshihito (Emperor Taisho)

1912–1926 TAISHO ERA
1914 Declaration of war on Germany
1918 End of World War I
1923 Great Kanto Earthquake
1925 Adoption of universal manhood suffrage
1926 Death of Emperor Taisho and succession of Hirohito (Emperor Showa)

1926–1988 SHOWA ERA
1931 Outbreak of Manchurian Incident
1932 Creation of Manchukuo
1936 Assassination and attempted *coup d'etat* ('2–26 incident')
1937 Shanghai campaign: Start of war with China
1939 Outbreak of World War II in Europe
1940 Tripartite Alliance with Germany and Italy
1941 Start of the Pacific War
1945 Surrender of Japan
1946 Promulgation of new constitution
1946–1952 Allied occupation
1947 Antimonopoly Law, Deconcentration Law
1949 Budgetary and fiscal retrenchment: 'Dodge Line' ($1 = ¥360)

1950–1953 Korean War
    1951 Peace treaty and security treaty with the US
    1956 Admission to United Nations
    1964 Admission to OECD
    1971 'Nixon Shock' ($1 = ¥308)
    1973 Adoption of floating exchange rate
          'Oil Shock' (Oil embargo by Arabs)
    1989 Death of Emperor Showa and succession by Akihito

    1989– HEISEI ERA
    1994 Further appreciation of yen ($1 < ¥100)

Source: Reischauer (1974) and others.

Bibliography

Note: Names at the opening of each entry are written with surnames first, followed by comma and then other names. Elsewhere, names are given as they appeared in the cited literature, namely, surname-first for books in Japanese and forename-first for those in English.

ABE, TAKESHI (1990), 'Men Kogyo' [Cotton Textile Industry], in Nishikawa Shunsaku and Abe Takeshi [eds.], *Nihon Keizaishi, 4: Sangyo Ka no Jidai, Jou* (Tokyo: Iwanami Shoten), 163–212.

ABEGGLEN, JAMES C. (1958), *The Japanese Factory: Aspects of Its Social Organization* (Glencoe, Ill.: Free Press), repr. in J. C. Abegglen, *Management and Worker: The Japanese Solution* (Tokyo: Sophia University, in cooperation with Kodansha International), 1973.

—— and STALK, GEORGE, JR. (1985), *Kaisha, The Japanese Corporation* (New York: Basic Books).

ABRAMOVITZ, MOSES (1986), 'Catching Up, Forging Ahead and Falling Behind', *Journal of Economic History*, 46, 385–406.

ADACHI, TETSUO (1981), 'Ririkuki o Mukaeta Nihon no Koukuki Kogyo' [The Japanese Aircraft Industry in a Takeoff Period], *Chogin Chosa Geppo*, No. 185 (Tokyo: The Long-Term Credit Bank of Japan).

Agency of Industrial Science and Technology, the Ministry of International Trade and Industry (1964), *Gijutsu Kakushin to Nihon no Kogyo: Kogyo Gijutsuin 15 Nen no Ayumi* [Innovation and Manufacturing Industries in Japan: The 15 Year History of the Agency of Industrial Science and Technology], (Tokyo: Nikkan Kogyo Shimbun Sha).

AIDA, HIROSHI (1991), *Denshi Rikkoku Nihon no Jijoden* [The Autobiography of Japan, a Country of Electronics], 4 vols (Tokyo: Nihon Hoso Shuppan Kyokai).

ALCHIAN, ARMEN A. (1950), 'Uncertainly, Evolution, and Economic Theory', *Journal of Political Economy*, 58, 211–21.

ARISAWA, HIROMI (1967), *Nihon Sangyo 100 Nen Shi* [The 100 Year History of Japanese Industries], 2 vols (Tokyo: Nihon Keizai Shimbun Sha).

ARROW, KENNETH J. (1962), 'Economic Welfare and the Allocation of Resources for Invention', in *The Rate and Direction of Inventive Activity* (Princeton: Princeton University Press), 609–25.

ASANUMA, BANRI (1985), 'The Contractual Framework for Parts Supply in the Japanese Automotive Industry', *Journal of Japanese Studies*, Summer, 54–78.

BABA, YASUNORI; KURODA, SHOICHI and YOSHIKI, HIROSHI (1996), 'Diffusion of Systemic Approach in Japan: The Case of Gauge and Industrial Standard', in A. Goto and H. Odagiri [eds.], *Innovation in Japan: Empirical Studies on the National and Corporate Activities* (Oxford: Oxford University Press).

BAUMOL, WILLIAM J., PANZAR, JOHN C. and WILLIG, ROBERT D. (1982), *Contestable Markets and the Theory of Industrial Structure* (New York: Harcourt Brace Jovanovich).

Business Week (1991), 'A Portrait of a CEO', (25 Nov.), 44–8.

Business Week (1993a), 'A Car Is Born', (13 Sept.), 38–44.

Business Week (1993b), 'Portrait of a CEO', (11 Oct.), 64–5.

CANTILLON, RICHARD (1755), *Essai sur la Nature du Commerce en Gènèral* (ed. with English trans. Henry Higgs, London: Macmillan, 1931. Repr. New York: Augustus M. Kelly, 1964).

CASPARY, SIGRUN (1995), 'Doitsu no Kouku Gijutsu ga Nihon Rikukaigun Koukuki ni Ataeta Eikyo' [The Influence of German Aircraft Technology on the Development of the Japanese Army and Navy Aircraft], unpublished.

CHANDLER, ALFRED D., JR. (1990), *Scale and Scope* (Cambridge, Mass.: Harvard University Press).

CHIDA, TOMOHEI and DAVIES, PETER N. (1990), *The Japanese Shipping and Shipbuilding Industries: A History of Their Modern Growth* (London: Athlone).

CLARK, KIM B. and FUJIMOTO, TAKAHIRO (1991), *Product Development Performance: Strategy, Organization, and Management in the World Auto Industry* (Boston: Harvard Business School Press).

COHEN, WESLEY M. and LEVINTHAL, DANIEL A. (1889), 'Innovation and Learning: The Two Faces of R&D', *Economic Journal*, 99, 569–96.

CORBETT, JENNY and JENKINSON, TIM (1994), 'The Financing of Industry, 1970–1989: An International Comparison', paper presented at the 11th ERI International Symposium: International Comparison of the Systems of Market Economy, Economic Research Institute, Economic Planning Agency, Tokyo.

CORDELL, ARTHUR J. (1973), 'Innovation, the Multinational Corporation: Some Implications for National Science Policy', *Long Range Planning*, 6, 22–9.

CUSUMANO, MICHAEL A. (1985), *The Japanese Automobile Industry: Technology and Management at Nissan and Toyota*, Harvard East Asian Monographs 122 (Cambridge, Mass.: Harvard University Press).

DAVID, PAUL A. (1985), 'Clio and the Economics of QWERTY', *American Economic Review: Papers and Proceedings*, 75, 332–7.

DEMSETZ, HAROLD (1973), 'Industry Structure, Market Rivalry, and Public Policy', *Journal of Law and Economics*, 16, 1–9.

DORE, RONALD (1973), *British Factory, Japanese Factory* (London: George Allen & Unwin).

—— (1976), *The Diploma Disease* (London: George Allen & Unwin).

EADS, GEORGE C. and NELSON, RICHARD R. (1986), 'Japanese High Technology Policy: What Lessons for the United States?' in H. Patrick [ed.], *Japan's High Technology Industries* (Seattle: University of Washington Press), 243–69.

Ekonomisuto (1984), *Shougen Kodo Seichoki no Nihon* [Testimony on Japan in the High Growth Era], (Tokyo: Mainichi Shimbun Sha).

Fair Trade Commission (1994), 'The Report on the Actual Conditions of the Six Major Corporate Groups', unpublished.

FRANSMAN, MARTIN (1990), *The Market and Beyond: Cooperation and Competition in Information Technology Development in the Japanese System* (Cambridge, UK: Cambridge University Press).

—— (1994), 'AT&T, BT, and NTT: Vision, Strategy, Corporate Competence, Path-Dependence, and the Role of R&D', in G. Pogorel [ed.], *Global Telecommunications Strategies and Technological Changes* (Amsterdam: North-Holland), 277–314.

FRUIN, W. MARK (1983), *Kikkoman: Company, Clan, and Community* (Cambridge, Mass.: Harvard University Press).

—— (1992), *The Japanese Enterprise System: Competitive Strategies and Cooperative Structures* (Oxford: Oxford University Press).

FUJIMOTO, TAKAHIRO and TIDD, JOSEPH (1993), 'The UK and Japanese Auto Industry: Adoption and Adaptation of Fordism', paper presented at the Tokyo University Conference on 'Entrepreneurial Activities and Corporate Systems: The Historical Perspective'. Japanese trans.: 'Ford Shisutemu no Donyu to Genchi Tekiou: Nichi-Ei Jidosha Sangyo no Hikaku Kenkyu', *Keizaigaku Ronshu*, 59, (2), 36–50; (3), 34–56.

FUJISHIRO, NAOTAKE (1988), 'Konpyuta Sangyo ni Okeru Kyodo-Kenkyu no Yakuwari' [The Role of Joint R&D in the Computer Industry], (unpublished master's thesis, University of Tsukuba).

FUKASAKU, YUKIKO (1992), *Technology and Industrial Development in Pre-War Japan: Mitsubishi Nagasaki Shipyard 1884–1934* (London: Routledge).

GENTHER, PHYLLIS A. (1990), *A History of Japan's Government-Business Relationship: The Passenger Car Industry* (Ann Arbor, Mich.: The University of Michigan).

GORT, MICHAEL and KLEPPER, STEVEN (1982), 'Time Paths in the Diffusion of Product Innovations', *Economic Journal*, 92, 630–53.

GOTO, AKIRA (1982), 'Business Groups in a Market Economy', *European Economic Review*, 19, 53–70.

—— (1988), 'Japan: A Sunset Industry', in M. Peck [ed.], *The World Aluminium Industry in a Changing Energy Era* (Washington: Resources for the Future), 90–120.

—— (1993), 'Technology Importation: Japan's Postwar Experience', in J. Teranishi and Y. Kosai [eds.], *The Japanese Experience of Economic Reforms* (New York: St. Martin's Press), 277–304.

—— (1996), 'Cooperative Research in Japanese Manufacturing Industries: Innovation in R&D System?', in A. Goto and H. Odagiri [eds.], *Innovation in Japan: Empirical Studies on the National and Corporate Activities* (Oxford: Oxford University Press).

—— and WAKASUGI, RYUHEI (1988), 'Technology Policy', in Komiya, Okuno, and Suzumura (1988), 183–204.

GRILICHES, ZVI (1992), 'The Search for R&D Spillovers', *Scandinavian Journal of Economics*, 94, S29–47.

GROSSMAN, GENE M. and HELPMAN, ELHANAN (1990), 'Comparative Advantage and Long-Run Growth', *American Economic Review*, 80, 796–815.

—— and —— (1991), *Innovation and Growth in the Global Economy* (Cambridge, Mass.: MIT Press).

—— and —— (1994), 'Endogenous Innovation in the Theory of Growth', *Journal of Economic Perspectives*, 8, 23–44.

HADLEY, ELEANOR M. (1970), *Antitrust in Japan* (Princeton: Princeton University Press).

HALBERSTAM, DAVID (1987), *The Reckoning* (New York: Avon).

HALL, G. R. and JOHNSON, R. E. (1970), 'Transfers of United States Aerospace Technology to Japan', in R. Vernon [ed.], *The Technology Factor in International Trade* (New York: National Bureau of Economic Research), 305–58.

HASEGAWA, HISASHI (1986), *Sangyo no Showa Shakaishi: Iyakuhin* [Social History of Industries during the Showa Era: Pharmaceuticals], (Tokyo: Nihon Keizai Hyoron Sha).

HAYASHI, IZUO; HIRANO, MASAHIRO and KATAYAMA, YOSHIFUMI (1989), 'Collaborative Semiconductor Research in Japan', *Proc. IEEE*, 77, 1430–41.

HAZAMA, HIROSHI (1964), *Nihon Roumu Kanri Shi Kenkyu* [A Study of the History of Labour Management in Japan], (Tokyo: Daiyamondo Sha).

HICKS, DIANA (1994), 'Regulation and Reality in University-Industry Cooperation in Japan', unpublished. Forthcoming in *A Productive Tension: University-Industry Research Collaborations in the Era of Knowledge-Based Economic Development* (Palo Alto, Calif.: Stanford University Press).

HIROSHIGE, TETSU (1973), *Kagaku no Shakaishi* [The Social History of Science], (Tokyo: Chuo Koron Sha).

HIRSCHMAN, ALBERT O. (1970), *Exit, Voice, and Loyalty* (Cambridge, Mass.: Harvard University Press).

HIRSCHMEIER, JOHANNES and YUI, TSUNEHIKO (1975), *The Development of Japanese Business, 1600–1973* (London: George Allen & Unwin).

—— and —— (1977), *Nihon no Keiei Hatten* [The Development of Business in Japan], (Tokyo: Toyo Keizai).

HODDER, JAMES E. (1988), 'Corporate Capital Structure in the United States and Japan: Financial Intermediation and Implications of Financial Deregulation', in J. B. Shoven [ed.], *Government Policy towards Industry in the*

United States and Japan (Cambridge, UK: Cambridge University Press), 241–63.

IIDA, KEN'ICHI (1979), *Nihon Tekkou Gijutsu Shi* [The History of Iron and Steel Technology in Japan], (Tokyo: Toyo Keizai).

—— (1982), *Nihonjin to Tetsu* [Japanese People and Iron], (Tokyo: Yuhikaku).

IMAI, KEN'ICHI (1984), *Joho Nettowaku Shakai* [Information Network Society], (Tokyo: Iwanami Shoten).

—— ; NONAKA, IKUJIRO and TAKEUCHI, HIROTAKA (1985), 'Managing the New Product Development Process: How Japanese Companies Learn and Unlearn', in K. B. Clark, R. H. Hayes and C. Lorenz [eds.], *The Uneasy Alliance* (Boston: Harvard Business School Press), 337–75.

IMATSU, KENJI (1992), *Karakuri Giemon* [Karakuri Giemon], (Tokyo: Daiya-mondo Sha).

INOUE, YOICHIRO (1990), *Nihon Kindai Zosen-Gyo no Tenkai* [The Development of the Japanese Modern Shipbuilding Industry], (Kyoto: Mineruva Shobo).

ISHIKAWA, KENJIRO (1974), 'Meiji-Ki ni Okeru Kigyosha Katsudo no Toukeiteki Kousatsu' [A Statistical Study of the Entrepreneurial Activity in the Meiji Era], *Osaka Daigaku Keizaigaku*, 23 (4), 85–118.

ITAMI, HIROYUKI (1988), *Gyakuten no Dainamizumu: Nichi-Bei Handoutai Sangyo no Hikaku Kenkyu* [The Dynamism of Turnaround: Comparative Study of Japan-US Semiconductor Industry], (Tokyo: NTT Shuppan).

Japan Pharmaceutical Manufacturers Association (JPMA); *see* Nihon Seiyaku Kogyo Kai.

JOHNSON, P. S. (1971/2), 'The Role of Co-Operative Research in British Industry', *Research Policy*, 1, 332–50.

KAIGO, MUNEOMI [ed.], (1971), *Nihon Kindai Kyouiku Jiten* [Encyclopedia of Modern Education in Japan], (Tokyo: Heibonsha).

KAJINISHI, MITSUHAYA (1964), *Gendai Nihon Sangyo Hattatsu Shi, XI: Sen'i* [The History of Industrial Development in Modern Japan, XI: Textiles], (Tokyo: Kojun Sha).

KAMATANI, CHIKAYOSHI (1988), *Gijutsu Taikoku 100 Nen no Kei: Nihon no Kindaika to Kokuritsu Kenkyu Kikan* [The 100 Year Strategy towards an Innovating Country: Japan's Modernization and the National Research Institutions], (Tokyo: Heibonsha).

KANDACHI, HARUKI (1982), 'Kindai Boseki-Gyo no Ishoku to Ringu-Gata Kojo no Seiritsu' [The Transfer of Modern Textile Industry and the Establishment of Ring-Type Mills] in Unno Fukuju [ed.], *Gijutsu no Shakaishi, 3: Seiou Gijutsu no Inyuu to Meiji Shakai* (Tokyo: Yuhikaku), 131–66.

KANEKO, EIICHI [ed.], (1964), *Gendai Nihon Sangyo Hattatsu Shi, IX: Zosen* [The History of Industrial Development in Modern Japan, IX: Shipbuilding], (Tokyo: Kojun Sha).

KAPLAN, STEVEN N. (1994), 'Top Executive Rewards and Firm Performance:

A Comparison of Japan and the United States', *Journal of Political Economy*, 102, 510–46.

KARASAWA, EIICHIRO (1986) 'Kouku Gijutsu no Hizumi' [Deficiencies in Aircraft Technology], in Hasegawa Keitaro [ed.], *Nihon Kindai to Senso, VI* (Kyoto: PHP), 193–224.

KATO, TAKAO and ROCKEL, MARK (1992), 'The Importance of Company Breeding in the U.S. and Japanese Managerial Labor Markets: A Statistical Comparison', *Japan and the World Economy*, 4, 39–45.

KAWAGOE, TOSHIHIKO (1993), 'Land Reform in Postwar Japan', in J. Teranishi and Y. Kosai [eds.], *The Japanese Experience of Economic Reforms* (New York: St. Martin's Press), 178–204.

KESTER, W. CARL (1991), *Japanese Takeovers* (Boston: Harvard Business School Press).

KEYNES, JOHN MAYNARD (1936), *The General Theory of Employment, Interest and Money* (London: Macmillan).

KIKUCHI, MAKOTO (1992), *Nihon no Handotai 40 Nen* [40 Years of Semiconductors in Japan], (Tokyo: Chuo Koron Sha).

KIMURA, YUI (1996), 'Technological Innovation and Competition in the Japanese Semiconductor Industry', in A. Goto and H. Odagiri [eds.], *Innovation in Japan: Empirical Studies on the National and Corporate Activities* (Oxford: Oxford University Press).

KINOSHITA, ETSUJI (1968), 'Shihon Shugi no Seiritsu to Gaikoku Boeki' [The Start of Capitalism and Foreign Trade], in Kawai Ichiro, Kinoshita Etsuji, Junno Shoichiro, Takahashi Makoto, and Hazama Genzo [eds.], *Koza Nihon Shihon Shugi Hattatsu Shi Ron, I* (Tokyo: Nihon Hyoron Sha), 219–58.

KINUKAWA, TAICHI (1937), *Honpo Menshi Boseki Shi* [The History of Cotton Textiles in Japan], 7 vols (Osaka: Nihon Mengyo Kurabu).

KIYOKAWA, YUKIHIKO (1973), 'Men Kogyo Gijutsu no Teichaku to Kokusan-Ka ni Tsuite' [On the Settlement of Cotton Textile Technology and its Domestic Production], *Keizai Kenkyu*, 24, 117–37.

—— (1987), 'Men Boseki-Gyo ni Okeru Gijutsu Sentaku: Myuru Bouki kara Ringu Bouki he' [Technology Choice in Cotton Spinning Industry: From Mule Spinning Machines to Ring Spinning Machines], in Minami Ryoshin and Kiyokawa Yukihiko [eds.], *Nihon no Kogyo-Ka to Gijutsu Hatten* (Tokyo: Toyo Keizai), 83–107.

KLEMPERER, PAUL (1990), 'How Broad Should the Scope of Patent Protection Be?', *Rand Journal of Economics*, 21, 113–30.

KLEPPER, STEVEN and GRADDY, ELIZABETH (1990), 'The Evolution of New Industries and the Determinants of Market Structure', *Rand Journal of Economics*, 21, 27–44.

KNIGHT, FRANK H. (1921), *Risk, Uncertainty and Profit* (Boston: Houghton Mifflin, repr. Chicago, Ill.: The University of Chicago Press, 1971).

KOBAYASHI, HIDEO (1973), '1930 Nendai Nihon Chisso Hiryo Kabushiki Kaisha no Chosen no Shinshutsu ni Tsuite' [Nitchitsu's Advance into Korea in the 1930s], in Yamada Hideo [ed.], *Shokuminchi Keizaishi no Shomondai* (Tokyo: Asia Keizai Kenkyusho).

KOIKE, KAZUO (1988), *Understanding Industrial Relations in Modern Japan* (London: Macmillan).

KOMIYA, RYUTARO (1972), 'Direct Foreign Investment in Postwar Japan', in P. Drysdale [ed.], *Direct Foreign Investment in Asia and the Pacific* (Canberra: Australian National University Press), 137–72.

—— (1988), 'Introduction', in Komiya, Okuno, and Suzumura (1988), 1–22.

—— ; OKUNO, MASAHIRO and SUZUMURA, KOTARO [eds.], (1988), *Industrial Policy of Japan* (New York: Academic Press).

—— and YOKOBORI, KEIICHI (1991), 'Japan's Industrial Policies in the 1980s', *Studies in International Trade and Industry*, vol. 5 (Tokyo: Research Institute of International Trade and Industry, Ministry of International Trade and Industry).

KONO, TOYOHIRO (1984), *Strategy and Structure of Japanese Enterprises* (London: Macmillan).

KOSAI, YUTAKA (1988), 'The Reconstruction Period', in Komiya, Okuno, and Suzumura (1988), 25–48.

—— (1989), 'Kodo Seicho he no Shuppatsu' [The Departure for High Growth], in Nakamura Takafusa [ed.], *Nihon Keizaishi, 7: Keikakuka to Minshuka* (Tokyo: Iwanami Shoten), 283–321.

—— and TERANISHI, JURO (1993), 'Introduction: Economic Reform and Stabilization in Postwar Japan', in J. Teranishi and Y. Kosai [eds.], *The Japanese Experience of Economic Reforms* (New York: St. Martin's Press), 1–27.

LIEBENAU, JONATHAN (1984), 'Industrial R&D in Pharmaceutical Firms in the Early Twentieth Century', *Business History*, 26, 329–46.

LYNN, LEONARD H. (1982), *How Japan Innovates* (Boulder, Colo.: Westview Press).

—— (1994), 'Japan's Systems of Innovation: A Framework for Theory Guided Research', forthcoming in Allan Bird and Schon Beechler [eds.], *Advances in Japanese Management* (New York: JAI Press).

MAEMA, TAKANORI (1993), *Man Mashin no Showa Densetsu: Koukuki kara Jidosha he* [The Showa Legend of Man and Machine: From Aircraft to Automobile], 2 vols (Tokyo: Kodansha).

—— (1994), *YS-11* [YS-11], (Tokyo: Kodansha).

MANNARI, HIROSHI (1974), *The Japanese Business Leaders* (Tokyo: University of Tokyo Press).

MANSFIELD, EDWIN (1985), 'Public Policy toward Industrial Innovation: An International Study of Direct Tax Incentives for Research and Development', in K. B. Clark, R. H. Hayes, and C. Lorenz [eds.], *The Uneasy Alliance* (Boston: Harvard Business School Press), 383–407.

MARRIS, ROBIN L. (1964), *An Economic Theory of 'Managerial' Capitalism* (London: Macmillan).

MARSHALL, ALFRED (1898), *Principles of Economics*, 4th edn, (London: Macmillan).

—— (1923), *Industry and Trade*, 4th edn, (London: Macmillan).

MASAKI, HISASHI (1976), 'Kabushiki Kaisha Seido no Donyu' [The Introduction of Joint-Stock Company System], in Miyamoto Mataji and Nakagawa Keiichiro [eds.], *Kogyoka to Kigyosha Katsudo* (Tokyo: Nihon Keizai Shimbun Sha), 219–44.

MATSUI, AKIHIKO (1989), 'Consumer-Benefited Cartels under Strategic Capital Investment Competition', *International Journal of Industrial Organization*, 7, 451–70.

MATSUSHITA, MITSUO (1990), *Introduction to Japanese Antimonopoly Law* (Tokyo: Yuhikaku).

MAURER, P. REED (1988), 'Ready for an R&D Breakout', *Business Tokyo*, May, 41–3.

MINAMI, RYOSHIN (1976), *Douryoku Kakumei to Gijutsu Shinpo* [The Power Revolution and Technical Progress], (Tokyo: Toyo Keizai).

—— (1992), *Nihon no Keizai Hatten* [The Economic Development of Japan], (Tokyo: Toyo Keizai).

Ministry of International Trade and Industry (MITI) (1985), *Shoko Seisaku Shi* [History of Commerce and Industrial Policy], vol. 19 (Tokyo: Shoko Seisaku Shi Kankokai).

—— (1989), *Tsusho Sangyo Seisaku Shi* [History of Trade and Industrial Policy], vol. 5 (Tokyo: Tsusho Sangyo Chosa Kai).

MISHIMA, YASUO (1980), 'Taisho-Showa Zenki no Keiei' [Management in the Taisho and Early Showa Era], in Sakudo Yotaro, Mishima Yasuo, Yasuoka Shigeaki, and Inoue Yoichiro [eds.], *Nihon Keieishi* (Kyoto: Minerva Shobo), 142–204.

MIYAZAKI, MASAYASU and ITO, OSAMU (1989), 'Senji Sengo no Sangyo to Kigyo' [Industries and Firms During and After the War], in Nakamura Takafusa [ed.], *Nihon Keizaishi, 7: Keikakuka to Minshuka* (Tokyo: Iwanami Shoten), 165–235.

MIYOSHI, NOBUHIRO (1979), *Nihon Kogyo Kyouiku Seiritsu Shi no Kenkyu* [A Study of the Early History of Engineering Education in Japan], (Tokyo: Kazama Shobo).

MIZOTA, SEIGO (1991), 'Zosen' [Shipbuilding], in Yonekawa Shin'ichi, Shimokawa Koji and Yamazaki Hiroaki [eds.], *Sengo Nihon Keieishi*, vol. 1 (Tokyo: Toyo Keizai), 185–262.

MOLONY, BARBARA (1990), *Technology and Investment: The Prewar Japanese Chemical Industry* (Cambridge, Mass.: Harvard University Press).

MONDEN, YASUHIRO (1983), *Toyota Production System* (Atlanta: Industrial Engineering and Management Press).

MORIKAWA, HIDEMASA (1973), 'Meiji-Ki ni Okeru Senmon Keieisha no Shinshutsu Katei' [The Process of Emergence of Professional Managers in the Meiji Era], *Business Review*, 21 (2), 12–27.

—— (1975), *Gijutsusha* [Technicians], (Tokyo: Nihon Keizai Shimbun Sha).

MORISHIMA, MICHIO (1982), *Why Has Japan 'Succeeded'?: Western Technology and the Japanese Ethos* (Cambridge, UK: Cambridge University Press).

MORITA, AKIO (1986), *Made in Japan: Akio Morita and Sony* (New York: E. P. Dutton).

MUTO, HIROMICHI (1988), 'The Automobile Industry', in Komiya, Okuno, and Suzumura (1988), 307–32.

MYERS, MARGARET G. (1970), *A Financial History of the United States* (New York: Columbia University Press).

NAKAGAWA, KEIICHIRO; MORIKAWA, HIDEMASA and YUI, TSUNEHIKO [eds.], (1979), *Kindai Nihon Keieishi no Kiso Chishiki* [The Basic Knowledge on the Business History of Modern Japan], revised edn, (Tokyo: Yuhikaku).

NAKAGAWA, MASANAO [ed.], (1984), *Antimonopoly Legislation of Japan* (Tokyo: Kousei Torihiki Kyokai).

NAKAGAWA, YASUZO (1981), *Nihon no Handotai Kaihatsu* [The Development of Semiconductors in Japan], (Tokyo: Daiyamondo Sha).

—— (1987), *Kaigun Gijutsu Kenkyusho* [Naval Research Institute], (Tokyo: Nihon Keizai Shimbun Sha).

NAKAI, NOBUHIKO (1966), 'Mitsui-ke no Keiei: Shiyonin Seido to Sono Unei' [Management at Mitsui: The Employment System], *Shakai Keizai Shigaku*, 31, (6), 88–101.

NAKAMURA, YOSHIAKI and SHIBUYA, MINORU (1995), 'Japan's Technology Policy: A Case Study of the Research and Development of the Fifth Generation Computer Systems', *Studies in International Trade and Industry*, vol. 18 (Tokyo: Research Institute of International Trade and Industry, Ministry of International Trade and Industry).

National Science Foundation (1988), *The Science and Technology Resources of Japan: A Comparison with the United States* (Washington: US Government Printing Office).

NEGISHI, TAKASHI (1968), 'Protection of the Infant Industry and Dynamic Internal Economies', *Economic Record*, 44, 56–67.

NELSON, RICHARD R. (1959), 'The Simple Economics of Basic Scientific Research', *Journal of Political Economy*, 67, 297–306.

—— and WINTER, SIDNEY G. (1982), *An Evolutionary Theory of Economic Change* (Cambridge, Mass.: Harvard Unversity Press).

Nichibo Kabushiki Kaisha (1966), *Nichibo 75 Nen Shi* [The 75 Year History of Nichibo], (Osaka: Nichibo Kabushiki Kaisha).

Nihon Denki Kabushiki Kaisha (1972), *Nihon Denki Kabushiki Kaisha 70 Nen Shi* [The 70 Year History of Nippon Electric Company], (Tokyo: Nihon Denki Kabushiki Kaisha).

Nihon Denshin Denwa Kosha (1960), *Denshin Denwa Jigyo Shi* [The History of Telegraph and Telephone Operation], vol. 3 (Tokyo: Nihon Denshin Denwa Kosha).

Nihon Jidosha Kogyo Kai (1988), *Nihon Jidosha Sangyo Shi* [The History of the Japanese Automobile Industry], (Tokyo: Nihon Jidosha Kogyo Kai).

Nihon Kagaku Gijutsushi Taikei [Outline of the History of Science and Technology in Japan], (1967), vol. 3 (Tokyo: Daiichi Hoki Shuppan).

Nihon Kouku Uchu Kogyo Kai (1994), *Nihon no Kouku Uchu Kogyo 1994* [The Japanese Aerospace Industry 1994], (Tokyo: Nihon Kouku Uchu Kogyo Kai).

Nihon Seiyaku Kogyo Kai (Japan Pharmaceutical Manufacturers Association, JPMA) (1987), *Waga Kuni Seiyaku Sangyo no Choki Bijon to Kihon Seisaku* [The Long-Term Vision and Basic Policies for the Japanese Pharmaceutical Industry], revised edn, (Tokyo: Nihon Seiyaku Kogyo Kai).

—— (1991), *Deta Bukku* [Data Book] (Tokyo: Nihon Seiyaku Kogyo Kai).

—— (1993), *Seiyaku Sangyo no Kokusai-Ka no Genjo* [The Current Situation on the Internationalization of the Pharmaceutical Industry], (Tokyo: Nihon Seiyaku Kogyo Kai).

Nissan Jidosha Kabushiki Kaisha (1965), *Nissan Jidosha 30 Nen Shi* [The 30 Year History of Nissan Motor], (Tokyo: Nissan Jidosha Kabushiki Kaisha).

ODAGIRI, HIROYUKI (1981), *The Theory of Growth in a Corporate Economy: Management Preference, Research and Development, and Economic Growth* (Cambridge, UK: Cambridge University Press).

—— (1983), 'R&D Expenditures, Royalty Payments, and Sales Growth in Japanese Manufacturing Corporations', *Journal of Industrial Economics*, 32, 61–71.

—— (1986), 'Industrial Policy in Theory and Reality', in H. W. de Jong and W. G. Shepherd [eds.], *Mainstreams in Industrial Organization* (Dordrecht: Martinus Nijhoff), 387–412.

—— (1992), *Growth through Competition, Competition through Growth: Strategic Management and the Economy in Japan* (Oxford: Oxford University Press).

—— (1993), 'Education as a Source of Network, Signal, or Nepotism: The Case of Managers and Engineers during Japan's Industrial Development', paper presented at the Network Conference, Whistler, Canada. To be published in M. Fruin [ed.], *Network Organization and Action in Japan* (Oxford: Oxford University Press).

—— (1994), 'Mergers and Acquisitions in Japan and the Antimonopoly Policy', paper presented at the Competition Policy Conference, Tokyo. To be published in W. S. Comanor, A. Goto, and L. Waverman [eds.], *Competition Policy in a Global Economy* (London: Routledge).

—— and MURAKAMI, NAOKI (1992), 'Private and Quasi-Social Rates of Return on Pharmaceutical R&D in Japan', *Research Policy*, 21, 335–45.

—— and YASUDA, HIDETO (1994), 'The Determinants of Overseas R&D by Japanese Firms: An Empirical Study at the Industry and Company Levels', Discussion Paper No. 594, Institute of Socio-Economic Planning, University of Tsukuba.

ODAKA, KONOSUKE (1989), 'Seicho no Kiseki: 2' [Path of Growth: 2], in Yasuba Yasukichi and Inoki Takenori [eds.], *Nihon Keizaishi, 8: Kodo Seicho* (Tokyo: Iwanami Shoten), 153–208.

OHSHIMA, TAKU and YAMAOKA, SHIGEKI (1987), *Sangyo no Showa Shakaishi: Jidosha* [Social History of Industry during the Showa Era: Automobiles], (Tokyo: Nihon Keizai Hyoron Sha).

OKAMURA, JUN, et al. (1976), *Kouku Gijutsu no Zenbo* [The Portrait of Aircraft Technology], 2 vols (Tokyo: Hara Shobo).

OKAZAKI, TETSUJI (1993a), 'Kigyo Shisutemu' [Corporate System], in Okazaki and Okuno (1993), 97–144.

—— (1993b), *Nihon no Kogyo-Ka to Tekkou Sangyo* [Japan's Industrialization and the Steel Industry], (Tokyo: University of Tokyo Press).

—— (1993c), 'Nihon no Seifu-Kigyo Kan Kankei' [The Government-Company Relationship in Japan], *Soshiki Kagaku*, 26 (4), 115–23.

—— and OKUNO, MASAHIRO [eds.], (1993), *Gendai Nihon Keizai Shisutemu no Genryu* [The Origins of the Contemporary Japanese Economic System], (Tokyo: Nihon Keizai Shimbun Sha).

OKIMOTO, DANIEL I. (1989), *Between MITI and the Market: Japanese Industrial Policy for High Technology* (Stanford, Calif.: Stanford University Press).

—— ; SUGANO, TAKUO and WEINSTEIN, FRANKLIN B. [eds.], (1984), *Competitive Edge: The Semiconductor Industry in the U.S. and Japan* (Stanford, Calif.: Stanford University Press).

OLSON, MANCUR (1982), *The Rise and Decline of Nations: Economic Growth, Stagflation, and Social Rigidities* (New Haven: Yale University Press).

ORDOVER, JANUSZ A. (1991), 'A Patent System for Both Diffusion and Exclusion', *Journal of Economic Perspectives*, 5, 43–60.

OTSUKA, KEIJIRO (1987), 'Men Kogyo no Hatten to Gijutsu Kakushin' [The Development of Cotton Textile Industry and Technological Innovation] in Minami Ryoshin and Kiyokawa Yukihiko [eds.], *Nihon no Kogyo-Ka to Gijutsu Hatten* (Tokyo: Toyo Keizai), 110–30.

OTSUKA, MASAO (1987), 'Zosen-Gyo no Gijutsu Sentaku' [The Choice of Technology in the Shipbuilding Industry], in Minami Ryoshin and Kiyokawa Yukihiko [eds.], *Nihon no Kogyo-Ka to Gijutsu Hatten* (Tokyo: Toyo Keizai), 150–73.

PASCALE, R. T. (1984), 'Perspectives on Strategy: The Real Story behind Honda's Success', *California Management Review*, 26, 47–72.

Patent Office (1955), *Tokkyo Seido 70 Nen Shi* [The 70 Year History of the Patent System], (Tokyo: Hatsumei Kyokai).

PATRICK, HUGH (ed.), (1986), *Japan's High Technology Industries: Lessons and Limitations of Industrial Policy* (Seattle: University of Washington Press).

PECK, MERTON J.; LEVIN, RICHARD C. and GOTO, AKIRA (1987), 'Picking Losers: Public Policy toward Declining Industries in Japan', *Journal of Japanese Studies*, 13, 79–123.

—— and TAMURA, SHUJI (1976), 'Technology', in H. Patrick and H. Rosovsky [eds.], *Asia's New Giant* (Washington: The Brookings Institution), 525–85.

PENROSE, EDITH T. (1959), *The Theory of the Growth of the Firm* (Oxford: Basil Blackwell).

PRAHALAD, C. K. and HAMEL, GARY (1990), 'The Core Competence of the Corporation', *Harvard Business Review*, May/June, 79–91.

REICH, MICHAEL R. (1990), 'Why the Japanese Don't Export More Pharmaceuticals: Health Policy as Industrial Policy', *California Management Review*, 32, 124–50.

REISCHAUER, EDWIN O. (1974), *Japan: The Story of a Nation*, revised edn, (New York: Alfred A. Knopf).

ROMER, PAUL M. (1990), 'Endogenous Technological Change', *Journal of Political Economy*, 98, S71–102.

—— (1994), 'The Origins of Endogenous Growth', *Journal of Economic Perspectives*, 8, 3–22.

ROSENBERG, NATHAN (1976), *Perspectives on Technology* (Cambridge, UK: Cambridge University Press).

—— and NELSON, RICHARD R. (1994), 'American Universities and Technical Advance in Industry', *Research Policy*, 23, 323–48.

SAKAKIBARA, KIYONORI (1995), *Nihon Kigyo no Kenkyu Kaihatsu Management* [R&D Management in the Japanese Firm], (Tokyo: Chikura Shobo).

—— and WESTNEY, D. ELEANOR (1985), 'Comparative Study of the Training, Careers, and Organization of Engineers in the Computer Industry in the United States and Japan', *Hitotsubashi Journal of Commerce and Management*, 20, 1–20.

SAKIYA, TETSUO (1982), *Honda Motor: The Men, the Management, the Machines* (Tokyo: Kodansha International).

SAKUDO, YOTARO (1980), 'Edo Jidai no Keiei' [Management during the Edo Era], in Sakudo Yotaro, Mishima Yasuo, Yasuoka Shigeaki, and Inoue Yoichiro [eds.], *Nihon Keieishi* (Kyoto: Minerva Shobo), 12–70.

SAMUELS, RICHARD J. (1994), *Rich Nation Strong Army* (Ithaca, NY: Cornell University Press).

SAWAI, MINORU (1990), 'Kikai Kogyo' [Machinery Industry], in Nishikawa Shunsaku and Abe Takeshi [eds.], *Nihon Keizaishi, 4: Sangyo-Ka no Jidai* (Tokyo: Iwanami Shoten), 213–53.

SAXONHOUSE, GARY (1974), 'A Tale of Japanese Technological Diffusion in the Meiji Period', *Journal of Economic History*, 34, 149–65.

—— (1977), 'Productivity Change and Labor Absorption in Japanese Cotton Spinning 1891–1935', *Quarterly Journal of Economics*, 91, 195–219.

—— (1985), 'Technology Choice in Cotton Textile Manufacturing', in Kazushi Ohkawa and Gustav Ranis [eds.], *Japan and the Developing Countries: A Comparative Study* (Oxford: Basil Blackwell), 212–31.

—— (1988), 'Japanese Cooperative R&D Ventures: A Market Evaluation', unpublished.

SCHERER, F. M. and ROSS, DAVID (1990), *Industrial Market Structure and Economic Performance*, 3rd edn, (Boston: Houghton Mifflin).

SCHUMPETER, JOSEPH A. (1942), *Capitalism, Socialism, and Democracy* (New York: Harper & Row).

Science and Technology Agency (STA) (various years), *Kagaku Gijutsu Hakusho* [White Paper on Science and Technology], (Tokyo: Printing Bureau of the Ministry of Finance).

SEKIGUCHI, SUEO (1986), 'Gijutsu Yunyusha to Shiteno Nihon' [Japan as a Technology Importer], in Sekiguchi Sueo and Tran Van Tho [eds.], *Chokusetsu Toshi to Gijutsu Iten* (Tokyo: Japan Center for Economic Research).

SHEARD, PAUL (1989), 'The Main Bank System and Corporate Monitoring and Control in Japan', *Journal of Economic Behavior and Organization*, 11, 399–422.

Shibaura Seisakusho (1940), *Sibaura Seisakusho 65 Nen Shi* [The 65 Year History of Shibaura Seisakusho], (Tokyo: Shibaura Seisakusho).

SHIMOKAWA, YOSHIO (1989), *Nihon Tekkou Gijutsu Shi* [The History of Iron and Steel Technology in Japan], (Tokyo: Agune).

SHINJO, KOJI (1988), 'The Computer Industry', in Komiya, Okuno, and Suzumura (1988), 333–68.

SMITKA, MICHAEL J. (1991), *Competitive Ties: Subcontracting in the Japanese Automotive Industry* (New York: Columbia University Press).

SUZUKI, TSUNEO (1991), 'Gosei Sen'i' [Synthetic Fibre], in Yonekawa Shin'ichi, Shimokawa Koichi, and Yamazaki Hiroaki [eds.], *Sengo Nihon Keieishi*, vol. 1 (Tokyo: Toyo Keizai), 117–84.

TAIRA, KOJI (1970), *Economic Development and the Labor Market in Japan* (New York: Columbia University Press).

TAKATERA, SADAO (1976), 'Kindai Kaikei no Donyu to Teichaku' [The Introduction and Diffusion of Modern Accounting], in Miyamoto Mataji and Nakagawa Keiichiro [eds.], *Kogyo-Ka to Kigyosha Katsudo* (Tokyo: Nihon Keizai Shimbun Sha), 245–66.

Takeda Yakuhin Kogyo Kabushiki Kaisha (1983), *Takeda 200 Nen Shi* [The 200 Year History of Takeda], (Osaka: Takeda Yakuhin Kogyo Kabushiki Kaisha).

TERANISHI, JURO (1993), 'Mein Banku Shisutemu' [The Main Bank System], in Okazaki and Okuno (1993), 61–95.

TIROLE, JEAN (1988), *The Theory of Industrial Organization* (Cambridge, Mass.: The MIT Press).

Tokyo Denki Kabushiki Kaisha (1940), *Tokyo Denki Kabushiki Kaisha 50 Nen Shi* [The 50 Year History of Tokyo Denki Co. Ltd.], (Tokyo: Tokyo Denki Kabushiki Kaisha).

Toyo Boseki Kabushiki Kaisha (1953), *Toyo Boseki 70 Nen Shi* [The 70 Year History of Toyo Boseki], (Osaka: Toyo Boseki Kabushiki Kaisha).

Toyo Keizai (1950), *Showa Sangyo Shi* [The History of Industries in the Showa Era], 3 vols, (Tokyo: Toyo Keizai).

Toyo Rayon Kabushiki Kaisha (1954), *Toyo Rayon Sha Shi* [Toyo Rayon Company History], (Tokyo: Toyo Rayon Kabushiki Kaisha).

Toyota Jidosha Kogyo Kabushiki Kaisha (1967), *Toyota Jidosha 30 Nen Shi* [The 30 Year History of Toyota Motor], (Toyota, Aichi: Toyota Jidosha Kogyo Kabushiki Kaisha).

TREZISE, PHILIP H. with the collaboration of Suzuki, Yukio (1976), 'Politics, Government, and Economic Growth in Japan', in H. Patrick and H. Rosovsky [eds.], *Asia's New Giant: How the Japanese Economy Works* (Washington: The Brookings Institution), 753–811.

UCHIDA, HOSHIMI (1983), 'Jinken Ohgon Jidai' [The Golden Age of Artificial Silk], in Uchida Hoshimi [ed.] *Gijutsu no Shakaishi, 5: Kogyo Shakai he no Henbo to Gijutsu* (Tokyo: Yuhikaku), 151–98.

UDAGAWA, MASARU (1984), *Shinko Zaibatsu* [New Zaibatsu], (Tokyo: Nihon Keizai Shimbun Sha).

UENOHARA, MICHIYUKI; SUGANO, TAKUO; LINVILL, JOHN G. and WEINSTEIN, FRANKLIN B. (1984), 'Background', in Okimoto, Sugano and Weinstein (1984), 9–34.

Umihara, Toru (1988), *Kinsei no Gakko to Kyouiku* [Schools and Education in the Tokugawa Japan], (Kyoto: Shibunkaku).

WAKASUGI, RYUHEI (1984), 'Sentan Gijutsu Sangyo no Kenkyu Kaihatsu Katsudo: Handotai Sangyo no Keisu' [Research and Development Activity of High-Technology Industry: The Case of Semiconductors], *Business Review*, 31, (3), 51–67.

—— (1986), *Gijutsu Kakushin to Kenkyu Kaihatsu no Keizai Bunseki* [Economic Analysis of Technological Innovation and R&D], (Tokyo: Toyo Keizai).

—— (1988), 'Kyodo Kenkyu Kaihatsu no Keizai-Teki Koka' [Economic Effects of Joint R&D], *Shinshu Daigaku Keizaigaku Ronshu*, 26, 1–26.

WALLICH, HENRY C. and WALLICH, MABLE I. (1976), 'Banking and Finance', in H. Patrick and H. Rosovsky [eds.], *Asia's New Giant: How the Japanese Economy Works* (Washington: The Brookings Institution), 249–315.

WEINSTEIN, FRANKLIN B.; UENOHARA, MICHIYUKI and LINVILL, JOHN G. (1984), 'Technological Resources', in Okimoto, Sugano and Weinstein (1984), 35–77.

WHITE, MICHAEL and TREVOR, MALCOLM (1983), *Under Japanese Management* (London: Heinemann).

WILKINS, MIRA (1990), 'Japanese Multinationals in the United States: Continuity and Change, 1879–1990', *Business History Review*, 64, 585–629.

WILLIAMSON, PETER J. and YAMAWAKI, HIDEKI (1991), 'Distribution: Japan's Hidden Advantage', *Business Strategy Review*, 2, 85–105.

WINTER, SIDNEY G. (1971), 'Satisficing, Selection, and the Innovating Remnant', *Quarterly Journal of Economics*, 85, 237–61.

World Bank (1993), *The East Asian Miracle: Economic Growth and Public Policy* (New York: Oxford University Press).

YAMAWAKI, HIDEKI (1988), 'Iron and Steel', in Komiya, Okuno and Suzumura (1988), 281–306.

YAMAZAWA, IPPEI (1988), 'Textile Industry', in Komiya, Okuno and Suzumura (1988), 395–424.

YASUBA, YASUKICHI (1989), 'Rekishi no Naka no Kodo Seicho' [High Growth in History], in Yasuba Yasukichi and Inoki Takenori [eds.], *Nihon Keizaishi, 8: Kodo Seicho* (Tokyo: Iwanami Shoten), 273–309.

YASUMURO, KEN'ICHI (1993), 'Engineers as Functional Alternatives to Entrepreneurs in Japanese Industrialisation', in J. Brown and M. B. Rose [eds.], *Entrepreneurship, Networks and Modern Business* (Manchester: Manchester University Press), 76–101.

YASUOKA, SHIGEAKI (1980), 'Meiji-Ki no Keiei' [Management in the Meiji Era], in Sakudo Yotaro, Mishima Yasuo, Yasuoka Shigeaki, and Inoue Yoichiro [eds.], *Nihon Keieishi* (Kyoto: Minerva Shobo), 71–141.

YONEKAWA, SHIN'ICHI (1984), 'University Graduates in Japanese Enterprises before the Second World War', *Business History*, 26, 193–218.

—— (1991), 'Men Boseki' [Cotton Textile], in Yonekawa Shin'ichi, Shimokawa Koichi, and Yamazaki Hiroaki [eds.], *Sengo Nihon Keieishi*, vol. 1 (Tokyo: Toyo Keizai), 55–116.

YONEKURA, SEIICHIRO (1983), 'Sengo Nihon Tekkou-Gyo ni Okeru Kawasaki Seitsu no Kakushinsei' [The Innovation of Kawasaki Steel in the Post-War Japanese Iron and Steel Industry], *Hitotsubashi Ronso*, 90 (3), 387–410.

—— (1986), 'Tekkou-Gyo ni Okeru Inobeshion Donyu Purosesu' [The Process of Innovation Adoption in the Iron and Steel Industry], in Imai Ken'ichi [ed.], *Inobeshion to Soshiki* (Tokyo: Toyo Keizai), 177–206.

—— (1991), 'Tekkou' [Iron and Steel] in Yonekawa Shin'ichi, Shimokawa Koji, and Yamazaki Hiroaki [eds.], *Sengo Nihon Keieishi*, vol. 1 (Tokyo: Toyo Keizai), 263–349.

—— (1994), *The Japanese Iron and Steel Industry, 1850–1990* (London: Macmillan).

YONEZAWA, YOSHIE (1988), 'The Shipbuilding Industry', in Komiya, Okuno and Suzumura [eds.], (1988), 425–50.

YUASA, MITSUTOMO (1980), *Nihon no Kagaku Gijutsu 100 Nen Shi* [The 100 Year History of Science and Technology in Japan], (Tokyo: Chuo Koron Sha).

Index of Names

Abe Takeshi 117, 122
Abegglen, James C. 271
Abramovitz, Moses 20
Adachi, Tetsuo 223
Agency for Industrial Science and
  Technology 32, 163
Aichi Aircraft 215–17
Aichi Clock and Electric Machinery 216
Aichi Horo 194
Aichi Kokuki, see Aichi Aircraft
Aida Hiroshi 168, 172–3, 274
Aikawa Yoshisuke 6, 27, 79, 185–7,
  192, 196, 202
Air Self Defence Force 211
Airbus 226, 232
Aircraft Production Council 222
Aishin Seiki 194
Alchian, Armen A. 257
All Japan Cotton Spinners Association,
  see Dai Nihon Boseki Rengo Kai
Amagasaki Boseki 116, 118, 120, 122,
  124
Amagasaki Seitetsu 147
American Export–Import Bank 131
American Motors 196
American Pharmaceutical Manufacturing
  Association 246
Anritsu 158
Arisawa Hiromi 19, 26, 78, 80
Armco 151–2
Army 26, 140, 144, 164–5, 174, 183–4,
  191–2, 194, 196, 203, 213–19, 260
Arrow, Kenneth J. 250
Asada Tsunesaburo 164
Asahi Beer 89
Asahi Boseki 130
Asahi Chemical, see Asahi Kasei
Asahi Kasei 126–7
Asahi Kenshoku, see Asahi Kasei
Asano (zaibatsu) 76–7
Asano Shipbuilding 143–4, 213
Asano Soichiro 73, 143
Asano Zozen, see Asano Shipbuilding
Asanuma Banri 101
Association for the Research on
  Transport Airplane 224

Association of National Universities 276
AT&T 176
Austin 41–2, 118, 187–8, 192, 195–6
Automobile Technology Association 195
Aviation Laboratory 215
Ayukawa Yoshisuke, see Aikawa
  Yoshisuke

Baba Yasunori 220
Bank of Japan 20, 25, 146, 148
Banyu Pharmaceutical 246
Banyu Seiyaku, see Banyu Parmaceutical
Bardeen, John 165
Baumol, William J. 258
Bayer 240
Beadle 125
Bell Laboratories 156, 165–6, 170
Bell, A. G. 155, 161
Bevan 125
Boeing 227–9, 232–3
Boren, see Dai Nihon Boseki Rengo Kai
Bratten, Walter 165
Bridgestone Tyres 97, 198
British Telecom 176
Busicom, see Nippon Calculating
  Machine Sales

Cadbury 83
Canon 172
Cantillon, Richard 270
Caro, N. 77–8
Casale, L. 78
Casio 172–3
Caspary, Sigrun 217
Chambers of Commerce and Industry 73
Chandler, Alfred D., Jr. 1–2, 80, 256
Chase Manhattan Bank 80
Chevrolet 189–90
Chida Tomohei 204–6, 210
Chrysler 181, 195–6
Chuo University 30
Citibank 80
Clark, Kim B. 101, 275
Cohen, Wesley M. 271
College of Engineering, see Kogakuryo
Corbett, Jenny 95

Index of Subjects

JAPAN BUSINESS AND ECONOMICS SERIES

This series provides a forum for books on the workings of Japan's economy, its business enterprises, its management practices, and its macroeconomic structure. Japan has achieved the status of a major economic world power and much can be learned from an understanding of how this has been accomplished and how it is being sustained.

The series aims to balance empirical and theoretical work. It also implicitly takes for granted that both the significant differences between Japan and other countries and the similarities between them are worth knowing about. The series will present a broad range of work on economics, politics, and systems of management, in analysing the performance of one of the major players in what may well be the largest economic region in the twenty-first century.